AF568162

ORIGINS OF MODERN EUROPE
Medieval National Consciousness

ORIGINS OF MODERN EUROPE
Medieval National Consciousness

Abida Shakoor

Edited by
Q.Z. Hasan
Hajira Kumar

AAKAR BOOKS

ORIGINS OF MODERN EUROPE
Medieval National Consciousness

First Published, 2004

ISBN 81-87879-33-5 (Hb)

Published by
AAKAR BOOKS
28-E Pocket-IV, Mayur Vihar Phase-I, Delhi-110 091
Phone : 011-22795505 Telefax : 011-22795641
E-mail : aakarb@del2.vsnl.net.in

Typeset at
Nidhi Laser Point, Shahdara, Delhi-110 032

Printed in India on behalf of M/s Aakar Books by
Arpit Printographers, B-7, Saraswati Complex,
Subhash Chowk, Laxmi Nagar, Delhi-110 092
Phones : 011-33339192, 30971860, 22825424

Preface

The book was written by Abida Shakoor during her stay in Europe and America. European History was her first love. A serious reader will find this book both interesting and knowledgeable.

The present work is neither a narrative nor a chronological account of European History. Rather some selected themes are taken up which had great bearing on the formation of the modern world. This is an in-depth study based on dispassionate use of secondary sources of selected events, people and issues of the period that translate the past into the present. The author provides fresh insights by utilizing wide-ranging sources on each theme. It should prove to be of immense value for research scholars, students and teachers of European History.

Acknowledgement

On behalf of my sister, late Abida Shakoor, I am grateful to all the professors at the various European and American universities under whose guidance she had worked on the topics dealt in this book.

My family members deserve special thanks as they searched and procured the material from various places. I am deeply obliged to all those who have silently provided technical assistance for preparing the draft. It is only due to their efforts that a manuscript could be transformed into this book.

Hajira Kumar

The book is dedicated to the fond memories of our father Prof. Abdul Shakoor. For us he was another name of an intellectual tradition. His vision inspired us, his academic standard dazzled us and his commitment set an example for us.

The topics discussed here is a continuation of his legacy. My sister Ms. Abida Shakoor inherited the major share of our father's talent.

I believe Samar will further strengthen this tradition in future.

Hajira Kumar

Contents

	Preface	*v*
	Acknowledgement	*vii*
1.	Nationalism in Medieval Europe	1
2.	Renaissance and its Periodization	49
3.	Economic Policy of Frederick the Great	78
4.	Napoleon III and Italy	108
5.	The Crimean War : A Study of the Origin	146
6.	British Liberalism in India	205
7.	Diplomatic History and International Relations 1871–1920	244
8.	Outbreak of the First World War : The Problem of Responsibility	257
9.	Foreign Political Ideas : The German Resistance Movement	303
10.	The Treaty of Rapallo	327
11.	Yalta : German Questions	344
12.	Towards Sarajevo	357
13.	British Radio and the Danish Resistance Movement, 1940–1945	391
14.	The Birth of New Europe	423
	Bibliography	437
	Index	453

Chapter I

Nationalism in Medieval Europe

PROLOGUE : MEDIEVAL NATIONAL CONSCIOUSNESS

It has been a tendency among some recent historians to disavow that the early centuries of the Middle Ages had any group consciousness at all, either national or racial.[1] This possibly stems as a reaction against romantic historiography. Historians and political scientists are prone to believe that both patriotism and national consciousness are cultural phenomena of a recent origin. This belief is based on the ground that the terms and the formulated concepts are themselves quite recent.[2] 'It is rather a simple acknowledgment of the fact that the term nationalism has no real synonym in the English language[3] says Tipton. The word 'patriotism' first appeared in the eighteenth century, and 'nationalism' only in the nineteenth. In French, *nationalisme* was first used in 1812 and the oldest example of 'nationalism' in English dates to 1836. Considering that the word later came to occupy a larger sphere of significance in English than in French, German or Dutch. The English word has achieved a place for itself in a single century.[4]

But to conclude that patriotism and nationalism are recent sentiments because the words and concepts are so, is misleading as one cannot grant existence to things only if they have a name. Can one question the existence of cosmic rays in the Middle Ages or the state in medieval times! It is true that the word and the concept 'state' originated during the Renaissance medieval society as Johan Huizinga points out and they made good use of the terms *regnum* and *civitas* ('kingdom' and 'union of citizens', that is Commonwealth) to express things political.[5]

Basically, Johan Huizinga believes that nationalism is an emotional state of mind, and so a counterpart concept existed in the medieval period. It is true, he admits, that modern nationalism is 'more clearly delineated' than the medieval variety, but he denies that it is something new.[6]

As a matter of fact, sentiments akin to nationalism are possibly as old and as prevalent as man and society. Every community, from the primitive tribe to the modern nation, seems to regard itself as the centre of the universe, as somehow distinct, as 'the chosen people', and each seems to have evinced some sort of group feeling.[7] A deep attachment to one's native soil, to local traditions, and to established territorial authority, has existed in varying degree throughout history.[8] And such sentiments did not require a very great refinement of mind. We know today that they showed themselves in the period of the Germanic invasions with much more force than Fustel de Coulanges,[9] for example, would have us believe. 'In the greatest example of conquest offered by the feudal era, that of Norman England,' says Marc Bloch, 'we see them clearly at work.' When the youngest son of William, Henry I, thought it prudent to marry a princess of the ancient dynasty of Wessex–of the 'direct' line of England, as it was called by a monk of Canterbury–the Norman knights mockingly loaded the royal couple with Saxon nicknames. But eulogizing this marriage* about half a century later, in the reign of the grandson of Henry and Edith, a hagiographer wrote: 'Now England has a king of English race; it finds among the same race bishops, abbots, barons, brave knights, born of both seeds.[10] The history of this assimilation is the history of English nationality, though this was destined to undergo many vicissitudes.

Nationalities are the products of the living forces of history, and therefore, fluctuating and never rigid. They are groups of the utmost complexity and baffle exact definition. Most of

* More will be said about this marriage infra.

them possess certain objective factors distinguishing them from others like common descent, language, territory, political entity, customs and traditions or religion. But clearly none of these factors are essential to the existence or definition of nationality. Although objective factors are of great importance for the formation of nationalities, the most essential element is a living and active corporate will. It is this will which we call nationalism, a state of mind inspiring the large majority of a people.

In the words of Halvdan Koht:

> That nationalism cannot exist without nations is self-evident. Historically, it means that the conditions of nationalism in Europe were present only with the establishment of separate nations after the dissolution of the Roman Empire.[11]

But in seeking to trace signs of nationalism within the nation so established, Koht continues, we should not feel bound by the modern conceptions and implications of the term. Like other ideological political terms, nationalism too has gone through many changes in the course of historical development, perhaps even more than others because it is just as much a psychological as a political term. In fact, primitive nationalism contains elements which have disappeared or are disappearing from the character of modern nationalism.[12]

Within the first kingdoms founded on the ruins of the Roman Empire, traditions were too strong to allow national separatism to dominate the ideas of the new leaders. Christianity, too, counteracted such a development. In this regard, historical analysis tends to confirm the view of Henry Pirenne according to which a definite breach between ancient and medieval civilizations did not occur until Carolingian times. Indeed, only with the collapse of the Carolingian Empire were, lasting conditions favourable to the growth of nationalistic ideas, finally created. From the ninth century onward, Koht opines, Europe organized itself into the kingdoms that were later to form the bases of modern political life. Natural, though surprising at so early a date, was the conclusion drawn about 830 AD, by a Frankish historian, Frechulf, bishop of Lisieux. Abandoning the almost sacred conception of the continuous existence of the Roman Empire, the bishop boldly asserted that the establishement of new kingdoms on Roman territory constituted the beginning of a new era in history. The ecclesiastical author perhaps recalled the hope of St. Augustine that the Roman Empire might be replaced by the establishment of a world of small states only. At any event, until several centuries later, he was the only one to express this view.[13]

To quote the same authority :

> Independent medieval thought, relying upon the genius of its own age, was not apparent until the twelfth century, the period that saw also the first expressions of European nationalism. It is a remarkable fact ... that a truly national consciousness, though limited in its scope, burst forth almost simultaneously in many of the European countries. It cannot be a simple coincidence, it must rather be the natural result of parallel evolution, and, in some cases, it is even possible to trace an influence from the country to another. The common fundamental reason must be the growth of national policies in most of the kingdoms of Europe.[14]

Marc Bloch, the renowned French medievalist, surveying the feudal society of medieval Europe, concludes that language played an intrinsic role in producing a highly developed sense of 'national-consciousness' among the peoples of Europe by the beginning of the twelfth century. Nothing is more preposterous than to confuse language with nationality; but it would be no less foolish to deny its role in the crystallization of national consciousness.

Bloch recognizes, of course, that there are marked differences in the attitudes and notions of medieval and modern men towards the concept of the *fatherland*, but he rightly observes that the idea of a fatherland is, in itself, proof of a crude national feeling.[15] 'The papacy itself admitted that war in defence of the *patria*', cites Gaines Post, 'was lawful even during Lent–a case of urgent–necessity (Nicholas I, 866).'[16]

If the cause is just, says Huguccio, famous as a teacher of Innocent III, laymen may engage in war at any time; and defining the just cause as *necessitas*, he adds that defence of the *patria* and winning and preserving the peace are among the necessities or just causes. This supreme necessity of defending the fatherland, it follows, makes lawful many things that are otherwise unlawful; if a man kills his father to defend the patria he is to be rewarded rather than punished.[17] About 1245, Johannes de Deo in his *Liber Poenitentiarius,* says that knights who fight against their own patria or are faithless to their Lord are guilty of sin. Defence of realm was of course a supreme necessity, and it made lawful the ruler's demand for extraordinary taxes to enable him to wage a just war against the aggressor.[18]

About 1338, in order to help forestall, probably, papal measures against the war plans of Edward III, William of Ockham declared that the Pope's *plenitudo potestatis* could not legally prevent the king of England from taxing the clergy for the defence of the patria.[19]

Among the canonists and legalists, we find further evidence of the rise, in thought as well in fact, of the national states in Europe, and this much earlier than once supposed. The new state is the common utility or welfare of all in the community of the realm.[20]

The earliest and most ardent statements of the theory of *dejure* as well as *defacto* independence of kingdoms came from canonists and theologians largely of England, Spain and France, from the late twelfth to the mid-thirteenth century and later. The canonists who started formulating the theory of the king as emperor who had no superior, were merely reflecting a long tradition. The early medieval barbarian kings imitated the late Roman imperial institutions and Spanish and English kings arrogated to themselves the proud title of *imperator*.[21]

By the twelfth century, an awareness of independence from the empire of Charlemagne and his successors had arisen. Joseph R. Strayer holds that although nationalism was not yet a 'respectable force at mid-thirteenth century', by the end of the same century, men were more and more inclined to give their primary allegiance to lay governments. 'Laicization', as he calls this process, necessarily involves the gradual decline of church power in terms of claims to universalism and a gradual development of royal power. The effect was to lift nationalism onto a new plateau and put the weight of the state behind it. Thus nationalism contributed to the formation of nations, and then emergence led to a heightened sense of national feeling. In this respect in turn nationalism was both a cause and effect of nation building.[22]

The relationship between nationalism and feudalism also needs to be examined. In Thomas F. Tout's view, the breakdown of the latter in the late thirteenth and early fourteenth centuries resulted in the transfer of the allegiance of the individual from the local lord to the king. In this way the decentralized and contractual feudal system, with its emphasis upon loyalty to a higher lord, was able to rise above localism and prepare the ground for national unity and a rudimentary national feeling. But the transition was neither short nor smooth.[23]

Tout points out that despite the general trend, 'English' barons followed Simon de Montfort, a 'Frenchman' when he rebelled against an 'English' monarch, and that the Burgundians sided with England and against France in the Hundred Years' War. When, as in the age of Phillip, the Fair and Edward I, they had established a real domination over an ordered and centralized community, the kings commanded allegiance much more as supreme lords than as political sovereigns. Great kings did not differ in kind but in degree from their nobles. Medieval potentates did not discriminate between the management of an estate and the government of a principality. The principle of allegiance remained personal rather than local.[24]

It seems whimsical to the modern Englishman that the barons who extorted *Magna Curta* from King John should have invited the future Louis VIII, the heir to the French throne, to deliver them and save English liberty from the English tyrant. But to the Middle Ages such things were natural enough, and no worse a crime than the normal 'defiance' by a vassal of his lord. Indeed the 'foreigner' was to the medieval man much less the alien of a distant land than the neighbour with whom he had constant bickerings. In the same way there seemed nothing outrageous to the fourteenth century mind that the king of England should claim the throne of France because of some supposititious claim of inheritance.

Nonetheless in the thirteenth, still more in the fourteenth century it was becoming perspicuous that proprietary monarchy would not do. The instinct which inspired England to expel Louis of France in 1217, the prudence which in 1327 impelled the barons of France to repudiate the detrimental doctrine that marriage might give a legal right to a foreigner to rule over their land, showed that national feeling was beginning to assert itself.[25]

The idea of national unity was most clearly realized and propagated by the great French statesman Abbot Suger. The Capetian kings of France put up a valiant struggle to bring the whole country under their sway. In this endeavour they met with resistance not only from some of the great vassals but also from France's neighbouring sovereigns, the king of England and the German emperor. The victories over the combined forces of such foreign enemies were hailed throughout the country as feats bringing honour to the whole people. Suger reports in his 'Life of King Louis VI' how, in 1124 this king appealed to the whole of France (*tota Francia*) to follow him against the invaders,[26] and the victory was a national triumph. It is significant how Suger exulted at the deed. Later by both the king and the people he was called 'the father of the fatherland' (*paterpatriae*).[27]

The decisive French victory at Bouvines in 1214 AD over the united English and German forces prompted exultations making it still more widespread and resounding than the triumphs of 1124AD. The boyish contempt of the enemy, characteristic of a juvenile national sentiment, is expressed by the exclamation of a French knight when warned, in 1200AD against the Germans: 'The Germans ! Even if armed they would not dare to attack an unarmed Frenchman!'[28]

Across the Channel, in England, the conditions of national development were in many respects dissimilar to those of France, particularly because the country, since the Norman conquest, was never threatened by invaders from abroad and nationalism could not be stimulated by the opposition to foreign enemies. The problem of reconciliation between Anglo-Saxons and Normans apparently was not so difficult as generally assumed in the period of national romanticism, and the unification of government and law as achieved by the Norman kings tended to foster a civic solidarity which could have easily grown into common national consciousness. The Anglo-Norman chroniclers of the twelfth and the thirteenth centuries uniformly gave the whole population of England the common name of *gens-Anglorum* without differentiating between the conquerors and the conqured. Nationalism in England was, in the opinion of Koht, however, at that time 'essentially a latent force'; it did not provoke passionate outbursts of enthusiasm or hatred.[29]

Different was the situation of the British race that was conquered by the English and their Norman kings. In their resistance against the aggressors, the Welshmen were roused to a fierce nationalism that not only helped maintain their own self-consciousness but even gave an impulse to similar movements in other countries. Towards the middle of the twelfth century, the Welshman Geoffrey of Monmouth wrote about the history of the Briton kings which became the most famous work of nationalistic historiography in the Middle Ages.

He aimed particularly at showing the Norman rulers of his country that the Britons as a race measured up very well with the Anglo-Saxons and had a most glorious past. For this purpose he created for them a more brilliant history than any other people could boast of. This confirms the general observation of Godefroid Kurth that defeats are more fruitful in national legends than are victories.[30]

In the words of Halvdan Koht :

> From the beginning of the twelfth century, European nationalism has a continuous history. From the simplicity of earlier times it grew to manifold complexity. New national institutions, such as a National Parliament and the Church placed themselves at the side of the king and attracted the devotion of the people. Civic interests multiplied and united the citizens for peaceful activities. Historic traditions conveyed to the people new

national symbols, heroes of independence, saints, laws. Trade and commerce fostered a powerful economic nationalism. Language and poetry created the basis of intellectual unity.[31]

I. Growth of National Consciousness in England 1066–1216

National consciousness evolves gradually and steadily through many generations. Premature and superficial indications may point towards a patriotism for which the nation is, as yet, unprepared. The human mind is so constituted that any vital and fundamental change in its thinking and approach is never abrupt; it is assimilated by an evolutionary process. It took more than a *Magna Carta* to guarantee England's liberties and more than a Lewes* to cement her nationalism.

Kemp Malone emphasizes the 'vigourous English nationalism of the eleventh century', and according to him, 'The foundation of this nationalism had been laid by Alfred the Great in the ninth century.'[32] It does not fall within the scope of this paper to inquire minutely into the nationalism of England before the conquest. Saxon nationalism was, after all, an unstable and fitful thing. The country was never properly united. A commanding personality like Alfred or Edgar, might have produced a semblance of union, but they were hampered by the slackness of his people. England under Harold hardly deserved to be called a nation–inspite of what Malone might say[33]–though a keen eye might have detected the germs of nationality.[34]

'Self-reliance in great and small alike', says Bishop Stubbs, 'without self-restraint, without the power of combination, with a national pride and yet no national spirit, laid England an easy, though unwilling, prey at the feet of the conqueror.'[35]

'The conquest tended to kill patriotism in the invaders, as it did in the conquered.'[36] William was holding down a sullen and humiliated people by means of a foreign garrison. The Normans were not as ready to become Englishmen, as their forefathers had been to become Frenchmen. They had every reason for treating the English with the contempt due to an

---

* For details *Battle Royal,* Tufton Beamish (London, 1965).

inferior civilization. This contempt died hard. But, as Wingfield-Stratford states, 'the English nation was dying for lack of discipline, and this was just what the Normans were qualified to give.'[37]

It is a favourite inquiry, as to what extent the conquest was responsible for the introduction of feudalism. There is every possibility that if England had been left to herself, she would have been fragmented into several loosely knit fiefs or earldoms, owing a more or less shadowy allegiance to some nominal overlord. The tendency towards feudalization was European, and it is difficult to see how England could have escaped its influence. But for its formal and definite establishment as a system of government, the conquest must be given credit. Luckily, however, England was saved from the worst effects of feudalism–which tantalized France and Germany–and she finally succeeded in steering clear alike of anarchy and despotism.

William's master stroke of policy was the summoning, at Salisbury, of all the landholders of the realm. All bowed down to him, became his men, and swore oaths of loyalty to him against all other men. Thus, from the very beginning, the hand of the king was heavy upon the nobles, and a central power took shape, which, except for the interlude of Stephen's reign, was to go on developing in expereince and complexity under his successors.[38] England was saved from the plague of disunion which ravaged her neighbours. The change made in 1066 AD was severely practical: it placed a stronger emphasis upon the part that kingship should play in the routine government.[39]

William had learned by long experience in Normandy that his nobles were not to be trusted. The conqueror managed to win over the English to his side. It soon became a matter of course that the English fought for the king against his Norman barons.[40] Before the first generation of the conquerors had passed away, however, the barrier between the Normans and Britons had considerably weakened. Forces were already at work, blending the foreign garrison with the subject population into one self-conscious whole, and building unity, which was imposed from the outside, but that gradually and steadily become implicit and spiritual.[41]

In the words of the eminent British medievalist, Edward Freeman :

> It came about that the descendants of the Normans who settled in England step by step become, as we may say, Englishmen, if not by blood yet by adoption. For several generations after the conquest the high places of the land, the great estates and chief offices, were almost always held by men of Norman or other foreign blood. But in a very few generations these men learned to speak English and to have the feelings of Englishmen. The effect of the Norman conquest of England was neither to make England subject to Normandy nor to make it a Norman land. It gave to England a much higher place in the world in general than it had held before. At home, Englishmen were neither driven out nor turned into Normans, but the Normans in England were turned into Englishmen. But in this work of turning themselves into Englishmen, they made, bit by bit, many changes in the laws of England, and in the language, manners, and thoughts of Englishmen.[42]

In order to secure the goowill of the English, the youngest son of the conqueror, Henry, married Edith, niece of Edgar the Atheling, sister of the king of Scotland, and a descendant of Alfred the Great. Thereby, he not only established friendly relations with Scotland, but grafted the Norman house on to the stock of the West Saxon royal line.[43] As a result of this marriage, all kings of England since the time of Henry, with the single exception of Stephen, became descendants of both Alfred and William the Conqueror.[44]

The marriage and its effects signified dramatically that the age of exploitation was drawing to its end, and the king began the process of wiping out distinctions between Normans and the English so successfully that the author of the *Dialogue of the Exchequer*, writing some seventy years later, declared, 'Nations are so mixed, that it is difficult today to discern which freemen are of English origin and which Norman.'[45] Henry insisted that he was not so much a Norman King as an Anglo-Norman King, who meant to rule over a homogeneous people. This marriage symbolized the fact that the monarchy would continue to devote its strength to obtaining the unification of the country.[46]

In the words of Freeman :

> The Norman conquest is the greatest turning-point in the history of the English nation ... it is impossible to exaggerate its importance. And yet there is no event whose true nature has been more commonly and more utterly mistaken. No event is less fitted to be taken, as it so often has been taken, for the beginning of our national history. For its whole importance is not the importance which belongs to a beginning, but the importance which belongs to a turning point. The Norman conquest brought with it a most extensive foreign infusion.... So, far from being the beginning of our national history, the Norman conquest was the temporary overthrow of our national being. But it was only a temporary overthrow. To a superficial observer the English people might seem for a while to be wiped out of the roll-call of the nations ... But in a few generations ... England was England once again, and the descendants of the Norman invaders were found to be among the truest of Englishmen.[47]

While, the Norman strain was becoming less and less, a seperate factor in the national being, the old Saxon spirit, which had received a sharp blow at the hands of William, was not dead. Saxon institutions were roughly handled, but there was no absolute breach of continuity. It did not suit the conqueror's policy to destroy more than was necessary, for he regarded himself as the lawful heir of the English kings, and it was more convenient to make use of the customs he found established, than to improvize or transport new ones.[48] He had not the resources to be a dictator who could afford to disregard the susceptibilities of his subjects. If he wished to establish himself as king he could not ride rough-shod over England. Wisely he accepted the past. He secured the formality of election by the witan and was consecrated by an Anglo-Saxon primate.[49] He accepted the the laws of the Anglo-Saxons and their institutions. In the words of Freeman: 'William conquered neither to destroy nor to found but to continue.'

William and his successors soon had an additional motive for fostering native institutions, for after the first risings had been suppressed, the real danger to the Crown came not from the people but from the magnates. And hence we find the Red King calling out the old shire levy aganist his rebel barons. The central government, which had been the weak point of the old system, was indeed practically reconstituted, and gradually extended its power over local franchises though the old machinery of the shire and hundred was preserved–if not intact, at least without revolutionary change. Localism persisted in England until modern times, but as Barnaby C. Keeney rightly observes, 'from the twelfth century onwards, the expansion of the royal court and with it the royal authority tended to break down provincial loyalties and made men aware of the king and his central government.'[50] Even Bishop Stubbs, for all his sense of the popular Anglo-Saxon background to English institutions believed that the Norman monarchy was essential to the creation of modern government.[51]

It was upon the towns, or big villages dignified with that name, that the conquest had the least permanent effect, inspite of the havoc wrought amongst them during its first few years. London, in particular, survived intact, and such was its importance, that the animosity of the Londoners was chiefly responsible for the failure of *Matilda*.[52]

In the reign of Henry I began the series of royal charters to towns and Henry II took his grandfather's charter of liberties as a model for his own grant.

He was French, not English–had many French possessions and stayed in England only about twelve years of his reign of more than thirty four–and never spoke the English language; yet England is heavily indebted to him for the many reforms he accomplished. His first task was to restore the good order of Henry I's reign. The barons were compelled to give up their castles or else to destroy them; the armed bands of foreign mercenaries were ordered to leave the country, and frightened, 'they disappeared like phantoms'; the crown lands that had been alienated under Stephen were reclaimed, the royal revenues increased and the central administration reinstituted. 'The good order that Henry had maintained', says Munro, 'the fusion he had brought about by his stern rule, made the English nation strong, rich and united.'[53]

William Stubbs calls Henry II 'one of the most conspicuous actors in the drama of English histroy.' He says :

> He (Henry II) was a link in the chain of great men by whom, through good and evil, the English nation was drawn on to constitutional government. He was the man the time required. It was a critical time, and his actions and policy determined crisis in a favourable way. He stands with Alfred, Canute, William the Conqueror, and Edward I, one of the conscious creators of English greatness.
>
> His reign was the period of amalgamation, the union of the different elements existing in the country, which, whether, it be looked on as chemical or mechanical, produced the national character and the national institutions.[54]

The reign of Henry II was also a time of crisis, and the hands which seized the happy moments were his own and those of his ministers. If Henry had been a better man, his work would have been second to that of no character in history; had he been a weaker one than he was, England might have had to undergo for six hundred years, the fate of France.[55] Such a speculation may be a mere flight of fancy, but it accords its main features with the facts of history, and, as Stubbs continues to say, 'if there be such a thing as national character it must be closely connected with national institutions.' 'In one state of society they grow out of it;' he says, 'in another it is fashioned by them until it seems to grow out of them: they develop together in a free state, in a subject one they affect one another by assimilation or opposition according to the nature and duration of the pressure.'[56]

What is merely a probable speculation at best, with regard to character, is, however, a true story applied to institutions. The Anglo-Saxon and the Norman institutions had been actually in a position to possibly come together since the conquest, and the reign of Henry was to give the united systems the character which has developed into the English constitution. It annihilated the undue preponderance of one power in the state over others; it secured the firm position of the central force, and opened the way for the growth of wealth in social security; it prevented England from falling under a military monarchy, or into a feudal anarchy; it so balanced the forces existing in the state as to give to each an opportunity for legitimate development. *Magna Carta* could never have been won by lawless barons for a frustrated and spiritless nation, nor would the people, when they discerned their strength, have remained satisfied with the temperate aims which gratified the heroes of the thirteenth century, had they been left too early without restraint, or been subjected to prolonged oppression. The Anjevin kings, the Norman nobles, the English churls, the Roman clergy, became in one century, the English people.[57]

The reign of Henry II also saw the end of feudalism, so far as it had ever prevailed in England, as a system of government. The executive power was taken altogether out of its hands; its military strength was subordinated to the general aims of government; the legislative capacities of the system were held in formal existence, but in practical abeyance. Feudalism continued to exist legally as the machinery of land tenure, and morally in its more wholesome results as a principle of national cohesion and the discipline of loyalty.[58] The oath of allegiance of 1086 was reaching its culmination.[59]

At this time England's industrial greatness only existed as an embryo. It was in the twelfth century that we first hear of associations of artisans, or craft guilds, The towns benefited almost immediately from the conquest. By this change of rule, the native part of the population had to suffer from a feeling of racial inferiority but not for long as prosperity visited them at once. The ships of the world came to their ports, and the wool of England gave them back higher standards of living. The Normans had a commercial—mind they were sharp dealers, acquisitive and shrewd. The power of the guilds developed rapidly from the time when Norman merchants and artisans were admitted to the ceremonies of the Craft-box and to a part in electing the portreeves and mayors. The towns were spreading out beyond their walls and their power grew to the extent that kings had to listen to them.[60]

The early medieval town in England thus was like a corporate fief, tended to be self-sufficient, and was more occupied with its own interests than those of the whole community. This led to a number of patriotic expansions, local and exclusive, but capable of being some day merged into a higher unity.

The Crown exercised the same restraining influence over this burgher exclusiveness, as over the great barons. In neither case was the feudal idea allowed to run to its logical extreme, as in Continental nations,[61] even in Scotland. The English towns never had the chance to break away altogether from the Government, to raise their own troops, make their own laws, and carry on bloody struggles with each other. The power of the Crown was always above them; we find Henry II, for instance, imposing a general fine upon all illegal guilds, and the repeated and highly esteemed charters are by themselves evidence of how dependent were the towns for their privileges upon royal favour. It is thus that the ground was laid for De Montfort's memorable policy of recognizing a burgher, or merchant interest, as a factor to be reckoned with in the Constitution, and for the subsequent pursuit by Edward I and Edward III of a definite national policy in respect of industry.[62]

In yet another direction, the policy of the Crown was working toward nationalism. The conqueror had been wise enough to impair the efficiency of the fief as a military unit. It is surprising how quickly the victors allowed themselves to be ruled by the military ideas of the vanquished. 'The Battle of the Standard was the triumph of an army mainly English, employing English dismounted tactics and proving, for the first time, the potency of the English bow.' observes Wingfield-Stratford

It was Henry II's great ambition that England should be a Military Power with the controls rested in the king himself. It was necessary to foster a military spirit without giving it the opportunity of being inimical to the royal power. Happily Henry saw a way, and had the means of maintaining such a spirit in the heart of the nation. If the national defence had been left at the mercy of feudalism, the country would have relapsed into anarchy; if it had been entrusted to mercenaries, a military despotism would have resulted: if, on the other hand, the modern principle of creating a national military spirit had been forestalled, England might have become a nation of soldiers, a scourge of the western world.[63] Henry's great contribution was the *Assize of Arms*, by which he reorganized the national militia. He had tested its use and loyalty during the rebellion of 1173 and hence, eight years later, history finds him proclaiming the duty of every free man to provide himself with arms according to his means. This was a notable act of trust in the people, this policy of the Crown to ally itself with the folk, in opposition to the magnates, and one of the major benefits of this was to draw country and town together, to enable the free burgher and free cultivator to stand side by side in the same levy, under the command of the sheriff. And to prevent the sheriffs themselves from becoming unruly, Henry took the precaution of dismissing them all at once, and replacing them for the most part by his own officials.[64]

A more difficult problem awaited consideration as regard the influence exercised by the Church in promoting or retarding nationalism. For not only in theory, but in practice too, was the spiritual power of paramount importance during the Middle Ages. The influence of the Church was, also in many respects, anti-national. The political theory of the age embraced both a temporal and a spiritual power that was universal. During the eleventh and twelfth centuries, especially, this common consciousness of Christianity was at its height, confronting everywhere, the growing national consciousness. But England, with her insular situation far away in the north-west, was less sensible of the common need, and less susceptible of Romanization. It was after the coming of the Normans, that made her practically a member of the European state system, and brought her within the pale of the Hildebrandine revival.[65] And yet the conqueror, who had fought under the gonfanon and with the blessing of the Holy Church, was by no means her slave. Though he took the important step of separating the ecclesiastical from the lay jurisdiction, he was no less determined than Henry VIII to be the master in his own house.[66] And this, by the tact and friendship of Lanfranc and with the tacit assent of the Church, he contrived to be, and the tussle of Crown and Church was, thus delayed.

The first great struggle for papal power in England occurred in the latter days of Henry II and John, terminating with a seeming papal victory; the religious crisis in John's reign blended with the political movement evoking the *Magna Carta* and further leading to the critical periods of the reign of Henry III. These were trying times for English national existence and the English system of representation, with the Pope being a steady critic of English liberty.[67] According to Oliver H. Richardson, the national character of the English church was preserved at the conquest mainly through two causes: *first*, the bulk of the lower clergy remained Saxon and retained Saxon speech. Their influence, largely expended in protecting the conquered race from the oppression of the nobles, became greater as the fusion of the races progressed; *second*, the admirable position of William I and Lanfranc toward one another assured their joint resistance to unreasonable papal demands.[68]

During the turbulent reign of Stephen, considerable encouragement had been given to papal interference and the clergy had become a body so independent of the king's control, that Henry II found himself facing a most difficult problem. Drastic measures were necessary if the secular authority was to remain potent. The result was the **Becket controversy**.

On the Becket and Henry II confrontation it is difficult to pass judgement. There is no doubt that Becket was impracticable and obstinate to the last degree, and his contention that anybody who had taken even minor orders might put himself outside the pale of the law was the negation of settled government. But, says Wingfield-Stratford, 'to treat Henry as a patriot king, contending for the integrity of his realm against a foreign power, is equally absurd. By birth and policy he was more than half a foreigner, and an Anjevin bureaucracy ... would have been a polity hardly less 'stark' for Englishmen than that of the conqueror.'[69]

Undoubtedly the constitution of Clarendon contained the true statement of English law and English custom. Henry's glorious victory, however, was ruined by his own rashness. Becket's murder was followed by popular reaction. In some vague way the people recognized that the cause of the church was that of the masses: the king was subjected to the double humiliation of Canterbury and Avranches. Appeals to Rome were henceforward allowed, and no clergy, despite being convicted of crime, was to be summoned before a temporal judge. In the words of Richardson:

> Important in form as these concessions were, other consequences still more important resulted indirectly from this struggle. First, a limit had been set to the royal absolutism. Second, Henry's attention had been drawn from foreign affairs, and his whole strength confined to England, at exactly that moment when projects of foreign conquest must have seemed, and were, most feasible ... it may well be that the controversy with Becket prevented England from sinking into the position of a French subject province. In a certain sense, therefore, ... the controversy must be ranked as analogous to the loss of Normandy in helping to make England, England. Third, to resist the archbishop successfully, the king had been forced to call upon the baronage for support; the appeal ultimately proved dangerous to the crown ... and after Normandy had been lost and race-fusion fairly begun, the movement culminated in the *Magna Carta*.[70]

But the conditions were changing, and the need for an independent Church was gradually becoming, as years passed, less urgent. As long as the central government retained the Norman tradition of a foreign power ruling an inferior race–and this idea was never quite absent from the polity of the early Anjevins–the struggle for ecclesiastical freedom, even when backed by Rome, made for national independence. But the more national the civil power, the more sensitive did Englishmen become to anti-national tendencies on part of the Church.

If the royal power was stark and alien in its sympathies, it made amends by fostering the growth of the toughest and most distinctively national of English institutions–the English Common Law. The tremendous strength of the central power enabled it to impose its own rule, in the strictest sense of the word, upon its subjects. This custom of justice became so much a part of the national being, as to take on a vitality of its own, impervious alike to the will of the monarch and the ardour of reformers, a dense growth of English liberties.

From the earliest times, reverence for the law had been characteristic of Englishmen. If we watch the gradual development of English legal institutions, we shall realize that the prime objective of the Crown was not justice, but power. But with such able and systematic monarchs as the first two Henries, the idea of justice follows inevitably from that of power. In the hands of an able monarch, justice becomes a powerful and remorseless engine; and in making his law felt all over the realm, Henry Plantagenet was taking the surest means of establishing his authority over the disruptive tendencies of feudalism.[71]

It is unlikely that he realized how surely, in establishing the rule of the Crown over its subjects, he was setting up a power that in the course of time would prove mightier than the Crown itself. But so well had 'the old warrior' done his work, that the law was already becoming strong enough to stand by itself. While the Poitevin King* was fighting the battle for Christendom–but not for England–against Sultan Salahuddin, it was found that the machinery of justice was able to work smoothly and automatically in his absence. Events were moving with extreme rapidity, and when the whole flimsy structure of the Anjevin empire lay prostrate before the might of Phillip Augustus, the magnates had got to be Englishmen or nothing. The tyranny and misfortunes of the depraved lackland did even more to cement the realm than the strong hand of his father. But so firm was the system of government John had inherited, that but for the disaster of Bouvines, his tyranny might have had the upper hand. The defeat of this tyrant abroad opened the doors of opportunities for his subjects at home; the three most important classes in the realm–barons, clergy and citizens–joined hands, and the

---

* Richard I *Coeur de Lion*.

result was *Magna Carta*. 'England for the first time spoke as a nation.'[72] Robert Vaughan has aptly remarked: 'The vices of our kings have often proved favourable to the liberties of the people.'[73]

In the opinion of Stubbs:

> The effect of his (John's) fifteen years of misrule had been to undo all that had been done to strengthen the royal power since the reign of Henry I; to undo the work of the twelfth century in England, as he had done in the continental territories of his house; and thus to set the nation at one with itself, in a way in which it had not since the conquest realized its identity. The sentence of Runnymede reversed the sentence of Hastings.[74]

Magna Carta was the first corporate act of the nation roused to the sense of its unity; the first act of the three estates discovering the true oneness of their interests and sinking their differences under the pressure of a common enemy.[75] Historians have recorded less of the action of the third estate, but the barons could not have done what they did without the help of the people, and the king would not have been so helpless as he was if he could, as William Rufus and Henry I had done, have made himself strong in the support of the people against the barons.[76] According to Edward-Cheyney: 'The date of the Great Charter, 1215, will always remain one of the most important in English history, not because it weakened the central government but because it took the first steps towards putting it under the control of the people.[77]

There is no need, however, to indulge in undue eulogy of the Charter or its authors. One would do well to note that the greatness of the Charter was less in its intention, than its results.[78] Commenting upon it, Vaughan observes: 'Many evils of that time were thus abated or abolished, many principles were avowed or assumed which were to be applied in after times upon a scale never suspected by those who had evoked them. The seeds were there, the vegetation and the growth would come in its season.'[79]

Considering that the barons were dictating their own terms, the wonder is not that they checked the central power, but that they accepted it as a whole, and left it pruned, but substantially intact. If they weakened the force of the law in some respects, they provided it also with its greatest triumph, for they put it definitely above the king. What the royal power did in respect of the magnates, the Charter did the respect of the king. And hence, while the feudal aspect of the Charter tends to recede with the gradual disappearance of feudalism, there emerges from it the concept of an impersonal and majestic law, dominating king and subject alike.[80] No lapse of time can detract from the grandeur and relevance of such words as: 'to no man will we sell, to no man will we deny or delay right or justice.' The spirit of the Charter is, in fact, the spirit of England. The mere fact that it deals in a practical manner with concrete grievances, and that it appeals not to the abstraction that ought to be, but to the custom that has been, makes it more English than ever.[81]

In one sense, it may be true to say that the efforts of the conqueror and the two great Henries were shattered at Runnymede. In a truer and deeper sense, it was crowned and brought to completion. The task of the Normans, and particularly the Norman kings, had been to bring method and order out of slovenliness and anarchy. That order was now established on impregnable foundations. The administrative machinery continued to function unimpaired, but so long as the Charter stood firm, it was forced to function by law and not according to any man's arbitrary whim. And that law was not the centralized despotism of Rome, but the Common Law of English liberties.[82]

The Norman conquest of England, says Davis Douglas, 'was perhaps the most revolutionary event in English history between the Conversion and the Reformation.'[83] In England, there has been in recent years a strong tendency among some scholars to minimize the results of the Norman impact upon English development. 'In the face of the deeper currents of continuity,' we are told, 'the Norman conquest and its immediate consequences were but ripples on a troubled surface.'[84] By contrast, states Douglas, 'two important lectures delivered in 1966 were concerned to emphasize the important contributions made by the Normans to English political and artistic growth, an a prominent legal historian has lately declared that the Norman conquest 'was not an episode but the most decisive event in English history with the most enduring consequeces'. 'A detached inquirer', Douglas continues to say, 'might well be excused if he felt bewildered by these conflicting voices, but he may be reassured by the judicious moderation of Sir Frank Stenton. That great scholar brought about an enhanced appreciation of the Anglo-Saxon achievement, but he also declared 'sooner or later every aspect of English life was changed by the Norman conquest.'[85]

Historians used to measure the sentiment of nationality, its growth and intensification, by the progress of the vernacular. Freeman long ago pointed out that no effort was made by the conqueror to 'strangle' the English tongue.[86] Latin supplanted English as the literary and official medium, we cannot doubt, with general approval, and French, too, rather later, won on its merits.[87] But, in the opinion of Thomas Costain: 'The emergence of English as the sole language of general use was delayed by the tendency of men like Thomas A Becket, Nicholas Brakespeare, and Stephen Langton to go abroad in search of learning, to Paris in particular, and to come back with French and Latin on their lips.'[88] 'Even in the stormy days of the sons of Henry, however,' Costain states, 'university was growing up around St. Frideswide's and St. Martin's at Oxford. In less than a century, the teaching of eager and poverty-stricken youths in the porches of the churches and in the *hospitia* formed by groups was helping in the gradual establishment of the native tongue.'[89]

The growing nationalism was not quite inarticulate. It found expression, not in the masterpieces of a regional literature, but in the work of men whose chief glory it is to have laid the foundations on which the masters could build. The important condition of nationalism is the sense of national continuity and it was futile to expect the Norman and the Englishman to amalgamate, unless they could boast of a common past, a common heritage of history and tradition. In course of time the anglicized Normans came to adopt not only the name but the very past of Englishmen. Alfred and Arthur were names more thrilling than those of Rollo or Charlemagne.[90] The medieval chroniclers were making history while they wrote it, and fulfilling that most dignified of the historian's functions in strengthening the bond between the generations, and deepening the same passions whose course they traced.

It was during the latter half of the twelfth century, when Norman as well as Saxon began to be glorified in the name of Englishman, that the activity of the chroniclers reached its zenith. The Anjevin empire, for all its shortcomings, at least did something towards nourishing a healthy pride, and the mere fact that the king of England was, with the possible exception of the emperor, the most powerful potentate in Europe, must itself have contributed to some extent towards healing the wound of the Conquest.

The foremost among Chroniclers, noted for accuracy, for command of materials, and ease of style, is William of Malmesbury, who died before Henry II came to the throne. A fervent patriot, he felt Norman and English blood in his veins, and was proud of both. But England was his true mother country, as we can see in his lament over Hastings. He took special pride in the success of his country and remarked that though the English had been conquered at home they always appeared invincible when they fought abroad.[91]

Malmesbury was perhaps the greatest patriot among the chroniclers. But he was not alone in loving his country, the fire of patriotism did indeed blaze among historians, amid the darkness of feudalism. It is hardly possible to chronicle the fortunes of a noble race without feeling a certain joy in its membership, and a longing to connect with its achievement. History does foster patriotism. A contemporary of Malmesbury, Ordericus Vitalis, is one of the longest and most diffused of historians but seldom tedious. The patriotism of Ordericus is tinged with a certain wistful pity that betrays his monkish sympathies, and while Malmesbury is proud of his countrymen, Ordericus is more often sorry for them.

There were more such other architects of patriotism, who invested this country's history with its background of legend, who gave to England, in King Arthur, what Theseus was to Athens and Aeneas to Rome. It was through them that the traditional story of English race was brought forth, and from whom gradually emerges the colossal figure of Arthur. We need not concern ourselves with the steps of this development, nor with the question of whether there was, or was not, a real Arthur. It may be said without exaggeration that every age has its own Arthur.[92]

If we are to judge Geoffrey of Monmouth on his claim of narrating things that actually happened, we must dismiss him as being either extremely credulous, or an unmitigated liar. But if we regard him in the light of a creative artist, consciously transforming legendary material into a prose epic and instinct with profound symbolism, we can hardly overestimate the value of what he accomplished. These legendary glories, which were the common property of baron and serf, and which survive as place names all over Britain, were the best possible means of touching the medieval imagination and effecting what the philosophic cant of our own day would call a transvaluation of values. The Normans would look back, not upon Rollo, but upon Arthur, whose career would exactly realize what he must have conceived as his ideal man of action. The Saxon would no longer think of himself as the member of a crushed race, but, illogically enough, as a countryman of the great king, and the descendant of Trojan Brutus, one of a people who

'In everything are sprung,
From earth's first blood,
Have titles manifold.'[93]

Gradually, painfully, but all the more surely for that, England was beginning to feel her soul.

The reign of John marks the end of the period[94] during which the effects of the conquest were felt.

In the words of Thomas Costain:

> In view of the terrible sufferings of the people in the first stages, and the monstrous injustice of the land seizure, it may seem callous to assert that the destructive aspects of 1066 were

outweighed by the benefits. Looking back over the centuries, however, it is easy to see that this was so.[95]

It is easy now to see that the defeat at Hastings was in the long run a great boon for the English people. If Harold had won, they would have been spared a long period of suffering: but there would have been a great loss. Would the Anglo-Saxons, left to themselves, have achieved in time all the objectives? Most probably not! According to Costain the Saxons had certain racial weaknesses which would have held them back. They were lacking in ambition, in dispatch, in commercial instincts. These lacks would have handicapped them, particularly as they lived in racial privacy, almost in a vacuum. It is futile to speculate what the future of England would have been if the Norman invasion had been a failure. 'This much is certain, however, Costain observes, 'the city of London would never have been the capital of a great empire.[96]

To quote the same authority:

> If Harold had not lost on the ridge of Senlac, there would never have been the opportunities which sent Drake around the world and Wolfe to the Plains of Abraham ... there would not have been a race of shopkeepers which could lead the world at the same time in political and scientific advance and produce a glittering roster of great names–Roger bacon, Francis Bacon, Wycliff, Shakespeare, Cromwell, Darwin and Winston Churchill. If the men who died on the ridge had been allowed a glimpse into the mists of the future and had seen great continents reclaimed, an empire built around their little island, the path of freedom won, they might have counted their lives well lost.[97]

II. England, A Nation: The Magnificent Century

The reigns of John and Henry III cannot be logically separated; both faced the same great problems. The growing nation had to grow into a national form of government, and the only government possible for reviving Anglo-Saxon community was a free one. 'This made the reign of Henry III, an epitome of English history.'[98] says Richardson.

After *Magna Carta*, the spirit of nationality became more and more pronounced. The barons did, indeed, send an invitation to Louis of France to come over and supplant John, but, says Wingfield, 'they were acting under as great provocation as the statesmen who called over William of Orange to deliver them from another *protege* of Rome.' It must be admitted, however, that 'the episide is one which reflects little credit on the barons.'[99] 'That the barons were able to contemplate and even favour such a result is an indication of the panic into which they had fallen',[100] says Costain.

A national hero had arisen in the person of Hubert de-Burgh, who despite his foreign name, is entitled to an honourable place on the roll of English patriots. Determined to prevent a new French army from getting across, he roused the fisherfolk of the country with burning words. 'If this folklands, England is lost', he told them, and added that, 'they might hang him if he surrendered the key of England, this brings the land of Arthur to the heels of Louis. The fishermen were moved to tears, and a victory, as complete and decisive as Trafalgar, was the result[101], and Louis was quickly disposed of. In the words of Wingfield-Stratford:

> This sea fight off Dover is important not only for the fact that it prevented another foreign conquest of England, but from the evidence it gives of England having begun to find herself and to glow with a spirit to which it would be pedantry to deny the name of patriotism. The existence of this spirit is a fact which the modern school of historians ... is a little prone to obscure.[102]

Wingfield admits that there were 'many forces making against what we now know as nationalism, and particularly in the beginning of the century ...nonetheless', he affirms, 'the thirteenth century is remarkable for the vigourous growth of this spirit, which was never more actively in being than during the regins of Henry and his son.'[103]

In the epoch of transition that comprised the fifty-six years of Henry III's reign, the main interest centred in the church. In truth, the country had been brought to a humiliating pass. For the greater part of his reign, Henry remained the passive tool of foreigners, and especially of the pope. It is a strange phenomenon in English history that the weakest of her kings should stand between the most obdurate and the ablest. Year by year, as royal misgovernment grew worse and worse, the alliance between the pope and king grew firmer. If every holy father had been animated by the pure ideals of an Innocent III, the subservience might have been less intolerable; but Rome herself was infected by the very canker of simony she professed to heal. And, indeed, the papacy was in desperate need of money for its struggles with the Caesars, and England, under the feeble Henry III, was a convenient milch cow. With the accession of Innocent IV, Roman extortion began to reach its climax. He went so far as to say, 'Is not the king of England our vassal, not to say slave, since we can, at our word, imprison or consign him to ignominy?' Surely it was ignomonious enough that such words could be used with the impunity of an English king![104]

But all Englishmen did not possess Henry's subservient temper. The situation was complicated by the fact that among churchmen too, the spirit of patriotism was beginning to conflict with that of Roman super-patriotism. In the words of Wingfield: 'Henry III's reign witnessed the growth of a militant nationalism even among clerics and magnates.'[105]

The greatest of all nationalist churchmen of this reign was undoubtedly Robert Grosseteste, a poor man's son who rose to be bishop of Lincoln. To the saintliness and learning of Anslem* he added something of Becket's fiery obstinacy: but Grosseteste proved himself different from Becket in that he showed himself as an Englishman first and a Roman Catholic afterwards; and towards the end of his life we find him among the foremost supporters of a national policy.

It was in 1247, that a parliament or assembly of magnates, lay and clerical, was held in London, from which letters of strong protest were sent, one to the pope and the other to the Cardinals, signed with the mark of the City of London. For London, now indisputably the capital city, had suffered more than any other part of the kingdom from the blundering partiality of Henry III, and her citizens were assuming the

* A pious and learned monk, Arch-bishop of Canterbury under William Rufus and Henry I.

character they were to maintain for centuries, of the most intractable and politically alive section of the community. The money extracted by the pope was, the remonstrance pointed out, wanted for defence against foreign enemies and to provide for the poor.[106]

The reign of Henry III is, on the whole, one of dissension and impotence, but nonetheless, from a patriotic standpoint, it is a period of fruitful and rapid growth. The distinction between an Englishman and a Norman was now practically obliterated; that between an Englishman and a foreigner was ever becoming more marked. Moreover, with the weakening of the feudal system, England stood in little need of the alien power of the papacy as a counteracting force.[107]

In the year 1257, it was calculated that the king had spent 950,000 marks since his days of pomp and wastefulness began–an immense sum, whose method of expenditure had rather injured, than profited, the kingdom.[108] Henry's shameful alliance with the papacy had resulted in draining England of its wealth, in turning Henry himself from the pursuit of national objects for the sake of a fictitious greatness on the continent, and, through the intrusion of foreigners into bishoprics and benefices,[109] in debasing and partially denationalizing the English church. As an indirect result of the impoverishment of the kingdom, and as the direct result of Henry's denationalizing policy, which had consistently favoured aliens in the church and state at the expense of his English subjects, the military vigour of the nation had been sapped–as the Welsh war had demonstrated. Seemingly, never since the days in which the barons had invoked Louis' aid against John, opines Richardson, had the liberties of the English nation been at a lower ebb.[110]

In 1258, the accumulated grievances of the realm came to a head. The king's policy had been discredited and his treasury was empty. It had assuredly been on account of no more fear of pope or king, that the realm had not long ago been liberated. The means of binding the king had been too hard to find, and the barons had lacked a leader. But now both the hour and the man[111] had come. 'The dangers which threatened the very existence of the nation compelled united action on part of its defenders, and the temper of the nation had been at length roused to such a point that drastic measures would not only be proposed, but enforced, if need be, at the point of the sword', says Richardson. The struggles of the English people against the papal exactions were the ground-swell which heralded the coming storm.

The postponement of the reforms had rendered its accomplishment certain, provided that success itself did not, as in the case of the Charter, bring in disunion. And so it came to pass that in a series of assemblies, stringent measures for the welfare of the land were adopted and so far enforced to rid the land of aliens. The power of the Crown was to be transferred to an oligarchy, consisting of a number of committees. The ambitious foreign policy was replaced by a strict 'Little Englandism.' But the system was too cumbrous to work, and the magnates had neither the unity nor the capacity for ruling the roost in the abeyance of monarchy. The members of the lesser baronage, the small country gentlemen, were by no means disposed to leave their destinies in the hands of their powerful neighbours. A third estate–if we may use the term in the modern sense–was, indeed, beginning to raise its head, an estate that after many vicissitudes was destined to dwarf the other two.

It now only remained to add to the representatives of the country gentry those of the town burgesses to complete, so far as that age would allow, the Commons of England. This was accomplished six years later. Simon de Montfort, leader of the nationalist coalition of barons and Londoners, was now virtually sovereign of England. He at once began to put into effect a policy of thorough going nationalism, including the protection of English craftsmen by keeping English wool for English looms, which were not as yet anything like numerous enough to absorb it, and by including Englishmen to sacrifice convenience to patriotism, and clothe themselves in the coarse fabrics of their native country.[112]

Simon was naturally anxious to establish such a policy on as broad a basis of national support as possible. It is for that reason that he summoned to the parliament not only the magnates, lay and ecclesiastical, and two knights from each shire to represent the lesser gentry, but also two burgesses from each of a number of towns selected for their loyalty to his cause. There is no need to credit the Earl with any particular love for constitutional principles in the abstract, or a desire to lay the foundation of representative government, and little need to stress the continental precedents that he may or may not have had in mind. He was doing what every ruler of England has had to do, squaring those sections of the community which were powerful enough to bring down his goverment if he did not. The towns were increasing rapidly in wealth and importance, and could no longer be left out of the reckoning. Once they had entered into the general assembly of the nation, they had come to stay.

Earl Simon's experiment of a nationalist government under his own auspices was doomed to failure. The magnates, though they had shown themselves capable of standing together for the law of the land, were too deeply infected with the feudal virus to hold together for very long, and least of all under one of themselves. Simon, too, was hot blooded and overbearing: perhaps his foreign blood disqualified him from the English faculty of compromise. He had been but a year in the saddle when he found himself faced by the necessity of fighting against the young Prince Edward, whose military genius was equal to his own. His little army was cut to pieces with its lealder. The virtual ruler of the country was now Edward, 'who was as thorough-paced a nationalist as Simon, and capable of continuing the Earl's policy of ruling England by her own laws and as the interpreter of her will.'[113]

By the time Simon died, several essential factors of patriotism had been established. Feudal anarchy was curbed; the anti-national claims of the church had grown odious; a trading class was beginning to flourish, and an industrial class struggling into existence; the towns were under control and the germ of a national policy planted; a national army was coming into being, and a sturdy and defiant racial pride was spreading through all classes.[114]

In the words of Richardson:

> He (Simon) was the pride of the minorities, the heralds of the popular movement, and the idol of the commune of London. The crowning act of his career was the construction of the parliament of 1265, with its rich freightage for all coming years. His sudden removal from the scene of action seemed to destroy in a moment the labours of a life; but the aspiration of one age proved to be the promise of fulfilment in the next, and the force of his one supreme creative act was never lost.[115]

Of Edward I, says Wingfield, 'England at last found herself under a sovereign whose good and bad qualities were equally characteristic of her ....He takes up the work of his great grandfather, Henry of Anjou; only now, instead of a foreigner setting up an efficient bureaucratic despotism, we have an Englishman, the type and hero of his people, acting in thorough harmony with them.'[116] In the words of Edward Cheyney: 'The most noteworthy feature of this period was its intensely national character.' And further: 'Edward, in striking contrast to his father, was strongly English. Along with his old English name he had a decided preference for Englishmen and English ways ....In Edward ... the English people at last had a truly national king, who loved England; one whose aim it was to carry out an English policy, to make England the centre of his interests, and to choose Englishmen as ministers of his government. This attitude of the king was in harmony with the condition of the country. The English were becoming more distinctly a single nation.[117]

Seldom had an English monarch such opportunities of influencing the course of history and few would have been so capable of rising to them. Edward I is rightly to be regarded not just as the successor of his father, but of Simon de Montfort, for it is in the Earl's spirit that he confronts his people and the Earl's policy of which his own is a continuation. The nation was ripe for such a leader. It was many times easier for it to follow an English king than to rally around the most admirable of rebels.

So great was the work accomplished by this 'English Justinian', that Mathew Hale thought that more had been done to settle the justice of the kingdom in the first thirteen years of his reign, than in all the three and a half centuries that succeeded it.[118] Every department of national policy had been taken in a firm and skilful hand. The power of the great feudatories, already shaken at Evesham*, was now decisively curbed. The Charter remained, but now as a national and not feudal document. Limits were set to the encroachments of Rome and the Church could no longer command the thunders of an Innocent or a Hildebrand. In the words of William Stubbs:

> Edward ... had to choose between the continuation of his vassalage (to pope) and his glorious status as a national king. Unlike John, he chose the latter, to the enormous increase of his own power in church and state, and to that adjustment of the relations between the papacy and England which continued to the Reformation, and which, read politically, without reference to the spiritual questions, continue in the direction of their course to the present day.[119]

Judged by its influence on England and other countries, the completion of the organization of parliament was vastly, in the opinion of Cheyney, the most importnat event of this time. The king and his ministers felt that the general approval of all the influential classes was desirable and even necessary for the successful carrying out of any measure. In one of his proclamations, Edward laid down his policy by declaring that, 'that which affects all should be approved by all.'[120]

Who were the 'all' whom the king had in his mind? In earlier times it had been simply the nobles and prelates. But a change had come over the country. The nation was beginning to claim a voice in its own government, and even a popular monarch, as Edward, was unable to enforce his will upon his subjects. If it was desirable for the king to obtain the agreement of all the important clases of the community to public measures, the substantial middle classes, which represented a large part of the solid strength of the country, could hardly be neglected. In the cities and boroughs, which

---

* The battle where the barons were defeated and Simon killed (1265).

had been growing in number and size, there were many rich, enterprising and intelligent merchants. From the point of view of taxation, these classes were even more important than the nobles and the great churchmen.

Edward was a great constitutional reformer not only interested in securing his own immediate ends and the money for the needs of his government, but devoted to the work of governing for its own sake, and anxious to introduce permanent arrangements for good government into England. In 1295, a regular system of representation was adopted, which became the standard and model for all later parliaments. Its membership consisted of the two archbishops, eighteen bishops, about seventy abbots, seven earls, and forty-one barons; and in addition to these, some seventy representatives of the shires and around two hundred representatives of the towns. All these classes were regularly summoned to parliament. The bishops and abbots sat in parliament not only as great churchmen but as representatives of the whole organized church. The nobility of England were the earls and barons who were summoned in person to parliament. The commons were considered to represent all the rest of the nation, though of course the great mass of the people had no influence in the elections or over the actions of the representatives in parliament.[121]

The reign of Edward I marked the coming of age of the English Constitution, and we may endorse the words of Blackstone: 'It is from this period, from the exact *observation* of *Magna Carta* rather than from its *making* or *renewal*, in the days of his grandfather and father, that the liberty of Englishmen again began to rear its head; though the weight of military tenures hung heavy upon it for many ages after.'[122]

And yet it was the same Edward of whom, after his overthrow by Simon at Lewes, an upholder of constitutional principles had been moved to write, 'O Edward! You want to be king without law; wretched indeed would they be who are ruled by such a king', and then, with an appreciation of the main issue that could not be bettered in the light of subsequent history, 'therefore, let the general body (*communitas*) of the kingdom be taken to counsel, and what the whole (*universitas*) feels, let it be known.' If the Earl Simon could, thirty years after his death, have been present in spirit at Edward's model of all subsequent parliaments, he might have well echoed the words he had used when caught in the trap at Evesham:

> 'By the arm of Saint James, they come on wisely, but it is from me that they learnt the method!'[123]

While England was taking remarkable strides in the direction of freedom and establishing principles of democratic rule which the world would accept later, Englishmen also had been sharing in other activities of this great and beneficent period.

Costain calls it 'the magnificent century' because it saw the beginnings of so much. Men began to think new thoughts, to dream again, to rediscover beauty which had almost been lost. Science, which had started with Plato and Aristotle, Euclid, Archimedes, and Pythagoras, may be said to have been born a second time in the thirteenth century, because it was then that the principles of scientific research were discovered. These years from 1200 to 1300 were to see progress in all directions.[124]

In architecutre, which usually reflects national life very clearly, this was the period of the introduction of the first truly national style of English building, that which is called 'Early English.' In France, as in England, the thirteenth century is the supreme period of Christian Gothic architecture. The 'Early English' Gothic style in the reign of Henry III has neither the outspoken virility nor the logical completeness of the contemporary French style. From this fact some critics have been tempted to write off the English builders as if they were incapable of applying the Gothic principle, and as if the English style were something second-rate and inferior to the French. If the pushing of one idea to its logical conclusion were essential to greatness, the inferiority of the English to the Latin mind would follow as a natural consequence.The Englishman has a temperamental aversion to extreme views or courses; he would rather strike a balance between several than commit himself unreservedly to one.[125] It is futile to prove the superiority of either the French or the English mind.

Whether we are to praise or blame them for it, the English builders failed to push the Gothic principle to its logical extreme, not because they could not but because they would not. No importation of foreign architects or ideas could avail against the unformulated English determination to express the national spirit in the national way. What must be evident to every student of English architecture is a certain reserve about the chief English buildings to which the French are strangers. The English Cathedral is shut off from the world in its close, or enclosed space, whereas the French stands in the heart of the city, jostled by houses, with its enormous doors inviting all and sundry to snatch a few moments of holy calm from the turmoil outside. The whole spirit of the English building is typified by its deliberate withdrawal into a closed peace. Not only are the heights less stupendous, the entrance less cavernous, but the openly displayed thrust of the buttress ribs is tempered, so that the form of the upper or clear story is more serenely apparent than in the typical French cathedral.[126]

With the interior it is the same. Only in Westminster is there any real apprach to the full steepness and uprush of the French Gothic, and even Westminster is, in this respect, a poor second to Amiens.[127] In so typically English a production as Salisbury, the eye is checked, as it mounts from floor to ceiling, by the restraining gesture of a continuous horizontal line at the base of triforium. The interior of walls, despite the exuberance and caprice of its detail carving, breathes an almost Anglican discreetness, there is such a deliberate aviodance of anything that could be remotely described as tumultuous–here the eye is guided, as if by some invisible sacristan, along and not upward.[128]

The English Gothic of the thirteenth century no doubt sacrifices much that is possessed by the French. Undoubtedly no architecture was ever great that did not give the most exact expression to the spirit that inspired it. The English buildings have a sweetness and solemnity of their own, that goes far to compensate for the more obvious attractions of the French style. And we must never forget that we see but the gaunt and mutilated skeletons of what were once veritable houses of God, aglow with colour and enriched with ornaments long since despoiled.[129]

It is not only in stone that England's spirit finds expression during these years of dawning nationhood. During a period of great intellectual progress throughout Western Europe, her thinkers and philosophers are in the van. The University of Oxford was acquiring a reputation scarcely inferior to that of Paris and Bologna. It was, however, very different from the home of aristocratic culture and monarchical sentiment it was afterwards to become; no one, in the thirteenth century, would have ventured to call it the home of lost causes. Its students were mostly poor men, fired with an insatiable zeal for knowledge, and robustly 'against the government'. They were in the forefront of the nationalist movement against Henry III and the pope. Robert Grosseteste sought to model Oxford after Paris and with brilliant success.[130] When we consider that Oxford probably counted thirty thousand students in these days, and weigh the political as well as the religious importance of the city in the troubles of the realm, we must assuredly rank Grosseteste's Oxford efforts high among the causes which made for the growth of English national sentiments and freedom.[131] The most revolutionary innovations in thought and politics are found in the works of medieval Oxonians.

When we talk of English or of Oxonian thought we must bear in mind that in no subsequent period was thought so European as in the days of schoolman (teacher in the medieval universities or Institution). Nevertheless, there is a sense in which we may speak of as definite a British contribution to thought as to architecture. Gothic is European but early English is national; scholasticism is European but the spirit of Bacon, Occam, and Wycliffe* is English, and this rich harvest of

* John Wycliffe was a religious preacher of the fourteenth century: he is called 'the morning star' of the Reformation.

thought and building springs from the soil of a patriotism newborn. The twist that English thinkers give to European thought is characteristic of the English contribution to thought throughout subsequent ages. 'Cut out the fine talk and get down to facts', has ever been the Englishman's motto. It reveals both his strength and weakness. The English mind is resolutely inductive, and most of all in dealing with the affairs of life. Where the Frenchman talks of the rights of man, the Englishman talks of *Magna Carta* and bases his liberties upon precedence.[132]

The thirteenth century was a century of great men in England as it was in other countries. At no time previously, during the middle ages, and scarcely since, have men thought in many fields more deeply or reasoned more closely. Indeed, many of the men who made the continental universities famous came from England.[133] Roger Bacon and a number of other learned Englishmen comprised a group of Oxford trained men, all whom later became famous as lecturers at Paris, Bologna, or other European universities.

The doctors of the thirteenth century were devoted admirers of Aristotle, considered him the philosopher of all times. The two intellectual champions of the Dominican order, Albert the Great and Thomas Aquinas, used his logic to build up a system of universal philosophy worked out with amazing thoroughness and ingenuity. 'The weakness of such a system of universal knowledge' in the opinion of Wingfield, 'lay in its divorce from the facts of life.' The criticism not unjustly levelled at St. Thomas was that he taught everything but knew nothing.[134]

The work of British thinkers like Duns, Occam and Bacon, in harmony with nationalist resistance to the claim of Rome, went a long way in breaking the shackles forged by St. Thomas. Bacon was no modern scientist; he was a man of manifest imperfections. He accepted the current assumption, that the end of all wisdom is to enable man to live according to God's will, and that all truth is contained in scripture. His very philology is marred by the strangest errors. The marvel is that he obtained such a *Pisgah*[135] view of subsequent developments and with true English practicality, he goes straight for the weak points in St. Thomas, He shows the absurdity of a blind acceptance of Aristotle through translations that distort his meaning, and reveal how far the schoolmen actually are from following the example of Aristotle when they neglect nature. 'If you want to know about God'—that is the gist of his message—'study God's works.'[136]

That national feeling and the regional had not yet come together in the thirteenth century is clear. The increase of some sort of political unity and the strengthening of national consciousness took place at a time when England enjoyed three literary languages; and (unless we throw over our Stubbs) the process of amalgamation was still continuous. The country was loyal, patriotic, anti-Welsh, anti-Scottish and anti-French and displayed all the essentials of national consciousness, except that, as Galbraith says, 'so far as education allowed, it preferred Latin to French, and French to English.'[137] Robert of Gloucester, writing towards the end of the century, complains that there is no land 'that holdeth not to its own speech save England only.'[138] But the exception is one that proves the rule, since of all European states, England was then the most highly developed national unit. 'The use of the mother tongue was not yet a criterion of national feeling.'[139]

To sum up, during this amazing span of years, the mind of man, awakening from its long stupor, had turned with vigourous energy towards progress. He was no longer content with what he had known before and was questing in all directions–thinking, asking, demanding and inventing. New weapons were being produced, new types of ships built. Clocks were put up in church towers, at Westminster, Canterbury, St. Albana, to the great wonderment of Englishmen, and one Robertus Anglicus was experimenting with a mechanical clock which would be operated with weights. Roger Bacon, that man of mighty intellect and fascinating mystery, was beginning to speak of curious things, of glasses which would make it possible to see clearly across the channel from Dover to France, of vehicles which would soar unsupported through the air, of a powder of the most secret kind, made up largely of saltpeter, which would explode with a flash of fire like lightning in the sky and a roar to equal the terror of winds at the end of the world.

III. Epilogue

Galbraith defines a nation as 'any considerable group of people who believe they are one': and their nationalism as 'the state of mind which sustains this belief.' Broadly speaking, the sentiment of nationality is 'much the same in quality at all times and in all places. Its minimum content is love, or at least awareness, of one's country, and pride in its past achievements, real or fictitious; and it springs from attachment to the known and familiar, stimulated by the perception of difference–difference of habits and customs, often too of speech, from those of neighbouring peoples.' The historical evidence for the existence of this positive sentiment in early times is largely inferred from the struggles and sentiment in early times is largely inferred from the struggles and mutual animosities of clans constantly at war. But by the tenth or eleventh century, says Galbraith, there is evidence that medieval man was faintly stirred by the same sort of national impulses as we are, though, as it is easy to see, he felt them in very different situations and environments, in a different degree and, often, in relation to other objects. 'By the thirteenth century the fully developed medieval state had reached a momentary equilibrium, and if it was still 'feudal', it was also, in its way, a national state.'[140]

Many of the symptoms of nationalism, B.C. Keeney observes, are evident in England at the turn of the fourteenth century. The consciousness of kind shared by a large group of people united in one state is present in the concept of the community of the realm[141] which consisted of individuals grouped into subordinate communities, such as the church, the country, the borough and the baronage. 'The subordinate communities were in the process of breaking down, and the loyalties attached to them were being bound to the community of the realm and the king, its head and personification', states Keeney. Though the king still dealt with the subordinate communities as groups, he was beginning on the one hand, as

Keeney points out, to handle their members as individual subjects with common obligations, and on the other hand, to deal with the community of the whole realm in parliament.[142]

A nation feels that it is entitled to determine its own destiny, and sometimes the destiny of inferior peoples. From the reign of Henry III on, the barons, at least, felt that they had thought to work out the country's destiny with the king, and without any outside help. There is a suggestion that the English thought they had a mission to rule the other peoples of the island. Edward I's 'imperialistic' plans, notwithstanding their failure, left a deep impression.

The most conspicuous symptom of nationalism in Edwardian England was a dislike for foreigners, but it was the least significant, since it existed among nearly all peoples, even primitive tribes who were indifferent to the feeling of nationalism. Dislike of real foreigners, as distinguished from the foreigner from the next county, was stimulated as a reaction against preferential treatment accorded to aliens among the retinue of Henry III, and by the long series of foreign wars beginning in the reign of Edward I. National characteristics were already etched; only they had to be channelized politically. Even today, emotions so vague and intangible as national feeling need symbols to give them definite expression. In 1300, as Keeney rightly observes, the symbol was the king. Loyalty to him manifested in the concept of the community of the realm. The king personified the country and, with the community of the realm–which was broadening out from the narrow baronial interpretation–was deemed responsible as the protector and defender of his people, in whose interests he acted. He tried to identify the interests of the people with the interests of the realm. Edward's memorable phrase, 'What touches all should be approved by all' and 'Common dangers should be met by measures provided in common', doubtless show that he was as concerned with common action as with general approval. In 1297, he ordered that anyone with twenty pounds income should be prepared to serve wherever the king should lead them to defend the realm. Common service in warfare made men aware that they were part of something larger than their local community, and this roused emotional attachment to the king and the country.[143]

By the first quarter of the fourteenth century, the phrase community of the realm at times identified the union of all individuals and subordinate communities, of which the baronage or peerage was one; in other texts it excluded the baronage and the church, and implied the Commons in parliament, who represented most of the rest of the free population. There is evidence that peasants were faithful to the community long before they became an active part of it. The feeling of obligation to the realm by all the members of its community became an important factor in royal politics when the king found it worthwhile to appeal to it to win support for his plans and policies.

NOTES AND REFERENCES

1. Marc Bloch. 'Medieval National Consciousness', *Nationalisn in the Middle Ages*–European Problem Studies–C. Leon Tipton, (ed.), (New York : Holt, Rinehart and Winston, 1972), p.25.
2. Johan Huizinga. 'Nationalism in the Middle Ages', Ibid, p.14.
3. C. Leon Tipton. 'Introduction', Ibid, p.2.
4. Huizinga. Ibid, p.14.
5. Ibid, pp.14-15.
6. Ibid, p.15.
7. Boyd C. Shafer. 'The Early Development of Nationality', Ibid, p.41.
8. Hans Kohn. *Nationalism : Its Meaning and History*, rev. edn., (New York : D. Van Nostrand Co., Inc., 1965), p. 9.
9. 'A nineteenth-century French historian who stressed the strength and continuation of Roman ideas and institutions in the early Middle Ages.' Tipton, op.cit. p.25.
10. Bloch, Ibid. pp. 25-26.
11. Halvdan Koht. 'The Dawn of Nationalism in Europe', *The American Historical Review*, Vol. 52, Oct., 1946 to July, 1947, p.265.
12. Ibid, p.265.
13. Ibid, p.265.
14. Ibid. p. 266.
15. Bloch, op.cit. p.28.

16. Decretum C 23 q. 8c. 15 Sinulla urget: J.E. 2812: cited by Gaines Post, 'Two Notes on Nationalism in the Middle Ages', *Traditio*—Studies in Ancient and Medieval History, Thought and Religion, 1953, Vol. 9, p.282.
17. Ibid, p.283.
18. Ibid, p.284.
19. Ibid, p.294.
20. Ibid, p.295. More will be said of 'community of the realm' infra.
21. Ibid, p.320.
22. Joseph R. Strayer. 'Laicization and Nationalism in the Thirteenth Century', Tipton, op.cit. pp.31–33.
23. Thomas F. Tout. 'Feudal Allegiance and National Sentiment', Ibid, pp.59–64.
24. Ibid, p.63.
25. Ibid, p.64.
26. *A.Lecoy de la Marche, (ed.), Oeuvres Completes de Suger* (Paris, 1867) p.116, cited by Koht, op.cit, p.266.
27. Ibid, p.266.
28. A. Luchaire. Innocent III (Paris, 1905), I, 175: cited by Ibid. p.269.
29. Ibid, p.270.
30. Ibid, pp.270–72.
31. Ibid, p.279.
32. Kemp Malone. Notes and Documents 'The Rise of English Nationalism' *Journal of the History of Ideas*, (Oct, 1940) Vol. I(4), p. 504.
33. Ibid, 505.
34. Esme Wingfield-Stratford, *The History of English Patriotism*, (New York: John Lane Co., 1913), Vol. I, p.7.
35. Ibid, p. 7.
36. Ibid, p. 8.
37. Ibid, p. 9.
38. Ibid, p.12.
39. G.O. Sayles. *The Medieval Foundations of England*, rev. edn.,(London: Methuen and Co. Ltd., 1952), p.218.
40. T.F. Tout, *A History of Great Britain*, (New York: Longman Green and Co., 1902), p.61.
41. Wingfield-Stratford. *English Patriotism*, op.cit, p.12.
42. Edward A. Freeman. *A Short History of the Norman Conquest of England*, 2nd. edn., (Oxford: Clarendon Press, 1880), p.5.
43. Sayles, op.cit, p.297.

44. Dana Carletin Munro. *The Middle Ages 395–1272*, (New York: The Century Co., 1923), p.257.
45. Philippe Wolff. *Western Languages A.D. 100–1500*, trans. from the French by Frances Partridge, (New York: Mc Graw-Hill Book Co., 1971), p.162.
46. Sayles, op.cit, p.297.
47. Edward A. Freeman. *The History of the Norman Conquest of England*, 2nd. rev. edn., (Oxford: Clarendon Press, 1869), Vol. I, pp. 1–2.
48. Wingfield-Stratford, '*Eng*. Pat. op. cit, p.14.
49. Sayles, op.cit, p.220.
50. Barnaby C. Keeney. '*England*', Tipton, op.cit, p.88.
51. D.J.A. Matthew. *The Norman Conquest*, (London: B.T. Batsford Ltd.,1966), p.288.
52. Wingfield-Stratford, op.cit, p.15: Henry I sought to persuade his barons to allow his daughter Matilda to reign after his death. The barons were very unwilling to agree to this, partly because they did not like to be ruled by a woman, and partly because Matilda was married to Geoffrey, Count of Anjou, and the Normans hated the Anjevins, as the men of Anjou were called. But the kings will prevailed, and all the barons took oaths to obey Matilda as their future queen. The barons, however, broke their promises, and choose as their king *Count Stephen of Boulogne*, Henry's nephew, and a grandson of the Conqueror. A long civil war followed. At last Matilda gave up the struggle in despair. Tout, op.cit, pp. 70–71.
53. Munro, op.cit, p.265.
54. William Stubbs. *Historical Introduction to the Rolls Series*, Arthur Hassal. (New York: Longman Green and Co., 1902), p.108.
55. Ibid, pp.109–10.
56. Ibid, p.110.
57. Ibid, p.110.
58. Ibid, p.110.
59. In the opinion of Robert Vaughan, however, 'Its effect, ... was not so much to augment the power of the crown, as to open the way to a gradual elevation of the people.' *Revolutions in English History*, 'Revolutions of Race' (London: John W. Parker and Son, West Strand, 1859), Vol.I, p.347.
60. Thomas B. Costain. *The Conquerors*, (NewYork: Doubleday and Co., Inc., 1949), pp.398–99.
61. In France and Germany, for example, the sovereign was simply *primus inter pares* (first among the equals) or more truly the

servants of his own servants: Stubbs, op.cit, p.113.

62. Wingfield-Stratford, Eng. Pat. op.cit, pp.16–17.
63. Stubbs, op.cit, p.158.
64. Wingfield-Stratford, op.cit, pp.18–19.
65. Ibid, pp.24–25.
66. Ibid, p.25.
67. Oliver H. Richardson. *The National Movement in the Reign Of Henry III and its Culmination in the Barons' War*, (New York: The Macmillan Co., 1897), p.5. 'That after victory he counselled moderation from motives of policy is the highest praise which he can rightly claim.' Ibid, p.5.
68. Ibid, p.6.
69. Wingfield-Stratford, Eng. Pat., op.cit, p.27.
70. Richardson, op.cit, pp. 9–10.
71. Wingfield-Stratford, op.cit, pp.29–30.
72. Ibid, pp.30–31.
73. Vaughan, op.cit, p.442.
74. Stubbs, op.cit, pp.484–85.
75. Ibid, p.484.
76. Ibid, p.485.
77. Edward P. Cheyney. *A Short History of England*, rev. enl. edn. (New York: Ginn and Co., 1944), p.184.
78. Wingfield-Stratford, Eng. Pat., op.cit, p.31.
79. Vaughan, op.cit, p.376.
80. Wingfield-Stratford, Eng. Pat., op.cit, pp.31–32.
81. Wingfield-Stratford. *The History of British Civilization*, (New York: Harcourt Brace and Co., 1928), Vol. I, p.168.
82. Ibid, p.168.
83. David C. Douglas. *William the Conqueror*, (Berkeley: University of California Press, 1964), p.367.
84. D.C. Douglas. *The Norman Achievement*, (Berkeley: University of California Press, 1969), p.169. 'The important work of F. Barlow also tends towards this interpretation. A learned though less balanced argument in the same direction will be found in H.G. Richardson and G. Sayles, "Governance of Medieval England", 1963, chs. 5 and 6, Ibid, p.2.
85. Ibid, pp.169–70.
86. Norman Conquest, V (1876), p.507. cited by V.H. Galbraith, *Nationality and Language in Medieval England*, 'Publications of the Royal Historical Society', (1941), Vol. 23, p.117.
87. Ibid, p.117.
88. Costain, op.cit. p.399.

89. Ibid, pp.399–400.
90. Wingfield-Stratford, op.cit, pp.43–44.
91. Ibid, pp.45–46. 'William of Malmesbury, ... breathes nationality, and excellent in Latin. His very grasp of English history ... marks a step forward in national consciousness, and a very slight study of the *Gesta Pontificum* reveals a historical interest rooted in English soil.' Galbraith, op.cit, p.122.
92. Ibid, pp.47–48.
93. Ibid, p.52.
94. The interval during which the great feature in English history consists in the ascendency of the Normans and the subjection of the Saxons, extends from the conquest to the age of the Great Charter. The reigns included in this interval are those of the conqueror, William Rufus, Henry I, and Stephen; also those of Henry II, and of his sons Richard and John. These reigns together cover a century and a half.
95. Costain, op.cit, p.398.
96. Ibid, pp.401–02.
97. Ibid, p.402.
98. Richardson, op.cit p.13.
99. Wingfield-Stratford, Eng. Pat. op.cit, p.35.
100. Costain, Conq., op.cit, p.388.
101. Wingfield-Stratford, Brit. Civil., op.cit, p.169, 'It is small wonder that when, fifteen years later, Hubert had fallen out of royal favour, so beloved was he by the common people that a poor smith refused, according to Mathew Paris, to strike fetters on the man who had saved England'. Ibid, p.170.
102. Ibid, p.170.
103. Ibid, p.171.
104. Wingfield-Stratford, Eng. Pat., op.cit, p.36.
105. Wingfield-Stratford, 'Brit. Civil., op.cit, p.176.
106. Ibid, p.178.
107. Wingfield-Stratford, Eng. Pat., op.cit, p.38–39. 'It was, at one time, quite conceivable that the work of the Reformation would have been anticipated, and England have snapped the bonds of Rome three centuries before the appointed time. the first half of the century witnessed a decline in religious fervour ... But the Church displayed the power ... of finding fresh source of vitality in the least promising circumstances ... And ... a way was found for the Church to continue her highest task and retrieve, by the poverty of her friars what the avarice of her pontiffs had so nearly lost'. Ibid, p.39.

108. Mathew Paris, V.p. 637, cited by Richardson, op.cit, p.152.
109. 'Of all Henry's oppressions, the misuse of ecclesiastical vacancies was perhaps the worst'. Richardson, op.cit, p.111.
110. Ibid, pp.152–53.
111. Simon de Montfort Earl of Leicester.
112. Wingfield-Stratford, Brit. Civil., op.cit, pp.179–80.
113. Ibid, pp.180–81.
114. Wingfield-Stratford, Eng. Pat., op.cit, p.43.
115. Richardson, op.cit, p.235.
116. Wingfield-Stratford, Brit. Civil, op.cit, p.197.
117. Cheyney, op.cit, pp.209–10.
118. Wingfield-Stratford, Eng. Pat., op.cit, p.58.
119. Stubbs, op.cit, p.486.
120. Cheyney, op.cit, p.210.
121. Ibid, pp.213–15. 'In speaking of the nation's will, we must not be misled by words, for the parliaments of the thirteenth century were no more representative than the caucus-driven majorities of the twentieth. The great mass of the agricultural labourers or serfs were without a voice, and even the towns sent representatives mainly drawn from the merchant, as distinguished from the growing industrial class. The elections were, at best, in the hands of a very few, and at worst, not elections at all, but nominations'. Wingfield Stratford, Eng. Pat., op.cit, p.59.
122. Ibid, p.60.
123. Wingfield-Stratford, op.cit, Brit. Civil., p.205.
124. Costain. *The Magnificent Century*, (New York : Doubleday and Co. Inc., 1951), pp.336–37.
125. Wingfield-Stratford, Brit. Civil., op.cit, p.182.
126. Ibid, pp. 182–83.
127. Ibid, p.183.
128. Ibid, p.183–84.
129. Ibid, p.184.
130. Rob. Gross, Epist. CXIV, p.335 cited by Richardson, op.cit, p.28.
131. Ibid, p.28.
132. Wingfield-Stratford, Brit. Civil., op.cit, p.191.
133. Cheyney, op.cit, p.190.
134. Wingfield-Stratford, Brit. Civil., op.cit, pp.192–93.
135. The mountain ridge east of Jordan from which Moses saw the Promised Land.
136. Wingfield-Stratford, Brit. Civil., op.cit, p.196.

137. Galbraith, op.cit, p.124.
138. J. Orr, French the third classic, p.11 : quoted in Ibid, p.124.
139. Ibid, 'It was only in fourteenth century that Europe began to be "vernacular conscious'. The change marks a clear stage in western development, and the beginning of an influence which, all over Europe, was to transform and intensify the national sentiment ...In England ... nationality and the vernacular come consciously and undeniably, if only momentarily, together for the first time in the reign of Henry V, whose despatches from France to the city of London were written, and so to speak deliberately written in English' Chambers and Daunt, London English (1931) p.139 : quoted in Ibid, p.125.
140. Galbraith, op.cit, pp.113–14.
141. Keeney, op.cit, p.88.
142. Ibid, p.96.
143. Ibid, pp.88, 89, 90 and 92.

Chapter 2

Renaissance and its Periodization

Renaissance presumably started in the fourteenth century when northern Italy was divided into cities. International trade was the main source of income. Florence depended on woollen cloth trade whereas Venice specialized in oriental goods. Here capitalist bankers and merchants had their own class groups.

'The class division was sharp in these city states. At the top were the wealthy merchants and bankers, the *popolo grasso* or 'fat people' as they were called. Beneath them were the lesser bourgeoisie, the *popolo minuto* or the 'little people'viz. craftsmen, shopkeepers and petty businessmen, and beneath them, was a growing *proletariat*, the workers.'[1] Conflict occurred in all forms : direct, indirect, anarchic and civilized. What distinguished northern Italy from the rest of Europe was the total independence of its city-states from any central authority or government. In these peculiar and unique cities of northern Italy a new society with new social ideals was flourishing which was different from the feudal society and its chivalric ideals. Their society had individualism, secularism and humanism as the newly developed values.[2]

In other words, achieved status, loose religiosity and a growing but vague concept of social justice were the features of the society. Secularism could be broken into two components; preoccupation with worthy pursuits and contempt for those who professed the ascetic ideal.[3] Humanists initiated a revolution in educational theory and practices, and Greco-Roman writers professed for liberal arts. Mean while the entire world was slowly and gradually changing.

There was also a fourth and final characteristic of this urban society–its historical self-consciousness. Humanists like Petrarch and his followers thought that the old civilization had completed its course of life. It had taken birth, existed and died and then in the fifteenth century there was a rebirth or revival of civilization. Rome had a golden age and they went into darkness with the passing of time, but life always exist after death. The Italian Humanists were followed by the Swiss Jacob Burkhardt who wrote a book *The Civilization of the Renaissance in Italy* (1860). This book agreed with the humanists and advocated the idea that after the Middle Ages there was a rebirth of civilization.

The term Renaissance is useful in the context of fine arts but it is not so meaningful for political thought and economic theories because there cannot be any gap in their history. In the political and economic context, Renaissance merely indicated less control of clergy over thinking process, do's and don'ts etc. It was intensely required in fine arts and social theories.

In Italy, France and Spain paintings were moving more and more towards realism and Giotto was first painter of this kind. In their search for realism, artists thought of shifting to three-dimensional perspectives in painting, sculpture and architecture. 'It was as if the sculptured prophets and many coloured saints had stepped down from their riches and stained glass windows in the great medieval cathedral to be reincarnated in bronze statues in Italian public squares or painted portraits in Italian palaces.[4]

The second characteristic development during the Renaissance was social prestige and individual importance given to artists. Michelangelo and Leonardo Da Vinci were the immortal artists of that time 'Picadella Mirandola in a famous oration or men's dignity (1486) pictured God as growing man–something he had given to no other creature, the unique gift of freedom.'[5]

Once again, it should be understood that in the fourteenth and the fifteenth century, a new tradition in art, literature and society was more pronounced and it can be called an exposition of the Renaissance because of its absolute dissimilarity with and superiority over everything medieval. Renaissance's influence on social and economic change is not so visible but art and literature were highly influenced.

Its very concept baffled Sellery[6] but he was optimistic and confident enough to observe that the problem of the Renaissance should not be regarded as insoluble.[7]

The attempt to ascertain a historical interpretation of the Renaissance, or of any other age, is based upon the acceptance of certain methodological presumptions. Although, history is an ever flowing stream of events and ideas, a record of adaptation and assimilation, it has to be synthesized and sifted. Even in a dynamic view of history, periodization may prove a very convenient instrument, if properly used. The slow transfor-mation resulting from a steady histroical development may be largely a change in degree, but once it has advanced far enough, it is sure to become to all intents and purposes, a change in quality.

There comes the menacing question as to what were the fundamental differences between medieval and the Renaissance civilization. The later economic historians draw attention to the dynamic revival of trade, urban life, and money economy in the midst of the agrarian feudal society of the high Middle Ages. Unfortunately these analysts have neglected the unfolding of intellectual and aesthetic culture. On the other hand, historians with special interest in religion, philosophy, literature, science or art have endeavoured to explain the progress in these spheres without corelating them with changes in the economic, social and political fabric of society. Nonetheless, in the past few years historians have understood and responded to the urgency of incorporating all phases of human activity in any general synthesis, an awareness conspicuous in Myron Gilmore's volume, *The World of Humanism*.[8]

> The popular myth that the Renaissance was the revival of light and joy after the bleak darkness of the Middle Ages was exploded by the better understanding of the great achievements of the twelfth and thirteenth centuries.[9]

That these centuries saw the development of a virile culture, is an established fact. But medieval civilization, based as it was on a system of land tenure and agriculture could not continue to imbibe an expanding urban society and money economy without losing its basic character. The revival of commerce and industry, accompanied by the growth of towns and money economy, introduced a novel and alien element into medieval agrarian feudal society. The first effect of this was to stimulate the existing civilization, emancipating it from the economic, social and cultural bondages of the purely agricultural society. As feudalism declined the political set-ups naturally also changed. The impact on the church was also immense. Its universal authority was rudely questioned and split up.

Few historians now-a-days would disclaim the value of periodization. In fact it is an intellectual tool essential to the historian's trade.[10] Its use, to quote Collingwood's dictum. 'is a mark of advanced and mature historical thought, not afraid to interpret facts instead of merely ascertaining them'.[11] Whether such periods be decades, centuries, or larger chronological areas like the Middle Ages or the Renaissance, the historian cannot think about history without them, much less interpret it for others. There is perhaps less agreement concerning the need for synthesis. Yet even for specialists, some general notion of the character of the age they are concerned with, seems necessary. In the opinion of Ferguson: 'Without some such general conception, the specialist may well find himself operating in a historical vacuum, in which the gravity of all objects seems equal.'[12]

A synthetic interpretation including all features of a particular civilization, is especially important for its bearing upon the problem of causation, even in the narrowest fields of enquiry. Painting, sculpture, music, poetry, science, philosophy or theology may each develop, to a certain extent, by a kind of inner logic, or by the activities of individual men of genius, yet the general trend of these can never be fully grasped without having an idea of other contemporaneous or antecedent changes in economic activity, political institutions, social configurations, religious beliefs, or modes of thought.[13] The scholar who ignores the possibility of a causal relation between them and the subject of his own special interest, or who is content to relate what happened without ever bothering himself to point out why it may have happened, is, in the words of Ferguson, 'using the concept of scientific objectivity as a pretext for avoiding the ncecessity of thought.'[14]

But, if we affirm the value of periodization and of synthesis, can these be applied successfully to the concept of the Renaissance? In many disciplines, like the history of art and music, the term Renaissance has been used as a style concept; in other fields, notably the history of literature and the history of ideas, it has been used to denote a movement of thought. Without getting embroiled into these confusing terms we must focus on the real problem which is not what the age should be called, but what were its most characteristic traits and chronological boundaries. How, in short, can we constitute a periodic concept of the Renaissance that may serve as a useful tool for the historian, and have practical value for the interpretation of history?

It would seem obvious that the foremost problem in periodization is to fix the chronological limits of the period in question. But this will not be possible without formulating some idea of the characteristics that distinguish it from the preceding and following ages. A period has to possess some conceptual content to encourage historical thought. It must correspond to a meaningful stage in the development of a civilization or a part thereof. Otherwise it is merely an arbitrarily selected and purposeless span of time. A perceptive and analytical historian can discern by close scrutiny, notable chagnes in the process of historical evolution; and he can do this only by forming a clear concept of the nature of these changes. He may then be in a better position to define the chronological limits of the period to which these characteristics apply. This process should not be regarded as the imposition upon historical reality of an arbitary scheme, based upon preconceived notions.[15] It merely implies that in historical analysis, close observation must result in the emergence of an hypothesis, if infinite isolated and scattered facts are to be systematized in some consistent form and order to be made accessible to thought.[16]

Coming to the problem of the Renaissance, the first step must be to form a hypothesis concerning its essential character. There is great divergence of opinion in this respect leading to an unending debate among historians of the last hundred years or so. Depending upon one's views, the Renaissance would seem to have lasted as much as four hundred years, or only twenty-seven years, not counting the views of those scholars who think that the Renaissance did not exist at all.[17] As we may see from Professor Ferguson's and Prof. Weisinger's studies, attempts to define and evaluate the meaning of the period have been so numerous and inconclusive that we might be tempted to fall back on the kind of definition that is sometimes offered in other fields as a sign of despair and define the Renaissance as that historical period of which Renaissance historians are talking. Kristeller, not being seriously satisfied with this definiton, would rather prefer to define the Renaissance as a period which understood itself as a renaissance or a rebirth of letters and of learning, whether the reality conformed to this claim or not. Or, avoiding even this questionable commitment, he would think it safer to identify the Renaisssance with the historical period that extends roughly from 1300 to 1600 A.D.[18]

Much of the chronological confusion around the Renaissance arose from erecting its conceptual edifice upon too narrow a foundation. Ferguson says:

> Viewing the Renaissance as an age in the history of Western Europe, I would define it as the age of transition from medieval to modern civilization, a period characterized primarily by the gradual shift from one fairly coordinated and clearly defined type of civilization to another, yet at the same time, possessing in its own right, certain distinctive traits and a high degree of cultural vitality. And on the basis of this concept or hypothesis, I would set the arbitrary dates from 1300 to 1600 as its chronological boundaries.[19]

To impregnate this definition with some significant content, it is imperative to indicate what may be considered the dominant elements of both medieval and modern civilization, and then to delineate the main lines of development within the transitional period.

Broadly speaking, the two predominant institutions of the Middle Ages were the feudal system and the universal church. Between them, they determined both the social structure and the ideological content. Into this land-ridden society, the commercial fermentation of the eleventh and twelfth centuries introduced the new and strange elements of commerce and skilled industry, leading to the growth of cities and expansion of money economy. This was also accompanied by a great whetting of cultural activity making the twelfth and thirteenth centuries the classic period of medieval civilization. The economic stimulus emanating from the expanding cities was, in the opinion of Ferguson, the material factor that made possible the immense cultural vigour witnessed in these two centuries. But the content and spirit of that culture did not generally come from the urban classes.[20]

Turning to the modern age, say by the beginning of the seventeenth century, the general texture of European civilization changed so radically that it was tantamount to a change in kind than in degree. The economic balance shifted from agriculture to commerce and industry. Money economy and capitalism become almost universal. In the political arena the national states replaced feudal particularism, while at the same time the unity of Christendom was permanently disrupted. Within the cities the growth of capital was working profound changes of which not the least significant was the emergence of an increasing number of enthusiasic laymen who had the wish and the resources to gratify their intellectual and aesthetic instincts.[21] The clerical monopoly of learning had been broken. The culture of the period, we call the Renaissance, was overwhelmingly the product of the cities, brought about by urban laymen who were in readiness to assume political and cultural leadership, and whose interests were different from those of the feudal and ecclesiastical aristocracy that dominated the culture of Middle Ages.[22]

Thus the medieval and the modern ages despite the common elements that have remained constant in the Western World for the past 2000 years or more are, in effect, two different types of civilizations, and the change from the one to other occurred during the three centuries of the Renaissance.[23]

However, the mere characterization of the types of civilization that preceded and followed the transitional stage, does nothing to show how and why the change took place. It brings us in confrontation with the crucial problem of causation. Here Ferguson would assume that the fundamental causes of change in the forms of culture are to be found in antecendent changes in economic and political institutions and in the whole structure of society: social change everywhere precedes cultural change, and that which is new in the Renaissance culture can most readily be explained as the product of a changed social milieu.[24]

By the beginning of the fourteenth century, agrarian society had already been replaced in Italy by an urban society with rapidly developing capitalist institutions. In the northern countries the expansion of money economy worked more slowly. The changes in the social structure were not projected immediately or in equal degree everywhere by changes in the forms of higher culture. But, with due margin to a natural cultural fluctuation, the lead in all forms of intellectual and aesthetic activity shifted from the clergy to the laity, from the feudal classes to the urban and the concentrated society of cities and princely courts.[25]

The Christian tradition certainly continued from the middle ages through the Renaissance and beyond but it did not persist unaltered, nor did it, in the same degree, dominate the culture of the age.[26] In the first place, whole vistas of secular knowledge were introduced into learning and art, a thing improperly represented in the middle ages. In the second place, the writer or artists, who worked for a predominantly lay audience or for lay patrons, had to satisfy the taste of men, free from clerical traditions. Even the religious art of the Renaissance was frequently according to the choice of lay patrons. Finally, religion itself was in some degree laicized.[27] The Protestant Reformation itself was partly a revolt against the sacerdotal ascendency of religion. By proclaiming the priesthood of all believers, Luther placed the believing layman on an equal footing with the cleric. In short, the Reformation must be interpreted as one aspect of the Renaissance, rather than as something running counter to it.[28]

The Renaissance as mentioned earlier, also possessed apart from the uneasy coexistence within it of medieval and modern characteristics, certain distinguishing traits and a high degree of cultural vitality. There can be innumerable questions posed by this latter aspect of the problem. We may attempt to answer a few. In the first place, whence sprouted the cultural vigour of the Renaissance? According to Ferguson:

> It was made possible by unprecedented wealth and by the participation of an unprecedented variety of social types. I would say, further, that it drew its positive inspiration from the intellectual excitement caused by the challenge of new conditions of life, of new potentialities in every field of culture, and, in general, of a sense of breaking new grounds and of scanning ever widening horizons. Within the civilization of the Renaissance there were, of course, innumerable cross-currents, inconsistencies, and apparent reactions. These, I think, were the natural results of the conflict, more intense in this age than in any other since the dawn of Christianity, between inherited traditions and a changing society. The Renaissance was an age of moral, religious, intellectual and aesthetic crisis. This has been recognized often enough. What has not always been so clearly recognized in this connection is that it was also an age of acute crisis in economic, political and social life.[29]

In the second place, was the Renaissance an age marked to a conspicuous degree by the spirit of individualism? This is indeed a hard question to answer, for individualism is a precariously variable concept. Nevertheless, there is no doubt that there was in this transitional age a growing consciousness of personality and a keener sense of individual autonomy than had been possible in the social and cultural environment of the medieval times; and it may also be asserted that this trait was more poignant in the Renaissance than in later ages, when man's right to self-determination was almost taken for granted. To individualism, many factors contributed besides those mentioned by Burckhardt; for there were more changes in the cosmos of Renaissance men than Burckhardt ever dreamt of–for example, the emergence of a lay piety that stressed man's direct communion with God, and at the other end of the moral spectrum, the growth of a capitalist spirit that stressed the individual man's direct communion with Mammon.[30] With the distintegration of European society men had to depend more upon their own personal mettle, where the increasing complexity of social set-up exposed them to more varied careers and opportunities for the cultivation of personal tastes and interests.

Finally, what is the role in the Renaissance of the revival of antiquity? According to Ferguson, its causative force, great though it was, was of a secondary character; that, indeed, the enthusiasm with which classical literature and learning were seized upon, was itself caused by antecedent changes in the social structure, which made themselves felt first in Italy, and later in the North.[31] The intense, almost excessive enthusiasm for classical culture, which was peculiar to the Renaissance, can be explained only by the fact that it was perfectly designed to meet the needs of educated, urban lay men, of a society that had ceased to be predominantly either feudal or ecclesiastical, yet had in its own immediate past, nothing to draw upon for inspiration but the feudal and ecclesiastical traditions of the middle ages.

In the words of Sellery:

> The abandonment of the theory ... that the revival of interest in and increased knowledge of antiquity ushered in modernity, leaves us ... with something much more real and more significant as the true cause of the advance of civilization in the era of the Renaissance, namely, the life, energies, hopes, and activities of vigourous people all over western Europe. A little detail will be useful at this point. The organization of life in the communes and capitals of the West (including all the inheritance from ancient times which had passed into customary use), its adornment with art and literature, and its integration with philosophy and history; the expansion of industry and of

> commercial enterprise, involving contact with other civilizations and lands; the growth of geographical knowledge and maritime skill from Marco Polo to Diaz and Columbus; the inventions of printing, the microscope, the telescope, and artillery; the demonstration of the heliocentric conception of our universe; the investigations into the nature of political authority which are marked by the insight of Marsilius of Padua and by the challenge to papal omnipotence–and, in truth, to all 'supreme authority'—by the Councils of Constance and Basel; the growing share of the laity in all the activities of learning–these are the main constituent elements of the true Renaissance. The Renaissance did not cause these phenomena; these phenomena constituted the Renaissance.[32]

Eugenio Garin interprets the situation as follows:

> The humanist wanted to learn from the classics not because he imagined that he shared a world with them but in order to define his own position as distinct from theirs .... The humanists ... found themselves vis-a-vis a historical past that was very different from their own world. It was precisely in this field of philosophy that there took place the conscious detachment from the past of which the humanists were so proud. It was a critic's detachment ... The face of ancient culture could no longer be simply reinterpreted. It had become once and for all, part of history ... there was detachment; and a result of this detachment a classical author ceased to be part of me and I began to define my own identity as something different from him. I found my own identity by discovering his. The Renaissance myth of ancient civilization was based upon a definition of the character of that civilization. And in defining that character the Renaissance reduced that civilization to something dead ....We had to define our own identity by defining the identity of another civilization.[33]

Thus we had to cultivate a sense of history and a sense of time. We had to learn to see both history and time as the dimensions proper to the life of man.[34] We had to relinquish forever the notion that the world was solid and fixed, that it was something definitive. We had to give up the notion that the world was a cosmos, continues Garin, which could be contemplated, indifferent to the passage of time, secure in eternity and forever rotating in continuing circles.[35] This old reality had been supposed to be totally solid and to have an eternal existence–so much that its very solidity had crushed all prophets of man's liberation.[36] It had led instead, says Garin, to the grand manner of medieval speculation and to the diabolical temptation to absorb the disquieting Christian message into the security of the Aristotelian world.[37]

From Petrarch onwards, humanism took up an entirely different turn. A truly fruitful renewal, it sought a way out of an insoluble problem, in the realms of poetry and philology, ethics and politics. In the end, it even sought a new way in a field which might appear antagonistic to humanism but which was nevertheless deeply connected with it: the fields of the arts which godlessly attempted to change and overturn the world.[38]

To sum up, in the above discussion there is implied a theory of historical interpretation, but not historical determinism. In the opinion of Ferguson, the growth of a wealthy urban society might well be regarded as a necessary conditioning factor in the development of *Quattrocento* art, but he finds it difficult to see how the development of the art of the *Quattrocento* could have been a necessay conditioning factor in the growth of a wealthy urban society.[39] There is no reason to believe that such a society must necessarily have produced a Donatello or a Ghirlandajo. To say that these things happend thus does not signify that they could not have happened otherwise.

'In seeking to discover the causes of cultural phenomena, the historian must often be content with permissive or partially effective causes[40]', observes Ferguson. In the words of Sellery, the problem of the Renaissance cannot, of course, receive a mathematical solution; it is a question of ideas and of movements in which ideas arc necessarily imbedded, and statistics are inapplicable.[41] A historian may be able to assert with some confidence what made a specific development possible, and what were the boundaries beyond which it could not go. But within that frame-work, he must always leave space for the unforseeable activity of the human spirit.[42]

According to Ferguson, the Renaissance was essentially an age of transition, containing much that was still medieval, much that was recognizably modern, and, also much that, because of the mixture of medieval and modern elements, was peculiar to itself and was responsible for its contradictions and contrasts as well as its amazing vitality.[43] His approach recognizes the dynamic character of both; and at the same time, to quote the same author, 'by suggesting a broad theory of causation in the gradual transformation of the economic and social structure of Western Europe, it tends to reduce the controversial questions regarding the primary influence of the classical revival, or the Italian genius, Germanic blood, medieval French culture, or Franciscan mysticism to a secondary, if not irrelevant, status.'[44]

Realization of the fact that he cannot hope to explain every thing fully and accurately, that history is not an exact science, should not, however, cause the historian to despair or lose confidence in his craft or cease to try to understand what can be understood. His reach must transcend his grasp, or what is the use of history.[45]

'In the last decade or so, Ferguson is happy to note, there has been 'a swing of the pendulum back towards appreciation of the originality of the Renaissance culture.'

Renaissance Historiography

The Renaissance is a prodigious concept. The achievements of our European ancestors which ushered in modern times have been frequently and variously listed; but how are they to be accounted for? That is another question. Burckhardt in his *Die Kultur der Renaissance in Italien*[46] (1860) argued that it were the Italians of the later middle ages who had freed themselves and, by precept and example, had subsequently freed the other Europeans from the varied restrictions of the middle ages. The Italians had done this through their own talents and the confidence they developed from the renewed study of ancient classics.

In 1859, George Voigt had already published his masterpiece on the revival of classical antiquity, *Die Wiederbelebung des klassischen Alter thums*.[47] The two books were read together as attributing overwhelming importance to the Revival of Learning. John Addington Symonds' *the Renaissance in Italy*, which began to appear in 1875, is indeed an eloquent testimony of the truth of the observation which Carl Neumann made in 1903: Since the appearance of Burckhardt's celebrated book, opinion has quite generally prevailed that the Renaissance was the mother of modern civilization, that the Italians were the first born people of the modern world, and that all this was due to the passionate zeal with which they overlapped the Middle Ages and sought, with success, to link themselves again to the ancient world.[48]

Numerous illustrations could be given to support Neumann's statement. George Burton Adams, in his *Civilization during the Middle Ages*, expressed thus in 1894: 'It was the work of the Renaissance ... to awaken in man a consciousness of his powers and to give him confidence in himself; to show him the beauty of the world and the joy of life; and to make him feel his living connection with the past, and the greatness of the future which he might create.'[49]

> Men began to realize that there lay behind them a most significant history, and that the men of the past had many things to teach them. When men became conscious of this the revival of learning began ... that intellectual and scientific transformation of Europe which we call the Revival of Learning or the Renaissance.[50]

More than forty years later, Conyers Read, in his informative book, *The Tudors*, reflects some, though little change, in the Burckhardtian concept: The Renaissance in its essence was a changed attitude of mind towards man and his environment, substituting for the medieval conception of man as a miserable sinner striving against the world and the flesh, man as an interesting and beautiful creature in a beautiful and interesting world...It was in short the impulse which set in motion the whole modern world...Man turned to the ancient models, not so much out of any reverence for the Greeks and the Romans *per se* as because they found in the classics the most satisfactory expression of what they themselves were trying to express ... But the impulse was universal and those who felt it merely turned to Italy as they turned to the classics for further inspiration and guidance.[51]

The most extensive commendation of Burckhardt in English was pronounced by the English encyclopedic author, G.P. Gooch:

> With the Renaissance, man discovered himself and became a spiritual individual. The fetters of a thousand years were burst, self-realization became the goal, and new valuations of the world and of man became current. Dazzling personalities of the type of the Emperor Frederick II had been witnessed but only once or twice in the middle ages. The complete man, *1'uome universale,* now became common in the world of action, of thought and of art. The fifteenth century is, above all, that of the many-sided man. ... With all its glaring faults, the Renaissance was the spring-time of the modern world.[52]

The Burckhardt-Voigt theory of the Renaissance did not enjoy such general acceptance as the foregoing comments would suggest. The main lines of hostile criticism have been two. *First,* it has been debated that many of the so-called Renaissance characteristics–for example, individualism, love of nature, and secularism–are to be found in broad reaches of the Middle Ages; and *secondly,* that many of the so-called medieval characteristics–submissiveness to authority, supernaturalism or interest in the transcendental, and superstition–were common in the Renaissance times. These lines of criticism stress the evolutionary rather than the revolutionary nature of the Renaissance, and they assert that Burckhardt's knowledge of the middle ages was faulty.

It was Carl Neumann who in his article, '*Byzantinische Kultur and the Renaissance Kultur*' published in 1903, took upon himself the taste of dismantling the Burckhardtian structure. He reached the conclusion that it was not the revival of antiquity but rather medieval Christianity and the realistic Teutonic 'barbarians' that had made possible the rise of true modern individualism. 'We must firmly grasp the idea', he wrote, 'that the medieval Christian training and the so-called barbarism were the life-strength of that which is traditionally called the Renaissance and that the revival of antiquity was productive and beneficient element only as long as it remained contented with the role of companion, with its pedagogical role.'[53]

Still more damaging was the attack of John Nordstrom in his *Moven Age et Renaissance*, published in 1933. He declares that medieval western Europe, under the guidance of France, had anticipated all the achievements attributed to Renaissance Italy, including the revival of classical learning, that Italy's debt to the North, especially to France, was enormous; in short, that the modern age evolved out of the medieval.[54] Nordstrom states: 'We must revise completely the traditional conception which makes us see in the Italian Renaissance the matrix of our civilization. And the so-called great contributions of this Renaissance to occidental culture is 'a simple continuation, or a transformation under the influence of the ethnic Italian character, of the traditions of the middle ages.'[55]

The 'revolt of the medievalists', as it was called, 'against the nineteenth-century conception of the Renaissance was in full swing in the early decades of the twentieth century. These 'medievalists' feared the perpetuation of an antiquate bias against the middle ages, and a false image of the unscrupulous, ruthless and lusty 'superman' of the Renaissance. Burckhardt's thesis was denounced as an irresponsible product of a period of historiography long passed.

Nordstrom's attack on the Burckhardtian thesis was vehemently challenged by Italo Siciliano in a little book *Medio Evoe Rinascimento*. He rejects Nordstrom's arguments in entirety, and ends his own analysis with this emphatic claim: 'When we think of all these we have no need of the astrologer to see why the Italian Renaissance issued from Italy to conquer the world, and why it is for modern civilization what Greco-Latin civilization was for antiquity.' Phrased a little differently the claim is this: 'In the middle ages one spirit and one universal culture nourished various peoples; in the Renaissance it is the 'elite of one nation which dominates and directs the whole world.[56] Burckhardt would not have put it quite so arrogantly.

Siciliano defends the Burckhardtian thesis with improved weapons. 'The spirit of the Italian Renaissance', Siciliano declares, 'is a fever of research, of discussion, of criticism, and a veritable frenzy for the new and the better, a mania for discovery, and a capacity for synthesis, which enrich the personality and refine the taste. These the middle ages lacked; and these the elite of Italy gave to the world.'[57]

The clash of opinion between Nordstrom and Siciliano can be paralleled, although on a much milder level in the writings of E.F. Jacob and A.S. Turberville in the English periodical-*History*, and many others.

It would be desirable to recall the general state of Renaissance studies before the Second World War as Renaissance scholarship has been transformed in the course of the last thirty odd years. This is by no means an easy task. In Volume VII of *The Cambridge Medieval History* (published in 1932) and in Volume VIII (1936) there are chapters by Arthur A. Tilly, dealing with 'The Early Renaissance and the 'Renaissance in Europe.'[58] These chapters give a tolerably updated (for the period) view of the subject. Here is the gist of his analysis: 'The early Renaissance' begins, in effect, with Petrarch, who was 'the first modern man' and was rightly termed the first humanist, for he was the first to find in ancient literature a larger measure than elsewhere of that learning and training which are peculiar to man.'[59] The resulting devotion to the Latin classics encouraged the existing Italian impulse to discover new manuscripts and form libraries. In this activity Petrarch was aided by Boccaccio, who excelled him in Greek. Tilly records Salutati's appointment as 'Latin Secretary' at Florence. There are a couple of pages on the study of Greek before we encounter Leonardo Bruni, whose 'chief service to learning was the translation into Latin of works by Plato, Plutarch and Aristotle.[60] There then follows a rather detailed account of Poggio and his discoveries. The description of Guarino's and Vittorino's educational programme comes next. The chapter concludes with a brief description of development in the arts of Florence. It leads on to the observation that secular art owed much to the way the despots had baroken away from the 'tutelage of the Church' in the cities of Northern Italy.

It is not unnatural that the literary ancestry of Tilly's approach should be found in Voigt, Burckhardt and Symonds. Tilly's dependence on Burckhardt group is conspicuous in his major generalizations:

> The Renaissance is 'transition from the medieval to the modern world'; it has special features which distinguish it from other historical periods ....Such was the Renaissance ... not a rebirth, not a sudden transformation from darkness to light, but a gradual transition ... stimulated by the advent of a new spirit ... a spirit of enthusiasm, of adventure, of pride in the dignity of man ... search for new knowledge, a spirit guided and sustained by intercourse with the great writers of antiquity ... many of whom had been disinterred from dust-laden repositories ...[61]

Now this description of the Renaissance is loose and rambling. Scholarship since 1880s was thrust into the Burckhardtian skeletal structure with little regard for the logical, let alone the aesthetic, form of the master's work. The obvious result was an amalgam of assertions of broad principles with antiquarian observation of detail, in which the structure of society and politics was all but ignored and, so to say, no distinction was drawn between the cultural developments to be found in republics, principates, and monarchies. The Renaissance is neither explained nor interpreted. It is treated as a collection of self-evident phenomena which need no justification as such.

However, if with recent scholarship at our back, we find Tilly's account flat, fragmented and detached from a solid social and political background, we should not be too hard to the author. Looking at Tilly with hind-sight, we may find him more sophisticated than the actual teaching on the subject in the 1930s when these Cambridge volumes were prepared and when the Renaissance was steadily treated as the prelude to the drama of the Reformation. 'At Oxford, when I expressed a desire (I suppose this must have been in 1936) to study the Italian Renaissance as my subject', so says Denis Hay, 'I was told by my tutor that only girls did that: I was to concentrate on the manly middle ages.[62]

Now, however, most of us take the Renaissance as a period

which ought to be studied in its own right rather than a protracted and tiresome transitionary phase from middle ages to modernity. Besides we also have a clearly more skeptical attitude to periods as such, emphasizing their subjectivity. Beyond that we have lately learnt to treat the changes implied in the word, Renaissance as serious factors in the public life of earlier times. 'And if the Renaissance is to be treated seriously then it clearly revolves round the moral imperatives and the political urgencies of the period of its development.[63]

Hans Baron's articles published just before the war make us realize just how profoundly important the Renaissance had been in the evolution of the conscience and the consciousness of Europe.[64] This novel approach gives an entirely new dimension to the processes of intellectual change and goes a long way to explain why the Renaissance is so important and why it grew and blossomed in Italy as it did.

Baron took a framework which stressed the chronological priority of Tuscany and more specifically of Florence in the evolution of new social and moral attitudes. This was indeed a very valuable shift in the traditional Burckhardtian concept. The tendency to ascribe the origin of the Renaissance to the development of capitalism, could be traced to the years between the wars. The main result was the important distinction between civic humanism and its later princely manifestations. This basic notion has proved methodologically extremely fruitful and has been generally adopted in post-war surveys of the period and its problems by scholars like Eugenio Garin and others.

It was proved that a vast amount of humanistic literature merited serious attention, not to be set aside as worthless, or stale imitation of antiquity. Once the basic sedateness in much of the literature of the period is appreciated, it is easy to understand that there were sound reasons motivating the Florentine bourgeoisie to patronize the humanist.

These readjustments necessitated casting a new and bold look at classical antiquity. Later writers sensed an unavoidable distinction between their own days and the days of the ancient world. From this arose on the one hand the feeling of identity with classsical civilization and on the other, the feeling of anachronism. These two elements sometimes clashed with each other. But the first undoubtedly moulded the new educational curriculum, whereas the second was a key force in the evolution of a new historiography. Moreover, this moral readjustment could easily be fitted in and adopted to societies quite different from that of the republican Florence, that is to say, the repercussions of Florentine civic humanism could be promptly transported in the monarchical parts of Italy and elsewhere in the continent at large.

Burckhardt had scarcely felt the need to account in any chronological or narrative sense for the emergence of the new ideas but had attempted rather to identify and analyze them.

In the words of Ferguson:

> Burckhardt's perception of the inner spirit of a civilization, which was at once the chief aim of his research and his sole guide to the selection and evaluation of sources, was based on nothing more than his own intuition and his undoubted familiarity with the literature of his chosen fields ....The peculiar character of Italian politics he ascribed in general to the conflict between the emperors and the popes. Causation, was not his major interest.[65]

Burckhardt concludes that in the Italian states 'the modern European state spirit appeared for the first time, free to follow its own inclinations', and that with them 'a new factor enters history, the state as a calculated conscious creation, the state as a work of art.[66] Interwoven with his major theme is the secondary one of the character of the Renaissance man as illustrated and conditioned by his political activity. The illegitimacy of despotic government and the party strife in republics bred a new type of individual, wholly dependent on his other resources and therefore developing them to the fullest extent seeking only egocentric ends, and uninhibited by sentimental or traditional standards.[67]

> The conscious calculation of all means, of which no prince outside of Italy had at that time any idea, combined with an almost absolute power within the limits of the state, produced here men and modes of life that were altogether peculiar.[68]

Baron stressed the existence long before Burckhardt's schemes of historical evolution which included the Renaissance, and explained that Burckhardt contributed to this prior pattern, a denial that the movement was to be received as an anticipation of the Enlightenment as well as 'rebuttals' of the 'classic belief' that the revival of ancient letters played a causal role.[69] Similarly, Burckhardt's stress on individualism had a long history. Nonetheless the synthesis was weighty and comprehensive. Burckhardt's main shortcoming according to Baron was his neglect of the rudimentary sociology of city-state life for which ground had been prepared by his predecessors of the preceding century. The reason was not, Baron is certain, that he misjudged the roles of Florence and Venice. On the other hand, his book contains some of the most impressive and sympathetic pages ever written on achievements in the Florentine republic: the spread of political raisonnement and a keen spirit of calculation among an entire people; the priority in time of the patronage of Florentine citizens to that of the princes; the contrast between Florentine historiography–written by citizens for citizens, as the ancients did–and the hired official historiography in most principalities.[70] This default on the part of Burckhardt was a consequence of his 'abhorrence for the then rising democratic trend.[71]

When he wrote this article, Baron's *The Crisis* was already published a lustrum back, with its supporting humanistic and political literature. The subtitle of the book, *Crisis–Civic Humanism and Republican Liberty in the Age of Classicism and Tyranny*–indicates the essence of these volumes. A further indication is the fact that the book is dedicated to Walter Goetz who taught the author that 'history should be a study of both politics and culture.' In these volumes, Baron investigated the connection between society and culture, political situations and concomitant developments in historiography and political and educational theory.[72]

It is true that Burckhardt treated the political situation in Italy as the perspective over which he built up his analysis of the spiritual and intellecutal state of the peninsula. But it is also true that he did not discriminate between the moral and cultural pressures exercised by different kinds of states to be found in Italy. He said, 'In the character of these states, whether republics or despotisms, lies not the only but the chief reason for the early development of the Italian.' Despotism, Burckhardt asserts, particularly favoured individuality in both the tyrant and his 'tools.'[73] This was tantamount to shutting the eyes to the plain fact that the first positive statements of the new moral attitudes and the first novel creations in painting, sculpture and architecture are to be found, not in the tyrannies, but in republican Florence around 1400 A.D.

In post-Burckhardtian research, the central theme has been the interminable controversy of the humanists about the merits of the *respublica romana* and the subsequent monarchy of the Roman emperors–a controversy culminating in the well-known quest of the historical justification of Cicero or Caesar. We have, perhaps, no better mirror than this controversy for studying the basic differences in the political-historical outlook developing in the city-republics and at the tyrants' courts. To Burchkardt all light and historical justification were on the side of Caesar. Thus, yet another window through which the reciprocity of thought and political experience in the Renaissance could be most clearly seen, was closed to the author of the *Civilization* of *the Renaissance*.[74]

The consequences extend even to the appraisal of humanism. Although Burckhardt had parted with the classical interpretation that the revival of ancient literature was the cause of the Renaissance, he did not change essentially the traditional view about the nature of humanistic contacts with the classical heritage. The notion of a renascence of something old after a long interval remained at the core of his concept of the humanistic movement. The essence of the classical revival, we read in *The Civilization of the Renaissance,* was an alliance between two distant epochs in the civilization of the same people, a 'partial reawakening of the old Italian genius ... the wondrous echo of a far-off strain.' By this token, those features of the humanistic movement which Burckhardt continued to call the humanistic 'reproduction of antiquity' remained in the foreground. Thus a lack of sympathetic interest is shown towards the forces by which the vital new philosophy of history was shaped; whereas neo-Latin poetry, oratory and epistolography were given more emphasis.[75]

The order of emphasis has practically been reversed in the study of the Renaissance Humanism during the twentieth century. An entire new branch of critical research has been devoted to the treatises, dialogues and works of historiography. And this has happened precisely because these *genera* of humanistic literature, which are probably the least successful as imitations of classical models, testify to the originality of the Renaissance, since through them humanists were able to express their own convictions and sense of life and to recreate the picture of the ancient past from fresh points of view. In revealing their authors' minds, these works often allow us deeper insight than any other sources into the differences in outlook that existed among the humanists in various social groups, especially between writers in the civic and courtly society. This transfer of interest has largely resulted in the questioning of Burckhardt's long-accepted estimate of the respective contributions of the communal and the 'individualistic' spirit to the culture of the Renaissance.[76]

Yet continued limitation of the role ascribed to the Renaissance 'individualism' has in the final count, not weakened but rather strengthened the validity of the thesis that the Italian Renaissance was prototype of life and thought in the modern world. For the conclusion that many of the 'modern' features of Renaissance Italy evolved out of the politics and culture of the city-state is in harmony with other persuasions of present-day historical philosophy. With respect to the ancient world, extension of our knowledge over the civilization of the East has only strengthened the interpretation that Greek and Roman culture was different–and in some way prototypical of many aspects of later European history–because it was founded on independent city-states; that in the tense and bracing atmosphere of those small commonwealths, many of the political, ethical, and cultural problems which were to become those of the modern western world were first explored and worked out. The more fully we realize the significance the city-state society had for the Italian Renaissance, the more the relationship of Renaissance culture to 'modern' life becomes a part of the general problem of the singular affiliation of western history with traditions inherited from early city-state republics.[77]

However, Baron would probably in the end be prepared to accept Burckhardt's basic approach as correct, suggesting that as sociology tremendously influences historical research, so 'the core of Burckhardtian conception of the Renaissance ... may still, eventually prove superior to the competing views about the nature of the transition to the modern age.[78] He opines that 'today' after more than a century 'little of that suspicion has survived'against him.

For at least twenty years before the appearance of *The Crisis*, Baron had been preparing himself for the stand he was to take in the early fifties. This was nothing very abrupt or entirely unheard of. He himself regarded this approach as a long lingering tradition faintly detectable in the writings of David Hume and Adam Ferguson, but more poignantly in Paolo Emiliani-Giudici whose book came in 1844.[79] This book certainly familiar to Burckhardt, definitely contains some significant statements on the connections between politics and cultural changes; but it seems a flimsy link. Baron's confident and sound thesis of 1955, supplemented by that of 1968, with its thorough scrutiny of the composition and dating of many of the major texts, has independent value.

The crucial question is whether Baron's interpretation of the cultural consequences of the Florentine-Milanese contest or the Florentine-Neopolitan tussle, is right:

> Baron's central argument is that the peril to the independence of Florence produced a radical shift in the tone of Florentine humanism; and accordingly his second distinction is moral and, to some degree, chronological. The humanist of the *trecento*, politically unawakened, aspired to live the *vita contemplativa*, looked to tyranny (local or imperial) for relief from the distractions of civic responsibility, preferred security, prosperity, and efficient government to liberty, and idealized the Roman Empire. The

> new Florentine humanist of the *quattrocento*, brought to a consciousness of his republican heritage by the Milanese peril, praised the *vita activa civilis*, accepted the obligations of citizenship, valued liberty above order, and found his ideals in the Roman Republic.[80]

Baron reflects:

> A fight for the liberty of the Respublica Florentina, and, at about the same time, a discovery of the historic role of the Respublica Romana; are generation of political morale in the crucible of the crisis of the Florentine Commonwealth, and, at about the same time, a revival of the memory of Roman citizenship among Florentine humanists ... these are elements so closely related to each other that it is hard to believe that they were not connected as cause to effect, co-related in time as well as spirit.[81]

The central issue is the nature of the relationship between ideas and experience. Gene Brucker, although quite sympathetic to Baron's conception of this relationship, is not persuaded by every part of his analysis. He says: 'One can accept his thesis that a fundamental change in human values and perception occurred in the early *Quattrocento*, and still be sceptical of his explanation for this intellectual revolution. Although the Milanese threat to Florentine independence was certainly a factor in this mental and psychological readjustment, it was not the sole–or perhaps even the most important–stimulus.[82]

In the words of Marvin Becker:

> The two commanding scholars of Florentine literary and philosophical culture of this period are Eugenio Garin and Hans Baron. Neither would stress economic depression as a causal factor. The former assumes the existence of a solid connection between politics and thought, always emphasizing continuity of development.... Baron would underscore discontinuity. He maintains that a particular set of circumstances ... served to galvanize a new intellectual world.
>
> Let me suggest that it may be possible to enlarge our understanding of the polis and its intellectual life, briefly described by Garin, as well as to dissent from Baron's thesis of discontinuity if we treat certain social, economic, and political changes after the 1340.[83]

Becker thinks that many of the elements quintessential for the rise of civic philosophy, art and literature were already abundantly evident long before the early *quattrocento*. 'If this hypothesis is untenable', observes Becker, 'Garin's observations on historical continuity would be more attractive. Although Baron's claims for the catalytic role of the Visconti war would then be scaled down, his valuable insights into the character of civic humanism would remain firm.[84] Becker's 'angle of vision reveals the strained and unmistakable birth pangs of the Renaissance policy alongwith the decay of the late medieval world.[85]

Baron has been criticized because, by making the Florence of Salutati and Bruni the deciding factor of the humanist story (as it obviously is in the evolution of the arts), he has relegated Petrarch to the background. To this he has himself replied[86] : 'Petrarch was more original ... in his earlier than in his later days, and could not take the final step towards the "New World" of which he was in many ways the prophet.' And in this same reply he goes on to indicate the telling fact that the politico-cultural relationship had been successfully used as a framework for enquiry by other recent writers besides himself.[87] Other than Baron's reassessment of the primary questions concerning the Renaissance, there are the imposing works of men like Cassirer, Kristeller, Garin and many others. Yet Baron's contribution appears enduring. Becker's stress on Baron's discontinuity is perhaps too uncharitable a view of the latter's analysis. The possibilities of synthesis afforded by Baron are fascinating and impressive. After all even today the social and political structures do affect our cultural interests. But we must express this enunciation of principle very discreetfully if we wish to avoid both Marxist and other forms of determinism or the grotesque assumption that such situations involve total transformations of every aspect of human life.

There should not be any doubt that in many respects what happened in Florence in the decades around 1400 was to colour deeply the whole picture of Europe. This illumination of Europe's life could only become possible when Florentine republicanism had ceased to shroud the fertilizing ideas which could bear fruitful results in a continent, where rulers, courtiers and the gentry were the cultural pace-setters. It represents fundamental ethical education and cultural motivation in the governing classes of virtually the whole continent, a thing largely provided by the new attitudes developed in Florence in the days of Salutati, Bruni, Masaccio, Brunelleschi, and all the other heroes and their patrons.

NOTES AND REFERENCES

1. Strayer., J.B. *The Main Stream of Civilization Since 1500-1974* (New York: Harcourt Braco Jovanivich, Inc), p. 346
2. Ibid, p. 347.
3. Ibid, p. 350.
4. Ibid, p. 356.
5. Ibid, p. 357.
6. Sellery., George Clarke. *The Renaissance: Its Nature and Origin*, (Wisconsin, 1949), p. 1.
7. Ibid, p. 13.
8. Gilmore., M. *The World of Humanism 1453-1527*, (New York, 1952).
9. Braduer., Leicester. *Renaissance News*, 1954, Vol. 7, p. 1.
10. Ferguson, *The Interpretation of the Renaissance-Suggestions for a Synthesis*, 1951, Renaissance Essays Kristeller and Wiener, (eds). (New York: *Journal of the History of Ideas*, 1968), p. 61.
11. Collingwood., R.G. *The Idea of History*. (Oxford, 1946), p. 53.
12. Ferguson. op.cit, p. 61.
13. Ibid, p. 62.
14. Ibid, p. 62.
15. Ibid, p. 63.
16. Ibid, p. 63.
17. Kristeller., Paul Oskar. *Renaissance Thought II: Papers on Humanism and the Arts* (New York, 1964), p. 2.
18. Ibid, p. 3.
19. Ferguson, op.cit, p. 64.
20. Ibid, pp. 65-66.
21. Ferguson, op.cit, p. 15.
22. Ibid, p. 16.
23. Ferguson, op.cit, p. 66.
24. Ibid, p. 67.

25. Ibid, p. 68.
26. Ibid, p. 69.
27. Ibid, p. 70.
28. Ibid, p. 70.
29. Ibid, pp. 70–71.
30. The False God of riches.
31. Ferguson, op.cit, p. 71.
32. Sellery, op.cit, pp. 259–60.
33. Garin, op.cit, pp. 18–19.
34. Ibid, p. 19.
35. Ibid, p. 19.
36. Ibid, p. 20.
37. Ibid, p. 20.
38. Ibid, p. 20.
39. Ferguson, op.cit, p. 73.
40. Ibid, p. 73.
41. Sellery, op.cit, p. 13.
42. Ferguson, op.cit, p. 73.
43. Ferguson, op.cit, p. 16.
44. Ibid, pp. 16–17.
45. Ferguson, op.cit, 73.
46. Sellery, op.cit, pp. 1–2.
47. Ibid, p. 2.
48. Neuman., Garl. *Byzantinische Kultur and Renaissance Kultur.* 1903, cited in Ibid, pp. 2–3.
49. Ibid, p. 2.
50. Ibid, p. 3.
51. Ibid, p. 4.
52. Ibid, pp. 5–6.
53. Ibid, p. 7.
54. Ibid, p. 8.
55. Ibid, p. 8.
56. Ibid, pp. 8–9.
57. Ibid, p. 11.
58. *Cambridge Medieval History,* 1932, Vol. 7, pp.751–76 and Vol. 8 pp. 773–802.
59. Ibid, Vol. 7, p. 754.
60. Ibid, p. 760.
61. Ibid, pp. 751 and 775.
62. Hay., Denis. *Hans Baron in Renaissance Historiography,* Renaissance studies in Honour of Hans Baron, Molho and Tedeschi, G.C. Sansani (eds.), 1971, p. 17.

63. Ibid, p. 18.
64. Ibid, p. 18.
65. Ferguson, The Renaissance in Historical Thought, op.cit, pp. 188–89.
66. Burckhardt, cited in Ibid, p. 188.
67. Ibid, p. 189.
68. Burckhardt cited in Ibid, p. 189.
69. Hay, op.cit, p. 22.
70. Baron., Hans. *Burckhardt's Civilization of the Renaissance: a century after its publication,* *Renaissance News*, 1960, Vol. 23, pp. 218–19.
71. Ibid, p. 219.
72. Hay, op.cit, p. 23.
73. Ibid, p. 23.
74. Baron, op.cit, pp. 218–20.
75. Ibid, p. 218.
76. Ibid, p. 220.
77. Ibid, p. 222.
78. Ibid, p. 222.
79. Hay, op.cit, pp. 24–25.
80. Bouwsma., William J. Review : *The Crisis of the Early Italian Renaissance,* Hans Baron, *Renaissance News*, (Spring, 1956), Vol. 9(1), p. 28.
81. Baron., Hans. *The Crisis of the Early Italian Renaissance* (Princeton, 1955), Vol. 7, p. 67.
82. Brucker., Gene. *Renaissance Florence* (New York, 1969), p. 236.
83. Becker., Marvin B. *Florence in Transition*, (Baltimore, 1968), p. 27.
84. Ibid, p. 27.
85. Ibid, p. 27.
86. Most problems of *Renaissance Interpretation* : An Answer to W.K. Ferguson, *Journal of the History of Ideas*, 1958, Vol. 19, pp. 26–34 esp. 28–29, cited in Hay, op.cit, p. 25.
87. In the *New Cambridge Modern History I*, 1957, pp. 50–75, and the note on p. 73, he names Garin, von Albertini, Renandet, Spongano and Ferguson.

Chapter 3

Economic Policy of Frederick the Great

A CRITICAL APPRAISAL (1763–1786)

Frederick, the Great was in his fifty-second year at the signing of the Peace of Hubertsburg. He survived the great conflict of twenty-three years and accomplished what was the most difficult, if not the most important, achievement of his career.[1]

'In 1763', as Leo Gershoy observes, 'Prussia was a bleeding stump, drained of vitality,[2] and all the fortitude of the hatchet-faced and iron-willed ruler was tested in his long effort to bind up the mutilated end.'[3] It was in that last half of his reign that he showed himself, according to his many admirers, as the 'personification of creative action' who 'completely transformed the modest and inferior milieu which he had inherited'.[4]

The economic effects of the Seven Years War upon Prussia were variegated. On the one hand there was severe devastation; the currency depreciated; prices of land, houses, foods and manufactured articles soared; agricultural and industrial output were dislocated and internal and foreign trade disrupted. According to Veale, 'A ninth of the adult male population had perished, three quarters of the country had been at one time or another, ravaged by invaders'.[5] Yet certain branches of the industry grew–metal, armament and woollen industries–and worked under intensified pressure to meet the orders for the army.[6]

To Prussia the cost of war amounted to about 140 million Thalers.[7] The money was raised in three ways. *First*, some 93 million Thalers came from previous savings: *secondly*, money was raised by taxation but income from this source was much less than in normal times[8]: *thirdly*, Frederick bridged the gap between income and expenditure by debasing the coinage.[9]

The effect of the last, currency depreciation led to inflation with all its attendant evils. The reorganization of the coinage system provided the king with an early opportunity of applying inexorably the strictest principles of a one-sided fiscalism. After 1764, better money was again minted; but the debased coinage of the war days was henceforth taken by the royal banks only at its actual (that is, at little more than twenty-five per cent of its nominal) value. This sweeping measure was the climax of pernicious manipulations comparable to the national bankruptcies of Louis XIV and Louis XV. During the war, fines and imprisonment, even corporal punishment, had been unreservedly inflicted on persons refusing to accept money utterly debased. Says Emil Daniels :

> The statement that in 1764 Prussia returned to a standard of full weight in her coinage, can only be accepted with considerable qualification.[10] For the reorganization of the coinage in that year inundated the country with small coins, the standard of which was so greatly lowered by amalgamation with base metals, that a nominal three Thalers' worth of this minor currency contained no greater proportion of silver than that required by law in two Thalers. In the absence of a sufficient supply of large coins, small change often had to be used even for the payment of large amounts. This unsound practice did much harm.[11]

Though the king inequitably threw upon the people the expense of restoring the coinage, his subjects were sending him sheaves of petitions for aid. Though he was of all monarchs the least addicted to pomp, nonetheless, three months after peace had been signed, he began to build a third palace at Potsdam, a singular extravagance which has been the subject of much criticism and conjecture.[12] Frederick's palace, Versailles, however, remains to this day both a monument to his absolutism and an enigma.

The building of the new palace helped to support the artists of Berlin, but Prussia did not escape the economic crisis which swept over Europe at the end of 1763. The king was deeply amazed by this crisis, the mechanism of which he could not understand, and at first he believed it was a traders' conspiracy. However, it hurt him most of all to feel that Prussia was dependent on foreign banks. As early as 1752, he had thought of setting up an issue, discount and credit bank in Berlin, but the business was too novel and difficult for the routine officials of the central offices. This time he was advised by a projector who came from the homeland of money-changers, a very obscure Italian called Calzabigi. Despite strong ministerial opposition, the king stuck to his guns–difficulties only stiffened his resolve. He would have preferred the bank to be independent of the state, but found no buyers for his shares and had to subscribe the whole of the capital himself. The foundation decree (June 17, 1765) expressly stated that the concern would not be under any branch of the administration, but the king alone.[13]

The early stages were very difficult, as no one had confidence in the institution. The public was sure that the king wished to draw the currency of the realm into his coffers and then pay out in paper. 'This dread of paper money was in fact the crux of the matter', observes Emil Daniels. The commercial world had not forgotten the catastrophe produced by the debased currency. The bank was started with 450,000 Thalers (£ 57,000) cash in public money and the right to issue bank notes up to 1,300,000 Thalers. The king further held out the prospect of making over to the bank 8,00,000 Thalers in cash out of the War Exchequer. The leading merchants of Breslau begged that a part of this sum might be put in circulation at once, but that the issue of paper money should be stopped; otherwise they would enter into no business transactions with the bank. But their request was turned down.[14]

The centre of the linen industry of Silesia was Hirschberg. In their distrust of paper money, the merchants there gave up sending their bills to the capital of the province for discounting, but sent them instead to Leipzig or Prague. The notes on the Prussian bank continued to fall in value; and the Breslau merchants after all had their way in the end. 'In business and general dealings', states Daniels, 'Prussian paper money counted for so little as to warrant Mirabeau's gibe that no scoundrel had ever yet counterfeited a Berlin bank note.[15]

The bank's statutes were modified, and under minister Hagen's control it gradually acquired connections, thanks to its businesslike conduct of operations. In 1768, its bills were accepted at Hamburg in preference to commercial drafts.[16] The royal deposit which was called *Fouragegelder* (forage moneys), constituted an apparent security for the voluntary and compulsory deposits of the general public flowing into the bank. The compulsory deposits were compulsory following the edict of 1768, 'directing the authorities to invest in the bank, at an interest of three per cent, all unemployed capital deposited with them belonging to widows, orphans, minors, institutions, hospitals, or charitable and educational foundations, unless such money could be placed in mortgages.' 'This was a serious enactment', continues Daniels, from the 'moral point of view; and its economic expediency is also open to grave question.' The trade of Prussia, hampered as it was by the system of monopolies and privileges and by tariff wars, could not profitably employ the capital which was to reach it through the bank. However, during Frederick's life-time, all seemed safe;[17] and the net profit from the bank was continued to grow.[18] The profits, which were only 22,000 Thalers for the financial year 1767–68, rose to 216,000 for 1785–86.[19]

II

Frederick's two Political Testaments, the first written in 1752, the second in 1768, were first published in full by Volz in 1920, 'when at last dynastic secrets could be safely revealed.' The royal author believed that poor governments never receive consideration.[20] The prince could increase his revenues, not by imposing new taxes, but by stimulating agriculture and developing industry. The whole of the year's revenue should not be spent, and the treasury should be ready to confront any calamity.[21]

After the war, Frederick was determined that the costs of reconstruction should not be financed by any further measures of devaluation. It was clear that new sources of revenue would have to be found to help pay for the cost of recuperation. He remained wedded to the cameralist precepts which he had penned in the *Considerations Sur 1'etat present du corps politique de* 1'Europe (1738) and in the *Refutation du prince Machiavel* (1739) when he was still the heir to the throne.[22]

To give himself a freer hand, Frederick began to withdraw large sums from the control of the general directory and the general audit office, placing them in a secret fund, the so-called 'Royal Disposition Fund.'[23] He used this secret fund with great practicality, not capriciously but according to firm principles. The most important of these was never to waste a penny, so that resources were always available for the pressing demands of the state, and so that he could afford to be generous whenever it seemed necessary. The ministers heading the general directory were reduced to the status of treasurers responsible for different areas of the exchequer, who lacked any real knowledge–let alone control of the overall budget. 'Income and expenditures of the state', states Gerhard Ritter, 'remained the king's secret.'[24]

Prussia's revenues rose from 13.8 million Thalers in 1768 to 23.7 million Thalers in 1786. At the close of the 'Seven Years War' the revenues of the king were derived mainly 'from the rents of the farms on his estates; from timber sold from his forests; and from the profits of the royal mint, manufacturers, and salt-works; from the land tax and the 'occupation tax'; and from custom duties, excise duties and tolls of various kinds.'[25] In the rural districts a land tax or 'contribution' was assessed as a proportion of the value of the harvest.

'In the towns no direct taxes were levied': as Henderson states: 'On the other hand, excisc duties had to be paid upon many consumer goods such as grain, leather, sugar, firewood, beer, spirits and wine.' From these revenues the king defrayed the expenses of his court, the civil administration, and the army. The most conspicuous change in the pattern of expenditure in Frederick's reign was the decline in the proportion of revenue allocated to the maintenance of the army.[26]

One of the most difficult problems with which Frederick was confronted in the period of reconstruction after the turmoil of the war was the woeful dearth of competent men. The teething troubles of the Bank of Berlin and the Overseas Trading Corporation (*Seehandlung*) were largely due to the failure of the king to find administrators of proper calibre to take charge of them. Among Frederick's ministers, 'Heinitz was the only man of learning and independent ideas; in his special province of mining, he was an authority of truly European stature. Other ministers ... were not men to pierce the heart of a problem or to propose incisive measures.'[27]

Frederick's dissatisfaction with the general directory came to a crisis in the first decade after the Seven Years War. The new position which this war had given to Prussia in Europe demanded, as Frederick saw it, a larger army and an increased public income. Whatever the limitations of a country notoriously poor and exhausted by the war, the monarch was very determined to enhance his revenues by two million Thalers.[28] The negative attitude of the general directory in this respect caused a complete breach between the king and the Prussian bureaucracy. The result was the formation of the French *Regie* under De Launay to collect excise tax throughout the Prussian monarchy., 'one of the most extraordinary acts of any monarch in the eighteenth century'[29]; as W.L. Dorn puts it. The handing over of a major department of state to foreign officials was so unwanted a proceeding that the significance of other aspects of this change were perhaps not fully appreciated at first. Since customs and excise duties were now levied on national and not on provincial basis, a great step forward had been taken towards unifying the fiscal administration of the various Prussian territories. 'The French official class, the pattern of all modern bureaucracies', in the words of Emil Daniels, 'was still superior to the Prussian in ability.' De Launay abolished the tax on rye-flour, and the duty on pork was at any rate not raised. Rye bread and pork were almost the bread and butter of the poor and the soldiers. Frederick cared for the material welfare of the private soldier and wished to distribute the burden of taxation more fairly among the different classes than had hitherto been the case; but his need of money was so pressing that the promptings of humanity were in the end abandoned. As what usually happens, De Launay's financial reforms amounted in the end to little more than an increase of taxation. The prosperity of the people increased but slowly. In 1779, Frederick reckoned that the sources of revenue opened since 1763 were yielding nearly 3 million Thalers and the total public revenue at this time reached 21 millions Thalers a year. The effective check on smuggling contributed to this thoroughly satisfactory result.[30]

The *Regie* was naturally very unpopular in Prussia, so much so that its officials had to go about armed and the British ambassador joked that the French were taking their revenge for Rossbach.[31] It can be said here that there was a temporary public reaction against his policies after his death, but many of the institutions established by Frederick endured.[32]

Although there was an increase in revenue from existing direct and indirect taxes, and the king was anxious to find new sources of income. The most important were the tobacco and coffee monopolies. The fact that Frederick was able to add to his income from these monopolies suggest that the standard of living in Prussia was rising at this time. Tobacco and coffee, once the luxuries of the rich, were now being consumed by a larger section of the population than before.[33]

In the words of Emil Daniels:

> There was economic progress in Prussia under Frederick II, ... though the figures of contemporary statistics, which should indicate a marked rise, are absolutely untrustworthy. It was no case of a rapid advance in material welfare ... but from certain facts it may be inferred that a certain improvement in the welfare of the people actually took place. Frederick the Great, once complained to De Launay that luxury was so much on the increase that every servant girl must now have a thread of silk in what she wore ... however, it must not be supposed that there was any very considerable increase in public prosperity between 1763 and 1786.[34]

Meanwhile, Frederick's critics condemned his policy of hoarding a large treasure in bullion.[35] The king, however, was adamant and considered that it was essential to have immediately available cash necessary to finance the first campaigns of a war. Although he may have appreciated the force of the arguments against permanently withdrawing from circulation large quantities of silver, he thought it essential for his comparatively poor country that a subsantial sum of money should be kept aside.[36]

It is to Frederick's credit that he:

> contrived to produce on the economic resources of what was then the least prosperous section of Germany, a public revenue which was greater than that of Russia on the accession of Catherine II, with a *per capita* burden of taxation no greater than that of Austria, and considerably less than that of France ... [And] managed to support the army of a first-rate power on the resources of a third-rate state and at the same time accumulated a large reserve in the public treasury.[37]

III

In the words of N.O. Henderson:

> There is something to be said for Ziekursch's view that the earliest signs of an industrial revolution in Prussia may be detected in the economic changes that took place just before and after the crisis of 1763. Agriculture, industry and finance had all been stimulated by war demands and by inflation.[38]

Further he states:

> The rise of Germany in the nineteenth century to the position of the leading manufacturing state on the continent was due largely to the expansion of the Prussian economy ... it was the Prussian authorities who took the initiative in establishing the customs union which played so important a part in bringing about the economic unification of the country[39] ... But the origins of the industrial revolution are to be sought in the second half of the eighteenth century rather than in the nineteenth century. It was the age of Frederick the Great that saw the rise of Prussia not only as a leading military power but also as a manufacturing country.[40]

When Frederick came to the throne Prussia had an agrarian economy but when he died the position was quite different. In Silesia he had acquired one of the greatest centres of factories east of the Elbe. The king called the Silesian linen industry his 'Peru'[41]. In West Prussia he had secured a link between East Prussia and the Mark Brandenburg. In Emden he had procured a window to the North Sea. He had obtained a long stretch of the Baltic coast and Prussia now controlled the important trade routes of the order and the Vistula. He had promoted the economic growth of both the hereditary dominions and the recently acquired territories by setting up the Bank of Berlin, the Overseas Trading Corporation and several priviledged commercial companies.[42]

The growth of the population was a factor of major importance in the economic expansion of the country. Frederick's lasting achievements in the colonization of Prussia 'have played the greatest part in establishing the reputation of his rule among contemporaries and posterity', says Ritter. He states :

> To the rationalistic spirit of the eighteenth century–always searching for clear concepts, which, if possible, could be mathematically proven–it seemed that the economic well-being of a country and the success of its government could be determined on the basis of statistical tables; how rapidly did population density increase? How many square miles of wasteland were made arable? Populating the country was therefore a primary objective of all enlightened governments. Each of the great Hohenzollern rulers had tried to settle foreign immigrants in their underpopulated, backward eastern provinces.[43]

Frederick's achievements greatly surpassed those of his predecessors. The density of population increased from 18.7 per square kilometre in 1740 to nearly 30 in 1793.[44] It has been estimated that during his reign, 300,000 individuals settled in Prussia,[45] and that as many as 900 new villages were founded for the colonists. At the end of his reign, every fifth person in Prussia belonged to a recently immigrated family. Gerhard Ritter finds close likeness in the extent of this colonization and the great eastward migration of the middle ages. It increased the German character of the population in the monarchy's territories to a very significant degree.[46] Hertzberg claimed in the 1780s that Prussia's population was increasing more rapidly than in any other country on the continent.[47] The artisans who came to Prussia included miners, metal workers, linen weavers, silk workers and makers of porcelain. The leading merchants of Berlin–men like Splitgerber and Gotzkowsky–co-operated with the king to allure skilled workers to Prussia.

But Frederick's policy of internal colonization met with obstruction both at home and abroad. Townmen and peasants viewed askance the immigrants as unwelcome intruders and potential competitors. The rulers of Austria, Saxony and Poland did their best to prevent their subjects from emigrating to Prussia.[48] Frederick, however, was not a man to be deterred or thwarted. He knew that besides the knowledge of husbandry and handicraft which in many cases surpassed that of the Prussians, the aliens brought with them substantial additions to the material wealth of the land.

It was necessary to expand agricultural production to provide additional food for the increased population. During the so-called 'halcyon years' between 1746 and 1756, Frederick launched agricultural schemes that were only to see full realization many years later. The greatest single achievement was the draining and the recovery for cultivation of the swampy area along the lower Oder River. The catastrophic war undid much of his early work but, undaunted, Frederick devised his famous '*Retablissements*' programme of post-war recovery.[49] Beginning with the first year of peace he made annual visits to his lands, devoting himself with physiocratic zeal to the many aspects of agricultural improvement.

In the words of Henderson:

> Frederick made strenuous efforts to improve the standard of agriculture in Prussia ... He made enquiries concerning up-to-date methods of agricultural production in England[50] and Holland and invited Dutch farmers to settle in his dominions to expand the output of dairy products. He favoured the

> consolidation of scattered strips and the enclosure of common fields though this might harm the interests of the small-holders whom he professed to support. Hertzberg stated in 1785 that the abolition of common fields and pastures had been carried out in hundreds of villages. The king tried to improve the breeding of horses, cattle and sheep.[51]...

It is characteristic of his real interest that in his correspondence with Voltaire Frederick, the enlightened prince *par excellence*, should argue the merits of different broods of laying hens and fertilizers with the prince of European intellectuals.[52] With the acquisition of the 'piece of anarchy', as Frederick called West Prussia, he gained control of the Warthe and the Netze as well as a considerable section of the lower Vistula. This territory was soon linked by the Bromberg Canal to the Oder, thus bringing the still politically independent Danzig–luckless shuttlecock of the Germanic and Slavic powers–via this all-power east-west system of transportation into the economic orbit of Prussia.[53] With Poland's chief outlet, his Prussia was reasonably safe against the stark dread of famine, for it was through Danzig that Poland exported her surplus grain. The increased productivity of the new territory soon made its acquisition as precious for agriculture as Silesia's had been for manufacture. Fifty new villages sprang up, settled by German peasants emigrated from the empire. Counting the foreigners who had entered the country earlier, twenty per cent of the total population of the country was non-German in its origin.[54] This 'racial pollution' seemingly did not disturb Frederick's complacence. He was mainly concerned that their manpower was put to profitable military[55] and agricultural purposes. Rivers were dredged and widened, dams built, canals cut, and marshes drained. He cleared away virgin forests and planted young firs and pines; cultivated estates running to waste. In these respects, as in so many others, he was following in the footsteps of his predecessors, but doing things on a much larger scale.

The king applied every art of governance to bring new land under cultivation and to increase the fertility of the old. No site for a farmstead was to be left vacant and in the forests–

so ran the decree–'no place where a tree can stand' should be unplanted. The sterile nature of the soil challanged the untiring industry of the king.[56] In the words of John Gillies: 'Brandenburg abounded with sandy hillocks, unmixed with loam, devoid of moisture, and long condemned to invincible barrenness. An English farmer undertook to cultivate this seemingly ungrateful subject.'[57] Thousands of acres had to be set with bushes, says Reddaway, to prevent its surface from being blown over the neighbouring field.[58] The agricultural reformers, such as the famous agronomist, J.C. Schubart, redoubled their efforts during the last two decades of the reign to introduce fodder crops and institute new farming techniques like scientific rotation.[59] In the words of Sidney B. Fay: 'It ... made possible more feeding of cattle in the stalls instead of in the fields, improved the quality and amount of milk, and produced more stable manure that could be used further to enrich the fields. He persuaded his people to make greater use of such cheap forms of food as potatoes and turnips.'[60]

The king took vigorous measures to preserve the forests in his kingdom and to regulate the timber industry.... After 1763, new edicts were issued to limit felling and to provide for reafforestation. It was Frederick's, concern 'that gave Germany a leading place in modern forestry methods.' as stated by Fay.

Much was accomplished. While there is scant evidence to warrant belief that the improvements corresponded to the highest expectations of the zealous ruler, undoubtedly they greatly strengthened the agricultural position of the state.[61]

Frederick attempted to do something to ameliorate the peasants' hard lot. In the rural areas, many peasant holdings operated at a marginal level even in good years, and were often heavily indebted in bad years. The usual source of rural capital, the noble landlord, was frequently as financially embarrassed as were his peasants. This situation of capital starvation had to be remedied. In the words of John G. Gagliardo:

> Frederick II ... established the credit institutes known as

> *Landschaften*, which consisted of a pooling of noble estates, on which members could borrow up to two-thirds the value of their estates. But rural credit remained a very serious problem ... In any case, the peasant cultivatior benefited at most only very little and very indirectly from these credit schemes.[62]

Reforms in the agrarian constitution of Prussia were praised in much of the agrarian publicistic literature of the late eighteenth century. But even if the lot of some of the most heavily oppressed peasants was eased somewhat, the most basic problems of the agrarian constitution had not been dealt with.[63] For all his detestation of serfdom, which he called an abomination, he shrank from the radcial legal remedy of liberating even his own serfs,[64] His efforts to help private serfs were still more unavailing. Innumerable royal edicts indicate that his humanitarian compassion was fortified by more sober considerations.[65]

His personal efforts were fruitless, because impersonal circumstances worked against him. Prussia had no agricultural revolution as in England's, but there was a marked trend toward large-scale capitalist farming. Peasant cultivators were foced out to less fertile areas or squeezed out entirely from their small parcels. They were forbidden to migrate to the towns or engage in competitive rural industry with the lord. The lord or his resident steward generally shirked the responsibilities to the state for the relief and the well-being of the men, while Frederick himself was often ignorant of the actual state of affairs and grievances. Not only was the monarchy incapable of checking this capitalistic development and only half-hearted in its efforts to temper the abuses, but it was obligated by its own fast-growing grain requirements to encourage and patronize it and to insure the Junkers an exclusive labour monopoly while keeping their feudal privileges intact. Frederick thus firmly consolidated the economic provileges of his landed aristocacry on whose support his state leaned so heavily.[66]

The core of Frederick's economic policy was the old mercantilist preoccupation with state building. A national policy was to supersede regional and private policies in order to achieve the goal of state self-sufficiency. He did away with the narrow fiscal point of view of the royal domain administration. More important, he set to work creating a systematic trade policy. Its guidelines were the then dominant principles of mercantilism, and their exemplary implementation in France under Colbert.

In 1749, Frederick personally assumed the direction of the state's commercial and trade policies. The detailed knowledge he acquired is miraculous.[67] He devoted special care to the silk industry, which he raised from insignficant beginnings to considerable–if somewhat artificial–prosperity. Exact regulations on the treatment of silk-worms, the spinning of the thread, and numerous other details were printed and in rural areas even announced from the pulpit.

In the words of Leo Gershoy:

> With the end of the war Frederick had his opportunity to integrate the whole of Prussian economic life by co-ordinating capital, men and resources. After stimulating recovery–his famous programme of '*Retablissements*'–by public spending, he would maintain and increase national prosperity by continuing to supply the same stimulus of state aid. With millions of Thalers from the state treasury at his disposition Frederick left little undone for the next quarter of a century to transform his essentially agricultural country into a major industrial power.[68]

Nor was he content to improve already existing industries, such as the Silesian linen weavers. Studying the trade balances of the various provinces, he deliberated on what might be done to manufacture articles that were presently imported. 'Luxury goods as well as necessities–fine damask and cotton fabrics, paper, sugar, porcelain–', writes Ritter, 'were to be produced at home to weaken foreign competition ... to bring export to the eastern markets under Prussian control, and to save Prussia from the fate of Poland, which in Frederick's opinion was being ruined by heavy imports that were not balanced by domestic production.'[69]

Not all of Frederick's projects succeeded or achieved permanency. But on the whole he accomplished a great deal; for some industries that subsequently crystallized, like the

Silesian mines, he actually created the conditions congenial for growth. Cadres of trained workers and competent enterpreneurs settled in Prussia; commercial ability and ambition were stimulated. 'Poverty-ridden Prussia had assumed her place as one of the great European producers, exporting roughly one-third of her manufactured products abroad'[70], states Leo Gershoy.

The existence of a large standing army stimulated the production of woollen cloth in Prussia. It was exported to various parts of Germany and was regularly sold at great fairs. The growth of the weaving branch of the industry was so considerable that there was a shortage of spinners. When it was suggested that English spinning machines should be introduced to increase output Frederick became doubtful. He allowed the importation of only a limited number of machines to spin fine wool or cotton and refrained from too quick an introduction of machinery lest it should lead to unemployment among the Prussian wool workers.[71]

The improvement of communications was an essential feature of Frederick's plans to promote both internal commerce and foreign trade. He saw the necessity of linking the agrarian parts of his kingdom with the provinces which were beginning to be industrialized. Transport facilities were provided by building canals rather than roads. The king also appreciated the need for improving the shipping facilities of Stettin: in a single year twenty ships were launched, some of which were sold abroad.[72] The acquisition of East Frisia gave Frederick the opportunity he desired to extend Prussia's overseas commerce. He dreamed of turning Emden into a new Amsterdam. The failure of Emden to develop its trade with India and China was due partly to the inexperience of Prussian entrepreneurs and partly to the opposition of England and other maritime states to those who intruded upon their preserves.[73]

Frederick was determined to see that Prussian subjects sold as much as possible to foreigners and bought as little as possible from them in return. The latter part of his task could be, and was, accomplished by prohibiting the importation of certain commodities, such as salt, porcelain and steel, and by appointing a host of custom officers to make the prohibition effective. But to sell to foreigners goods which were produced in Prussia, simply because the king wished that his subjects should forego the convenience of buying them from foreigners was a herculean task which taxed Frederick's statecraft to the utmost. His greatest pride nevertheless was that Prussia's passive trade balance was converted into an active one. By the most conservative estimate the surplus for 1783 amounted to 3 million Thalers, and the total value of industrial production three years later to 29 million Thalers.[74]

In general, Frederick's commercial policy, especially during the last years of his reign, suffered from the fact that his primary concern was the rapid development of industry. A complicated system of protective tariffs and transit tolls simply could not be combined with the best interests of commerce. The barriers to import and export were particularly damaging to Silesia which had lost her old ties with Austria and Galicia. Nor did Frederick succeed in imposing uniformity upon the domestic market–something that no government before the French Revolution was able to achieve.[75] 'It often appeared ... that there were spheres in which statecraft, even when practised by a Frederick, could accomplish little', says Reddaway.

IV

In the opinion of Walter L. Dorn:

> The ultimate test of any system of administration is its management and control of finance ....The success of the Prussian monarchy in the eighteenth century must finally be explained in terms of its financial history. Edmund Burke was profoundly impressed with the excellence of the Prussian financial system and admonished the British Parliament to emulate the example of Prussia.[76] 'Carlyle defined Frederick in a single word: he said he was a Reality ... a reality too strong, too active, too independent[77] ...

A decent respect toward Frederick's economic policy does

not preclude a searching analysis of its various phases, nor does it forbid raising the question of how much he sacrificed of the aggregate good in pursuit of his goals. Frederick's methods, as already discussed, were those followed by all governments in the age of mercantilism, an age which was in its death throes at that time in Western Europe. Even during Frederick's lifetime a new school of French economic theorists, the Physiocrats, was beginning its criticism of his economic policies in which the Prussian king showed less originality. He appears to have learned little from experience and the views of the Physiocrates and of Adam Smith, but these did not deflect him from pursuing the mercantilist policy which he had inherited from his father.

Shortly after Frederick's death, Mirabeau's book *De la monarchie prussienne sous Frederic le Grand* appeared in London. The author passed a crushing judgment on Frederick's economic measures by applying the standard of those theories of political economy which had lately come to the fore in Western Europe and obscured mercantilism.[78] Frederick was shown to have committed numerous blunders of the sort that are inevitable when the state tries to direct industries that are rapidly expanding, increasing in complexity, and becoming more cumbrous. Trade and agriculture had suffered by prohibiting the export of raw wool and the import of manufactured goods, and by the whole system of protective tariffs and transit duties.

The harsh jurisdical relations between Junker and peasant were not relaxed. The stupendous expansion of industrial and commercial enterprise under the aegis of a state working paramountly for its military fabric unfailingly gave a vitalizing concussion to the more smart villagers and accelerated the capitalist zeal of the urban entrepreneur. By crushing the old medieaval and communal torpor, Frederick's Prussia opened the vistas of boundless opportunities of free enterprise for the talented and the ambitious. But the monarch frustrated the aspirations that he roused in the capitalist producer.[79] It was against the political system of absolutism in general that the most poignant criticism was laid: the free initiative of the people was not sufficiently trusted, while too much reliance was laid on rules and regulations.[80]

It is preposterous to deny that Frederick began the transformation of Prussia into a modern industrialized state; and it would be equally preposterous to deny, says Gershoy, 'that the policy of sterilizing money and hoarding specie ... seriously retarded a potentially still more rapid extension than took place ... he treated public finance in the manner that a householder considered a family budget, regarding public debt as a liability instead of the obverse of national investment.[81] The time-honoured practice of total or partial tax exemption for the priviledged groups put the burden of taxes upon those least qualified to bear it and at the same time depressed the living standard of many. 'The failure of the venture [Regie] to bring about the alleviation of popular hardship was pronounced. The reductions were largely on paper[82], observes Gershoy. No wonder the free born and free trading English envoy, Sir James Harris (Lord Malmesbury), was shocked and uttered angrily: (1776).

> The king of Prussia never can be taught to believe that a large treasure laying (sic) dormant in his coffers impoverishes his kingdom; that riches increase by circulation; that trade cannot subsist without reciprocal profit; that monopolies and exclusive grants put a stop to emulation and, of course, to industry; and, in short, that the real wealth of a sovereign consists in the ease and affluence of his subjects. These errors, however capital they are, have rather served to augment the misery of these subjects than impede the progress of his own grandeur.[83]

Lord Dalrymple, the British Minister in Berlin, declared in 1786 that Frederick's system of protection was 'too complicated and confused.'[84] Responsible Prussian officials were conscious of the drawbacks of some aspects of Frederick's version of 'mercantilism. This is clear from the report by Ursinus on the inefficiency of the Berlin silk industry–artificial creation of the king's.[85]

Viewed in retrospect the imposing might of militarized Prussia was already hollow when Fredrick died. Set upon crumbling foundations, Prussia confronted the new world that was dawning. It collapsed during the stress of the Napoleonic wars, because in a world increasingly based upon individual enterprise, already revolutionary before the upheaval in France, the great Prussian ruler kept its bases unchanged.[86]

The tragedy of Frederick's position in history–that he represented the apogee and at the same time the end of his epoch–is poignantly clear. 'Frederick was the greatest ruler of the age of the *Aufklarung*, but', as G.P. Gooch observes, 'distant horizons were beyond his gaze.'[87] If we wish to do full justice to Frederick's actions in the economic sphere, we must keep in mind that they were less concerned with promoting the economic well-being of the population–which was to be the first goal of the liberal age–than with inceasing the power of the state. In addition, his policies were characterized by the belief that the country's economic forces could be strengthened only in conflict with and at the cost of one's neighbours, not by peaceful collaboration. To this end, Frederick waged relentless economic wars for decades, accepted the ruin of Silesia's transit trade, and crippled the commerce on the Elbe River. These were ruthless measures, which in the end failed to achieve their purpose. Later generations dubbed them as shortsighted. 'Today when it is more difficult than it was in the nineteenth century to master the severe conflicts among vast economic interest groups, Frederick's methods may again meet with greater understanding.'[88] says Ritter.

'We have ... no accurate means of comparing the standard of living in Prussia at that time with her neighbours.'[89] Yet the way in which Frederick was able to carry out so many of his plans compares very favourably with the achievements of other monarchs in the second half of the eighteenth century. Failure to balance the budget, inability to find suitable officials, and irresolution in the face of the opposition of vested interests led to the downfall of many impressive schemes of economic amelioration by contemporary sovereigns. Frederick too worked against heavy odds[90]: economic, geographical and social factors sometimes created circumstances over which he could exercise little control. Yet alone among the rulers of his age he left his country with a far more flourishing economy than it had when he ascended the throne.[91]

NOTES AND REFERENCES

1. It can be no mere coincidence that this period of Frederick's life is passed over so casually 'by all his non-German biographers'. Philip Guedalla rather maliciously suggest that the reason is that most of them have wriiten for the express purpose of misrepresenting Frederick as a crude militarist delighting only in war and bloodshed and during this period "he was not quite sufficiently the Hun." This, no doubt, is one reason, but it does not explain why Thomas Carlyle, who frankly regarded Frederick as the most heroic figure of his age, devotes nine volumes to the first fifty one years of Frederick's life and only one to the remaining twenty-three.' 'Yet during these last two decades Frederick succeeded', in the opinion of F.J.P. Veale, 'in recreating Prussia—a work essential if his previous achievements were to have permanent influence—and during these years he was 'never more the Hohenzollern in his versatility or the German in his thoroughness.' The main reason why the last quarter of Frederick's life has been thus overlooked, not only by writers of propaganda but by genuine biographers, is obvious. This period while economically and politically important is lacking in interest and colour. Frederick's zest for life, his most attractive quality, perished with the Seven Years War. It was as if some dark cloud had descended upon him. 'It is a poor old man who is coming home', he said when the great war ended. But if Frederick's former zest for life had perished, his capacity for hardwork remained unimpaired. In the eyes of posterity, nearly every great man is stabilised at one 1stage of his life. We think of Napoleon as he was on the eve of Austerlitz and not of the corpulent invalid of St. Helena. 'It may well be that with regard to Frederick the Great, the posterity has displayed a keener discernment than Frederick's biographers. It is the Frederick of the period which they neglect who survives in the memory of mankind... "small in stature, shruken and bent with the work of the so many years, but the fire in his eyes showing that his mind had not aged." Instinctively posterity seems to have realised that the really significant period of his

life was that in which ... he saved Prussia from economic collapse.' F.J.P. Veale, *Frederick the Great : His Life and Place in History* (Rochester : The Stanhope Press Ltd., 1935) pp. 224–30.

2. Yet 'In finance, the Prussian Government suffered less from the war than France, Australia or even England' : Norwood Young, *The Life of Frederick the Great* (New York : Henry Holt and Company, 1919), p.360. 'The war left all belligerent powers excepting Prussia deeply in debt : Frederick alone had no creditor to satisfy; nay more-while all his adversaries were prostrated by exhaustion, he could expend large sums on magnificent buildings as if to show his enemies that, after the prodigious efforts which he had been obliged to make during the war, he still possessed resources against any new aggressions which they might mediate' : Thomas Campbell (ed.), *Frederick the Great, His court and Times* (London : Henry Colburn Publishers, 1843), p.68. There had been no 'increased taxation, and when the war ended there was a sum equivalent to Pound 4,000,000 in the Prussian treasury, more than enough to pay for another campaign, while the necessary military stores of all kinds were already with the army.' Young, op.cit, p.360. In the opinion of Pierre Gaxotte : 'If Frederick could stand the expenses of reconstruction calculated at the lowest possible price to be sure, it was because his finances were not in too bad a way. England and Saxony had financed Prussia. After Kunersdorf he had himself advised "Prosperous folk" to fly to Hamburg with their capital: it served as a reserve ... ' Pierre Gaxotte, *Frederick the Great*, trans. R.A. Bell (London : G. Bell and Sons Ltd., 1941) p. 375..
3. Leo Gershoy, *From Despotism to Revolution 1763–1789, The Rise of Modern Europe*, William L. Langer (ed.) (New York : Harper and Brothers Publishers, 1944), Vol. 10, p. 5.
4. Veit Valentin. *'Some Interpretations of Frederick the Great'*, In : *History* (1934), Vol. 19, pp. 122–23.
5. Veale, op.cit, p. 230.
6. W.O. Henderson. *Studies in the Economic Policy of Frederick the Great*, (New York : Augustus M. Kalley Publisher, 1965), p. 38.
7. Ibid (on the authority of R. Koser), p. 39.
8. As 'no revenue came from East Prussia during the Russian occupation. The annual receipts of the General Domains Fund fell far short of the 3.5 million Thalers secured in peacetime. Only Silesia paid its usual contribution throughout the war.

The income from customs, excise and tolls and from the profits of nationalised undertakings declined sharply' : Ibid, p. 40.

9. Ibid, p. 40.
10. 'By a Royal edict the debased coins for which the king's subjects had been compelled to pay three times their value, were, after a near date, to be no longer legal tender. They could be sold for one-third of their face value. New coins, for which the full price had to be paid were issued. A similar repudiation by the prince of his own coinage had been perpetrated by the Great Elector. 'It is a characteristically Prussian expedient', says Norwood Young, 'for it wipes out a Government debt, at the expense of the people, in an indirect manner. The people are cheated but they have no redress. "Mitchell [Andrew Mitchell, British Ambassador to Berlin] wrote to a friend : "His Prussian Majesty affirms that he had laid no taxes whatever upon his subjects, though at the same time it is evident that by the alteration and diminution of the coin, his subjects have, since the beginning of the war, lost two-thirds of their personal estate, being paid at the rate of thirty-three per hundred,... "Nothing the king ever did has so much disgusted and alienated the affections of his people as the rash and inconsiderable steps he has taken with regard to the coin', the people want bread ... ": Young, op.cit, pp. 360–61.
11. Emil Daniels. 'Frederick the Great and His Successor (1) Home and Foreign Policy 1763–97', *The Cambridge Modern History*, planned by Lord Acton, A.W. Ward (ed.), *The Eighteenth Century* (New York : The Macmillan Company, 1909) Vol. 6, pp. 710–11.
12. 'Those who insist that he did nothing without a motive of State may find it in his desire to convince foreign Powers that it was dangerous to attack a nation which could afford luxuries while its enemies were deep in debt. Other conjectures are possible. Frederick loved to indulge the hope that the sciences, which had visited Greece and Italy; France and England, in turn, might settle for a while in Prussia, and the new palace ... might be regarded as a sacrifice at their altar. The claims of the new Prussian Industries, especially the manufacture of silk, which was largely used in adorning the interior, may have induced the king to provide an artificial market in this way.' W.F. Reddaway, *Frederick the Great and the Rise of Prussia* (New York : Haskell House Publisher Ltd., 1969), pp. 307–8, vide supra (1) p. 2.

13. Gaxotte, op.cit, p. 377.
14. Daniels, '*Cambridge Modern History*'. op.cit, p. 721.
15. Ibid, p. 722.
16. Gaxotte, op.cit, p. 378.
17. Daniels, op.cit, 'Under the two Kings who followed on Frederick II, the directors of the bank [who searched in vain for an opportunity to make suitable investments] found themselves driven further and further along this precipitious path. There was all the less chance of safeguarding the deposit holders, when the avalanche of the Napoleonic invasion descended upon the kingdom of Prussia... The institution of this bank was manifestly premature from an economic standpoint ... there was no palpable result from the foundation of Prussian bank beyond the creation of a new surplus in favour of the royal finances.' Ibid, p. 722.
18. Ibid, p. 722.
19. Gaxotte, op.cit, p. 378,
20. 'The Emperor Maximilian whom the Italians called ... *senza denari* was the laughing stock of Europe. More recently the Emperor Charles VI left his state in such disorder that Maria Theresa was compelled to accept English subsides, which made her the slave of King George and cost her the loss of fine provinces ... If France continued her unwise practices she too would be abased and despised by her rivals. What was true of other countries was particularly applicable to Prussia, which possessed neither colonies, nor rich companies, nor a bank, nor many other resources at the disposal of France, England, and Spain. Even in an emergency only a small loan could be raised ... The Second Political Testament, .. covering the same ground as the first, reflects the anxious experiences of the Seven Years War. In his new survey of the resources of the state Frederick laments the destruction of forests during the recent conflict ...' cited by G.P. Gooch, *Frederick The Great : the Ruler, the Writer, the Man* (New York : Alfred A. Knopf, 1947), pp. 291–304.
21. Ibid, pp. 293–94.
22. Gershoy, op.cit, p. 73.
23. Gerhard Ritter. *Frederick the Great : A Historical Profile*, trans. Peter Paret (Berkeley: Univ. of California Press, 1968), p.151.
24. Ibid, p. 152.
25. Henderson, op.cit, p. 66.
26. 'It has been estimated that this proportion sank from 80 per

cent in 1740 to just over 50 per cent in 1786', Ibid, p. 68.

27. Walter L. Dorn. 'The Prussian Bureaucracy in the Eighteenth Century III', *Political Science Quarterly*, (1932), Vol. 47, p. 272.
28. Ibid, 'Press Bur in 18th Century II'. p. 79, vide Thomas Carlyle, *History of Frederick II of Prussia called Frederick the Great*, in seven volumes, (London : Chapman and Hall 193, Piccadilly, 1869), Vol. 7, Part III, p. 21.
29. Dorn, Ibid, p.89. In the words of Rosenberg: 'The establishment of the Regie was precipitated, in part, by the General Directory's courteous refusal to cooperate with Frederick's plan for starting postwar reconstruction in the midst of deep economic depression by increasing taxes. In turning down this ill-conceived programme of fiscal reform, the Directory, by implication ventured to treat His Royal Majesty like an amateur', Hans Rosenberg, *Bureaucracy, Aristocracy and Autocracy : The Prussian Experience 1660–1815* (Cambridge : Harvard Univ. Press, 1966), p. 196.
30. Daniels, op.cit, p. 712.
31. Sir Andrew Mitchell wrote to his government : 'The new projects of excise have really alienated the affections of the people from their sovereign to a degree hardly to be described.' *Memoirs and Papers of sir Andrew Mitchell*, A. Bissett (ed.) two Vols. (London, 1850)' quoted in Young, op.cit, p. 363, vide also Ludwig Reiners, *Frederick the Great : A Biography*, trans. Lawrence P. R. Wilson (New York : G.P. Putnam's Sons, 1960), p.232. In the words of Rosenberg : 'The opposition ended in 1786 with the dissolution of the Regie and the formal reappropriation of its powers and emoluments by the old hierarchy', op.cit, p.197. 'When his successor had abolished this administrative machine public opinion accused Launay of the worst misdeeds. Contemporary historians have done justice to his capacities and his character. As for the system, it has been judged in a variety of ways. Prof. Smoller portrays the State Department as one of the pillars of the idea of monarchy ... Walter Schultz, the specialist, writes that it was a 'completely useless' institution. One thing stands out clearly, it was a costly institution and it involved a disproportionate increase of rigour and inspection to produce a very small increase of revenue.' Gaxotte op.cit, p. 383. 'La Haye de Launay himself wrote a defence of the French system of State Department in answer to Mirabeau, *Justification du systeme d'economie politique et financiere de Frederic II*' Ibid, p. 438.

32. 'The Mining Office, the Forestry Department, the Royal Bank of Berlin, and the Overseas Trading Corporation continued in the nineteenth century to foster the industrial and commercial development of the country.' Henderson, op.cit, p. 65.
33. Ibid, p. 72. The General Tobacco Administration 'had the exclusive right to import, process and sell tobacco and snuff ... A preventive force, largely staffed by French officials, was established to stop both smuggling and other infringements of the monopoly. There were complaints concerning the high price of tobacco products ... In 1776 the king stated that the tobacco monopoly was bringing in one million Thalers a year and by the end of the reign this income had risen to 1,286,000 Thalers', Ibid, pp. 71–72.
34. Daniels, op.cit, pp. 722–23.
35. 'According to Koser the total reserves kept in readiness for war amounted to 50 million Thalers' : cited by Henderson, op.cit, p. 74.
36. Ibid, pp. 74–75 'Of the 100,000,000 or more Thalers that were minted during the second half of his reign, Only 66,000,000 were in circulation' : 'Schrotter', cited by Gershoy, op.cit, p. 87, vide infra, p. 30.
37. W.L. Dorn. 'The Prussian Bureaucracy in the Eighteenth Century', *Political Science Quarterly*' Vol. 46, (1931), p. 404.
38. Henderson, op.cit, p. 58.
39. Vide Supra, op.cit, p. 11.
40. Henderson, op.cit, p. 123.
41. Daniels, op.cit, p. 719. 'He said that in the linen-manufacturing districts he would permit no mining, not even for gold, lest the supply of wood should be diverted from the bleachereis. Recruits for filling up the gaps made by the Seven Years War in the ranks of the weavers were sought abroad not less energetically than they were for the army. Every immigrant weaver received a loom as a free gift. Of course, he was not allowed to leave Prussia at his option. The position of the linen weavers was mostly unfavourable in Prussia as indeed all over Germany. The king was ignorant of those social ills which the eighteenth century in general was little capable of understanding. In his eyes, the salient point was that Silesian linen should reach the Spanish market at a low enough price to be able to undersell that manufactured across the frontier in France close by'. Ibid, pp. 719–20.
42. Henderson, op.cit, p. 124.

43. Ritter, op.cit, p. 179.
44. Henderson, op.cit, pp. 125–26.
45. 'Even if that figure is an exaggeration, it is at all events certain that Frederick's colonization policy very considerably increased moderate sized and small rural holdings. Under Frederick II ... large number of immigrants were settled on comparatively unproductive soil.' Daniels, op.cit, pp. 716–17.
46. Ritter, op.cit, p. 179.
47. Henderson, op.cit, p. 126. According to him : 'The expansion of Prussia's population—particularly after 1763—was due to the excess of births over deaths, the acquisition of new provinces and the arrival of thousands of new settlers in Frederick's Dominions' : Ibid. In the words of W.L. Dorn : 'Before they [The provincial chambers] could settle the colonists who came from all the quarters of Europe, they had first to reclaim sandy wastes, drain swamps and morasses, and that in such a way 'that not an acre of arable land from which a family can sustain itself remains unoccupied: Their parole was : more colonists, more people, more industries, more commerce and greater production. The end in view always to achieve that substantial 'plus' in revenues which the king never ceased to demand from them.' Dorn, op.cit, Vol. 47, p. 84.
48. Henderson, op.cit, p. 128.
49. Gershoy, op.cit, pp. 76–77 'Drawing upon his dwindled ... metallic reserve, he disbursed millions of Thalers to succour the devastated areas ... ' Ibid, p. 77.
50. In the words of John Gillies 'In imitation of the great conquerors and civilisers of Europe, Frederick borrowed from neighbouring nations the institutions in which they respectively excelled. In rural economy, England, of course formed his principal model; and when he divided the extensive commons in Prussia and Pomerania, he thought, that a German prince who followed the example of a British parliament, could not be accused of despotism. Yet this accusation was made and repeated, until the benefits of his regulations began to be sensibly felt by those who had most loudly condemned them' : (View of a contemporary British, written soon after Frederick's death) : John Gillies, *A veiw of the Reign of Frederick II of Prussia* (Dublin : William Porter, 1789), p. 318.

51. Henderson, op.cit, p. 132.
52. Gershoy, op.cit, p. 77. It may be added : 'The spectacle of the royal philosopher writing to Voltaire about manure and walking almost daily from Sans Souci to his turnip-field is a visible proof of Frederick's devotion to 'this branch of his stewardship. He was wont to speak with authority as the leading agriculturist of the realm ....Having once attained his object by teaching his subjects to produce an article at home, he imperatively forbade them to import it from abroad. The full reward of his policy would be reaped when Prussia began to supply it to other counties in exchange for gold and silver.' Reddaway op.cit, p.310.
53. Gershoy, op.cit, p. 77.
54. Ibid, pp. 77–78.
55. Rosenberg aptly calls Prussia 'the Sparta of the North' op.cit, 40.
56. 'Many centuries before blotting-paper came to be known, Brandenburg was nicknamed "the sand box" of the Holy Roman Empire.' Reddaway, op.cit, pp. 309–10.
57. Gillies, op.cit, p.321. To quote Henderson : 'The problem of making the best use of the sandy soil of Brandenburg was tackled in various ways. On one of the royal estates an English expert grew turnips and allowed them to rot in the ground. He then planted the fields with various grasses and clover and turned them into pastures on which cattle and sheep could graze. The fields subsequently supported one-third more cattle than before. On soil too sandy for either arable or dairy farming, trees were planted. About 13,000 acres of pine were planted between 1776 ans 1782.' Henderson, op.cit, p. 133.
58. Reddaway, op.cit, pp. 310.
59. Gershoy, op.cit, p. 78.
60. Sidney B. Fay. *The rise of Brandenburg–Prussia to 1786*, rev. edn., by Klaus Epstien (New York : Holt, Rinehert and Winston, 1964), p. 124.
61. The success of Frederick's agricultural policy was seen in 1770–71 when the harvest failed and there was a serious grain shortage in many parts of Germany. Saxony and Bohemia suffered so severely that some 40,000 persons migrated to Prussia where more food was available. On the other hand though the breed of cattle was improved by experimentation, 'Frederick did not succeed–as the rulers of Saxony succeeded in developing a native breed of sheep which produced wool of really high quality'. Henderson, op.cit, p. 133–34.

62. John G. Gagliardo. *From Pariah to Patriot : The changing Image of the German Peasant 1770–1840* (The Univ. Press of Kentucky, 1969), p.5. But 'Frederick II, after all, having foreseen the ravages his wars would bring to peasant lands, had remitted or reduced taxes, and was duly praised for it. In the absence of special funds assuring credit for the peasant who had become impecunious due to natural disasters, it was asked, why could other princes not take a page from Frederick's book and remit taxes for a greater or lesser period of time?, Ibid, p. 50.
63. Ibid, p. 17.
64. Gershoy, op.cit, p.78. 'On the royal domain Frederick was able to put limits on the onerous labour dues of his own serfs, many of whom obtained hereditary rights of possession'. Ibid, In the words of Gagliardo 'The ... major reform undertaken on the Domains occurred in East Prussia and Lithuania, in 1763, when Frederick II forbade the royal officials who leased his domains to make use of *Gesindezwangsdienst*, the right require services from the families of servile peasants. This order, together with the earlier reforms, in effect abolished hereditary personal servitude ... in 1777, hereditary tenure was granted to all other domains peasants in the monarchy ... .' Gagliardo, op.cit, p.15. It may be added that 'he failed utterly to win hereditary possessional rights for the peasantry in Pomerania and Upper Silesia', though he planned to improve their condition without changing their legal status, that problem was equally baffling; Gershoy, op. cit, p. 78. For some further details of the agrarian scene of Frederick's Prussia Gagliardo's *From Pariah to Patriot*, Part-I 'The Background', pp. 3–57, may be consulted.
65. Lessing in a private letter of 1769, calls Prussia 'The most enslaved country of Europe until the present day': cited by Rosenberg, op.cit, pp. 41–42. According to W.L. Dorn 'Mirabeau could truthfully say that the Prussian government had become for the science of despotism what Egypt was to the ancients in search of knowledge.' Dorn, op.cit, (1931), Vol. 46, p. 408.
66. Gershoy, op.cit, pp. 79–80.
67. Ritter, op.cit, p. 173. 'The discussion of economic questions in his first political testament extended to the manufacture of shoe laces and the problem of guild opposition to modern looms.' Ibid, p. 174.
68. Gershoy, op.cit, p. 82, 'Inspite of this considerable

industrialization under Frederick the Great which raised Prussia to be the fourth manufacturing country of the world, Prussia still remained essentially an agrarian state.' Fay, op.cit, p. 123.

69. Ritter, op.cit, p. 174.
70. Gershoy, op.cit, p. 83.
71. 'C. Ergang': cited by Henderson op.cit, p. 145.
72. Fay, op.cit, p. 122.
73. Henderson, op.cit, pp. 155-56.
74. Ritter, op.cit, p. 174.
75. Ibid, pp. 176–77.
76. Dorn, op.cit, Vol. 47, p. 256.
77. Gaxotte, op.cit, p. 326.
78. 'But, for the present, the English and French in practical politics applied the new doctrines only very cautiously and not even consistently ... The Prussian nation, which was far behind the nations of Western Europe in almost every respect, seemed for a long time yet to require direction from above in economic matters.' Daniels, op.cit, p. 723.
79. It may be added : 'Though the economic changes cleared the way for the disciplined labour force of a later day and prepared the way for the transformation of social power relationship, it was in Frederick's own day, as Treitschke candidly noted, 'an unnoticed and an undesired transformation.' Whatever the future relations were to be, for the present the state hemmed producer and production in the strait jacket of regulation and control.' Gershoy, op.cit, p. 87.
80. Ritter, op.cit, p. 175.
81. Gershoy, op.cit, p. 87.
82. Ibid, p. 84.
83. Lord Malmesbury (ed.), *Diaries and Correspondence of James Harris, first Earl of Malmesbury* (London, 1945), Vol. I, p. 123.
84. Henderson, op.cit, p. 160.
85. Ibid, p. 61.
86. In the words of Pierre Gaxotte: 'This [serfdom] was perhaps the true reason for the collapse of Prussia at the beginning of the nineteenth century. The Napoleonic conquest encountered a rural population which was amorphous, almost indifferent and incapable of a spontaneous outburst of the patriotism and self-sacrifice. It needed the landslide of 1806 to bring about a remodelling of the social structure. The men who revived Prussia after Jena endeavoured to free the peasants, or at the

very least to reduce their hardships; it was only then that they became one of the living forces of the nation.' Gaxotte, op.cit, p. 381.

87. Gooch, op.cit, p. 308.
88. Ritter, op.cit, p. 176.
89. Reiners, op.cit, p. 233.
90. 'It proved to be much more difficult than Frederick had imagined to wrest control of Prussia's foreign trade from the stronger and more experienced West European competition. Their traditional ways, inexperience, and lack of working capital made Prussia's merchants reluctant to face the dangers of long-term foreign projects. Even the time-tested technique of reducing risks by founding joint stock companes holding government monopolies could not overcome Prussia's natural weaknesses. Repeatedly Frederick found that granting a monopoly reduced rather than stimulated initiative. But as interim measures, monopolies were necessary—a point not grasped by the later criticism of the Physiocrats' Ritter, op.cit, p. 176.
91. Henderson, op.cit, p. 12.

Chapter 4

Napoleon III and Italy

FROM PLOMBIERES TO VILLAFRANCA

Louis Napoleon Bonaparte, President of the French Republic from 1848 to 1852 and, as Napoleon III, Emperor of the France from 1852 to 1870, was neither the first nor the last[1] of the France's rulers to be called an enigma.[2] His complex character and contradictory policies can never fail to fascinate, and men will not cease to argue about his intentions and whether or not his rule was preponderantly beneficent or calamitous to his country and to Europe at large.

Albert Guerard states:

> According to all 'realistic' historians, Napoleon III was 'woefully disinterested'; and they blame him roundly for preferring the golden haze of principles to the plain facts of national interest.[3]

According to Guerard, he was sincere in repudiating any thought of conquest: it was France's mission to liberate, not to enslave. Self-determination, ascertained through a plebiscite, was his goal; then free nations could live as happy neighbours. The kinship between his 'doctrine of nationalities' and Wilsonism is undeniable, although Woodrow Wilson never acknowledged so embarrassing a forerunner.[4]

It was a principle with Napoleon III that ethnic groups with common language and tradition, had the right to become *nations*.'In the case of Italy this conviction assumed the ardour of a personal faith: he was an Italian patriot ...Patriotism is not necessarily jealous and exclusive: there were many ardent 'Polish patriots' among the French throughout the nineteenth century.'[5] says Guerard.

The man whose principles were so lofty, and whose temper was so kind, turned into a disturbing element, a universal menace, all the more pervasive because of its vagueness. What frightened Europe about Napoleon III was that 'he had a dynamic faith. His motto was not *Quieta non movere*–in plain English, *Let sleeping dogs lie*–but Injustices need not be eternal.'[6] To his fellow rulers, continues Guerard, the impenetrable eyes of the French emperor became lakes of unfathomable deceit. His opportunistic tacking was interpreted as deviousness. When he spoke in the clearest tones, he was not believed: his utterances were scrutinized for the meaning cloaked there-in-to. When he remained silent, it proved that 'the Sphinx of the Tuileries' was harbouring mysterious designs.[7] After all, he had been a conspirator until he ascended the throne: why not a crowned conspirator? The sovereign who in the depth of his being was a Woodrow Wilson, only less smug and of a warmer heart, created the impression of a Hitler.[8]

Berry observed in 1908 (prior to the outbreak of World War I) : 'No man is more entitled than Napoleon to be called the maker of contemporary Europe ....the map of Europe, as it now is drawn, is largely the work of this man, among the most wonderful of adventurers.[9]

Napoleon III initiated seven wars or military expeditions.[10] As the heir of the great Emperor, and for the consolidation of his popularity and his potition, he was bound to minister to his countrymen's love of glory.[11] Few self-made rulers have resisted the temptation to pursue an ambitious foreign policy in the hope of achieving abroad the success which might lead to stability at home. That such a course would be followed by Louis Napoleon III was widely expected and feared, and his desire that his regime should have the lustre which the July Monarchy had so signally lacked, suggested that he would seek to undermine the existing order based upon the treaties of 1815, which, he told the British ambassador, were galling to France, But how this 'strange unaccountable man', who seemed to the Prince Consort to resemble 'a German Savant rather than a sovereign of France', would go about his task and what were his ultimate intentions was indeed uncertain.[12]

In the words of J.P.T. Bury:

> What was to be made of this man ... whose immobility of feature formed 'an impenetrable mask and breastplate' ... the mask was often as impenetrable to his own ministers as to foreign envoys .... the Emperor liked to employ unofficial agents and bypass the regular channels of the Foreign Ministry, he liked also to preseve the maximum flexibility of movement until the last moment ... thus, in the realm of foreign policy, still more than in any other department of state, his ministers were often, as a French historian has said, 'not counsellors, but mere executors of designs of which they only see fragments.'[13]

'Foreign policy thus was his peculiar prerogative, the emperor's secret, just as it had been sometimes in the eighteenth century the 'secret of the king',[14] states Bury.

Bury points out :

> In the past many historians sought to unlock the door to this secret with a single key. For Emile Bourgeois that key was the drive to 'do something' for Italy, for Hermann Oncken it was the ambition to recover the Rhine frontier, for Albert Pingaud the search for a grand alliance, for Heinrich Von Sybel Mediterranean hegemony. But modern historian prefer the view that Napoleon III was too complex a character to have a single aim, and believe rather that he had several aims, by no means all compatible, and that he sought to achieve now one and now another accordingly as opportunity offered.[15]

Men who wished to preserve the status quo were right in fearing that the treaties of Vienna would be torn by the heir of the great Corsican.[16] Although others besides Cavour believed that while he never forgot a service, he never forgave an injury and it was not just the personal resentment of a 'parvenu' Emperor, whom the conservative powers were slow to recognize, that impelled him to policies that would change the European map.[17]

At first, however, the obstructions to change seemed formidable. The great powers, liberal England as much as the conservative 'Northern' courts of Austria, Russia, and Prussia, were as determined as ever, to uphold the settlement of 1815, and France was relatively isolated and suspect. Thus Louis

Napoleon III had at first little room for manoeuvre. But he had two great assets. Unlike his dynamic and impetuous uncle, he was possessed of infinite patience, and in France he more than anyone else came to represent order and stability. His patience meant that he was willing to wait, watch and probe. His being a 'man of order' meant that he earned the goodwill of conservative governments, who feared that prolonged unrest in France would lead to some new and more dangerously radical French revolution.[18]

His patience did not, however, in any sense mean that he was content with a purely passive foreign policy. On the contrary, he made it clear that he expected to have a controlling say and to act as the arbiter of Europe.

Of all foreign lands it was Italy that lay nearest to Napoleon's heart. 'Every man', wrote Prince Louis Napoleon III at the age of thirty, 'is a slave to the memories of childhood. He obeys through life, without question, the impressions he received as a boy, the trails and influences he had to face.'[19] On grounds of sentiment as well as of revolutionary principle or ideology it irked him that two of her fairest northern provinces should still be ruled by the Austrians into whose hands he had nearly fallen in 1831.[20]

Robert Sencourt calls the Italian venture of Louis Napoleon 'at once his most radical mistake, and his most pregnant achievement.'[21] The Crimean War had left him with a craving to correct the map of Europe unappeased. Although the Italian question had been ventilated, the territorial status quo in the peninsula remained intact. Napoleon's foreign minister for much of the time since 1848 had been the traditionalist Drouyn de Lhuys, who distrusted England, and whose triumph during the Crimean War had been to negotiate the alliance with Austria. Together with Austria, he had urged, Napoleon could be the master of Europe and contain both 'ambitious Prussia' and 'revolutionary Italy.'[22] This was not, however, the Napoleonic ideal for Europe. Drouyn de Lhuys was dropped before the war ended, 'and the Congress of Paris marked the end of one phase in Napoleon's foreign policy and the beginning of a new one in which the emperor was to show himself at his most 'revolutionary'.[23] The new phase was one in which the Anglo-French alliance of the Crimean War would soon seem to have been, in Palmerston's phrase, 'but a summer season's partnership', for relations between the two countries rapidly deteriorated in consequence of the Orsini affair of 1858[24], and of the new French naval programme, which led to a veritable invasion scare in England.[25]

II

As a youth Napoleon had fought in Italy and, as an outlaw in New York, had sworn to serve the Italian cause; but no sooner did he come into power than he overthrew the young Roman Republic, and, as time went on, it became more and more evident that he was currying favour with the pope. This being so, it was not often that Italy was mentioned in his presence until, during the Paris Congress, Cavour raised his sonorous voice. Whispering campaign for Italy had been going on all the time, however, Cavour's cause had many zealous supporters in the emperor's entourage, and the most enthusiastic among them had, uptil then, not borne Italian names. There was Conneau, for instance, to whom Hortense Cornu (Napoleon's mother) had committed her son : he had carried out that trust, and believed in persuading the emperor to be faithful to his earlier dreams. He was in touch with Cavour. Then there was Hortense who had come to regard the cause of oppressed peoples as her life interest. Another supporter, though not so fanatic, was Prince Napoleon. Finally, there was Countess Walewska who, as the wife of one of the most influential diplomats, lost no opportunity of serving the Italian cause. And so, while empress Eugenie was working vigorously for a closer union between the emperor and the pope and the strengthening of the power of the Church in France, these other influences were working cautiously on the emperor and reviving his sympathy for Italy. But these methods were too wary for Cavour. When his well-organized spy system informed him that the emperor's faithfulness to Eugenie was worn out, he decided to play on Napoleon's weakness for charming women and quickly laid hands on what appeared to him the desirable tool. This was the lovely countess Castiglione, then hardly twenty, who came of a distinguished Florentine family.[26] The countess, burning with ambition and thirsting for admiration and adventure, fell in with Cavour's proposal and gained a firm hold on Napoleon. 'Yet with it all' says Rheinhardt, 'Napoleon proved a harder nut to crack than Cavour had suspected.'[27]

As regards Napoleon's impressionability, of which much has been made, it would seem that, while some persistent influence was pressing him towards a decision, he certainly could not be brought to say yes straightaway, but at least his reasons for saying no were apt to dissolve gradually, until as a rule his yes came tardily to the surface. So Cavour's words, spoken by those lovely lips at such receptive moments, had intensified the half-impression received from the many undertones around him and the whole conviction that was stirring within him; in other words they had shaken his opposition to taking action on the Italian problem. And if Eugenie's opposing influence had not proved stronger in the end,[28] something might have come out. But at this point there came a warning of such terrible force that all the emperor's instinctive hesitation dissolved and his good prophetic instinct was silenced.

It was on the evening of January 14, 1858 that some conspirators, fearing that the caresses of the countess were insufficient to win back the old insurgent, attacked him on way to the opera. Though Napoleon was unharmed, he usually so dauntless, was at once and forever after, quite unnerved: he could not face the accusation, so sharply driven home, of having been a traitor to the cause to which he had sworn allegiance in his earlier days.[29]

The attempt failed, but it undoubtedly played an important part in crystallizing the Italian problem. Taylor sees it as the decisive turning point in Napoleon III's international policy.[30] 'Not because he had broken his pledge to the French Republic, but because he had deserted the standards of his youth', so says D'Auvergne. 'His life was forfeit. The French might forgive, the Italians never.[31]

But to those around the emperor, the culprits, appeared as the arm of the Revolution. They knew very well that had the bomb been truly thrown, the empire would have collapsed that very night. A law was immediately drafted which allowed the government to deport without trial practically any person suspected of disaffection, especially those who had already been exiled or otherwise punished.[32]

It soon emerged that the conspirators were all Italians, the ringleader being Orsini. Their weapons were British made : Orsini had lately come from London. Napoleon sought to teach Britain a lesson over the refugee question. This had already embittered relations previously, notably in 1852 and 1853; it was only six months since he had remonstrated with Cowley–the British ambassador to Paris–on Ledru-Rollin and Mazzini being allowed to suborn people to assassinate him, with the British authorities' connivance.[33] The emperor now insisted on a law to curb the machinations of such refugees. To make matters worse, the French ambassador in London was the last person to preach reasonableness or bring about such a state; for Persigny was at once the Emperor's most loyal friend and his most impossible diplomat. Palmerston's cabinet, which was prepared to make conscessions, had to resign. The new cabinet–containing Lord Derby, Malmesbury, and Disraeli–was determined to forbid at any cost any intervention in English affairs. The emperor wished to avoid a breach with England above all things, and France took the first step towards ending it by recalling Persigny. Very slowly the tension relaxed.

The shock of the attempt on his life and the subsequent recriminations with Britain left Napoleon preoccupied and in low spirits. The hostile tone of the British press, especially *The Times*, irritated him.[34] Yet his mind was stirring towards his cherished object in foreign affairs: to bring the question of Italy before European consciousness.

Here is one of the few truly inexplicable questions of Napoleon's life. Why did this attempt on his life, made by a man furious at his destruction of the Roman Republic, drive him into making common cause with Piedmont to crush Austrian power in Italy?

In the words of Corley:

> This seemingly paradoxical act is usually explained as follows: the romantic emperor, once a fellow-conspirator and fellow-exile with Orsini, now accepted the present occurrence as an omen. Such as interpretation tallies with the customary conception of Napoleon as a quixotic character, goaded by a quest for his star into a fitful combination of lethargy and activity.[35]

But as Corley continues to say: 'The true story of how his Italian policy developed is more prosaic than romantic. His repeated promises to Piedmont ... had so far not been translated into deeds. Yet his restless mind had never left the problem alone.'[36]

In the words of Bury:

> The strong pro-Italian group in his entourage strained every nerve to ... persuade their fatalistic master that here, paradoxically, was the opportunity indicated by destiny 'to do something' for Italy. The economic recession of 1857 and the continuance of opposition in the towns had caused him anxiety, and, if the not very reliable Prince Napoleon is to be believed, his cousin actually told him after the Orsini attempt that the new empire and the emperor personally needed fresh glory since the successes of the Crimea no longer sufficed ... While his government openly took a strong line with England and Sardinia ...he secretly prepared for action at Sardinia's side.[37]

Immediately after the bombing incident, threatening looks were turned on Piedmont. As soon as Cavour heard of it, he cried: 'If only they are not Italians!' Simultaneously with the confirmation of his fears he began to feel the results of this attack by Italians on the life of the very man on whom all his hopes for Italy rested. The notes from Paris became more and more pressing, the demands for the surveillance of all suspects and the suppression of papers unfavourable to France became more and more difficult; and when Victor Emmanuel's special ambassador failed to conciliate the imperial government, Cavour saw small hope of saving the structure he had built up with such pains. For he flattered himself on knowing Napoleon.

France's demands meant a monstrous encroachment upon Victor Emmanuel's rights. It was as impossible to meet them as it was to allow a definite breach with the emperor. Finally the king (or was it Cavour?) thought of the psychological way of dealing with this apparently hopeless deadlock. He ordered his ambassador, Della Rocca, to go and see the emperor once more, sending him at the same time an ostensibly private letter, in which, referring to the honour of the House of Savoy, which had remained unsullied for eight and a half centuries, he repudiated the emperor's words and made it clear that, despite the alliance and their personal friendship, he would in no circumstances allow himself to be humiliated. He had added a note to request Della Rocca to commit the indiscretion of showing the letter to the emperor. Napoleon was impressed. The allusion to the long reign of the Savoy dynasty had its effect, and a little yielding on both sides then had the result all at once of allowing Cavour's aspirations to take a more concrete form than ever before.[38]

On February 25, the trial of the four Italians before the Paris jurors began. Orsini confessed proudly and frankly that he had been the originator of the attack. He is stated to have declared that the emperor's death would certainly bring about a revolution in France, and that would be the surest means of provoking a revolution in Italy.[39] Orsini had this obsession and his reasoning was confused, but it followed closely the teachings of Mazzini.[40] No one is so free to speak his mind as the man who has nothing more to fear and nothing more to hope for. Perhaps the despot was still a little frightened of his prisoner. Orsini, a man of romantic presence, disdained to plead for mercy. His handsomeness, composure, and dignity formed so strong a contrast to the whimpering, crawling misery of his fellow prisoners that the audience conceived a vivid sympathy for him, which became even more marked when his counsel, Jules Favre, spoke holding him up to the admiration of posterity as a patriot and a martyr. The doomed man appealed to Napoleon to do nothing against the independence of Italy, which had been destroyed in 1849 by the French themselves. 'Remember, Your Majesty', continued

His Majesty's would-be-slayer, 'how the Italians, among them my own father, shed their blood joyfully for Napoleon the Great; how they remained faithful to the end; remember that till the cause of Italian freedom is gained, the peace of Europe and your own security will be an empty dream ... Deliver my country, and the blessings of twenty-five million of my countrymen will follow you into posterity.'[41]

The wrongs of Italy could not, however, blind the Parisian jurors to the injuries inflicted on one hundred and fifty-six Frenchmen (the victims of assassination attempt). Orsini and two others—Pieri and di Rudio were sentenced to death, the fourth, Gomez to penal servitude for life. All eyes were turned on the emperor. Orsini's gallant bearing had made him almost a popular hero. It distressed Napoleon that Orsini should misunderstand and distrust him. More than once, he (Napoleon) had come near to sacrificing the interests of France to those of Italy. And that policy he would pursue, though he had so narrowly escaped death at Italian hands. *Though* he said to himself, not *because;* yet nothing the assassin had said would have left a deeper impression than Orsini's last moment appeal interweaving threats with entreaties[42], that appealed to the emperor's conscience to remember Italy. And Napoleon did remember Italy.

Why was Napoleon III such a good Italian? Albert Guerard tries to explain: 'Perhaps because his uncle Eugene had been a very acceptable Viceroy of Italy; perhaps because Rome was the gathering point of the exiled Bonapartes ... in 1831, the two sons of Louis (Louis Bonaparte) had taken part in an insurrection ultimately intended to liberate the whole of Italy. So, in this case, principles and sentiments were in accord; and they were not in manifest antagonism with French interests. A united Italy would be, not a rival, but a steadfast ally. Napoleon III nursed, among his vaguer dreams, the idea of a 'Latin Union'. The hegemony of France in such a regional understanding was at that time beyond challenge.'[43]

> No romantic explanation therefore is needed to account for Napoleon III's determination: neither a secret oath he might have sworn as a youthful *carbonaro* nor Orsini's bomb ... nor the

> dazzling young charms of countess de Castiglione. Napoleon simply believed in the Italian cause, and he thought that providence expected his cooperation.[44]

Taylor realistically thinks that the economic crisis of 1857 was a grave challenge to the stability of the second empire: 'to stave off revolution in France he must launch the revolution abroad.'[45]

III

Less than six weeks elapsed between Orsini's attempt and the emperor's pledge to fight side by side with Piedmont in any future war with Austria. By late February, therefore, Napoleon had irrevocably decided to intervene in Italy.[46] He was fifty years of age and not particularly in good health. 'I shall go down in history as a despot ... It's about time I established some claim on the gratitude of mankind': Louis Napoleon brooded over.[47]

Unknown to the rest of the world, Napoleon was at last on the move over Italy. To Cavour's private Secretary, Nigra, he unfolded his plans. *First,* France and Piedmont would together fight Austria to recover Lombardy and Venetia; *secondly,* Piedmont would be transformed into the Kingdom of Upper Italy; *thirdly,* Prince Jerome would marry Victor Emmanuel's daughter, Clotilde. Napoleon had raised the last point obviously for finding his tiresome cousin, a throne in some distant land.[48]

Cavour accepted in principle all three points, whereupon Napoleon raised several consequential matters. Russia's goodwill would be needed towards the war; Italy must be organized ultimately into a federation consisting of three states; that is a smaller number of more compact states than he had at first envisaged. These negotiations between Paris and Turin continued in the utmost secrecy throughout the spring.[49]

On July 20, 1858, at Plombieres, a spa in eastern France Napoleon interviewed Cavour. 'This famous meeting owes its place in the folklore of history', says Corley, 'to the conspiratorial aura surrounding it rather than to what it actually achieved. Its chief value lay in the opportunity it afforded the two men of sizing one another up in their new relationship.'[50] They had already arrived at the crucial decisions months before; the present meeting was mainly confined to points of detail and finishing touches, such as a pretext for war with Austria and questions of finance and military supply. The anxious quest of the two men for the most plausible means of justifying their war in the eyes of the world would have been richly comic, had they not been staking tens of thousands of lives in the venture. In the words of Guedalla: 'The two men talked for five hours; and when they rose, the future of Italy had taken shape under their hands.'[51] There was to be a war, of course; but France must have a reputable *Casus belli*. The Austrians might be goaded into war with Sardinia, and then it would be simple for France to come in with a fine gesture of protection. When the war was over Italy could be remade. Sardinia might take the northern plain from the Alps to Venice; there would be kingdom of Central Italy for somebody; one must leave the pope at Rome, but he would hardly need his territory; the emperor agreed that the papal marches, for whose freedom he had once fought, should belong to the sceptre of Savoy[52], perhaps the pope would care to be president of a new Italian Confederation: then there was Naples–the Russians were always so peculiar about Naples, and one might safely leave it to become Italian by a revolution of its own.[53]

For want of a better pretext for war it was decided that a Piedmontese rising in the strip of Modena which ran into Piedmontese territory and was under Austrian protection, should be made to create the quarrel. If these could be incited to revolt in favour of annexation to Piedmont; this should set the Austrian armies in motion.[54]

Cavour proposed to shorten the existence of the other Italian states as soon as he was rid of the Austrian double eagle, but their affairs seemed to him to be of an extremely provisional nature and he wasted no explanations on them at this point.[55] For him the main thing was to know what Napoleon wanted in return for his promised assistance. The counter-demands in this conspiracy were soon put forward, first of all, Savoy would have to be given up, because although the cradle of the ruling dynasty, it was really a French province.[56] Then the county of Nice would have to fall to France. When Cavour protested that by the seizure of so purely Italian a province, Napoleon would be outraging the principle of nationality for which they were fighting, Napoleon said that those were questions of secondary importance, which could be dealt with later.[57] He must have envied the old-fashioned diplomatists of the old regime, who were never embarrassed by principles.

Further the question of Prince Jerome's marriage was thrashed out. The spectacle of these two seasoned men of the world using the hand of a fifteen-year-old girl not yet out of a convent as a pawn in decision making is of significance.

As it is obvious Cavour was not interested so much in the unification of Italy but in extending the power of Piedmont in the North. This he imagined could be done at the expense of Austria. To create public sympathy for the Italian question, he managed participation of Piedmontese troops in the Crimean war. He could also organize a discussion on Italian problems in the Peace Conference. Then he looked towards Napoleon III who had a peculiar liking for Italy.

Much later on, Cavour tried to find out a pretext for war with Austria. He and Napoleon III continued their preparations while rumours were in the air about the possibility of war. The Austrian authorities were not worried but England and Prussia were anxious and, started planning for the evacuation of Austrian troops from the Peninsula. Cavour and Napoleon III were concerned about other neighbouring countries and what would happen in case of war in countries like Austria and Russia. They visualized the situation on the Austrian frontier, which would drain off troops from Italy, and Russia which would well paid by a revision of the Black Sea Clauses of the Treaty of Paris.[58] 'If the Germans gave trouble and there was a general war, she might even (the emperor was a practising nationalist in Italy, but one could hardly be sentimental about Poland) get Galicia.'[59] It was a queer transaction'; says

Guedalla, but the isolation of Russia during the Crimean war, had left her with no love of Austria, and the Russians didn't mind watching the blow fall on Vienna. There was even an attempt to buy the neutrality of Prussia; but the Hohenzollerns were nervous of the Bonapartes, and on that side nothing was arranged.[60] 'Here was the risk', as Bury rightly observes, 'which was one of the factors which accounted for the emperor's hesitations both before and during the coming war.'[61] Russia would thus help to contain Austria, but she was under no obligation to prevent any other German state, in particular Prussia, from coming to Austria's rescue when embroiled in a war with France.

The year 1858, which had begun so sensationally for Napoleon with a narrow escape from death, ended with Austria nervously apprehensive, Britain hostile, Russia not yet bound to him as an ally, Piedmont dangerously provocative and France sullenly opposed to any war.[62] The monarch did not lack faith and determination to go ahead with his cherished project, but the doubt lurked as to whether his political and diplomatic skill was great enough to overcome the tremendous obstacles to its realization. This then was to be great question-mark of 1859.

The new year began with a sinister omen. At the New Year's reception, the emperor, 'with a rare mastery of that meaningless diction of which royalty possesses the secret, startled the world by addressing to the amiable widower who represented Austria in Paris in expression of hollow solemnity.'[63] 'I regret that our relations with your government are not so good as in the past, but I beg you will tell the emperor that my personal feelings have not changed.'[64]

Whether this was a prepared speech or the impulse of the moment no one could say. The occasion on which those words were spoken ensured their being spread abroad with fatal velocity. There was a nervous scurry among the diplomats[65], for in April 1812, a few months before launching his Russian expedition, Napoleon I had addressed a similar message to Czar Alexander I.[66] 'The air was thick with dementis and explanations.' In France a wave of alarm spread through the country and the emperor hastened to protest that he had been misunderstood.

Napoleon's words heralded to Italy's mastermind at Turin, the coming of his country's deliverance.[67] The war, however, did not come so easily as Cavour had planned and hoped as England, under the new Tory Government, was on excellent terms with Austria.[68] The emperor has above all resolved that events should not move forward too quickly. He was disgusted at Piedmontese impatience, and was still anxious about Germany. As he told Nigra, 'people were afraid that an Italian war might be a prelude to one in Germany: 'after Marengo comes Jena.' 'If things of this kind continue', he threatened, referring to Piedmont's provocative conduct, "I will begin with Jena and will launch a great war over the Rhine." In such a case he could not spare for Italy more than a handful of men.'[69]

Napoleon had arrived somewhat belatedly at an agreement with Russia. So far as it went the treaty was a triumph for Napoleon; 'indeed it alone made possible', Taylor observes, 'the liberation of Italy.' Though it did not hold out much prospect of Russia's support, it secured him against her opposition.[70]

Things were less congenial on the Prussian side. Indeed German intervention in support of Austria was beginning to be a real menace. Prince William pinned his faith to an alliance with Great Britain; he thought this would be bulwark aganist France and Russia, the restless peripheral powers. Moreover, William in his liberal mood, wished to satisfy national sentiment in Germany; and this demanded solidarity with Austria (despite the fact that she was still governed despotically). German liberals believed that a 'German' cause was at stake in Italy. The regent intended to use German sentiment in order to improve Prussia's position.

Napoleon hoped that Russia might help to keep Prussia neutral by a mixture of promises and threats; but this was a feeble hope–as Napoleon knew, Russia's alliance was directed exclusively against Austria. But if Great Britain remained neutral, Prussia might also remain so, and in order to guarantee this neutrality, Austria had to be made to appear the aggressor–a herculean task, since the sole object of Austrian policy was to retain what she possessed. At Plombieres, Cavour and Napoleon had arranged a vision of labour–Cavour was to devise a 'respectable', that is to say a non-revolutionary cause for war with Austria and Napoleon was to ensure that she was diplomatically isolated. These tactical problems turned out to be more troublesome than the conspirators had imagined. It was almost impossible to devise a respectable cause for war with Austria. The only argument against her was the 'revolutionary' argument of nationality–a non-Italian state ruling over Italians. Every right of treaty and law was on Austria's side, and Cavour was on weak technical ground. The conspirators had to count on Austria to provide an excuse and get entrapped.

As winter faded into spring, there was a last whirl of diplomacy: England offered mediation, Russia proposed a Congress.[71] French policy seemed to sway in the grip of a minister who worked for peace and Prince Jerome whose desire was war. The emperor played for time. The Cowley mission certainly brought a temporary improvement to Austria's position by making the British Government believe erroneously in Austrian goodwill; but it could not achieve anything concrete. Hardly had Cowley returned to Paris than the Russians proposed a European Congress to settle the affairs of Italy (18 March).[72] The Russians were determined to localizing the war in Italy; this implied in practice repressing Prussia from attacking France on the Rhine. But the Russians were all along resolved not to be entangled into war with Prussia for the sake of their friendship with France.

England and Prussia subscribed to the idea of Congress without enthusiasm: 'a Congress implied the recognition that the problem existed.'[73] The Austrians saw that the Congress involved their humiliation. It had taken eighteen months of war to make the Russians attend the Congress of Paris; Austria was being asked to attend a Congress and necessarily to acquiesce in an undermining of her Italian position before a shot had been fired. She accepted the proposal with drastic reservations and demanded that Sardinia should be forced to disarm before the Congress met; this would substantiate her premise that Sardinia was the sole disturbing element in Italy. Cavour was disgruntled.[74] He insisted that both Austria and Sardinia should withdraw their armies from the frontiers, and that Sardinia be admitted to the Congress. However, the technicalities were of little importance; for this was the first open clash between the two principles of treaty—rights and national liberty. Cavour seemed to be losing the game as Austria would only go to a Congress if Sardinia first agreed to disarm. On April 19, British and French pressure induced the reluctant Cavour to consent–he accepted the disarmament proposal with very bad grace[75] and it looked as though the war had been averted.

Cavour was saved by his enemies from his difficulties. Sensibly enough, he and his ally had decided to rely a little on luck and on Austria's mistakes. These fluctuations were probably calculated. The Austrians wished Sardinia to be disarmed by Austrian threats, not by British inducement and still less by French coaxing. At this time the Austrians overreached themselves–it seemed intolerable that Sardinia should emerge from its impertinence without humiliation–and they pressed their advantage as they were to press it more than fifty years away in a disastrous future, overcome with a conviction that Germany was behind them, and pushed it too far.[76] On April 20, Austria cut the knot: a strongly worded ultimatum to Sardinia amounted to a declaration of war. 'This was stupendous miscalculation', as Corley observes: 'Austria believed that any terms dictated by the Congress would irrevocably weaken her whole position in Europe, crippled as she was by the cost of protracted mobilization and facing constant trouble from her subject races.'[77] Cavour's moment had come.[78] Napoleon would have his war.

By the time Austria realized her grave error, it was too late. Napoleon, having declared war on the third of May, was already despatching his expeditionary forces. While Piedmont was thus fully supported by her ally, Austria found herself completely isolated. 'Yet for all Cavour's venturesome activity', says Corley, 'it was Napoleon whose efforts had brought about this satisfactory outcome.'[79]

The emperor was not yet certain how his own people would react to the war. "For all his apparent sluggishness', Guerard observes, 'Napoleon III was extremely sensitive to public opinion."[80] He could probe beneath the official surface. After so many months of hostility or complete apathy towards the war, French public opinion was not impressed by the attempt he now made to show that France had clean hands in the quarrel or that the war could remain localized. However, the legislative body docilely approved the grant of war credits. To the dismay of everyone concerned, Napoleon's forces were now revealed as being ill-prepared and ill-equipped.[81] (Admittedly at that time no great power could mobilize men and war supplies in a matter of days). Inspite of painful memories of shortages and breakdowns during the Crimean war, Napoleon had achieved little in the way of overhauling his cumbersome military system. Nor during his war of nerves, had he dared to resort to overt war preparations.

Yet Austria seemed bent on self-annihilation. She committed a second blunder by allowing much precious time to elapse before she sent her troops over the Ticino. Where five days' marching would have enabled them to outstrip the weak Piedmontese army and invest Turin before a Frenchman had arrived on Piedmontese soil, the clash with France had now become inevitable.[82] To the French declaration of war Napoleon had added the solemn but very rash assurance: 'that Italy would be free to the Adriatic, that the disorders in the peninsula would receive no support, and that the power of the Holy Father would not be shaken.[83] Together with this came the announcement that the emperor would take his place at the head of the army.[84]

The war, which had been unpopular in France when first bruited, became so popular when once it was entered upon, that the French people watched all movements of the troops with eager enthusiasm, and crowded to the *mairies* to subscribe to the loan.[85] Napoleon III was hailed by the Parisian workingmen. For the moment, the *Coup d'Etat* was pardoned.

Actually, the popularity of this war had been secured, in the opinion of Rheinhardt, by the secret leaders of the masses because it was a 'revolutionary' war, 'and the profound contradiction implied in the circumstances of its being led by their dictator, left room for all kinds of hope on more egoistical grounds.'[86]

In the political direction of a great war, affirms Corley, Napoleon would undoubtedly have excelled.

> Here his diplomatic gifts, fertility of ideas and grasp of strategy on a world scale ... would have been of the greatest value. As it was, while his technical capacity for war was indeed greater than his critics would admit, ... he had no practical experience since his Roman exploits of 1831 ... he could not grasp the dispositions and movements of large bodies of troops ... or even read a map intelligently.[87]

With a supreme gesture of Bonapartism, the emperor had taken the command: was it not in Italy that General Bonaparte first rose to fame? He too must fight in Italy. And when a Napoleon took the field, it would be as well for him to be Napoleonic.

The expected great battles were slow in coming, however; and once in field, he found himself confused by the practical business of war. The player on the other side of the great game, Gyulay, suspecting some big feint and, disconcerted by the fact that history was repeating itself in the name of Napoleon and the threat of war, felt obliged to wait and see what would happen, and lost his advantage in doing so. After three battles, favourable to the French, but insignificant in themselves, Gyulay withdrew his troops to Magenta across the Ticino. But the bridge was not completely blown up, and the French followed close behind.[88] 'Contact had been established almost by accident'; observes Guedalla, 'and strategy seemed to have been replaced, as in the middle ages, by mere collision.[89] Then, in a long summer day of fighting, the issue was left without control or generalship to the bayonet.[90] The losses were extraordinarily heavy on both sides, and although the day was saved, an onlooker reported that the French won 'purely on lucky chances, in which the military talent of their leaders had no say.'[91]

In the words of Sencourt:

> The emperor was waiting, baffled, even stupefied ... Italian reinforncements were expected but failed to appear. He waited, disgusted at the carnage, fearful of failure ... But ... by evening the emperor's generals had won him the battle.[92]

Napoleon's complacence at his own generalship was marred by distress at the sight of the physical horror of the battlefield; and this emperor, who had his uncle's tenderness for his soldiers without that ruthless concentration which made him so decisive in his aims at victory, could not help noticing that the Lombard peasantry and villagers cared little for the rescue which had been effected at such a frightful cost.[93] The stark memory shadowed even the triumph which awaited him at Milan. For a moment recovering his enthusiasm, he called on the Italians to close up their ranks. This was the proudest and not the least moving moment of the second empire, for the emperor received a completely spontaneous and heartfelt welcome from the Milanese,[94] as the earlier Napoleon had received on May 15, 1796, but a striking contrast with the rehearsed and calculated pomp and glitter which marred so many great occasions of the era. An equestrian statue was commissioned on the spot to celebrate the victorious entry.[95]

But the situation, so brilliant in official dispatches, was in fact extremely dark. Prussia was arming, and France had no troops left to face a menace on the Rhine. On the eve of the next battle Napoleon received a disturbing letter to this effect from Eugenie. It was urgent to end the war. But how? The French could hardly retire as long as, nominally at least, they were victorious. On the other hand they could not impose peace on the strength of a confused battle like Magenta. Not far behind the Austrian lines stood a formidable array of fortresses to be reduced, the famous Quadrilateral: Mantua, Peschiera, Legnago, Verona. Fortunately, the Austrians again played into the hands of the French. They accepted another major contest at Solferino. It was almost as chaotic as Magenta.[96] 'Once more the bayonets thrust and lunged in the sunshine, as the Emperor sat watching on his horse and smoked, gave an order, smoked again, and watched, muttering, "*Les pauvres gens! les pauvres gens! guelle horrible chose que querre!"* It cost him more than fifty cigarettes to sit the day out', says Guedalla. But at the right moment Napoleon III did launch the Guard in the right direction. It was decidedly a victory, although very far from a decisive one.

In this way, Napoleon managed to extricate himself from the Italian trap with all the appearances of magnanimity. Diplomacy had been fumbling in the dark: he addressed himself directly to Franz Josef.

IV

'*Grande bataille, grande victoire*' : those were the words of the emperor; he and his army could drink for a moment the sparkling wine of glory: but the next morning, his ecstasy was over. The dead, lying thickest around the Spy of Italy, told silently how hard the day was won.[97]

The army moved slowly forward through the scorching Italian summer, and the emperor rode on with his doubts. It was not easy: if France was to be protected on the eastern frontier, to thrust after the Austrians into Venetia where war would be, by the very nature of the ground, more costly still. If one succeeded, the Germans would regard any serious defeat of Austria in Italy, as a danger to the left flank of the German position, and they might be in Paris in a month.[98] If one failed, Lombardy was lost and France would not be merciful to a defeated Bonaparte.

The grim sight of the field of slaughter could not have failed to bring to Napoleon's mind an agonizing reappraisal of his Italian engagement. The risks were too great, and further he began to doubt both Cavour and his king. 'Massimo d'Azeglio had been on a mission to Bologna to persuade the people to declare for Piedmont. If they were to annex the duchies, the Romagna, perhaps even the papal States, they would begin to be a formidable neighbour.'[99] He wanted the Italians free, but not the dangerous Piedmont. In addition, Piedmont's greed and bad faith had forefeited all sympathy towards her in France.[100] But, above all, the most disquieting news came from across the Rhine. A week before the Solferino win, Prussia had mobilized. 'She had done so', wrote Schleinitz to Prince Reuse at Paris, simply as a precaution. She wanted simply to take those prudent diplomatic measures which prevent complications by foreseeing them.'[101] But the news of Solferino woke in Berlin 'an echo from ancestral voices', and seemed to call to war. 'For it was the habit of diplomatists and politicians at that time to regard with a certain satisfaction the quarrels of their neighbours, unless one of those neighbours became so successful as to threaten the onlooker. By winning Solferino, Napoleon suddenly took the guise of a menace to the whole German-speaking world.'[102] If there was one thing that Napoleon had reason to fear (was he not the modern emperor?) it was a combination of the German-speaking world: a combination all the more fearsome if, as he now saw, the Italians were not amenable as allies.

Then the Czar, of whose goodwill Napoleon had felt assured, seemed to consider that enough had now been done in support of the Italians and therefore, left the Prussians to do as they liked, contenting himself with warning the emperor on the German alliance.[103] In addition, the Austrians, though beaten, were by no means knocked out. Protected as they were by the fortresses of the Quadrilateral, which would stand a long and stiff siege, they would still be able to procure one army after another from the huge reservoir of forces–and, inspite of all the confident prophecies, there was no Hungarian rising. Franz Joseph could face a long war, Napoleon could not.[104] He saw, all at once, behind these dream-like victories which had left a dark horror behind them, a panorama of new wars, of defeat[105] leading to destruction and fall–and he did not hesitate long. He was still the winner and would come as a donor when he desired peace. And had he not done all that was possbile for Italy? He could leave Venetia to be settled later; he could ensure reform in the papal states: he had now won Lombardy: he had gone as far towards uniting Italy as he felt it discreet for a Frenchman to do. The Crimean war he had ended by making an ally of the Czar: this time he would endear himself to the other emperor. With England stiff, and the thought of those hundred thousand Prussians on the Rhine and of France bereft of her troops, like a chilling physical pain, Napoleon decided to act himself.

In the words of Rheinhardt:

> The Plombieres account did not, after all, add up quite satisfactorily, partly because Cavour had felt a little too sure of his imperial fellow-conspirator, and partly because they had both been far too optimistic in counting upon certain factors. In particular they had taken the attitude of the powers towards such a war as a constant, not foreseeing that their policy might be one of wait-and-see.[106]

On July 11, to the general astonishment and to the rage and mortification of his Italian allies, Napoleon met the Austrian Emperor at Villafranca. The two monarchs, both of them disillusioned generals, discussed like chieftains, the conditions for ending the war whose beginning had been determined in much the same way. To young Franz Joseph this meeting signified the first loss in a life so rich in losses. He was to cede Lombardy to Napoleon, who would hand it over to Sardinia. Venetia was to remain under Austrian rule but as member of a new Italian Confederation presided over by the Pope (as Gioberti had suggested in his great book of thirteen years earlier, *I'l Primato*)[107]: and the whole settlement was ultimately to be approved by a European Congress.[108] The settlement was frankly a compromise. Franz Josef 'had lost a game and paid with a province.' The fate of the rest of Italy remained vague.[109]

Rheinhardt writes:

> To come to an agreement with the enemy was the easiest thing in the world compared with what awaited Napoleon on the part of his friends. As the most important historian of the time has said: 'It is a bad thing to render a half-service, even though a great war may have been brought to a good end thereby; for the party who has benefited counts what he has received as nothing and believes himself to have been let down over the more that he might have had.' ... the part which the Piedmontese army played in the victories achieved was none too great, and Lombardy, which Franz Josef called his finest province, was a superabundant reward for it. And now that they had their

> Lombardy, neither Cavour ... nor his king stopped to reflect that they could not have conquered it themselves, but harped on that unlucky bond which the Emperor had given them with his: 'Italy free from the Alps to the Adriatic.'[110]

'Yet a good deed half done', Guedalla says, 'was better than no deed. There was always time to resume; and the Emperor had only drawn back within a week of war with Germany.'[111] Piedmont's rapacity had throughout been so blatant that, as Corley says, it would not harm her to be denied the province for the time being. His political objectives in Europe were now quite clear and simple. Venetia should be eventually transferred–preferably by peaceful means–to Piedmont, but as part of an overall settlement of the peninsula into a federation.[112]

'So Napoleon had taken the decisvie step toward the liberation of Italy' scored hollow but resounding victories, avoided a general war, reached a settlement that left no bitterness.[113] 'The enemies of the emperor have striven, not without success, to lessen his just share in the glory of Italy's emancipation': Jerrold observes: 'he left Italy free to work out her own emancipation.[114]

Victor Emmanuel and especially Cavour were furious at Napoleon's 'betrayal'. 'Yet it was Napoleon', in the opinion of Guerard, 'who could have complained of a betrayal. He had been betrayed by England ... so jealous of the emperor's prestige that she refused him her diplomatic support.[115] He had been betrayed by Piedmont, and particularly by Cavour. For Italy Napoleon III envisaged was to be free and united, but not *unitary*': whereas Cavour would cheerfully promote a 'unitary' solution for his country, a centralized monarchy on the French model. 'Napoleon III was probably right', Guerard continues; the federal solution adopted by Germany in 1871, might have been the best for Italy.[116] But a French sovereign could hardly complain if a neighbourig country paid France the compliment of imitating her institutions.

At Plombieres, Napoleon III and Cavour had understood themselves, but not each other. Foreshadowing disagreement, they had thought it wiser to ask no delicate questions. To govern is to foresee. Napoleon III had not foreseen that the nature of Cavour's ambition and Cavour had not foreseen that the French ruler might understand him in time and leave him in the lurch.

On his way back through Italy the liberator of Lombardy was received with an icy reserve. It was in Turin that Napoleon III saw Cavour again, and explained to him the grounds on which he had been forced to conclude the truce. This was the last meeting between the emperor and his partner of plombieres. But as long as Cavour lived, and even afterwards 'Napoleon III frequently felt that, in obedience to a sense of guilt and ideology, he had conceded to this great intellect and mighty will a certain stake in the drama which he had hitherto regarded as sacred to himself and his star.'[117] says Rheindhardt.

V

Amid acclamations with which France greeted him and his victorious legions, despite the glory which he had personally acquired, even to those who congratulated him upon his moderation and statecraft, Napoleon III betrayed his doubts and uneasiness of mind. 'He was too much at pains to justify himself for having made peace; he multiplied his reasons as though aware that no one of them could be accounted sufficient.'[118] In the words of Forbes: 'His reasons for stopping short were very forceful in themselves, but they were susceptible of this complete answer–that they should all have been foreseen and should have entered into his calculations when he published his programme of freedom of Italy 'from the Alps to the Adriatic.'[119]

Jerrold writes:

> Sir Theodor Martin tells us that, in a letter to Lord Malmesbury (June 8), Lord Cowley mentions, on the authority of a person who learned the fact from Count Walewski, that when this proclamation was under consideration, Count Walewski had passed many hours in endeavouring to persuade the Emperor to omit all reference to the Adriatic, observing that the expression would alarm all Europe, and moreover render it exceedingly

> difficult for the emperor to conclude a peace which should fall short of his own words. The emperor, we are told, demurred to Count Walewski's interpretation of the passage, which, he said, was simply the expression of an opinion, but did not bind him in any way to maintain that opinion by sword', ...It is true that on his return from Italy, after the Peace of Villafranca, he said ...that he felt great reluctance in withdrawing from his programme 'the territory from the Mincio to the Adriatic', but this declaration is in strict accordance with His Majesty's original interpretation of his phrase.[120]

One criticism frequently directed against the emperor, we cannot admit to be justified. The spectacle of the author of the *Coup d'Etat* battling side by side with Mazzini and the Carbonari seems, at the first glance, bizarre and incongruous. How could the man who had robbed his country of her liberty be himself zealous for the liberty of Italy? The question arises from a confusion of terms. There is no real inconsistency in the conduct of the emperor. The cause that Napoleon III championed was the nationality of Italy; it was only incidentally, from his point of view, that the individual liberty of her citizens was involved in this crusade. 'It was the liberation of Italy from a brood of foreign kings that formed the avowed objective of Napoleons' wars and policy; his intent was to help her to win her Bannockburn*, not necessarily to secure her *Magna Carta* or her Reform Bill. National independence and personal liberty are two distinct things'[121] says Berry. Robert Sencourt calls the Italian policy of Louis Napoleon III 'at once his most radical mistake, and his most pregnant achievement.'[122] Emile Lousse gives him credit for 'restoring to Italy the political unity lost since the time of the Romans.'[123]

The future was to show that, in helping to secure the unity of Italy, Napoleon III was aiding and abetting the silent, relentless, persevering ambitions of Prussia, and biulding up the storm of destruction which was to burst in consuming fury upon his own head.

---

* The Scottish war of independence against England (1314).

NOTES AND REFERENCES

1. In the words of T.A.B. Corley : 'The parallels between the General (de Gaulle) and the Emperor are, indeed, most striking. Both men share a deliberately cold and aloof personality, one which conceals deep feelings and passionately held convictions and even a rich vein of sardonic humour that is rarely allowed to come to the surface. Both are possessed by an almost mystical sense of history.' *Democratic Despot A Life of Napoleon III*, (London : Barrie and Rockliff, 1961), p. 10.
2. W. Grinton Berry however observes 'We are not impressed by the air of mystery his character so often wore: ... A silent man with a pensive cast of countenance sometimes acquires reputation as the possessor of deep revolving thoughts, when the simple and sufficient explanation of his taciturnity is that his inward parts closely resemble the interior of the Grenadier's big drum' *France Since Waterloo* (New York: Charles Scribner's Sons, 1909), p. 197.
3. Albert Guerard. *Napoleon III: A Great Life in Brief* (New York : Alfred A. Knopf, 1966), p. 103.
4. Ibid, p. 104.
5. Ibid, p. 113.
6. Ibid, p. 102.
7. Ibid, p. 105.
8. 'Queen Victoria, who liked him personally, was never able to trust him'. Ibid, p. 105.
9. Berry, op.cit, p. 221.
10. 'War against Russia in the Crimea (1854–1856); war aganist Austria in Italy (1859); an expedition to Syria for the protection of Christians in that country against the fanaticism of the Moslems (1860); an expedition to China in order to open the ports of that country to foreign trade (1860); three campaigns against the Emperor of Annam, which ended in the cession of Cochin-China (1867); war with Maxico, ... and the war with Prussia (1870)' Ibid, pp. 221–22.
11. 'He regarded himself as set apart by Providence' observes R.H. Patterson, to vindicate, by completing, the Napoleonic Scheme for regenerating Europe and exalting France. Having placed himself upon the throne and consolidated his power, he now applies himself in earnest to the accomplishment of his 'mission'. *The New Revolution or The Napoleonic Policy in Europe* (Edinburgh: William Blackwood and Sons (1860), p. 44.

12. J.P.T. Bury. *Napoleon III and the Second Empire* (London E.C., The English Universities Press Ltd., 1964), p. 63.
13. Ibid, pp. 63–64.
14. Ibid, p. 64. Edmund B.D' Auvergne however holds a different view : he says 'Accused by his detractors of dissimulation, Louis Napoleon at no time during his reign took any trouble to disguise his intentions from his enemy. He let Cavour's visit be known through the Press'. *Napoleon The Third* (New York : Dodd Mead and Co., 1929), p. 161.
15. Bury, op.cit, p. 64.
16. 'The Emperor took great pains' to quote Archibald Forbes, 'to effect the removal of this impression, (that the Imperial policy would be guided by a spirit of war and conquest) especially from the minds of English statesmen; but with slight success'. *The Life of Napoleon The Third* (New York : Dodd Mead and Co., 1897), p. 200.
17. Bury, op.cit, pp. 64–65.
18. Ibid, p. 65.
19. 'Life and works of Louis Napoleon Bonaparte (1852) I, p. 259' cited by Corley, op.cit, p. 1.
20. Napoleon disliked Austria, the power who had been the chief architect of the 1815 treaties, and who dominated Northern Italy. Austria, as he said, was 'a cabinet for whom I have always felt ... The most lively repugnance.' Bury, op.cit, p. 68.
21. Sencourt continues : 'France remembers him today, and Thiers recognised him long since, as *l'accoucheur de l'enfant terrible*: that child is Italy' *Napoleon III : The Modern Emperor* (New York : D. Appleton-Century Co., 1933). p. 190. Emile Lousse gives Napoleon III credit for 'restoring to Italy the political unity lost since the time of the Romans'. He calls him a great European and 'a true European' 'because of his active, direct interest in the whole continent'. 'The True Place of Napoleon. III in *the History of Europe*, In : *Napoleon. III and Europe*, pp. 135–40. Bibliographical Studies (Oxford : Pergamon Press, 1965)
22. Bury, op.cit, pp. 76–77.
23. Ibid, p. 77.
24. In the words of Corley : 'The Orsini incident left behind in Britain a legacy of increased mistrust of Napoleon'. op.cit, p.200. For details of the Orsini affair vide infra, pp. 10–16.
25. Although, good relationship with England was the corner-stone of Napoleon's foreign policy.
26. E.A. Rheinhardt. *Napoleon And Eugenie*, trans. from German

by Hannah Waller (New York : Alfred A. Knopf, 1931), pp. 177–78. The Countess had been married at sixteen to the rich young Count Castiglione. His passion for her made him so docile that he bore patiently her cruel caprices and held his peace when she became the mistress of King Victor Emmanuel; and looked on from a distance while she set about the conquest of the Emperor, Ibid.

27. Ibid, p.179. 'He lent a willing ear to his mistress's oft repeated tales, nodded his appreciation of her accounts of the degradation of the Italian provinces under foreign rule, and no doubt sighed a little when some latent instructions from Cavour had lent the speaker peculiar eloquence; but at the end, when she would implore his help, plead for a promise, he only murmured something vaguely affirmative, while his face became blank, so that she could find nothing definite in either his words or his looks, to hand on to the man at her back.' It was 'the Emperor's conviction, which he could not shake off, that his mistress's perpetual pleading for Italy had probably some basis other than her suffering patriotism.' Ibid, pp. 179–80. 'Prince Metternich describes Napoleon III's technique of evasion as follows :

    "The Emperor knows admirably how to alter the focus of the main problem, evade inconvenient intrusions, and produce amazing ideas for the future when it is a question of securing the present". Ibid, p. 180.'

28. 'It had not occurred to him (Cavour) that, although love no longer tied him to Eugenie, they were united by another very powerful tie which the Emperor, though he might be in love, was careful not to imperil'. Ibid, p. 179.
29. Hubner, *Neuf Ans II*, 92, 3 : cited by R. Sencourt, op.cit, p. 196. 'It was on this tune, ... that Orsini, the assassin, played with satanic skill'. Ibid, p. 179.
30. A.J.P. Taylor. *The Struggle for Mastery in Europe 1848–1918* (Oxford : Clarendon Press, 1954), p. 101.
31. D'Auvergne, op.cit, p. 154.
32. Ibid, p. 154.
33. Corley, op.cit, pp. 193–94. Count de Morny, Louis Napoleon's half brother, 'though usually so cautious, had spoken of England as the 'murderers laboratory'. Rheinhardt, op.cit, p. 185.
34. Corley, op.cit, p. 194.
35. Ibid, p. 194.

36. Ibid, p. 195.
37. Bury, op.cit, p. 79–80.
38. Rheinhardt, op.cit, pp. 185–86.
39. D'Auvergne, op.cit, p. 153.
40. Philip Guedalla. *The Second Empire* 2nd. rev. edn. (New York: G.P. Putnam's Sons, 1922) p. 264.
41. D'Auvergne, op.cit, p. 156. 'His (Orsini's) letters to the Emperor, calling upon him to free his country, were sent by Napoleon to Cavour for publication in the '*Gazetta Piemontese*'; and they produced exactly the sensation they were intended to create. Their publication was the Emperor's endorsement of them; and they gave fresh hope and courage to the Italians.' Blanchard Jerrold, *The Life of Napoleon III* (London : Longman Green and Co., 1882) Vol. 4, pp. 169–70. Napoleon also allowed Orsini's appeal to be published in the official *Moniteur Universal*'. Bury, op.cit, p. 79.
42. D'Auvergne, op.cit, p. 158–59. 'Kossuth in his *Memoirs of my Exile*, gives the story of the Emperor's relations with Orsini, as they were given to him by Senator Pietri, on their way to meet the Emperor at Valeggio, during the Italian war', cited by Jerrold, op.cit, p. 170.
43. Guerard, op.cit, p. 113.
44. Ibid, p. 114, 'Italian historians writing of the *Risorgimento* were for a long time influenced by a quite understandable and national pride in the 'miracle' of the unification. They attributed to Camillo di Cavour and Victor Emmanuel II a far-sighted and systematic policy with a positive aim, that of making use of Napoleon III and, to a lesser extent, of England to further their design for a great Kingdom of Italy. 'This entirely unilateral interpretation thus saw, in Napoleon III, a more or less unconscious tool of Cavour, while from this narrow viewpoint general evaluations of the Emperor's policy were made on the sole criterion of his 'usefulness'. 'However, this interpretation of the making of Italy is now rejected. The process of Italian unification is today considered to be that aspect of European politics during Napoleon III's reign (at least up until the summer of 1859) in which the Emperor's nationalist policy best coincided and harmonised with an already developed conscious national movement in the Italian peninsula ... 'It is another matter, which we will not enter into, whether Napoleon III's European policy of making new nations, and in particular his handling of the Italian problem,

were in the French interest. What is important to note, however, is that, given this preliminary general conception of the Emperor's European policy, his policy towards Italy (again up until the summer of 1859) was a more or less logical development, which, happily for Cavour, happened to fit in conveniently with his own policy ....This is the view of the process of Italian unification now taken by the most authoritative recent historical criticism. Without wishing to burden the text with references to individual historians and specific works, it is sufficient to say that this version has been put forward in various studies and papers published in Italy and abroad by Franco Valsecchi, and that it has been brilliantly synthesised in two general works, recently published in France and England respectively : *L'Histoire des Relations Internationales* by Pierre Renouvin and *The Struggle for Mastery in Europe, 1848–1914* by A.J.P. Taylor. *Napoleon III and Europe* : Bibliographical Studies (London : Pergamon Press, 1965), 'Cavour, Napoleon III and the Unification of Italy' by Ottavio Barie, pp. 79–80.

45. Taylor, op.cit, p. 101.
46. A.J. Whyte. *Political Life and Letters of Cavour 1848–61* (London : Oxford Univ. Press, H. Milford, 1930), p. 250. Whyte suggests that Napoleon decided to intervene in Italy sometimes between January 14, and February 25, 1858.
47. 'Decidedly, Napoleon Bonaparte was thinking, "I ought to do something for Italy. It was not merely for my personal aggrandisement that, as a boy, I aimed at power. I have shed ideals enough, God knows! All the men of letters in France are against me ....D'Auvergne, op.cit, p. 159.
48. Corley, op.cit, p. 201.
49. Ibid, p. 201.
50. Ibid, p. 202.
51. Guedalla, op.cit, p. 269.
52. Rheinhardt, op.cit, p. 190.
53. Guedalla, op.cit, p. 270. 'Napoleon had promised Alexander not to disturb King Ferdinard in Naplas ... One must keep one's words, of course, but men of affairs have a way of getting what they want, even while they hold to the letter of their engagement ... If a revolution in Naplas dethroned the king, how would the Czar hold the Emperor of the France responsible?" Sencourt, op.cit, p. 197.
54. Corley, op.cit, p. 202; Rheinhardt op.cit, p.190. 'The solution

worked out between Napoleon and Cavour was a 'legal' war against Austria'. Ottavio Barie, Napoleon and Europe. op.cit, p. 82.

55. Rheinhardt, op.cit, p. 190.
56. 'In Napoleon's mind it was present also that the possession of this magnificently defensible mountain country would protect him against any possible show of ingratitude on Italy's part'. Ibid, p. 190.
57. Ibid. Corley, op.cit, p. 202; D'Auvergne, op.cit, p. 160.
58. Guedalla, *The Second Empire*, p. 272. 'It was incidentally a vivid example of Napoleon's opportunism that the neutralisation of the Black Sea, which he was now ready to abandon, was the peace condition on which he had been most insistent in 1856'. Bury, *Napoleon Second Empire*, 81.
59. Guedalla, *Second Empire*, p. 272.
60. Ibid, pp. 272–73.
61. For the step he was about to take was far more hazardous than a distant war against Russia in alliance with England and Trukey: Bury, *Napoleon Second Empire*, p. 81.
62. Corley, *Dem. Des.*, p. 206. Emperor's efforts to build up a secret treaty with Russia, on the basis of Vague declarations 'were not successful until March 1859, when Russia finally agreed, with no explicit reference to the Black Sea, to adopt a benevolent neutrality, both political and military, towards a war in Italy. It was none too soon, for the war was due to begin in May' : Corley, *Dem. Des.* p. 206. For negotiations vide Sumner, *Secret Franco-Russian Treaty, Eurp. Hist. Rev.*, 1933, p. 65. Sencourt views askance at the entente of France and Russia : 'The man who, as the champion of the people, was to free Lombardy and Venetia from the honest cleansing control of Vienna was to do so by joining hands with the very monarch whose rule looked furthest backward into absolutism, and whose subjects of all in Christendom came nearest to being slaves ... *Nap. III Mod. Emp.* p. 200.
63. Guedalla, *Sec. Emp.* p. 273. According to Sencourt the Austrian Ambassador, Hubner, had never won the Emperor's confidence. 'It was not only that Hubner had a way of lecturing Napoleon, but his origin was so obscure that his presence at the French Court seemed a reminder to the Sovereign that Franz Josef looked askance at him'. 'Cowley papers : Cowley to Malmesbury, December 26, 1858', cited by Sencourt, *Nap. Mod. Emp.* p. 192.

64. Rheinhardt, *Nap. Eug.* p. 192.
65. 'The shock created in Paris, the disastrous fall in funds, the immediate stop put to trade, the swift interchanges of diplomatic notes, the refusal of England and Prussia to promise neutrality and the wild hopes which found expression among the Italian patriots so startled the Emperor, that he hastened to protest that his meaning had been exaggerated. The "*Moniteur*"declared that the alarm was irrational ... But the fears which had been conjured up would not be laid : Jerrold, *Life Nap.*, pp.181–82.
66. 'Napoleon I's actual words to Alexander I of Russia on April 25, 1812 were : "If unfortunately war becomes inevitable between us, it will in no way alter those feelings with which Your Majesty has inspired me, and which are secure from all vicissitudes and all change" : Corley, *Dem. Des.* Ch.18, p. 378.
67. Cavour said quietly, 'Il parait que l' Empereur veut alleren avant' cited by Jerrold, *Life Nap.*, p. 181.
68. On January 10, 1859, Lord Malmesbury, in a long letter to Lord Cowley, pointed out that England's interest in the question of a change in Italy stopped short of at improvements in the administration of the Papal States, ...With Austria they could have no quarrel; and Malmesbury felt that a war with Austria would soon become a war not of nations but of opinions. It would lead to a contempt for authority, inflame sentimentalism, and finally encourage anarchists'. 'Quai d' Orsay (Angleterre); Malmesbury to Cowley' cited by Sencourt, *Nap. III Mod. Emp.* pp. 204–5.
69. 'Hallberg : Franz Josef, p. 176' cited by Corley, *Dem. Des.* p. 211.
70. The Russians aimed at overthrowing the settlement in the Near East, and for this they 'hoped to cheat Napoleon at some time in future; they therefore, gave Napoleon an immediate opportunity to cheat them'. Taylor, *Str. Mast. Eur.* p. 106.
71. 'It is often said that the Russians proposed the congress on French prompting; but there seems no evidence of this' Taylor, *Str. Mast. Eur.*, p. 110.
72. There was an important consideration for Russian in holding a congress. It would be a method of regaining their freedom. Even though it was meant for Italy, they could bring in the Near East, just as in the reverse way Italian question had been brought into the congress of Paris; and Napoleon could not but support them.

73. Guerard, *Nap. Brief*, p. 115.
74. 'Napoleon had to issue a sharp reminder to Cavour that Europe was full of rumours that France was using Piedmont as an instrument for promoting war and self-aggrandisement. These rumours, the Emperor declared, were turning all Europe against himself': Corley, *Dem. Des.*, p. 211. 'That the Emperor did his utmost to moderate the ardour of Cavour, and to turn him to a less vehement course, the tenor of subsequent negotiations demonstrates. The Italian minister saw how the French Sovereign was surrounded with difficulties and dangers; and that the great powers were one and all against him'. Jerrold, *Life of Napoleon*, p. 194.
75. Corley, *Dem. Des.*, p.212. Bury, *Nap. Sec. Emp.*, p. 82.
76. Men always learn from their mistakes how to make new ones. The Austrian mistake in the Crimean War seemed to have been the reluctance to go to war; therefore, they determined to overdo things on the other side. They expected Cavour to reject the ultimatum, so that Sardinia could be broken in isolation; if (against expectation) Napoleon went to Sardinia's help, they counted confidently on Prussian, and even on British support. In the words of Jerrold, 'The action of Austria, taken in the hope of finding France unready, and Italy an easy prey for her splended army, turned public opinion, as the Prince Consort had predicted, against her at a stroke and transferred the sympathies of the nations of Europe to Sardinia.' *Life of Napoleon*, p. 195.
77. Corley, *Dem. Des.*, p. 212.
78. 'There was sheer exultation in Turin over this blunder, which gave the Piedmontese ... the welcome pretext for appealing to France ... and putting Austria completely in the wrong'. Rheinhardt, *Nap. Eug.*, p. 193–94.
79. Corley, *Dem. Des.*, p. 212.
80. Corley, *Nap. in Brief*, p. 115.
81. In all its civil activities the Second Empire was remarkable for its efficiency. The army, the show piece of the regime, was in a hopeless condition. For this strange contradiction, three causes may be adduced. The first was that the army lived on the grandeur of Napoleon the First, if France had succumbed in the end, it was under the combined effort of all Europe. This was the Grand Army : what else was needed? 'The second was that the commanders under the Second Empire had received their training under Louis Philipoe in Algerian

warfare: a second lieutenant's paradise, in which reckless courage counted for more than strategy or logistics. The third was that Napoleon III and France wanted peace; it was impossible to prepare, thoroughly and ostensibly for war.' Guerard, Ibid, p. 115–16.

82. Rheinhardt, *Nap. Eug.*, p. 194.
83. Ibid, p. 194.
84. In the opinion of Taylor, Napoleon 'at heart ... was resolved on the Italian war, as on nothing before or afterwards' *Str. Mast Eur.*, p.109. It seems Taylor has overstated his point. In the opinion of Archibald Forbes 'Louis Napoleon had given his pledges to Cavour, but it seemed as if he were fain that they would not be exacted. He was disconcerted by the precipitate march of events. He was not ready for action ... The French people were not at all eager to make heavy sacrifices for the deliverance of Italy.' Forbes, *Life of Napoleon*, p.199. Jerrold puts it thus : 'The Emperor had never denied this promise, nor threatened to break it ... He only persisted in regarding war as the last resource; and with his habitual patience he tried every means by which the Italian cause might be won without drawing the sword". Jerrold, *Life Nap.*, p. 193.
85. Jerrold, *Life Nap.*, p. 196.
86. Rheinhardt, *Napoleon and Eug.*, pp. 194–95.
87. Corley, *Dem. Des.*, p. 214. In the words of Rheinhardt: 'The Emperor was now fifty-one years of age; his military experience was limited to the skirmishes in the Romagna, thirty years before, and his Swiss artillery training'. *Nap. Eug.*, p. 194.
88. Ibid, pp. 195–96.
89. Guedalla, *Sec. Emp.*, p. 279.
90. Ibid, p. 280.
91. 'The same Captain d'Herisson stated, further, that never had an army had worse reconnaissance than the French on this occasion, for it was never able to locate the enemy': cited by Rheinhardt, *Napoleon and Eugenie*, p. 196.' It has been for two centuries the misfortune of Austrian generalship to provide with victories the armies of other nation, and in 1859 its traditions were well maintained...' the French enjoyed in 1859 the pleasing experience of defeating with the methods of 1809 an adversary whose military thought was that of 1759 ... over generalship which had advanced no further than the Seven Years' War; but if the Austrians had been Prussians or if

General Von Moltke had ridden to Pavia with the Feldzeugmeister Gyulay, the French would have been swept against the Alps'. Guedalla, *Second Empire*, pp.277–79. According to Captain d'Herisson': The only general who in this unorganized confusion showed anything like initiative was MacMahon, to whose timely intervention at the most threatening point of the battle the victory was ascribed. For this, he was made Marshal of France and Duke of Magenta by the Emperor' : Rheinhardt *Napoleon and Eugenie*, p.196. D'Auvergne, however, thinks that Napoleon 'might fairly have allotted a part of the credit to himself. It was the Guard, fighting under his own eyes and with his direct encouragement, which by their desperate resistance to the Austrian advance had gained time for MacMahon to carry out his turning movement': D'Auvergne, *Napoleon III*, p. 166.

92. Sencourt, *Nap. Mod. Emp.*, p. 210.
93. Ibid, p. 212.
94. Corley, *Dem. Des.*, p. 216.
95. 'In the events which followed, the monument was as completely forgotten by the Milanese, however, as were the Emperor's services by the majority of the Italians.' Rheinhardt, *Nap. Eug.*, p. 197.
96. Guerard, *Napoleon Life in Brief*, pp. 116–17.
97. 'Sixteen hundred Frenchmen lay dead, seven hundred Italians. The allied losses were 17,000, the Austrians 22,000': Sencourt, *Nap. Mod. Emp.*, pp.216–17.' The sight of these slopes, which had become a shambles, aroused in him a resolution of which the outcome was the creation of the Geneva Convention and the establishment of the International Red Cross Society'. Reinhardt, *Napoleon Eugenie*, p.199 vide also Corley, *Dem. Des.*, p. 217.
98. Guedalla, *Sec. Emp.*, p. 282.
99. 'Cowley Papers : Cowley to John Russell, July 28, 1859' cited by Sencourt, *Nap. Mod. Emp.*, p. 217. 'French clerical opinion was alarmed by the revolt of the Romagna against Papal government' : Bury, *Nap. Sec. Emp.*, p. 82.
100. After Magenta when Victor Emmanuel apologized to Napoleon at the failure of his troops to appear in the battle, Napoleon made the terse and chilly reply; 'Sire, when one is duty bound to join forces before the enemy, a scrupulous adherence to one's obligation and instructions is to be expected. I regret that your Majesty has not done this. "It was

a clear warning to the king that he and Cavour would be ill-advised to try Napoleon's patience much further'. Corley, *Dem, Des.*, pp. 215–17.

101. 'Archives du Quai d'Orsay : Prussia': cited by Sencourt, *Nap. Mod. Emp.*, p. 217.
102. 'Schleinitz to Prince Reuss, June 17, 1859'. Ibid, 'Napoleon could not fail to see that he had only Prussia's jealousy of Austria between him and an European armed coalition': Jerrold, *Life Nap.*, p. 192.
103. Rheinhardt, *Napoleon and Eugenie,* pp. 200–1. In the words of D'Auvergne 'Russia herself was annoyed by the presence of Kossuth in the Emperor's camp, and said bluntly that she would not tolerate another insurrection in Hungary.' *Napoleon III*, pp. 168–69.
104. Rheinhardt, *Napoleon and Eugenie,* p. 201.
105. According to Bury, Napoleon's successes were due rather to the blundering Austrian command than to any brilliant generalship on his part. His instructions for his field orders to be destroyed at the end of the campaign were sad recognition of his discovery that, when the test came, he had none of his uncle's military genius: Bury, *Napoleon Second Empire,* p. 82. 'He certainly deprived posterity of the best evidence as to his military capacity' Corely, *Democratic Despot,* p. 214.
106. Rheinhardt, *Nap. Eug.*, p. 195.
107. Sencourt, *Nap. Mod. Emp.*, p. 221.
108. Bury, *Nap. Sec. Emp.*, p. 83.
109. Guerard, *Nap. Brief,* p. 117. 'The rulers of some of the lesser Central Italian States, who at the outset of the war had been expelled by their subjects, were to be reinstated' Bury, *Nap. Sec. Emp.*, p. 83.
110. Rheinhardt, *Napoleon and Eugenie,* p.203. According to the Grinton Berry, Napoleon spent his prestige in a vain attempt to satisfy two opposite parties the party that would be contented with nothing less than the complete unification of Italy, and the other party which resented any menace upon the integrity of the Papal dominions : *Fr. Waterloo,* p. 226.
111. It may be added that 'Not a single power in Europe was ready to help the cause of Italian freedom if the further success of French brought Germany (her forces being already mobilized) into the field. The Prussians were clamouring for a war, and shouting for Alsace and Lorraine with a vast army of observation on the frontier, Russia had massed 200,000 men

on the Austrian frontier, who would not have been on the side of France if she had helped the Magyars to begin a war of independence; Switzerland had 100,000 men under arms; and even Denmark had raised her forces to 70,000; while England promised, at most neutrality, and would not even risk the proposition of an armistice, Jerrold, *Life of Napoleon*, pp. 219–220; Guedalla, *Second Empire*, p. 284.

112. Corley, *Dem. Des.*, p. 219.
113. Guerard, *Napoleon Life in Brief*, p. 119.
114. Jerrold, *Life Nap.*, p. 223–24.
115. Napoleon 'telegraphed armistice proposals for Persigny to submit to the British government, whose mediation was requested. Receive no helpful reply from Palmerston, now back in office as Prime Minister he sent Fleury direct to Franz Josef's headquarters' Corley, *Dem. Des.*, p. 218.
116. Guerard, *Napoleon Life in Brief*, p. 118.
117. Rheinhardt, *Nap. Eug.*, p. 204.
118. D'Auvergne, *Napoleon III*, p. 170–71.
119. 'Yet it appeared that even when he addressed the Italians at Milan as their deliverer, the new light had not been broken in upon him ... That new light seems to have flashed upon Napoleon for the first time from the stern Austrian ranks on the day of Solferino' Forbes, *Life Nap. III*, p. 213.
120. Jerrold, *Life Nap. III*, pp. 200–1.
121. Berry, *Fr. Watl*, p. 229.
122. Sencourt, *Nap. Mod. Emp.*, p. 190.
123. Lousse calls him 'a great European' and 'a true European', because of his active, direct interest in the whole continent' and also 'becuase, in his foreign policy, it was the interest of the Europe in general which always took precedence' : Emile Lousse, 'The True Place of Napoleon III in the History of Europe' In: *Napoleon and Europe*, pp. 135–40.

Chapter 5

The Crimean War : A Study of the Origin

The study of the circumstances which led to the Crimean War has proved to be one of modern historiography's thorniest problem. The tangled and danger-laden situation of Europe in 1854 has been rivalled only by that of 1914 in its intrigue for students of diplomacy and war origins. Harold Temperley accurately summed up the academic effort of eighty years, observing that 'the origins of the Crimean War are not even yet wholly revealed'[1]. Many writers, contemporary and later, agree that the war was useless,[2] but as to its origin, as Bernadotte Schmitt pointed out, 'the most diverse views', sponsored with varying motives and concentration, have gained currency and favour.[3] Responsibility for the war is attributed to a number of statesmen, to religious and political complications, to economic rivalries, to simple miscalculation, and to sheer blundering.

An aged and innocuous dispute over the Holy Places served as a magnet to entice the major European governments, drawing them together in such a way that the prospects of open conflict proved all too fatal. The widely prevailed view regarding the cause of the Crimean war is that it was fought in defence of the Ottoman Empire, a war for the maintenance of the *status quo* and against Russian encroachment. Europe by 1852 had come around to the view that Russia was intent upon Ottoman destruction. The Turks themselves enthusiastically sought to identify the Ottoman independence with European safety.[4] The pretence that France and Britain were fighting the battle of all Europe against Russian 'aggression' was an attempt to put their real position in its best, most attractive light, and to persuade others to join their cause.[5] Alyce Mange, in her well-documented work, found that, basically, 'the Crimean War (1854–1856), was a war fought ostensibly for the preservation of the integrity of the Ottoman Empire but actually for the curtailment of Russian encroachment'[6]. J.A.R. Marriott spoke of the Czar Nicholas I as 'unquestionably the prime author of the war'[7]. Interestingly enough, this obviously oversimplified anti-Russian view survives as a continuing dominant explanation of the war.

The Russian *Diplomatic Study of the Crimean War*[8] found the villain in the Emperor Napoleon III, with Lord Stratford de Redcliffe, the British ambassador in Constantinople, as accessory to the plot. Sergei M. Goriainov definitely asserts the right of Russia to occupy the Danubian principalities; while the passage of the Dardanelles by the French and British fleets, which was the rejoinder to the Russian occupation, is denounced as illegal.[9] The critics of Napoleon III explained the war as largely the result of his machinations.[10] In fomenting a crisis from the prosaic details of the continuing dispute about the Holy Places, his penchant for plotting came to the fore as he manipulated the Turks, Russian and English into a situation where war was virtually assured. Since he profited so much from the struggle, he appeared as a prime suspect.

On the other hand, the historian of the second empire, M. Pierre de la Gorce, writing before the turn of the century, regards 'the distant days of 1853' as 'the last when French diplomacy spoke a language worthy of itself.'[11] So also M. Edmond Bapst's objective is a defence of Napoleon III.[12]

The 'Great Elchi', Stratford Canning, is suspect as the major culprit. His critics have insisted that this imperious and distinguished diplomat, who had nursed a personal grudge against the Russian Czar for over twenty years, manipulated things to mortify Nicholas I. A further point of interest centres on the limited control which the cabinet in London exercised over Redcliffe. In addition to the unfortunate ambiguity within the English Government itself, and the dissensions of the Aberdeen ministry–which could not formulate a policy definite and downright enough to make Russia modify her demands– the problem of evaluation is further complicated by the fact that Redcliffe purposely carried on measures at variance with the instructions of his home government and acted in Constantinople as a law unto himself. While to insist that the war came as a result of his wounded vanity would perhaps be an oversimplification of the situation, it would be worthwhile to scrutinize his role.

It has often been suggested that short-tempered individuals in Constantinople were caught up in issues requiring the patience of job; but while the conduct of particular personalities is open to criticism, the overall crisis was far too complicated to be adjudged a personality conflict.

Pivotal to the whole issue was the question of Ottoman vitality. How sick was the sick man of Europe? The sickness of Turkey and the 'growing health' of her northern neighour are both crucial points in this study. It is surely ironic that in opposing Nicholas I's contention that the Turk was in imminent danger, possibly unable to maintain himself, the English and the French were in effect proving the Czar's point in the manner in which they coerced the Turk. A substantial part of Turkey's difficulties came because, in an accident of geography and history, her lying astride the Bosphorus and the Dardanelles made her liable to demands from several outside powers who all happend to be markedly stronger than she. Turkey's problem may well have been that in Austria and Russia she had predatory neighbours. It is interesting to study how much of a pawn was she, and how much was she forced to yield to the desires of other powers?

This brings the intriguing question of what indeed were the legitimate interests of outside powers in the Near East. The answer to this would obviously be relative to our basic views regarding Nicholas I and Napoleon III. In the case of England, even if we ignore the effect of Redcliffe, an ambiguity emerges which certainly misguided Nicholas I, namely, who in London really spoke for England? Was it Aberdeen or was it Palmerston? And how did England become involved anyway in a quarrel which in its early phases was based on a dispute between Orthodox and Latin Christians? Added to this is the problem of how to evaluate the endeavours at peace carried on in Vienna. Did the various powers earnestly wish for peace by this time? Did the attmepts at Vienna have to fail? And what of the role of the Turk through it all? Does the crisis have to be explained in balance-of-power terminology?

A perceptive observer and critic of the nineteenth century scene was Karl Marx.[13] As could be imagined, he found the war developing out of conflicting economic drives. Danubian commerce was all important, control of Constantinople and the outlet into the Mediterranean was crucial, and the developing patterns of the economic life made the struggle well-nigh inevitable. During the thirties of the last century, Vernon J. Puryear searchingly explored the involvement of each of the major powers in the trade of south-eastern Europe over a period of thirty years prior to the war.[14] When Puryear combined his economic findings with his interpretation of the 1844 dis-cussions–between Nicholas I and English statesmen– the result was an implied challenge to other more staid and traditional views.[15] Is economic interpretation inconsistent with other analyses which focus on strictly diplomatic and personal con-siderations? It is the purpose of this study to resolve these points.

I

The turn of the mid-century seemed to augur peace in Europe. In England it had been marked by a spectacle profoundly impressive to contemporary observers, the Great Exhibition of 1851. In that novel conglomeration of cosmopolitan industry, following upon a generation of peace and unprecedented commercial development, the English radicals read the opening of a new chapter in world's history. War after all had been but the folly of princes; its days therefore were numbered with the recent attainment of power by the people and the triumphs of industrialism.

It was not in England only that the continuance of peace seemed assured. 'Peace and cheap corn', was the the Prince

Consort's reading of Louis Napoleon III's ambition; 'Peace with dishonour', was the taunt levelled against the new empire by its exiled enemies during its early months.[16]

Such hopes were not unreasonable in view of the history of Europe since Waterloo. For nearly four decades, no real war had disrupted the peace of the continent, save for the picturesque but brutal struggle which resulted in the independence of Greece : a struggle culminating in the armed and successful intervention of Russia which betokened the triumphal inauguration of the reign of Nicholas. In Turkey, defeat had produced its usual consequence of internal reform; the personal initiative of the sultan, in the reign of Mahmoud, and the activities of a reforming minister under his successor, gave to the Ottoman Empire not only a period of relative prosperity and peace, but even the apparent prospect of some development towards constitutional government. It is natural with hindsight to pronounce such promise foredoomed to disappointment; it does not necessarily follow that contemporary observers ought to have condemned such prospects as hopeless in advance. A reforming Sultan, no less than a reforming pope, received and perhaps deserved more generous treatment from his contemporaries than from posterity.

In the case of the porte no less than of the papacy, general promise of internal reform was accompanied by a single dramatic act, which appeared for an instant to bestow on either government the championship of national liberties as well. Pius IX in 1847 had protested against Austria's occupation of Ferrara, and by the success of that protest had won the gratitude of all Italy. Two years later, against the yet more audacious intervention of an even more reactionary Austria–backed this time by the now declared ally of all reaction, Czar Nicholas I–the sultan appeared to play an even nobler role; refusing to hand over to the joint subjugators of Hungary her fugitive defenders. Kossuth and his followers owed it to the more kindly Turk that they were not delivered up to the wrath of the Catholic emperor and the orthodox Czar.

While England and France had watched with sympathy

and sustained by armed support this liberalism of Turkey, these same signs of Ottoman revival were looked upon askance by Nicholas I. When any state adjoining Russia showed signs of 'breaking up', it normally became an object of gracious solititude on the part of its giant neighbour. No matter how long the illness, the patient could count in all bedside attentions upon the inexhaustible patience of the east. But suffer him at this stage to show symptoms of setting his house in order for himself, and the self-summoned physician would at once pronounce death imminent and inevitable.[17] The present case proved no exception.

Between 1838 and 1844 Reschid Pasha had introduced in Turkey a series of civil and administrative reforms. In 1844, Nicholas I on his visit to England remarked to Aberdeen, 'We have a sick man on our hands.' In the following years the reforms continued on the whole to make headway: tax-farming was prohibited, black slave-markets abolished, education improved and secularized, and the army in particular radically reorganized. This in a neighbour of Russia could clearly be nothing less than the delirium which presaged approaching dissolution. In January, 1853 the Czar thought the time opportune for a second consultation. Addressing himself to the British ambassador at Petersburg, he pronounced the sick man to be now in *extremis;* this time he added proposals as to a division of the estate. By these, Russia would establish protectorates not only over the Danubian principalities but over Serbia and Bulgaria: England, in return for her acquiescence in this, and in view of a possible temporary occupation by Russia of Constantinople, might annex Egypt and Crete.[18]

But England was now in no mood to assist such schemes either as a spectator or as an accomplice. Aberdeen's amicable reception of his earlier overture had, it is true, given Nicholas I some basis for presuming a similar complaisance in 1853; but much water had flowed under the bridge since 1844. Russia, then merely the most gigantic of world-states, had now clearly emerged as the most despotic.

Russia at this time was not only the greatest Empire in

the world, but the greatest Empire the world had ever seen. Its territories–which contemporary statisticians gravely computed to be of an area equal to the moon[19]–stretched their unbroken bulk over three conterminous continents. In Europe alone the Russian Dominions more than doubled the extreme size ever attained by Napoleon Bonaparte's brief Empire; and were nearly ten times the size of the next largest existing continental power, the patchwork Empire of Austria: considerably more than half of Europe was already Russian. And behind these vast European territories lay others in unbroken stretch three times their size in Asia; which in their turn were separated only by the narrow Behring Strait from an expanse of another half a million square miles of Russia in America. Enormous in itself, this empire looked more enormous still at a time when Europe in general had already lost America and not yet acquired Africa. And this empire, in appearance at once so colossal and compact, was not merely great but growing: with a growth only the more awesome that it was gradual; expanding unthwarted and to all appearances irresistibly at the expense of every state bordering it. And this steady process of advance was more disquieting in that as yet, no power or combination of powers had ever finally succeeded in compelling Russia to disgorge her gains. With rampant serfdom and obscurantist Christianity, being actual threats to civilization, the 'devouring monster' was threatening to become amphibious. Externally its moral influence was cast upon the side of oppressive reaction. And inside its ever-enlarging frontiers–a fact perhaps most obnoxious of all–it was the very essence of the Muscovite rule, as viewed from Europe, that it persistently sought to obliterate, by subjection to its orthodox slavonic servitude, cultures both superior and more European than its own. Hence this half-barbarous power, 'hanging like a pall upon the confines of civilization, seemed then as a century later, an instrument less fitted to leaven Asia with Europe, than to submerge Europe once more with Asia.'[20] Crimean War was, thus, the answer of 'Europe' to this situation.

II

The official position of every power which participated in or directly influenced the Crimean war presents a striking paradox. England at first favoured Russia, then switched to France; France had opposed Russia in Turkey and had thus aggravated the situation, but before the war ended was rather in sympathy with Russia. At the beginning of the war, Austria was linked with Russia and owed her a political debt, but Francis Joseph's government abrogated the Metternichian policy and remained neutral, finally entering an alliance with the western powers and delivering an ultimatum to Russia which ended the war.[21] Prussia was indirectly concerned with the conflict but veered from a previous close concert with Austria to benevolent neutrality toward Russia. Turkey, a victim of circumstances, as ruler of the Straits committed a series of contradictions in the pre-war developments which in general may be said to have reacted more strongly against Russia than against France.

'The untimely disruption' of the understanding of 1844 between Russia and England[22] was, in Vernon Puryear's words, 'the principal cause of the Crimean War.' The agreement was based on two definite concepts given currency in Russian foreign policy under Nicholas I : conservation of a weak Turkish Empire as long as possible, and of concerted action in an ultimate partition of Ottoman dominions, the later to be effected by pacific methods.[23] Preceding the joint Anglo-Russian sanction of these concepts in 1844, an international basis had been given to them in an extensive alliance programme in which Austria and Russia were determined to cooperate in all matters regarding Turkey.[24]

The diplomatic preliminaries of the Crimean war began with the Treaty of Unkiar-Iskelessi, signed on July 8, 1833, which gave Russia a decided political preponderance in the Straits. In the event of a war in which Russia was engaged, the Sultan was to close the Straits against the enemies of the Czar. Ten weeks later Nicholas I found it expedient, on account of Franco-British opposition to the treaty, to make a secret agreement with Austria, wherby a part of the political gains Russia had acquired at Unkiar was transferred to Austria. The Convention of Munchengratz of 1833 provided for concerted action on the part of Russia and Austria in the maintenance of Turkey as long as possible. The two powers also agreed to cooperate in an eventual partition of Turkey. It was now possible, therefore, for the moribund Ottoman Empire to be given external support to prevent dissolution after 1833, in a joint Austro-Russian convention.

The admission of Austria into full partnership with Russia in everything concerning Turkey nullified the advantages secured by Russia at Unkiar-Iskelessi. It is safe to conclude that Russia's position secured at Iskelessi–which was the highest point of achievement of Russian diplomacy in its relations with Turkey–while in theory continuing for eight years, in fact continued only for ten weeks. Such was the result of the prompt and vigourous opposition of the western powers to Russian aggrandizement in Turkey in 1833.[25]

The Austro-Russian Convention of Munchengratz respecting Turkey is one of the two great diplomatic landmarks in the history of Russian foreign relations before the Crimean War. The second landmark was the adhesion of England to the plan, after 1844.[26]

The marked hostility between Russia and England in the decade after the Treaty of Adrianople definitely abated with the isolation of France in 1840. The European Straits Convention of 1841[27]–which closed the Straits to warships of all powers while the porte remained at peace–in which France acquiesced, temporarily halted any diplomatic activity regarding a possible designation of successors to the component parts of the Turkish Empire. Nevertheless, the political events of 1838-41 may be said to have provided the basis for an extension of the Russo-Austrian programme to include England as a participant in the settlement of Turkish affairs, to the exclusion of France.

When a series of world political conflicts between France and England were raised in the summer of 1844, Czar Nicholas I utilized the opportunity to explain to the British statesmen that Russian and British interests in the Near East were harmonious, and that war could be averted in the event of the collapse of Turkey only if the three powers most involved acted in concert.

Conditions favoured an Anglo-Russian Entente, and Nicholas utilized the occasion to its fullest. With Aberdeen at the British foreign office, things were congenial and relations with Russia were marked by intimacy. In the face of continued French threatening interest in Egypt and expansion in Africa, the Anglo-Russian Asian rivalry appeared insignificant. Even in economic matters, the Anglo-Russian relations were based on diplomatic friendliness.[28]

The French were alienating England in many spheres. British influence was undermined in Spain. In the Southern Pacific a serious situation developed over the status of Tahiti. England had started her free trade policy in 1842, but France clung to the protectionist system. Efforts to smooth the differences failed largely because of the hostility engendered in 1840. Russia too was protectionist, but the infant industries in the Czar's Dominions hardly matched with British manufacturers, and Britain continued to dominate the Russian market.[29]

It was under these circumstances that Nicholas I quite candidly inaugurated a series of confidential conversations on world politics with the leading British statesmen of the day. The occasion was the visit of the Czar to England in June 1844. Great Britain and Russia resolved to adjust amicably their most troublesome common problem through a partition of Turkey. This decision was simply the result of an admission of the fact that by land, Russia exercises over Turkey a preponderant position; by sea, England occupies the same position. Isolated, the action of these two powers might do a great deal of harm; combined, it may do much good.[30]

The outcome was the establishment of a secret understanding, directed against France, which outlined the bases for an ultimate partition of Turkey through the joint action of Russia, England and Austria. Puryear goes so far as to call it 'a world alliance between Russia and England because the contemplated isolation of France in Turkish questions would have as its corollary an Anglo-Russian cooperation in every other matter.[31] In the words of Puryear :

> The secret understanding consisted of three parts: the verbal agreement made while Nicholas I was in England; the Nesselrode Memorandum which summarized in written form the points of agreement on the most hazardous of Anglo-Russian friction zones; and the ministerial letters of confirmation of the Memorandum, exchanged between Nesselrode and Aberdeen, with the attendant correspondence.[32]

Like the alliance of Munchengratz, it was specified in advance that the terms of succession to Turkey should neither threaten the security of either contracting party nor imperil the maintenance of European equilibrium. If, however, accidental or precipitated disintegration of Turkey took place in advance of such preparations, or an attack from outside threatened the existence of Turkey–if anything untoward should occur in Turkey–Russia and England would act together. These conclusions with England, states Puryear, were simply an extension of the principles of the Austrian convention, but Nicholas I corrected the most serious defect of Munchengratz by the provision that the terms of succession to Turkey were to be arranged in advance to the actual dissolution of the decadent empire.[33]

Puryear further writes :

> Guarded as a great state secret by each cabinet, the Nesselrode Memorandum was transmitted to successive foreign secretaries in England, with each of whom Brunnow [the Russian ambassador at London] entered into confidential conversations. The document passed through the hands of Aberdeen, Palmerston, Granville, Malmesbury and Russel in order without being repudiated.[34]

Cavin Henderson feels that the agreement of 1844 ended when Palmerston became foreign secretary in 1846. He says :

> The British Cabinet knew nothing of it. It had no validity, save that given to it by an exchange of letters between Nesselrode and Aberdeen ...The letters were completely personal; and, though they are to be found in the Aberdeen Papers at the British Museum, they are not in the Foreign Office archives, and were not published in the Parliamentary Papers of 1854. They are in

no sense a proper diplomatic instrument.[35] In the opinion of Temperley, Palmerston 'seems to have repudiated the memo.'[36]

Political agreements quite naturally have varying degrees of effectiveness over a period of years. In the case of the secret agreement of 1844 the high points of intimacy between England and Russia were reached under Aberdeen. The low point was during the foreign office tenure of Palmerston.[37] Thus it was that when Aberdeen became Prime Minister at the end of 1852 there began a distinctly new period of intimate relationship between the two powers, providing the immediate occasion, paradoxical as it may seem, for what later developed into the Crimean war.

Aberdeen assured Brunnow that he had in no way changed since 1844 in his principles and in his views regarding Turkey. He expressed a hatred for the oppressive governmental system in Turkey and evinced neither sympathy nor esteem for Napoleon III. The Russian ambassador at London believed that British public opinion would not support the maintenance of Turkey. During January 1853, word reached Nicholas that England was preparing to defend her coasts against a possible French attack. To all appearances, a complete return to the conditions for an application of the policy so clearly enunciated in 1844 had been brought about. The agreement of 1844 was no formal treaty, yet it was a gentlemen's agreement; and Aberdeen's coming back to power and his assuarances gave Nicholas I a sense of security. Nicholas, Nesselrode, and even Brunnow thought they had established a new political system, and Great Britain would now consult with Russia before cooperating with any one else in Europe. The Czar felt he had achieved a concrete agreement with Great Britain. He believed he had pinned Aberdeen down to a specific understanding–in fact, this was exactly what he had not achieved.[38] That the Czar misunderstood this point is the real tragedy. These talks, Seton-Watson says referring to the 1844 agreement, 'did more harm than good.'[39] Aberdeen's bungling diplomacy and unfortunate methods brought for much criticism. 'Nicholas thought', writes Temperley, 'that he could rely upon Aberdeen first to induce the British Cabinet to acquiesce in Russia's demands, next to prevent any working arrangement with France, and at any rate to keep England out of war. Nicholas I found reason to believe that Aberdeen might fail in the first two aims. But he never believed, until too late, that he could possibly fail in the last.'[40] Czar assumed a menacing attitude in Turkey from which Russia could not retreat with honour after it became clear that England could no longer be considered her ally. 'So, in a rather tragic sense, Aberdeen was, 'concludes Temperley, 'responsible for the war and it seems that he felt the responsibility.'[41]

III

Commercial opportunity for foreigners in free trade, non-competing Turkey, in contrast to the high-tariff handicaps and mercantile competition in Russia, was one of the main reasons for the British policy of maintenance of the Ottoman Empire. Karl Marx pointed out the importance of the Black Sea in European trade and the fact that two-thirds of Europe was using it in the process of exchanging goods. Through Constantinople and Trebizond (in Asia Minor) British trade had greatly increased so that by 1852 Britain was an equal participant in areas that in 1840 were Russian monopolies. A commerical battleground had been established, and, since British trade depended on confidence in the power holding the Dardanelles and Bosphorus, the diplomatic position of Great Britain could never be seriously in doubt. Russia clearly could not be expected to allow the door to remain open for British competition if it were in her power to close it.[42] Puryear corroborated Marxian thesis: with painstaking and elaborate documentation he examined Anglo-Russian commerce and made a potent case for economic determinism. His probe is illuminating.[43]

To a country like England, with a full grown industrial system, and world markets since 1600, the total annual volume of foreign trade enjoyed by Russia in 1853, and the slowly increasing trade balances in favour of that country, would have seemed a small matter. Yet it indicated beginnings–

potentialities–a real problem for the future and so one of vital concern for Great Britain. To the Russian bureaucrat too it must have appeared to be of momentous significance. While examining the commercial preliminaries of the Crimean war, one has to keep in mind the industrial backwardness of Russia, and her natural and normal ambition for commercial growth in which she would become Britain's rival. The focal point of this great problem was Constantinople and the Straits.

If Great Britain won anything in the Crimean War, it was commercial pre-eminence in the eastern Mediterranean. For years, she had debated what her policy towards Russia and the Near East should be. She might support Russia, being thus assured preponderance in Russian markets for decades; and to cooperate with Nicholas I in a peaceful partition of Turkey on the basis of the understanding of 1844, thus subjecting the trade of that empire to a positive share with her rising trade rival in eastern Europe, western Asia, central Asia and far East, she could support the Ottoman Empire, thereby jeopardizing the British trade with Russia but achieving a dominant position in the trade with the near East, and placing a check upon Russian commercial expansion in Asia.[44]

Of the two propositions, it appeared that cooperation with Russia was the better plan: a partition of Turkey commercially would still leave ample scope for a free development of the superior British industrial equipment and marketing organization for competition with Russia on favourable terms. Moreover, the moral question of western Christianity could not but be meliorated by this solution of a perplexing problem. But the far-reaching repercussions of Russia's commercial expansion and political penetration into the Near East and Middle East would be hazardous; it would constitute a permanent threat to India. The two lines of action had their adherents, and the vacillation of British policy reflects this basic dilemma. Throughout the period 1930-54 the opposing groups saw their ideas projected by the British government as Palmerston and Aberdeen alternated in the control of foreign affairs. England ultimately accepted the second alternative as of paramount importance.

So also in Russia two groups of partisans, pro-British and anti-British, disputed over the problem. The main concern was the relative advantages of England or France as an ally in fulfilling 'manifest destiny' for the gigantic Slavic Empire. The 'Great Russia Party', to which most of the large landowners and capitalists in Russia belonged, saw that there was no possible limit to the progressive aggrandizement of British India and that ultimately Russia and England must have a tussle over that issue. Hence this group wished that the government stick to a policy of simple courtesy toward England but alliance with France. Nicholas I and those at the helm of affairs, however, decided upon a different policy, for a different reason. Nicholas I upheld Russia's economic expansion, but was averse to foster a course of action which implied inevitable conflict with Britain. By means of a cordial relationship with England crucial world problems might be amicably adjusted between the two. To Nicholas, France had no concern in the whole matter. From 1844 on, he always had said that he did not care what France thought or did as long as England was in agreement with him.[45]

What are the factors which presaged a future conflict between Russia and England over the former's southern commerce? 'The fundamental factor was', as Puryear has persuasively argued, 'the international grain exchange situation after the Napoleonic period. In this the part played by Russia was conspicuous.[46]

The development of the grain export of southern Russia was delayed after 1815 on account of the deteriorating relations of Russia toward Turkey. After 1830, the southern provinces increased their annual output of produce both for internal and foreign consumption, and Russian publicists suggested some form of governmental support of the region. However, there were factors which were working to retard Russia's profitable grain export trade, despite average annual increases in volume. In the first place, the international tariff system was operating against its interests : British and other protectionist grain laws worked with disfavour towards it. Secondly, the problem of Turkish competition acted as a deadweight. After the Treaty of Adrianople had freed Moldavia and Wallachia from their obligation to sell their wheat exclusively to Turkey at fixed rates, these provinces entered the international competitive market.

The Danubian principalities increased their output, exporting wheat on English and Austrian ships into countries where earlier Russian grain was exported almost exclusively. Thus Russia faced a strong rival now. 'Despite these factors', to quote the same authority, 'the grain exports from Russia did not decline, but steadily expanded even before the repeal of the British corn laws. Russian grain commerce increased 56 per cent as an annual average from 1832–40 ... the available supply of grain for export doubled.[47]

Great Britain, meanwhile, was purchasing grain to the value of more than twice the sales to Russia at the port of Odessa. Russia's prohibitive system was doing much harm to England, whose diplomats sought to procure a new commerical convention with Russia which would favour British sales of manufactured products to the latter. But the Russians were reluctant to negotiate except on the basis of strict reciprocity.[48]

The two countries after 1840 also confronted each other in the textile manufacturing industry. Russia was seeking new markets in Asia and was replacing England in the supply of domestic consumption of manufactured fabrics. Besides, Russian trade balances steadily became more favourable to the empire, because of increased grain exports from Odessa which became the greatest Russian port for exports by 1847.[49] 'In the twenty-six years preceding the Crimean war, the rise of importance of Russia's ports on the Black and Azov seas in wheat commerce was remarkable.'[50]

From 1846 to 1852, with the abolition of the grain tariff restrictions in England, Belgium, Holland, and other countries, the Russian grain trade became more stable, and witnessed a striking development as well. An exchange on a basis theretofore unknown was ushered in. Wheat became more than ever, the standard export from Russia's southern ports.[51] In addition, however, certain articles not able to bear the inconvenient land transit–rough iron, steel, manufactured iron, copper, tin, brass, earthenware, silk, prepared fish, and some raw materials–were being shipped by sea as far as possible.[52]

In the meantime, two other common commercial problems of the Near East were being faced by the foreign secretaries of Great Britain and Russia. One was the question of unequal benefits of English and Russian retail dealers in Turkey. Aberdeen started using the new political status between the two powers as a lever to secure Russia's acquiescence in a position which would place their traders on a parity in Turkey, as regards retail transactions. He strongly pressed Russia to adopt a commercial attitude towards Turkey, identical with that formulated between England and Turkey at Balta Liman.[53] Russia complied and signed a commercial treaty with Turkey, duplicating the English convention in April 1846. The other issue was the trade with Persia. In February, 1845 a secret Russian commission of investigation approved the expediency of granting the facilities of a Russian port in the the Black Sea for the transit trade from Persia. But evidence does not reveal an English diplomatic objection to this purely Russian measure.[54]

Commercial statistics usually were two or three years behind the events tabulated, and so, it was impossible for the diplomats in 1853 to calculate the commercial advancement of Russia down to the actual crisis preceding the Crimean War. Enough data were accessible, however, to show the lines of development with fair accuracy.[55]

In 1853 the most valid comparison possible in the commercial relations of England and Russia was this : The total volume of trade between the two countries was not evincing vital gains, but was undergoing a change in which England in reality was becoming a customer of Russia. At the same time British trade with other parts of the world was augmenting at an enormous speed. Particularly in the Straits, English trade with Turkey was increasing quite fast, the balance favouring Great Britain. Turkish territories, both European and Asiatic, were better customers of England than was Russia. Further, the Ottoman Empire was being developed as a region of supply for grain and other produce normally furnished by Russia, since the Russian protectionist system did not provide reciprocal advantages for Britain's free trade policy. Russia naturally was antagonistic to this development.[56]

In the first decade (1842–52) of the free trade era, official values of English imports and exports enhanced by sixty-five per cent. This heavy increase may be compared with an actual diminution of England's exports to Russia, and an increase in purchases (notably wheat) from Russia despite England's evident efforts to purchase more British Empire products and Turkish grain.

The evidence shows conclusively that after 1838 there had developed a natural competition between Russia and European Turkey for procuring the markets of western Europe in identic items; that Turkey, becoming a better customer for British manufactured goods, was progressing more rapidly than Russia. Alongwith this contest of sorts, Russia and England were entering an epoch of industrial competition for domination of the potential markets of Asia. These significant economic considerations, according to Puryear, 'go farther in explaining the causes of the Crimean War than any diplomatic or moral considerations.'[57]

Evidence is extant to prove the tremendous importance being given to a consideration of these factors by the British foreign office in 1853 following the collpase of the diplomatic combination between Russia and England in the spring of 1853.[58] If England decided to oppose Russia on economic grounds, she would find herself linked with France, still more highly protectionist, in sustaining Turkey against Russia.[59]

Of the great powers more directly interested in the commercial aspects of the problem of the Straits, Austria comes up for a brief consideration. On a simple basis of international reciprocity for the aid accorded by Russia in the Hungarian rising of 1849, Austria's political obligation demanded that she support Russia. But her economic interest agreed with those of England making her take a firm stand in preventing a permanent occupation of the Danubian principalities by Czar Nicholas I. In 1853, a free Danube was more important for

Austria than for any other European power. The conclusion reached by Austrian and English writers on the eve of the Crimean War, that a deliberate attempt was being made by Russia to expand her own commercial interests at Odessa at the expense of the Danubian ports seemed to have good ground.[60] Thus an identity of purely economic interests between Austria and England had aligned these two powers against Russia.[61]

Russia had a vast interest at stake. Her chief trade route had shifted to the Black Sea and the Straits. Commercial prosperity could only be achieved if that outlet for her produce were kept open. Besides, her infant industries could grow only if their outlet were sure. The same held true for her problem of a continuous supply of raw materials to be used in manufacture within Russia.

The position of Great Britain in the matter was entirely different. It was simply a question of choosing between Turkey and Russia as a permanent source for the supply of wheat. Grain qualities and prices being about the same, other factors were involved in a decision. For one thing, Turkey had become a better British customer than Russia. Russia was not only becoming a relatively poorer customer; she was developing into a British competitor in the budding markets in the east, a situation never to be apprehended from Turkey after the treaty of Balta Liman.

The fundamental economic factors herein sketched partly explain the origin of the Crimean war. 'But economic analysis, however, exhaustive', to quote our authority, 'will go only part way in explaining one of the world's most curious and unnecessary conflicts.'[62]

IV

A.W. Kinglake saw the Crimean war as having been mainly brought about by the artful scheming of Napoleon III. He said that 'by his ambiguous ways of acting and speaking, the French Emperor came to have a chief share in the kindling of the war.'[63] Kinglake[64] and the English opponents of the Second

Empire knew that they could not better estrange England from Napoleon III than by convincing her that in the Crimean war she had been used and tricked by him. A generation later, Louis Napoleon III's brilliant French apologist[65] interpreted the same thesis as evidence of his superb statecraft; the Emperor had goaded England into the war in order to destroy the last vestiges of the Holy Alliance, and so to make possible the later developments of his foreign policy.[66] In fact the figure of Napoleon III fits neither praise nor blame such as this. In their appraisement of political leaders, historians tend to exaggerate the element of design and underestimate the element of accident in the conduct of human affairs. Nor are any people more encouraging to them in this tendency than leaders themselves. The historian is propense to the process because in this way, he seems to magnify his office; but incidentally he magnifies also the personality to whom he attributes such deep and prophetical designs.'[67]

Perhaps Emile Bourgeois was not much farther from truth when he wrote :

> Napoleon III was sincere when he declared his intention of founding a peaceful Empire, for he was not in the least desirous of staking his unexpected stroke of luck on the uncertainty of battle. If he thought of abolishing the treaties of 1815, and restoring France to the glorious position of arbiter between nations and sovereigns ...he ...wished to see the remodelling effected by diplomatic congresses, not by war.[68]

That the French emperor had a sincere desire for the English alliance in general, and for alignment with England on the eastern question in particular, is no doubt true. And he was no less certainly determined that France, under him, should not submit to such humiliation on that question as she had suffered under Louis Philippe in 1840.[69] 'But that he had any consistent desire to lead both countries into war, is a contention which can now be conclusively disproved.'[70] as Simpson observed.

The first rift between the Czar and the French Emperor occurred over 'the dynastic numeral'. Nicholas I had been alarmed and antagonized more than any other sovereign by the creation of the empire and had personally warned Louis Napoleon III from taking such a step. Now his assumption of the title, 'Napoleon III' seemed to Nicholas I an additional piece of arrogance, since the Allies had never recognized Napoleon II. Spurred on by Austria, the Czar refused to treat Napoleon III as a legitimate sovereign, and greeted the new ruler not in the traditional form as his 'brother' but merely as his 'friend'. At one moment it looked as though 'the dynastic numeral' would lead to a rupture of diplomatic relations, but the French monarch had the good sense not to let a matter of protocol provoke a crisis. He adroitly let the incident pass with a famous repartee: 'We have to put up with our brothers, but we can choose our friends.' The incident, moreover, turned to his advantage, for, when it came to the point, the rulers of Austria and Prussia had followed Queen Victoria and not the Czar in giving Napoleon III the customary credentials. 'The significance of the rift', J.P.T. Bury observes, 'was hardly likely to be lost on the new emperor.'[71]

T.A.B. Corley writes :

> Napoleon III did not bring about the Crimean War in order to secure prestige for his *parvenu* dynasty or for his Empress, or for any other of the many reasons which historians and writers of memoirs have suggested. He, like the other combatants, merely drifted into the war. To him, at least at this time, the empire really did mean peace, but as he gained power and experience, so his ideas on foreign policy were developing. Now, partly under the influence of the followers of Saint-Simon, they leapt forward to take account of the new economic conditions lately created in the world.[72]

The first half of the nineteenth century saw an unprecedented opening up of the whole world. In Europe, and in other developed areas–such as the eastern United States–roads, canals, and railways, were being multiplied into inter-woven networks which would soon provide easy communications with remote places. Steam power was beginning to replace sail, with momentous impact on international trade and migration.

During the period in which this revolution in transport

was being crystallized, Napoleon III was the ruler of France and fully cognizant of its profound implications to all countries and to every citizen of countries. He was determined to build up France into a powerful nation. Meanwhile, 'the centre of the old world was, as it has been almost since the beginning of history, the Mediterranean, across which ran the two great axes of this rapidly growing network of communications: from north to south, London-Marseilles-Algiers, and from west to east, Bordeaux-Marseilles-Alexanderia'. These axes both passed through France, which now received a new importance because they entailed considerable shortening of distance compared with the alternative sea route through the Straits of Gibraltar. Thus, with her political revival and parallel to her enhanced economic importance as a source of funds for international investment, France was attaining a unique status in the world as one of its great and thriving arteries.[73]

The concern of France in the Mediterranean, which her expanding role in the world helped to intensify, was nothing new. Even the cautious Louis Philippe pursued this policy–of conquering Algiers, which had laid the foundation stone of a vast new African Empire. It was inevitable that a more enterprising regime in France would soon be regarding the Mediterranean as what Napoleon III had described as 'a French lake'.[74] If the Levant and particularly Syria and Egypt were of concern to France, then certainly Constantinople, the 'key to the Mediterranean', was of such strategic importance that its fall must affect not only France but the entire continent.

All writers on diplomacy preceding the Crimean war explain the flurry and tension created by the resurrection of the Napoleonic dynasty. Few self-made rulers have resisted the temptation to pursue an ambitious foreign policy in the hope of achieving abroad the glory which might lead to stability at home. Men were right in apprehending that the *status quo* might be disrupted by the heir of the great Corsican. Nesselrode warned the Czar that a dangerous time was approaching. 'It is peace, but armed peace with all its expenses and uncertainty. Only the union of the Great Powers is capable of maintaining it.' Still this improved Russia's position : a solidarity against France was necessarily a solidarity in Russia's favour. French threat must make Prussia and Austria dependent on Russian support.[75] Further Nicholas I was trying to drive a wedge between France and Britain..

The most serious criticism against Napoleon III was for sending the French fleet to the Near East. 'Nor was he ... seeking', so says Corley, 'to propitiate the French Catholic vote. This he already possessed to a considerable extent.'[76] He was merely acting in France's interests as he had done over various issues in the past.[77] He had to do something in the face of the arrogant appearance of Prince Menshikov. Failure to act vigorously in foreign affairs had cost Louis Philippe his throne. The Napoleonic programme could not allow Russian ultimatums to be meekly accepted,[78] and he could take no chances that a minor Russian success might appear as a defeat for France and himself. Castelbajac's report that Russia genuinely did not want war appeared to minimize the real danger in the situation and tended to encourage Napoleon III to more forward action.[79] 'There is one word which is fatal to the welfare of a great nation. Lord Cowley breathed it: *Honour*.'[80] Napoleon's more positive reactions to Russian threats found greater favour at Constantinople on the whole than Britain's half-hearted attitude; moreover, the powerful French naval forces, with such vessels as the *Charlemagne*, testified that she was capable of backing up his firmness.

The French king could find few signs of war-like feelings among his subjects: a kind of sullen indifference prevailed throughout France. Most industrialists and businessmen regarded the prospect of hostilities as little short of disastrous just when economic conditions were on the mend; to the common people war could only mean further hardships and the long casualty list of the first empire. According to Guerard: 'No one in France, from the sovereign to the most humble peasant, had the slightest desire for war.'[81] Besides, the new *Entente* with Britain was generally unpopular. Throughout the Crimean war Napoleon III, by the unstinted expenditure of his personal popularity, was engaged in forcing France, in unison with the nation whom at the time she most despised, into an assault upon the nation whom she held least vulnerable.[82] But he was, in fact, daily growing more experienced in the art of shaping public opinion. The limitation of Russian sea-power did genuinely concern Englishmen; but it left France entirely cold. Nor was there even in France any real religious ardour for the war such as a crusade on behalf of fellow Christians nurtured in Russia. The dispute to the Holy Places, it is sometimes forgotten, had been settled nearly a year before the war began. Of the clerical and reactionary parties, Orleanists generally were bitterly anti-English,[83] and Legitimists were pro-Russian to the core. As a matter of fact those who in France disapproved of the war least were probably the socialists and liberals; to bring down Russia was to shatter despotism everywhere, 'and the same fact which made the war repugnant to clear-sighted royalists made it welcome to clear-sighted Republicans. But royalists were many and Republicans few; and clear-sight was an even rarer merit among the latter than among the former.'[84]

It is not surprising therefore that at the beginning of 1854, the Prince Consort should have described the Emperor as being in anything but a belligerent mood,[85] though his disinclination to war was but a pale reflection of his people. So obvious was this situation that Russia, in Simpson's words, 'made repeated efforts to detach France from the English alliance', Napoleon III determined to address Nicholas I publicly and directly; dispatched at the end of January, 1854 an autographed letter to the Czar. 'It urged that only definite efforts in the direction of peace could now avert difinite war; it then proposed for this purpose a scheme of pacification based upon an immediate armistice, and the simultaneous abandonment of the principalities by the Russian troops, and of the Black Sea by the allied fleets.' Further, the Czar could deal directly with the Turks; when they had settled matters between themselves, their arrangement should be submitted for final ratification to the four powers. This letter was conciliatory in tone, and its proposal offered Russia a decorous escape from her troubles.

But the Czar rejected the offer, and taunted that the Russia of 1854 would be found the same as that of 1812.[86]

The chief criticisms to which the French monarch's overture exposed him are that it smacked of self-advertisement; that in seeking peace in this outrageously public manner he was departing from all the decent norms of diplomacy; that his action was pompous. These criticisms are probably just. But some higher criticisms may also be noted. Bernadotte Schmitt states: 'One cannot ... avoid a suspicion that the French Emperor was playing a deep game ... the language of his letter to the Czar was not exactly calculated to appease the irritation of that proud prince... It could not have been a matter of surprise that this language... proved too much for the temper and dignity of Nicholas I... He replied in a tone so haughty as to destroy all chances of negotiation. And further that 'the policy of Napoleon ... made a peaceful solution difficult, perhaps even impossible'.[87]

The 'open letter', it is true, is less commonly a harbinger of peace than of the sword; and it has long been a device practised by those who praise the one and seek the other. 'But with many small crookednesses of method contracted during his long training as conspirator, Napoleon III yet retained in some larger matters an almost childish simplicity of motive; and in the present instance, there is abundance even of published evidence that the Czar's rejection of his overture occasioned its author only an extreme and naive disappointment'.[88] Edmund B. D'Auvergne writes in his biography, *Napoleon the Third :*

> It was a bloodless victory at which he aimed–a triumph of diplomacy which should make him appear the conservator of the peace of Europe and a welcome member of the concert of kings. He tried to talk over the Czar; but Nicholas I did not think he meant to fight, and for that reason made no show of yielding ...So patiently did the Emperor pursue peace that many people in England suspected him of bad faith and really favouring Russia. Had the two Central Powers come in on the side of the new allies, the Czar must certainly have given way ... King Frederick William rejected the parvenu's overtures with disdain.[89]

V

According to L.C.B. Seaman:

> European peace after 1815 had depended in part on the successful use by Metternich of the fear of revolution as a means of hypnotizing Russia into a passive policy towards Turkey.[90]

By 1853 the Holy Alliance was decrepit.[91] 'The disappearance of Metternich from the diplomatic scene', continues Seaman, 'had deprived the Habsburgs of their last lingering scrap of intelligence ...A Hohenzollern halfwit and a handsome Habsburg dimwit ... recently racked with revolution, were not so much a restraint upon Nicholas I as an incitement to him to adventure forward in the belief that they could do nothing to stop him.'[92]

The other guarantor of Near Eastern peace had been Great Britain. But now it was in a chaos. In the words of Seton-Watson: 'Nothing contributed so much towards the impending disaster as the confused state of party politics at home'. The fact that a number of the most eminent public men did not see eye to eye on vital issues, served to increase the tension in public mind. And if there was one question upon which British public opinion, from Lord Palmerston downwards, was woefully misinformed and unbalanced, it was that very eastern question which now exploded in the Crimean war.[93] The foreign secretary was now Lord John Russell. His views on foreign policy were those of a whig idealist, hating Czars as he hated popes. Worse still, he was ill-informed on matters of elementary geography. He advanced the odd theory that if Britain did not fight the Russians on the Danube, she would have to fight them on the Indus; although Danube was not on Russia's most clear route to the Indus.[94]

There can be no doubt that the Czar was entirely sincere in his profession of friendliness to England. 'The real trouble was the difference in atmosphere between London and St. Petersburg, or it may be said, the difference in point of departure.' The Czar as a close neighbour casting covetous glances on Turkey, was imbued with the idea that nothing could save her from precipitate destruction, while the British statesmen wishfully maintained a really pathetic belief in Turkey's reformability.[95] In the opinion of Seaman: 'The Crimean War was based not so much on the eastern question as on the ideological breach between the East and West.'[96]

The British cabinet throughout the summer was paralyzed by internal divisions. In season and out of season, Aberdeen professed a horror of war. Such men can be dangerous enough and the Czar believed that, as then led, England would not dream of war. 'It is a matter of history', George MacMunn observes, 'that our liberal governments have usually been those to have war on their hands.'[97] Nor was Nicholas the first or the last European ruler 'to think that in her preoccupation with trade and money-making, England would decline' to fight in a cause not directly affecting her purse.[98] Aberdeen was not strong enough to impose himself upon all his colleagues or to insist upon warning Turkey that Britain would be no party to a war, while Palmerston and John Russell were not strong to warn the Czar that in the event of war Britain would place herself on the Turkish side. Either attitude might have led one or other of the disputants to recoil before it was too late.

It is said that 'Aberdeen allowed his riper judgment to be over-ruled' on the vital issue of the reappointment of Stratford Canning to Constantinople.[99] The role of Stratford has been a subject of acute controversy.[100] He was believed to be 'an expert on the eastern mind, and a keen opponent of Russian ambitions in Turkey.'[101] Alfred Rambaud writes: 'In the Queen's Cabinet his despatches had the weight of law; in the Sultan's Council his opinions were held as oracles.'[102]

It would be worthwhile to examine here briefly the earlier diplomatic career of Stratford Canning. Towards the close of the year 1832, Palmerston had promoted him to the embassy of St. Petersburg: 'an unwarrantable act on his part since the Czar had already privately intimated to him that Canning was the only man in England to whose appointment he would object. The fact of this previous protest was however generally unknown.' Hence, it was a matter of general astonishment when Nicholas I refused to receive him at St. Petersburg.

Stratford on his part refused to smoothen the situation by any act of voluntary retirement: so the embarrassed Premier sent him as a special envoy to Madrid, but still styled in his letters of credence, 'Ambassador to the Emperor of All the Russia's.' It is likely that Palmerston resented the rebuff to which he had gratuitously exposed his friend: it is certain that Stratford felt himself to have been viciously used by Nicholas.[103] Such memories no doubt contributed to his conviction 'that there could be no real settlement in the Near East until the pretensions of Russia had been publicly repudiated and until the Czar had sustained an unmistakable defeat either in diplomacy or in war.

If without war so much the better, but by war if necessary.'[104]

Let us see what Temperley the great apologist of Redcliffe, says on this intriguing legend. He writes:

> Stratford was a strong man, but not, in this instance, a warlike one. It has often been asserted that he wanted war between Turkey and Russia and ultimately got it. If that theory was true, the sending of Stratford to Constantinople would have been a fatal mistake. Aberdeen thought it was and repented in sackcloth. He and his colleagues were not sorry to escape the responsibility of the war. But contemporaries do not always select the right scape goat. The Stratford legend ...does not stand the criticism of later research. Stratford had no part in the military and naval demonstrations which did so much to produce war... In the first half of 1853 there were two serious diplomatic steps and two armed demonstrations. These were the Leiningen and Menshikov missions, the despatch of French naval squadron to Salamis in March and of the Franco-British fleet to Besika Bay at the end of May. Over two of these, Stratford had no control and the third was done against his advice. So much for three incidents. Over the fourth, Stratford exercised a real influence by helping the Turks to reject Manshikov mission, but that action was approved by his government. Until June, the governments of England, France and Russia had proved more warlike than Stratford. After June, the situation got out of hand and neither Stratford nor anyone else could stay the drift towards war.[105]

Temperley's reasoning does not appear very sound and convincing. In reply to him, F.A. Simpson congently argues:

> It is no doubt possible, as Professor Temperley seems to have held, that Stratford was altogether immune, in his conduct of the negotiations which preceded the Crimean war, from any desire to have his 'tit for tat' with Nicholas. On the other hand, it is also possible that in the course of them, the great ambassador was profoundly, even if unconsciously, affected by the unprecedented personal rebuff which the Czar had earlier inflicted on him. After a careful reading of all the evidence amassed by Professor Temperley, in addition to that which I had already examined for myself, I am still of the deliberate opinion that the latter is the more probable interpretation. I neither think, indeed, nor thought ... that Stratford was guilty of the enormity of seeking to avenge a private injury by a European war. But I both thought, and think, that he was not unwilling to confront Nicholas in 1853 ... with the alternative between war and a public and humuliating retreat, at a time when to build a bridge for that retreat was the true task of diplomacy.
>
> ... the difference between Professor Temperley's view and mine is a difference less on facts, than on the proper interpretation of facts. He did not, for example, question the authenticity of the doubly attested utterance of Stratford ... You have brought good news, for that means war. The Emperor of Russia chose to make it a personal quarrel with me; and now I am avenged. What he did do was to explain: this last utterance, once the war was certain, seems a legitimate outburst due to war psychology, possibly. But ... it is also possible that it was precisely in such moments of rare excitement that the real mind of this polished and formidable diplomatist was most truly revealed.[106]

VI

The extremely impressive and in certain ways dominant position which Russia obtained with the collapse of the revolutions of 1848–49 on the continent, did not last long. In fact, the international image of the gendarme of Europe and of the country he represented was much stronger in appearance than in reality: the forces of liberalism and nationalism, although scotched, were by no means crushed, and they carried European public opinion with them.[107] Even the usual friends of the Czar complained of his interference with their interests, as in the case of Prussia, or at least were irritated with his overbearing solicitude, as was true of Austria. Nicholas I himself, on the other hand–in the opinion of some specialists–reacted to his success by becoming 'more blunt, uncompromising, doctrinaire, and domineering than ever before.'[108] The stage was set for a political debacle, if not exactly for the climactic act of a Greek tragedy.

But the circumstances of this debacle turned out to be anything but obvious, simple, or straightforward. The original issue was a three-cornered dispute between Russia, France and Turkey over certain Holy Places at Jerusalem and Bethlehem associated with the life of Christ. By 1850, the Catholic population of Jerusalem was less than six per cent and Catholic pilgrims numbered less than a hundred out of twelve thousand making the journey each year to the Holy City.[109] By the capitulations of 1535, the custody of the Holy Places had been entrusted to French Catholics, and this French protectorate, reaffirmed in 1673, had been solemnly confirmed and enlarged by the famous capitulations of 1740. William Miller calls the last 'the *magna Carta* of the French in the Levant.'[110] It provided that the French religious orders should not be molested in their occupation of the church of the Holy Sepulchre at Jerusalem, and that, whenever the monuments of the Holy Places required repair, the requisite leave should be granted at the request of the French ambassador. These exclusive privileges of 'the eldest daughter of the church', derived from a period when the Russian Empire had not yet sprung into being, had been undermined by certain 'firmans' conceded to the Greek Church from 1634 onwards, at times when France was either hostile to Turkey, or indifferent to ecclesiastical questions.[111] The Latins had been neglectful of their responsibilities in the East and the Greeks had monopolized many of their functions of maintenance and repair. For this the Sultan had given the Greeks special guarantees and titles which conflicted with existing treaties and capitulations and could be revoked at will. When Louis Napoleon III became President of Second French Republic, the support of the

French Catholics was essential to him. Alike in Rome and at Jerusalem he came forward as the champion of the Catholic cause and instructed his ambassador at Constantinople to insist upon the strict execution of the capitulations of 1740; thus, in the words of the British foreign secretary, 'making the tomb of Christ a cause of quarrel among Christians.'[112] In the heated discussions over specific points on issues that followed, the French were technically correct, but current practice since 1759 showed that the 'firmans' better represented justice. The Czar's specific rights originated from the treaty of Kuckuk Kainarji in 1774 with reaffirmations of his position in subsequent treaties; in 1812 at Bucharest, in 1826 at Akkerman, in 1829 at Adrianople, and in 1833 at Unkiar-Iskelessi. In the Five Power Convention of 1841, Russia renounced only her new rights (of 1833) and not those previously granted.[113] Actually, however, 'neither Nicholas I nor Nesselrode nor Brunnow knew much about the treaty [Kuchuk Kainarji] or the claim which it put forward.... The Czar and his advisers ultimately went to war over a claim they had never troubled to examine.' It would not be fair to say that the question of religious protection was a pretext, for Nicholas I felt deeply about the Holy Places. He often said that he had no political views on Turkey and wished only to satisfy the conscience of his subjects. But no religious claim, urged with threats and backed with force, can remain purely religious. The demand for a religious protectorate over the Orthodox subjects of the Porte had a political implication. 'Thus the motives of Nicholas I, even if purely religious to begin with, could not remain so. And for this reason, though he sought peace, he found war.'[114] The Muslim Sultan, caught in the vortex of a christian dispute, finally (February, 1852) sought to satisfy all parties by awarding the keys to the French while assuring the Greeks that in effect the *status quo* was intact. This obvious inconsistency aggravated the situation, giving rise to further complaints from both the French and the Russians.[115] A.J.P. Taylor has called this decision favouring the French simply *Realpolitik*; the Turks concluded that in the last resort the

French fleet could defeat the Russians. Fear of French power had become greater in Constantinople than fear of Russian power, and hence, Taylor concludes, overt Russian action became imperative. 'The French success was not merely a challenge to the Czar's religious prestige; it threatened the basis of Russia's policy towards Turkey... the essential condition of this policy was that Turkey should fear Russia more than any other power. Now the Turks had shown that they feared France more than Russia. The Czar would have reacted, no doubt, Taylor continues, to such a challenge from any great power; but he would not have reacted so violently if the challenge had not come from France.[116] In his eyes (and not in his alone), the struggle between France and Russia was merely a cloak for the far greater struggle between conservatism and 'the revolution'. When the Czar flung himself into the Turkish conflict, he sincerely supposed that he was championing a European cause as well as his own.[117]

He also assumed that this European cause would make his victory easier and surer. Nesselrode warned him that neither England nor Austria would support Russia in a war against France; but Nicholas I was confident that he could deal with France so long as the other powers stayed neutral, and he was confident of their neutrality.

At this juncture Nicholas made two important advances:

(1) He inaugurated a new series of secret conversations with England regarding plans for a peaceful partition of Turkey, using Sir Hamilton Seymour at St. Petersburg as an intermediary.

(2) Prince Menshikov was ordered to Constantinople to retrieve the lost Russian political ascendancy, his demands being supported by the amassing of large numbers of Russian troops on the Turkish frontier.

Nicholas I was playing a dangerous game, but in so doing, 'he determined to trust no one but himself. Never before in the history of the world did a monarch so absolutely and directly take upon himself a responsibility.[118] He referred to Turkey as 'a sick man', and defying the advice of his wisest counsellor, who spoke from experience–Nesselrode had seen Czar Alexander 'of glorious memory' fail in an overture to Castlereagh at Vienna, and he knew that history would repeat itself–Nicholas I decided to be his own negotiator.[119] He spoke to Seymour his desire to reach an agreement with the British government on the disposal of the Turkish empire before its collapse. He did not wish to take Constantinople, but would not consent to its being taken by any other great power or by an enlarged Greek state. Serbia and Bulgaria might be given the same status as the Rumanian principalities, which were 'in fact an independent state under my protection.' Egypt, and perhaps also Crete, might go to Britain. Nicholas declared that the interests of Russia and Austria were identical. His evident intention was to isolate France. Seymour reported these talks to London, but the British government would not be drawn. Clarendon, the foreign secretary, told Seymour that Britain desired no gains of territory, and that Britain and Russia should cooperate in upholding the independence and integrity of Turkey. The British cabinet did not like the Emperor's attitude towards France, but, on the whole, his assurances were considered satisfactory. 'Englishmen considered that his overture proved his disinterestedness and pledged his honour to make no attack on the Turkish empire. In that sense the overture did positive good, for it enabled England and Russia to have more confidence in one another.'[120]

In the words of Temperley:

> The efforts of Nicholas I to arrive at a good understanding with England were inspired by a sincere and even noble emotion... It was unwise to try to discuss potentialities with parliamentarians. But the suggestion that there was anything criminal in such an attempt is ridiculous ... Though not a crime on the part of Nicholas I, it was nonetheless a blunder. And the penalty for blunders is exacted in this world.[121]

Thus terminated, Rambaud describes it as, 'the strangest series of negotiations known among the archives of diplomacy.'[122]

In February, 1853 the Czar sent Prince Menshikov as his

special envoy to Constantinople. With an escort so impressive as to give a foretaste of invasion, and with calculated insolence, Menshikov attempted to cajole or coerce the sublime Porte into agreement. 'At Constantinople, the attitude of Prince Menshikov was threatening and mysterious; on the Danube, the movements of the Russian forces were threatening and significant.'[123] All these had produced in the Turkish capital a feeling bordering on panic. At Russia's request, Fuad Effendi, the Ottoman Foreign Minister who had actually given the keys to the French, was retired.[124] Excitement ran high as Menshikov presented his emperor's views on the Holy Places. He then presented a new note, virtually an ultimatum, demanding a treaty which would confirm Russian protection of all Greek Orthodox Christians in the Ottoman Empire. This demand of protective rights in itself was nothing new, it had been vaguely understood by everyone since 1774. That it now came as a shock must be attributed to the existing tension.

The demands of Menshikov had alarmed both the British and the French governments. England sent back to Constantinople Stratford de Redcliffe armed with a somewhat vague authority to order the Admiral of the Fleet at Malta to hold his fleet in readiness to sail for the Near East. The general European situation under the Second Empire gave to official diplomacy greater powers than it had under the Armed Peace; and those powers, thanks to the still complete freedom of diplomacy from popular control, were concentrated in fewer hands. Of those greater powers, moreover, a far larger portion was centred at this time in the person of the ambassador; since the common use of telegraphy had not yet accomplished its inevitable work of centralization, by subordinating every embassy to the immediate control of the foreign office. 'From this fact it followed also that the importance of an ambassador's initiative varied in direct ratio with his distance from his own capital; and in all Europe there was no capital so distant from St. James' as Constantinople.'[125]

In an attempt to believe the Russian assurances that Menshikov's mission had no other object than a solution to the troubled issue of the Holy Places, Stratford induced that unseasoned diplomatist to present to the Porte separately the avowed portion of his demands: with the result that in less than three weeks this tedious ecclesiastical dispute was settled. 'The problems of keys, stars, doorkeepers, gardens, domes, and outbuildings', to quote F.J.C. Hearnshaw,[126] were decided to the satisfaction of the orthodox. Menshikov, however, had committed a fatal error in separating the old and avowed grievance of Russia as to the Holy Places, from her new and ominous demand for a formal and exclusive protectorate over all Greek Christians. He had achieved the professed object of his mission: but thereby he was forced to produce openly and separately the demand for the protectorate; a demand hitherto disavowed, and in its present form and situation clearly indefensible. This he did. Stratford communicated to the Sultan the fact that he was authorized to order the fleet at Malta to be in readiness to sail. 'This had a magical effect, and the Russian demands were rejected.'[127]

The Menshikov mission appears to have been nothing more than a bluff by the Czar. Bluffing, indeed, seemed to be the order of the day. During the earlier phases of negotiations on the Holy Places, Lavalette[128] had used threats to bolster the French argument; and the Austrians had just succeeded in a mission identical to that of Menshikov. A show of force was getting desirable results for those who used it. In the Danish Question direct threats by Russia had produced the armistice of Malmo. Upon its expiration, a Russian naval demonstration brought about the Conference of London in 1852. The victory of the French in the battle of the Holy Places had wounded Nicholas I too deeply for him to accept defeat. Rioting mobs in Constantinople, Jerusalem, and St. Petersburg asked whether 'millions of Greeks' were to stand quietly and 'be robbed by these wretched Turks to gratify a few French tourists.'[129] It was imperative that Nicholas do something to restore his influence in the East without provoking a European conflict. In early February 1853, Austria's Count Leiningen demanded concessions from the sultan. This suggested an answer for Nicholas I, who only wanted a diplomatic success. In St. Petersburg early in 1853, both a declaration of war against the Ottoman Empire and a surprise occupation of the Danubian principalities were regarded as inconvenient courses to pursue.* Menshikov was chosen as a 'pure Russian'. After some fumbling, the Russian diplomats hit on the idea of enforcing Russia's protectorate over the othodox peoples of Turkey, a claim allegedly based on the treaty of Kuchuk Kainarji. Some of the Russian diplomats knew that they were running a forced claim.[130] These technicalities were of little significance: the religious protectorate was the first idea that came to hand. A conflict of prestige with France had, in fact to be tied up with religious sentiment before it could appeal to an orthodox and obscurantist public indifferent to the danger from 'revolution'.[131]

Why had the Turks refused? The natural answer is that Menshikov's claims were incompatible with Ottoman independence. Taylor says that 'the Turks were bound to refuse, if the Ottoman Empire was to remain an independent power; and Stratford was bound to advise them as he did, so long as the independence of Turkey was part of British policy.'[132] Temperley feels that 'the Turks, having yielded twice to Napoleon in 1852 and once to Austria in 1853,** could not yield to Russia or to anyone else a fourth time.' Besides, 'Leiningen prudently gave way on ... [two] points, while insisting on the others.' And the French had never claimed or demanded political protection of Ottoman Roman Catholics. 'France limited her claims to what was narrowly ecclesiastical, just when Russia extended hers to what was dangerously political... The Sultan had feared the *Charlemagne*, but he feared Kuchuk Kainarji even more.'[133]

Finally, there were personalities involved. Redcliffe's preponderance at Constantinople and his temper invited

---

* Vide Florinsky, *Russia II*, p. 865.

** The Turks 'had twice been coerced by France in 1852, once by the threat to bombard Tripoli, and again by the arrival of the *Charlemagne* on the Bosphorus. During 1853 the Porte were for a time studiously moderate, giving way to count Leiningen.' Temperley, *Crimea*, p. 507.

suspicion. He in many ways, as W.F. Reddaway puts it, 'resembled an independent potentate rather than an ordinary public servant.'[134] To Florinsky 'there is little doubt that his passionate Russophobia was important among the factors working against the preservation of peace.'[135] Not only Redcliffe, there were other short-tempered men on the spot working to solve problems that needed the utmost patience and understanding. Menshikov and Colonel Rose, the British attache, were numbered among the 'three most violent men in Europe, and... it would be extraordinary indeed if they could come in contact without an explosion.' Another fiery personality was added when General Baraguay d'Hilliers arrived as the new French ambassador.[136] It looked as though the stage was set for an explosion.

When the Menshikov mission failed, Nicholas I turned to a second stratagem and ordered troops into the Danubian principalities, a war-like act, which the Czar protested was prompted by motives entirely pacific. The news of the invasion, notwithstanding the explanations with which it was accompanied, gave rise in England to an outburst of popular excitement; but Aberdeen, as premier, was working for peace. In France too, even Drouyn de Lhuys, one of the most war-like of the imperial advisers, was still inclined to a pacific policy. The occupation of the principalities violated no specific agreement and did not necessitate a war. The action belongs to the same category as French aid in the war of Greek independence, French and British action in the issue of Belgian independence. Even the Porte did not regard it as a cause for war at the outset. But Russian troops in the principalities had more to do with the outbreak of war than any other single incident. 'By taking Menshikov's threatening appearances and the Czar's demands literally, thereby closing the door to the latter's solution, the Ottoman Empire and the rest of Europe forced him to further action and ultimately promoted a war which Nicholas I had not wanted and had actually sought to prevent.'[137]

On June 2, the British fleet was ordered to Besika Bay. It was joined by the French fleet a few days later; the Anglo-

French alliance thus came into being. In seeking to maintain Turkish independence, Great Britain and France were fighting for a pretence, which they knew to be such; but it was a pretence which had to be kept up for lack of an alternative. Once it was admitted that Turkey was not truly independent (and every event of the Crimean war testified to it), the Russians were justified in their demands for the sake of their own security.[138]

Alfred Rambaud writes:

> This understanding between France and England, which the Czar had never believed possible, was not the first nor perhaps the bitterest of his miscalculations: Russia saw Austria and Prussia fall away... Neither Prince Menshikov at Constantinople, nor the Czar at St. Petersburg, nor his envoys at Berlin and Vienna, had found among the representatives or ministers of those two powers that support upon which Russian policy had a right, or supposed it had a right, to depend.[139]

To Nicholas I directly, Austria owed Hungary: yet Russia at the mouth of the Danube was already threatening her in the nineteenth century with the fate which Holland at the mouth of the Scheldt had inflicted on the Austrian Netherlands in the eighteenth: the deliberate throttling of her trade by the one great waterway which she possessed. But Russia's acquisition of the whole Danubian principalities would have added an immediate and formidable political threat. It would have given Russia extensive frontiers not only to the east of Austria but to the south; and poised semi-Slavonic subjects of the one between the outstretched finger and thumb of the other. It needed a tougher constitution than Austira's to contemplate with equanimity the friendly but ineluctable hand-grip that would ensue.

Napoleon III on his side was dreaming of a dramatic act of mediation by which he might win Russian favour. Diplomats saw, to quote Alfred Rambaud, 'the heir of Napoleon using as an argument against Russia the obligation of treaties, and calling upon all Europe to maintain the equilibrium, and the heir of Alexander threatening the established order of things[140] ... ' Therewith, began the characteristic diplomatic pattern of the Crimean war: the attempt by the two conflicting sides to involve the Central Powers. Both Prussia and Austria aimed at neutrality, Prussia because she had no interests at stake, Austria because she had too many.[141] Prussia's only concern was not to become the battleground in the tussle between conservatism and 'the revolution'; Austrian's that Nicholas should drop his demands on Turkey without being humiliated.[142]

On August 1, the four powers agreed to the proposals drafted by the Austrian Foreign Minister, Count Buol, and known as the 'Vienna Note'. This note, a vague reaffirmation of previous treaties, embodied the concessions which in the opinion of the powers, Turkey could make to Russia without risking her independence. The note was accepted by Nicholas I; and all Europe with a sigh of relief pronounced the question settled, and peace assured.

But to the common amazement, this note was refused by the usually complacent Turkey; unless certain apparently trivial[143] modifications were introduced into three clauses of it. This was a strange situation, in which Russia accepted and Turkey rejected a scheme devised by Europe for Turkey's protection against Russia. Since however, the alterations in the note merely served to render explicit the loosely-worded text, England now urged the acceptance of the revised version upon the Czar. But Nicholas I now very naturally refused to accept the revised version as derogatory to the dignity of Russia: 'Either the alterations which the Porte requires are important, in which case it is plain that we must refuse to accede to them; or they are unimportant, and then the question arises, "Why should the Porte unnecessarily make its acceptance dependent on them?"[144] What answer could be found to this? Europe acquiesced, and Turkey was evidently lost.

Why did the Porte refuse? When on the news of Russia's acceptance of the Vienna note all England was speaking of the entire question as 'settled', the following entry in C.F.G. Greville's diary was found: 'I saw Clarendon yesterday. Nothing new, but he said he fully expected Stratford Canning would play some trick at Constantinople, and throw obstacles in the way of settlement.'[145] Nor was Clarendon alone to have premonitions of the sinister developments at Constantinople. Aberdeen, the Premier, wrote that autumn to Sir James Graham, his close frirend and the First Lord of the Admiralty: 'I thought we should have been able to conquer Stratford, but I begin to fear that the reverse will be the case.' The premier was shaky about the presence of Stratford at the Turkish capital. That inspite of this opinion he left him at Constantinople was due to his conviction that when directly challenged, Stratford must prove more dangerous. His recall would entail the resignation of Russell and of Palmerston: and a new cabinet would emerge with Palmerston as its premier and war as its object. By remaining in office himself, even at the cost of some minor concessions to Stratford and to the war-like desires of the people, Aberdeen could still hope to counteract them both finally in the actual realization of their end.[146]

About the same time, Lord Cowley transmitted home the sense of M. de Lacour's reports to Paris on his British colleague's 'strange conduct.' Stratford, he stated, 'while nominally complying with his instructions and urging the Porte to accept the Vienna Note, "let it be seen at the same time that his private opinion is at variance with his official language, and does not bring that personal influence to bear which would have been so useful at the present moment." '[147]

Unfortunately for the cause of peace, the Czar proceeded at this point to cast aside all the advantage which he had earned by his ready acceptance of the Vienna Note, by explaining his reasons for accepting it. Simpson observes: 'Russia's position in opposing a bare refusal to the suggestion that she should modify to her own disadvantage at the instance of Turkey an international award, recommended to her by the great powers as a fair settlement of the dispute, was technically one of extraordinary strength.' But Nesselrode, the Russian Chancellor, was anxious to show that Russia had won the battle of prestige. He sent to Vienna 'a reasoned analysis of Turkey's proposed modifications, and Russia's grounds for rejecting them. This analysis revealed the fact that Russia had interpreted ambiguities in the original note in a sense not intended by its framers, though only explicitly excluded by the proposed Turkish alterations.'[148] 'This "violent interpretation" killed the Vienna Note.'[149] England and France refused to folllow Austria and Prussia in pressing Turkey to accept the original note.

Before further action could be taken, Turkey, confident that France and Great Britain would not leave her to the mercy of Russia, declared war on Russia on October 4, 1853. The diplomacy of the powers was now exerted to find a formula which would restore peace between Russia and Turkey before any overt hostilities. This last attempt was the meeting of the Czar and Francis Joseph at Olomouc. The Russian monarch was now in retreat, he repudiated Nesselrode's 'violent interpretation', and displayed great moderation and willingness to consider the interests of Turkey and of all the other powers. Taylor feels that 'this moderation was a bait': Nicholas I now wanted the alliance of the three 'Northern Courts.' He even suggested to Austria a joint protectorate of the Danubian principalities, anything, in fact, to break the 'solidarity of Europe.' Nothing could be more disquieting to the Austrians than to have the Russians permanently on the Danube even as partners. Frederick William IV proved evasive; his policy would be one of 'strong neutrality.' Taylor writes : 'Neither of the two German rulers could bring themselves to point out that Russia's withdrawal from the principalities was the first condition of any co-operation; and withdrawal would have made cooperation unnecessary.' Thus 'once the Eastern Question was raised, the Holy Alliance was a ghost, no more.'[150]

But even the ghost alarmed the western powers, though they reacted in different ways. Napoleon III wanted to accept in good faith the moderation which Nicholas I had evinced and to call off the conflict on the basis of a new version of the Vienna Note which Buol had prepared. The British government rejected Buol's proposals and ordered the fleet to pass the Dardanelles. They were convinced that Austria and Russia had planned a partition of Turkey, and, further, they wanted to assure the French emperor of the reality of the British alliance. The latter thereupon dropped the 'Buol project' and ordered his fleet to follow the British.

Even so, hopes of a pacific solution were not dead. The Czar announced that it was not he who had declared the war: his troops would refrain during the winter from taking the offensive: the principalities, however, Russia must continue to occupy; not necessarily for annexation, but as a guarantee of her adversary's good faith[151]

But the Turks possessed no such 'material guarantee' for the good conduct of Russia, whose mere presence in the principalities they deemed as in itself an outrageous affront. They defeated the Russians, having crossed the Danube, at Oltenitza in the first pitched battle of the war.

Mortifying as was the news of this Turkish victory to the Czar, it at any rate appeared to him a complete release from his pledge to refrain from taking the offensive. On November 30, the Turkish squadron on its way from the Bosphorus to Eatoum was assaulted in the Turkish harbour of Sinope by the Russian fleet, and blown out of the water.[152]

This was a challenge to the maritime powers, with their fleets at Constantinople supposedly to protect the Turks. It produced a wave of indignation throughout England, and was regarded as a breach of the Czar's engagement to refrain from taking the offensive. The 'massacre' of Sinope was decisive in its effect on British public opinion: it was the symbol which cleared all doubts. The war-party in the English Cabinet, hitherto restrained by the premier, now definitely came to the fore. Unfortunately too at this juncture, the French Emperor was enthused with a fresh desire to do something spectacular with the fleets.[153] He threatened that, if necessary, he would act alone, and the British Cabinet was pushed into decision.[154]

In the end, a word may be said of the outraged religious feelings and the newly awakened patriotism of the Turks. The religious feeling of Paris is known to have excited fanaticism at Petersburg, but the frenzy of religious fervour awakened at Stambol is often forgotten.

Temperley describes the situation thus:

> On September 25, Constantinople learned that the Czar had refused all the Turkish amendements to the Vienna Note. The very next day the Grand Council met. Its members... passed to their deliberations through the streets crowded with soldiers flourishing modern weapons and with bravos flourishing ancient ones, with dervishes praying aloud for vengeance on the infidel... Everyone knew of Nesselrode's violent interpretation of the Vienna Note. The other great powers were thought to condone it. Stratford himself was suspect. As the debates proceeded, the naked ugly face of fanaticism peered forth. Not a man dared to oppose the general feeling... In the end with absolute unanimity, 'a recourse to war has been declared indispensable.'
>
> ... The Sultan himself had inspired or permitted the decisions of the Grand Council. If he now wished to set them aside he would be ... placing himself in opposition to the chief notabilities of the empire. Compliance might save him from immediate danger of war, but only at the risk of disturbing the public tranquility and finally losing both his throne and his life. The reasoning was sound. The Sultan had gone too far to draw back. He speedily assented to the decision of the Grand Council for war, to which the *fatwa*[155] of the *Sheikh-ul-Islam*[156] gave legal sanction. Once the fatwa had been issued, it was irrevocable. The Sultan himself could not then have stopped the declaration. He might have delayed it. But he did not wish to do so. His throat might be cut by his own subjects if he showed hesitation. He preferred war to insurrection, and fighting foreigners to fighting his own subjects.[157]

VII

The Crimean War thus, was the result of miscalculations and muddle rather than deliberate aggression by any party. It was a war caused by ill-considered threats which personal and national prestige insisted had to be made good, by a 'show of force' which unexpectedly and tragically turned into the use of force by indecision, shortsightedness, and public hysteria. Diplomacy struggled valiantly to avert the war, but failed for lack of diplomats and because of flared-up passions among all the protagonists. The nature of conditions in the Near East made some sort of action imperative and the cumulative momentum of resulting developments pushed things to the extreme. Napoleon III's need for prestige, to strengthen his internal position, was an important factor. Because the prestige was sought at the expense of Russia, the Czar was determined to reassert himself at the expense of France. This position as defender of the Orthodox Church complicated matters. Despite warning from Edouard Thouvenel[158] that for Russia the question was one of life or death, it is certain that Louis Napoleon III did not fully realize that Nicholas I could not retreat.[159] The vacillation of Aberdeen misled the Czar and deceived him on the possibility of an effective Anglo-French alliance. That Russian policy depended to a large extent upon British relations with France was clear. Nicholas I read reports of mistrust in Great Britain over the establishment of the second empire and that the British were debating the possibility of a French invasion. There were also rumours that Louis Napoleon III really had designs on Belgium.

We must remember further that Brunnow did not report to the Czar conditions and things as he actually saw them, and the latter felt justified in continuing to think wishfully that an alliance between Great Britain and France was unlikely. Brunnow was a very keen observer, he understood the effect of public opinion on the British government, and the making of Anglo-French *Entente Cordiale* could not have escaped his notice. It is probable that he knew his monarch too well to think the report of an ambassador would deter him from his resolution.[160] If the Czar had understood British institutions better, or if the tougher Palmerston had been incharge of British foreign policy in 1853, things might conceivably have been different. His view that 'to threaten a European war was the best way of rendering Nicholas I less war-like'[161], carries weight.

Even so, some real issues were involved. Though Nicholas I did not intend to destroy Turkey immediately, the Menshikov demands–which deeply disturbed the British government–manifested a policy of extensive Russian interference in Turkish affairs. If Turkey were to be turned into a Russian satellite,

Russia would before long emerge as a dangerous naval power in the eastern Mediterranean; and London could not contemplate with equanimity this growth of Russia's power. Further, Britain was sensitive to the international commercial rivalry in the Near East. In fact, 'the Ottoman Empire was an enigma because of the inter-related political, strategic, economic, religious, nationalistic and imperial problems which it presented', problems which baffled statesman.[162]

Also in both the western countries, a large section of public opinion was bitterly hostile to Russia. The reason for this was essentially ideological. Nicholas I was hated as the 'gendarme of Europe', the commander-in-chief of all the reactionary forces which in 1849 had prevailed against the forces of liberty. He was considered 'an anachronism in the new Europe.'[163] This ideological rift made the Czar's actions suspect. Finally, even those who had no sympathy for any sort of liberalism were impressed by the apparent might of Russia. The failure of revolution in 1849 had caused the Czar to overrate his strength and to act more boldly in Europe: it had also caused the European governments to overrate him. Since 1849, the balance of power had appeared to be upset in a Europe which was beginning to interpret the diplomatic catchword of the balance of power in a new and more dangerous manner, owing to the telegraph and the rapidly growing railway system. It was time to call a halt to the great eastern power. Napoleon III's dictum, 'who is to have Constantinople? That is always the crux of the problem'[164], supplies the vital clue to the Crimean War.

NOTES AND REFERENCES

1. Harold Temperley. *England and the Near East : The Crimea* (London, 1936), p.9.
2. J.A.R. Marriott. *The Eastern Question*, 4th edn., (Oxford, 1940) p.249; Bernadotte E. Schmitt, 'The Diplomatic Preliminaries of the Crimean War', *Am. Hist. Rev.*, 25 (October, 1919), p.36; Nassau William Senior, *Conversations With M. Thiers*, M.Guizot and *Other Distinguished Persons during the Second Empire*, 2 Vol., (London, 1878), Vol. I, p.214.

3. Schmitt, 'Dip. Prel.', *Am. Hist. Rev.*, pp.36–37. One of the best summaries of each country's guilt is presented in Temperley, *Eng. Near East*, pp.507–13.
4. Brison D. Gooch. 'A Century of Historiography on the Origins of the Crimean War', *Am. Hist. Rev.*, 62 (1) (October, 1956), p.33.
5. Gavin Burns Henderson, *Crimean War Diplomacy and Other Historical Essays*, Glasgow University Publications No. 68 (Glasgow, 1947), p.99.
6. Alyce Edythe Mange. *The Near Eastern Policy of Emperor Napoleon III*, Illinois, Studies in the Social Sciences, No. 25 (Urbana; Univ. Press, 1940), p.14; vide also *The Cambridge History of British Foreign Policy, 1783–1919*, A.W. Ward and G.P. Gooch (eds.) (New York, 1922–23) Vol. 2, pp.340–76. F.T.O. Hearnshaw and W.F. Reddaway accept this thesis.
7. J.A.R. Marriott. *The Eastern Question* (Oxford, 1940), p.242.
8. Written in 1862, but not published till 1878: English translation, 1882.
9. Sergei Mikhailovich Goriainov. *Le Bosphore et les Dardanelles*, (Paris, 1910), p.92.
10. The Most brilliantly vicious indictment of Napoleon III is to be found in Alexander W.Kinglake's *The Invasion of the Crimea* (6 Vol.), London, 1863–80), In his famous chapter 14 (Vol.1 pp.142–209) he depicts Louis Napoleon as the master conspirator, resorting to violence to further his egocentric ends. 'Many writers' as B.D. Gooch observes 'still accept this view and it has continued, despite a growing body of revisionist scholarship favouring Louis Napoleon' : Brison D. Gooch *The Origin of the Crimean War*, Problems in European Civilization (D.C. Heath and Co. Massachusetts, 1969), p. 8.
11. 'Qu'on nous pardonne de nous etre arretes avec quelque complaisance a ces jours de ja lointains de 1853, les derniers ou la diplomatie francaise ait parle un langage digne d'elle... ' Pierre Francois Gustave de la Gorce, *Histoire du second Empire* (7 Vol.) (New York : Reprint of the edition published in Paris 1899–1905, 1969), vol. I, p. 216.
12. Edmond Bapst. *Les Origines de la Guerre Crimee: La France et la Russie de 1848 a 1854* (Paris, 1912).
13. Karl Marx. *The Eastern Question* (London, 1897).
14. Vernon John Puryear. *England, Russia and the Straits Question 1844–1856* (Archon Books, 1965, originally published 1931); Puryear, *International Economics and Diplomacy in the Near East* :

A Study of British Commercial Policy in the Levant 1834–53, (Archon Books, 1969 originally published 1935).

15. V.J. Puryear. 'New Light on the Origin of the Crimean War', *Journal of Modern History*, Vol. 3(2) (June, 1931), pp. 219–34.
16. F.A. Simpson. *Louis Napoleon and the Recovery of France* 3rd. edn. (Longman 1951), p. 217. 'It was the opposition, now in exile, that was bellicose: Victor Hugo poured contempt on Napoleon's 'cowardice'. Albert Guerard, Napoleon III (New York, 1966), p. 108.
17. And in such circumstances Poland before and Persia afterwards could testify to the accuracy of the imperial diagnosis.
18. Vide infra, p. 43.
19. E.H. Nolan. *The History of the War against Russia*, 2 Vol. (London, 1857), I, Vol.I, p.5; Robert Sencourt, *Napoleon III : The Modern Emperor* (New York, 1933), pp. 145–46.
20. Simpson, *L.Nap.Rec. France*, pp. 217–23.
21. The consequences are well known and momentous. Austria lost the friendship of Russia, never again to secure it permanently; but no compensating support was gained from England and France.
22. 'In the literature of the Crimean War there does not exist a comprehensive analysis of this fundamental aspect of Anglo-Russian relations in the nine years which preceded the conflict in the Crimea. The reason is obvious: the agreement was secret and verbal. Certain parts of the conversations which inaugurated the secret understanding were committed to writing, however, in a formal document known as the Nesselrode Memorandum of 1844, and later there was an exhange of ministerial letters and other correspondence in acceptance of the tenets of this Memorandum. These papers were guarded carefully while the agreement was effective, moreover, on account of the extreme secrecy necessary in an arrangement which excluded France, through a sheer preponderance of power, from a share in the ultimate partition of Turkey. They were not made available even to statesmen in the respective British and Russian cabinets or to their diplomatic representatives, much less to historians. When the agreement collapsed, prior to the outbreak of the Crimean War, the letters of acceptance and the correspondence immediately concerned were eliminated from the British archives, records, leaving only the Memorandum–in itself not intelligible except

through conjecture on account of its unilateral character. The set of pertinent documents in Russia was hidden carefully in the archives and was not rediscovered until the twentieth century. Hence historians have treated the whole subject in a fashion which all but eliminated consideration of the Anglo-Russian secret agreement of 1844 as an element of importance preceding the Crimean War. The sum of available information on the problem prior to 1908 consisted of an official publication of the text of the Nesselrode Memorandum in 1854, parliamentary diatribes against the makers of it after the outbreak of war that year, a letter in Baron Stockmar's Memoirs published in 1872, spasmodic outburts in the memoirs of certain British statesmen of the period Malmesbury, for example—in themselves inadequate to trace the history of the negotiations, and sketchy paragraphs of suspicion in a few historical treatments—notably that by Tatishchev in 1886. In 1908 the discoveries of S.M. Goriainov, director of the Russian archives, were published in St. Petersburg, and in 1912 an English publication of the documents was made. Since that time the British archives on the period of the Crimean War have been opened for inspection, revealing several unpublished documents having a direct bearing upon the problem. It now is possible to trace, with historical accuracy, the outlines of the origin, making and collapse of the secret agreement ... 'The conclusions inevitably have led to a new interpretation of the whole of Crimean War diplomacy': Puryear, *Eng. Rus. Str. Ques.*, pp.2–4.

23. 'Clearly the latter alternative, a partition of Turkey had been the major Russian thesis from the eighteenth century, and the adoption of the policy of preserving Turkey was in contrast to what usually is called the "historic mission" of the Czars. It is this problem which is not well understood... In the first half of the nineteenth century, and notably after the peace of Adrianople, Russia consistently maintained a vigorous policy of preservation of the Turkish Empire as it was then constituted.' ... The three great Powers most interested in the Question of the Straits before 1853 were Russia, England and Austria, The direct interest of the two eastern European empires is evident ... while Britain's interest came logically from her naval and commercial strength and the location of India ... Austria had no active policy in the Straits from 1815 to 1854 ... Hence the concern for diplomatic history largely

centres about the activity of the only two powers. 'In general, it is clear from incontrovertible Russian sources, notably the archive researches of Professor F.F. Martens, that the Imperial government at St. Petersburg reversed the policy of Catherine II' regarding Turkey : Ibid, pp. 4–7 vide Temperley, *Crimea*, p. 273.

24. Ibid, pp. 1–6 (Puryear)
25. Ibid, pp. 22–23.
26. Ibid, p. 21.
27. N. Dascovici says 'The Straits Convention was the first European act which made a barrier to Russian ambitions in the Orient', cited by Ibid, n.1 p. 36.
28. Puryear, 'New Light on the Origin of the Crimean War', *Journal. Mod.Hist.* pp. 221–22.
29. Ibid, p. 223.
30. Ibid, p. 224 (A section of the Nesselrode Memorandum of 1844, cited by Puryear).
31. Ibid, p. 225.
32. Ibid, pp. 224–25.
33. Ibid, p. 226. The wording of the treaty of Munchengratz is, in Puryear's words, 'defective in regard to the partition of Turkey, because it stipulates that an agreement on the details of succession is to be effected only after the dissolution of the Ottoman Empire' Puryear, *Eng. Russia St,. Ques.;* p. 22. For the text of the secret interest of the treaty, vide Ibid, Appendix B, p.435. It may be added: 'Two important points were not agreed upon in 1844: (1) The ultimate possessor of Constantinople and the Straits was not fixed, but Nicholas specifically excluded Russia, England, France, or a reconstructed Byzantine Empire ...(2) The time at which the agreement was to be completed through an arrangement of terms for the succession to Turkey was not definitely stated. The qualification simply was "in advance of dissolution'. This became a matter of controversy in the crisis of 1853, and was the British basis for nullification of the alliance. These factors would convince any Russian pessimist that Nicholas steadily relinquished his control of traditional Russian policy from 1829 onward: that Austria gained at Munchengratz, the powers in general gained in 1840 and 1841, while England was the distinct beneficiary in 1844. The Russian optimist, on the other hand, might well conclude that Nicholas pursued a consistent and well defined policy aiming at a peaceful

solution of the most difficult Russian foreign problem and the most hazardous of Anglo-Russian friction zones.' Ibid, p. 56.

34. Puryear, *'New Light'*, *J.Mod. Hist.*, p. 227.
35. Henderson, *Crim. Dip.*, pp. 34.
36. Temperley, *Crimea.* p. 257.
37. Puryear, *Eng., Rus., Str. Ques.* p. 139.
38. Temperley, *Crimea*, pp. 255–57; Michel T. Florinsky, *Russia : A History and an Interpretation* (New York, 1953), 2 Vol. pp. 849–50; Seton-Watson R.W. *Britain in Europe*, 1789–1914 (New York, 1937), p.205, Affairs in the Near East were thus in a state of delicate "suspense" which was upset by the vigorous revival of French claims regarding Holy Places.
39. Hugh Seton-Watson. *The Russian Empire 1801–1917* (Oxford, 1967), p. 310.
40. Temperley, *Crimea*, p. 513.
41. Ibid, pp. 385 and 513.
42. Marx, *Eastern Question*, pp. 14-19.
43. In his day Marx was virtually alone. No voice added documented support to his analysis until 1931 when Puryear's *England Russia, and the Straits Questions* appeared. Here Puryear summarized the exhaustive study which was to follow, *International Economics and Diplomacy in the Near East.* R.J. Kerner regarded the latter work as the 'first thorough analysis' of the economic background of the Crimean War': Puryear, *International Economics*, p.15. R.W. Seton Watson *Britain in Europe,* and Temperley did not seriously accept Puryear's economic analysis.
44. Puryear, *Eng., Rus., Str. Ques.*, pp. 75-76.
45. 'But that unilateral conclusion', in Puryear's words, 'did not contemplate what England might think of what France did in Western Europe at a time when Russia was evading a categorical pronouncement on the ultimate disposition of Constantinople and the Straits. Herein seems to lie the basis of the collapse of the secret agreement of 1844'. *'New Light'*. *J.Mod. Hist.* pp. 231–32. Moreover, it was not high statesmanship and good policy to ignore completely a great power in such important matters as the future of Turkey.
46. Puryear, *Eng. Rus. Str. Ques.*, p. 86.
47. Ibid, pp.87–88. Yet this acceleration was not constant, and in some years natural mishaps caused reverses.
48. An impossibility for England while the grain laws were in force : Ibid, pp. 88–89.

49. Ibid, pp. 89, 90 and 93.
50. Ibid, p. 94.
51. Ibid, p. 102. Florinsky holds a different view. He states that the export of wheat 'had increased from 1825 to 1850' but it still remained relatively insignificant, and further, that there is nothing to indicate that grain exporters had any part in determining the government's near eastern policy'. Florinsky *Russia II*, p.864.
52. Puryear, *Eng. Rus. Str. Ques.*, p. 102.
53. 'The Anglo-Turkish convention of navigation and commerce signed at Balta Liman on August 16, 1938, may be said to be the initial official activity in an English plan of commercial expansion in Turkey as an answer to Russian political penetration and commercial growth.... The treaty specifically provided for the passage of British merchant vessels through the Dardanelles and Bosphorus 'with the least possible delay' without charge for passage of British goods through the Straits, or for transshipment within the Straits ... The right of British 'purchase, removal and sale of Turkish growth, produce, and manufacture' was not to be restricted in any way, the sole obligation being to remit duties as paid by the most favoured class of the Sultan's subjects, all trade monopolies expressly being abolished ... The treaty of Balta Liman atonce became the basis of European commercial relations with Turkey. The main obstacle to unanimity was Russia. One of the benefits to accrue to England from the treaty with Turkey was the right to procure gain from Turkish provinces without restriction or interference by Turkey'. Ibid, pp. 118–21.
54. Ibid, pp. 102–4.
55. Ibid, p. 104.
56. Ibid, pp. 125–26.
57. Ibid, pp. 127–28.
58. Ibid, p. 128.
59. Ibid, p. 129.
60. Ibid, pp. 131–35. By 1851, the export of grain from Moldavia and Wallachia was equal to that exported by Russia. With this in mind, the Russian occupation of the principalities has added significance.
61. Conflicting opinions are held on Austria's economic interests. While Vernon Puryear finds that Austria had more interests in common with Great Britain than with Russia (*Eng., Rus., Straits Question*, p. 135). Eugene Horvath points out that Austria

had never co-operated with Great Britain in tariff matters and had even forced closure of Ottoman ports to the British (*Origin of the Crimean War :Documents Relative to the Russian Intervention in Hungary and Transylvania, 1848–1849*), Budapest, 1937, pp. 290–92. However, Austrian interest in Danubian shipping is obvious, and it was she who really forced the evacuation of the principalities.

62. Puryear, *Eng. Rus. Str. Question*, pp.136–38. With no apparent regard for the imposing array of evidence which Puryear presented, A.J.P. Taylor found his ideas 'novel, if unreliable' (*The Struggle for Mastery in Europe 1848–1918*, Oxford, 1954), p.595), while E.L. Woodward thought that Puryear's work contained 'interesting material, though the conclusions drawn are often controversial' (*The Age of Reform*, 1815–1870, Oxford, 1938), p.621. Russia's government accepted in 1940, most of the economic factors as basic. The official Soviet account of nineteenth century Russia saw the Eastern Question as 'above all a question of economic and political mastery in the eastern part of the Mediterranean and the adjoining basins'. It pictured industrial capitalism as intensifying a feverish drive for foreign markets and noted that Great Britain was ahead of the rest of Europe in this respect.' An uninterrupted advance in the Near and Middle East became an essential condition to the growth of English capitalism'. This pursuit of markets ran headlong into the 'military and feudal aggressions of Czarism' and the Crimean War was one of its products'. M.V. Nechkina (ed.) *The History of Russia* (Moscow, 1940; Eng. trans. Oliver J. Frederiksen and Bernard Pares, Ann Arbor, 1953), Vol. II pp.315, 405–06, 'An old diplomatic cliché describes the eternal contest between Russia and England as 'the duel of the elephant and the whale'. Albert Guerard, *Napoleon III : A Great Life in Brief* (New York, 1966), p. 109.
63. Kinglake, *Invasion*, I, p. 309.
64. Simpson's comment *Nap. Rec. France*, p. 382. The problem has been to ascertain what specific source material Alexander Kinglake used for his attack on Louis Napoleon. Kinglake himself tells us that 'this portion of the book' (which contains invectives against Napoleon) 'must rest upon statement of one who had good means of knowing the truth.' He promises to leave the clue whereby his statements 'may be traced by their sources' (*Invasion*, p. 24). However, he did not leave any

such clue, and his most telling charges against Napoleon are undocumented. It is possible that Kinglake's work was written with a prejudice against the French Monarch. In 1868, Kinglake was unseated from parliament on charge for bribery: an insinuation of a character defect. He was ill–disposed to Napoleon as he had competed unsuccessfully with him for the favour of 'Miss Howard': B.D. Gooch, '*Cent. Hist. Cr. War. Am. Hist. Rev.* p. 45.

65. Emilie Olliver.
66. That is the unification of Italy.
67. Simpson, *L.Napoleon*, p. 230.
68. Emile Bourgeois '*Early Years of the Second Empire* : *Crimean War Origins*', *Gooch, Crimean War*, p. 42.
69. 'A strong policy in the east and a sure alliance with Britain would give the young Second Empire the international prestige is badly needed if it was to survive'. H. Hearder, *Europe in the Nineteenth Century 1830–1880* (London : Longman, 1966), p. 145.
70. Simpson, *L. Nap. Rec.* p. 231.
71. J.P.T. Bury. *Napoleon III and the Second Empire* (London, 1964), p. 70.
72. T.A.B. Corley. *Democratic Despot : A Life of Napoleon III* (London, 1961), p. 146.
73. Ibid, pp. 146–47.
74. 'Michel Chevalier, a friend of the Emperor and a Saint-Simonian, saw the eastern Mediterranean as comparable to the Middle West of the United States, then being developed as a granary for the whole world'. Ibid, p. 147.
75. Taylor, *Str. Mast. Eur.*, pp. 46–47.
76. But as B.D. Gooch states : 'That Louis Napoleon's motive was to maintain and increase support for his programme from the clerical party ... has been clearly established'. *Cent. Hist. Origins, Am. Hist. Rev.*, p.36.
77. Corley, *Dem. Des.*, pp.149. A firm stand by Napoleon in 1850 had brought Palmerston 'to his sense during the Don Pacifico affair', Ibid, p.150.
78. Puryear, *Straits Question*, p.242–44. It may be added that Napoleon 'had early divined the value of the sea power in a dispute of this kind. During 1852 he twice ordered the powerful screw-propelled battleship *Charlemagne* up the Staits to Constantinople ...'The appearance of the *Charlemagne* conveying her mass of artillery and men against the most

rapid current of the Bosphorus by the sole power of the screw, produced a great effect here... The Turks, gaping incredulously at this evidence of French armed might, immediately saw—'how a little instrument, like the screw, affects, and will probably still more affect, great political events'. Corley, *Dem. Des.* p. 150.

79. Gooch, *Cent. Hist. Origins, Am. Hist. Rev.*, p. 47; Temperley, *Crimea*, p. 508.
80. Sencourt, *Napoleon III*, p. 150.
81. Guerard, *Great Life*, p.108; Corley, *Dem. Des.* p. 154.
82. 'Surely it was foolish as M. Hugo suggested, to begin one's empire with 1812'. Simpson, *Nap. Rec.*, p. 243.
83. 'But Thiers favoured the alliance'. Ibid, p. 244.
84. Ibid, p. 244.
85. 'He is so anxious to preserve peace, that the desire to see the question terminated may overrule all other considerations', Cowley Papers : Cowley to Clarendon, November 11, 1853, 'cited by Sencourt, *Napoleon III*, p.149; Simpson, *Nap. Rec.* p. 244.
86. Ibid, pp.244–45; Sencourt, Ibid, pp. 149–50.
87. Schmitt, *'Dip. Prel. Cr. War' Am. Hist. Rev.*, pp. 53–54.
88. Simpson, *Nap. Rec.*, p. 246.' Admitted by the Russian *Diplomatic Study, Invasion*, p. 284. 'It seems positive that he expected great results from it, and that he was much hurt at the failure of this personal effort at conciliation.' And even by Kinglake; *Invasion*, p. 399' Ibid, n. 2.
89. Edmund B.D.'Auvergne, *Napoleon the Third : A Biography* (New York, 1929), pp. 142–43.
90. L.C.B. Seaman. 'Causes of the Crimean War' *The Origin of the Crimean War*, Gooch, p. 1.
91. 'The Czar supposed that the time had come to invoke the Holy Alliance in earnest. What he wanted from Prussia and Austria was their armed neutrality' : Taylor, *Struggle*, p. 59.
92. Seaman, *Causes*, p. 1.
93. R.W. Seton-Watson, The Origin of the Crimean War, *Origins*, Gooch, p. 24.
94. Seaman, *Causes*, p. 1.
95. Seton-Watson, *'Origins'*, Gooch, p. 26.
96. Seaman, *'Causes'*, p. 2.
97. George MacMunn, *The Crimea in Perspective* (London, 1935), p.10.
98. W.Baring Pemberton. *Battles of the Crimean War* (New York,

1962), p. 16. According to Philip Warner, 'The Csar... felt that Britain was going through a pacifist phase and was unlikely to use force' *The Crimean War: A Reappraisal* (Arthur Barker Limited, 1972), p.11. Moreover, as Nicholas V. Riasanovsky states, "The entire complex and unfortunate entanglement with Great Britain contributed hugely to Nicholas I's mistaken belief that his near Eastern policy had strong backing in Europe", *Nicholas I and Official Nationality in Russia,* 1325-1855 (University of California Press, Berkeley, 1961), p. 252.

99. Seton-Watson '*Origins*' p.28. 'At a later stage Russell defended this action (the appointment of Stratford), in his driest manner. On previous occasions, he said, Aberdeen and Palmerston had each had an opportunity of getting rid of Stratford, but had each reappointed him to Constantinople ... He was only imitating them in reappointing Stratford a third time ... On previous occasions, when not serving as a diplomat, Stratford had made things awkward for the government of the day by going into parliament. Aberdeen thought he would not be formidable at a distance. It was typical politician's error. Stratford was far more powerful on the Bosphorus than he could ever be at Westminster'. Temperley, *Crimea,* p.313.

100. 'The most thorough treatment by an English historian' of the Stratford role, as Hugh Seton-Watson states 'is H.V. Temperley, *England and the Near East : the Crimea*'. 'The distinguished Soviet historian the late Professor E.V. Tarle ... takes a diametrically opposite view ... Tarle sees fit to describe Temperley's version as' an impudent lie' ... In Tarle's veiw Temperley deliberately ignores the' double book keeping' of Palmerston and Aberdeen ... Aberdeen's pacific and Palmerston's belligerent attitude were an elaborate pretence ...'The two men played their roles in agreement with the aim of deceiving the Czar and trapping him in a disastrous war' : Hugh Seton-Watson, *The Russian Empire,* p. 318 n.2. There seems absolutely no justification for the latter presumption of E.V. Tarle.

101. Warner, *The Crimean War*, p. 11.

102. Alfred Rambaud, *A popular History of Russia from the Earliest Times to* 1882, trans by L.B. Lang, ed. enl., by Nathan Haskell Dole (Boston, 1882), Vol. 3, p. 105.

103. Simpson, *Nap. Rec.* pp. 232–33.

104. J.A.R. Marroitt, *The Eastern Question*: An Historical Study in European Diplomacy (Oxford, 1917), p. 231.

105. Temperley, *Crimea*, p. 314. Both Taylor (*Struggle*, p. 53) and Henderson (*Cr, War Dip*).p. 9, exonerate Stratford. R.W. Seton-Watson finds his influence at Constantinople baneful. He cites Prince Albert who told Stockmar, 'Lord Stratford fulfils his instructions to the letter, but he so contrives that we are constantly getting deeper into a war policy': '*Origins*', pp. 29–30.
106. Simpson, *Nap. Rec.*,p. 391.
107. The development of the hatred of Russia of Nicholas I in one major European nation is presented in Gleason, *The Genesis of Russophobia in Great Britain*, vide also T. McNally '*The Origins of Russphobia in France* : 1812–1830. *American Slavic and East European Review*, Vol. 17 (2), (1958), pp. 173–89.
108. Riasanovsky, *Official Nationality*, p. 250. In the words of Alfred Rambaud : Nicholas 'was a man of another age, an anachronism in the new Europe', *Hist. Russia*, Vol. 3, p. 172.
109. Gooch, *Cent. Hist. Origins*, p. 35.
110. William Miller. *The Ottoman Empire and its Successors 1801–1927* (London, 1966) pp.199–200, (rev. enl. edn.) of *The Ottoman Empire 1801–1913*). The latest capitulation had granted, among other things, permission to all "Christian and hostile nations" to continue to visit Jerusalem under the protection of the French Flag: Mange, *Near East. Pol. Nap.* p. 10
111. 'The Orthodox naturally gained ground during seasons when pure reason directed French Foreign policy, for it is a result of anti-clericalism in Latin countries that it cripples the national influence otherwise exercised by the Church abroad' Miller, *Ott. Emp.*p. 200.
112. Ibid, p. 201.
113. Mange, *N. East. Pol. Nap.* p. 19; Temperley, p. 466. According to Temperley 'Apart from the older prescriptive rights of the Orthodox there is another weak point in the French case. Their privileges under the treaty rights of 1740 were, in fact, mostly abandoned in 1757. The Orthodox resumed their old position and the latin claims dropped. The attempt to revive them ninety years later was dangerous. For, if obsolete or abandoned claims can thus suddenly be revived and enforced, there is an end to all diplomacy and to prospects of peace. As regards ... the Russian view that the Treaty of Kuchuk Kainarji gave them the rights of a religious protectorate is certainly too extreme': *Crimea*, p.466. For Article VII of the Treaty and its Interpretation vide Ibid, pp. 467–69.

114. Ibid, p. 304.
115. Woodward, *Age of Reform*, p. 245.
116. 'After all he had tolerated a pretty strong British influence at Constantinople in the preceding decade', Taylor, *Str. Mast*, pp. 49–50.
117. Ibid, p. 50.
118. Rambaud, *Hist. Russia*, Vol. 3, p. 67.
119. Temperley, *Crimea*, p. 271.
120. 'The next year, when the war fever was at its height, one Blue Book published the Seymour conversations and the next one published the Nesselrode memo of 1844. ... Both were interpreted by an angry press as revealing the dark ambitions of a foreign despot. The Czar's wickedness was stressed in historical textbooks. He was the tempter whom England had virtuously withstood, and the legend of his wickedness was bequeathed to posterity'. Ibid, pp. 272–78.
121. Ibid, p. 279.
122. Rambaud, *Hist. Russia*, p. 99.
123. Ibid, p. 105.
124. Taylor, *Str. Mast. Eur.*, p. 52.
125. Simpson, *Nap. Rec.* p. 225.
126. Reddaway, *Camb. Hist. Br. For. Pol. II*, p. 348.
127. R.W. Seton-Watson *'Origins'*, p. 27.
128. French Foreign Minister.
129. Bourgeois, *'Cr. War Origins'*p. 44.
130. The Czar explained later that 'his conduct would have been different but for the error into which he had been led' cited by Taylor, *Struggle*, p. 52.
131. Ibid, p. 51–53, Temperley, *Crimea*, pp. 301–5.
132. Taylor, Struggle, p. 53.
133. Temperley, *Crimea*, pp. 296, 303 and 511.
134. Reddaway, *Camb. Hist. Br. For. Pol. II*, p. 365.
135. Florinsky, *Russia II*, p. 869.
136. B.D. Gooch, *'Cent. Hist. Origins'Am. Hist. Rev.*, pp.40–41.
137. B.D. Gooch, *'Cent. Hist.'* pp.41–42; Simpson, *Nap. Rec.* p. 227.
138. Taylor, *Struggle*, p. 54.
139. Rambaud, *Hist. Russia III*, p. 114.
140. Ibid, p. 115.
141. 'On general grounds the declared object of the allies, the maintenance in its integrity of the Ottoman Empire, was one which harmonized admirably with the Austrian policy of immobility' : Simpson, *Nap. Rec.* 251.

142. Taylor, *Struggle,* pp. 54–55. For details of Austria's role on the eve of the war Paul Schroeder's *Austria, Great Britain and the Crimean War,* may be consulted.
143. 'Though verbally slight, the modifications were not really trivial. The most important was the addition of the words 'by the sublime Prote' to Turkey's undertaking to observe the terms of previous treaties as to 'the protection of the Christian religion.' This addition excluded the assumption of a Russian protectorate'. Simpson, *Nap. Rec.*, p. 228.
144. Rambaud, *Hist. Russia III,* pp. 121–22.
145. Simpson, *Nap. Rec.*, p. 235. 'In fact Clarendon throughout displayed an accuracy as a prophet which is the measure of his condemnation as minister of foreign affairs. The real excuse for retaining Stratford at Constantinople would have been either ignorance of his probable course of action or approval of it. Of these, Clarendon could plead neither. He was wise, not after the event. but during it and before. Open-eyed he suffered himself to be led into the ditch'. Ibid, p. 235.
146. Ibid, pp. 235–36.
147. R.W. Seton-Watson *'Origins'*, p. 29. Seton-Watson says; 'on this point there is abundant evidence from inside the British cabinet'; Ibid, vide Miller, *Ott. Emp.* p. 210 (That is 'the baneful influence of Lord Stratford upon the Turks).
148. Simpson, *Nap. Rec.*, p. 236; Hugh Seton-Watson, *Rus, Empire,* p. 319.
149. Taylor; *Struggle*, p. 56. Temperley seeks to acquit his subject of war guilt saying that the Note was objectionable and its rejection reasonable. However, his arguments are untenable. For details Simpson, *Nap. Rec.*, pp. 592–93.
150. Ibid, p. 57.
151. Simpson, *Nap. Rec.*, p. 237; Taylor, *Struggle,* pp. 57–58.
152. Simpson, *Nap. Rec.*, pp. 237–38.
153. Ibid, pp. 238–39.
154. Taylor, *Struggle,* pp. 58–59. For 'Napoleon III's explanations on his Threat to Act Alone' vide Temperley, p.515. In the words of Taylor : 'The maritime Powers were drawn along from first to last by the need to prove to each other their mutual good faith. The British had led the way up the Straits in October; now the French pulled the British fleet into the Black Sea'. *Struggle,* p.59.
155. The written decision of a mufti (an expounder of Muslim religious law) on some legal point in the interpretation of the

Koran. In Temperley's words : 'Decision by a jurisconsult on a point of law. Official confirmation by the Sheikh-ul-Islam of the acts or decrees of the Sultan.' p.387.

156. 'Chief or elder of Islam, interprets the law and issues the *fetwa* sanctioning the Sultan's acts'. Ibid, p. 388.
157. Ibid, Temperley, pp. 360–61.
158. French Ambassador at Constantinople (1855–60), Foreign Minister (1860–62).
159. Gooch, *Cent. Hist. Origins*, p. 37. 'There is evidence that Napoleon bitterly regretted having raised the question' of the Holy Places. Temperley, *Crimea*, p. 508.
160. Gooch, *Cent. Hist. Origins*, pp. 55–57.
161. H.C.F. Bell. 'The Home Secretary in Foreign Affairs' *Origins*, Gooch, p. 37.
162. Puryear, *Int. Ec. Dipl. N. East*, pp. 1–2.
163. Rambaud, *Russia*, p.172. cf. supra n. 1, p. 39.
164. 'Le fond de la grande question est toujours la Qui aura Constantinople?' So wrote Napoleon to his ambassador in St. Petersburg in May 1808: 'Lettres inedites de Napoleon Ier, Leon Lecestre, Tome I, No. 286': Quoted in A.J. Barker *The War against Russia 1854–1856* (New York, 1970), pp. 1 and 318.

Chapter 6

British Liberalism in India

Before and After The Mutiny of 1857

The revolt of 1857 exercised a decisive influence on British attitude to India quite outside specific questions of land policy or social reform. It changed the whole nature of the British position in India by producing in them racial animosities and an attitude of social exclusiveness which undermined the confident reformism of the pre-Mutiny era, leaving a disillusioned liberalism and an authoritarian paternalism. This was the intangible but pervasive psychological influence of the mutiny; and it provided an atmosphere of distrust and distaste for things Indian and under this flourished the disillusioned and authoritarian liberalism of James Fitzjames Stephen.

Even before the mutiny, the British in Indian had formed themselves into a close community, which was almost, indeed, like a separate and superior caste in the Indian tradition. As a small ruling group, they were very much aware of their difference from the swarming masses around them, but it was hastened by the arrival of English wives and an evangelical religion with its stern disapproval of Indian ways. The women from home and a stricter moral code worked together to put an end to the old free and easy association of British officers with native society. By 1840's this ruling class in India had become small, quite self-contained communities, which had little contact with Indians except as servants and sepoys. This exclusiveness did not, however, imply any feelings of racial antagonism or arrogant superiority. It was more of a benevolent paternalism in which the natives were trusted and their growth and education solicitously cared for. As George Otto Trevelyan remarked in 1864, 'Thirty years ago the education of the people of the country was the favourite subject of conversation and occupied the spare time of men who had little enough of that commodity ... and the hopes entertained concerning the future of the race were proportionate to the interest which it excited.' This attitude of trust and confidence in the Indian was reflected in the assumptions of pre-mutiny British policy, which looked forward to the regeneration of Indian society on a British model. Towards this end the social, educational, and religious policies of the pre-mutiny decades had conduced; 'at the commencement of 1857, humanity and philanthropy were the order of the day.'[1]

Across this idyllic scene the mutiny cut a violent swath. The faithful bearer and the complaisant sepoy overnight became rapacious murderers, and the British found themselves unable to trust anyone with a brown face. This sudden revelation of Indian character produced an immediate and complete reaction against the old benevolence and solicitous affection. The bonds of race were drawn tighter, as survival itself was seen to depend upon it; and the English from their entrenchments looked out at the Indians with increasing bitterness and hatred. Racial antagonism grew by leaps and bounds as the English saw themselves betrayed by those whom they had trusted, and this ill feeling was exacerbated beyond all measure by reports of atrocities and massacres, when English women and children were murdered in cold blood. Suspicion and dislike soon reigned supreme and expressed themselves in the cry for indiscriminate vengeance against all natives especially after the Cawnpore massacre in particular. G.O. Trevelyan relates a story, which in its grim humour is only too indicative of the alienation and hatred wrought by the mutiny :

> Two soldiers fresh from England reported a mutiny of the bullock drivers ... The story was simple : 'I see two Moors talking in a cart. Presently I heard one of' em say, "Cawnpore." I knowed what that meant; so I fetched Tom Walker, and he heard 'em say

> "Cawnpore." And he knowed what that meant. So we polished 'em both off.[2]

The Cawnpore massacre did not itself, however, account for the extreme vengeance which the English took in India, an unprincipled revenge which led them to kill suspicious looking natives at random with no pretence of a trial. Underneath the provocation of the massacres lay hidden elements of the English character, which surged forth as 'English fury' when the precarious nature of their position in India was made clear. When their implicit faith in the trustworthiness of the Indians was destroyed, they struck out madly and wildly in all directions in an attempt to regain some sense of security and stability in an alien society which they no longer understood but only feared. John Lawrence saw how the mutiny as a war of races, in which the English were hopelessly outnumbered, had called forth 'all the bad passions of our nature.'[3] Writing to Canning on December 4, 1857 he commented that 'In the English, as in all imperial races, there is an element of the wild beast. There is a disposition in the hour of provocation or panic to indulge in wild reprisals, or even deliberate revenge, long after all justification, or even excuse, for it has ceased.'[4] Canning himself had earlier noticed 'the violent rancour of a very large proportion of the English community against every native Indian of every class.' He wrote to the Queen that 'There is a rabid and indiscriminate vindictiveness abroad, even amongst many who ought to set a better example, which it is impossible to contemplate without something like a feeling of shame for one's countrymen.'[5]

In the first impulse of terror and panic Englishmen at home were generally roused to emulate their brethren in India. 'Intense compassion, intense wrath, the injured pride of a great nation, combative propensities ... surged in upon the agitated community.'[6] Even Macaulay was swept along by the current and found himself admitting that 'It is painful to be so revengeful as I feel myself. I, who cannot bear to see a beast or bird in pain, could look on without winking while Nana Sahib underwent all the tortures of Ravaillao. And these feelings are not mine alone.'[7] In England this mood of vengeance wore off quickly, however, and was succeeded by a clamour for clemency quite as strong as the previous demand for vengeance.

Lord Canning, however, never succumbed to such vengeful passion but stood firm against this trend from the beginning. For this he earned himself the title 'Clemency Canning', at first applied bitterly by those who disapproved his moderate policy, but later applauded as an epithet worthy of a great statesman. Canning's steadfast opposition to the cries for vengeance sprang from his perception of the fact that British rule could not continue in India if no native was ever to be trusted and a black skin was to be considered the mark of a murderer. As he wrote to Earl Granville:

> In Bengal we are still dependent (mainly) upon the goodwill (I cannot say affection) and interests (well understood by themselves) of the natives. Suppose that hostilities train on ... will it not be the part of a wise government to keep such a population as that of the three great lower provinces in a loyal frame of temper? Can you do so if you proscribe and scout as untrustworthy whole classes?
>
> I will pursue no other policy than that which I have been following : not only for the reason of expediency and policy above stated, but because it is just. I will not govern in anger ...
>
> Impossible it is that for generations to come Englishmen should be more than a handful (more or less small) in this vast country, and how powerless for good they will be (to say nothing of the risks and other drawbacks of their position) if they ... take up as their means of defence the mistrusting, branding, and proscribing of whole classes. We shall do what no government has ever done in any country (so far as I know) without repenting it.[8]

Canning therefore refused to punish indiscriminately 'whether by wholesale hangings and burnings, or by the less violent but not one jotless offensive course of refusing trust and countenance and favour and honour to any man, because he is of a class or creed.' In measures designed to restore order, therefore, Canning made no distinction between Europeans and Indians. All newspapers were subjected to the same censorship; and no blanket exception in favour of Europeans was made in the law prohibiting the carrying of arms. This naturally exasperated the Calcutta European community, who raged furiously against Canning and even presented a petition to the Parliament demanding his recall. But Canning stood by his policy and even widened it in 1858 by declaring a large scale amnesty for all rebels except leaders of the mutiny and those implicated in the murder of Europeans.

The racism against which Canning set himself meant nothing less than the permanent consignment of the Indian to an inferior, and the Briton to a superior place in India simply by virtue of race alone. As he wrote to the Queen in his letter of September 25, 1857 :

> It is no exaggeration to say that a vast majority of the European community would hear with pleasure and approval that every Hindoo and Mahomedan had been proscribed, and that none would be admitted to serve the Government except in a menial office. That which they desire to see is a broad line of separation, and of declared distrust drawn between us Englishmen, and every subject of your Majesty who is not a Christian and who has a dark skin.[9]

Such a policy Canning would not countenance, if for no other reason than that 'if that spirit makes head, isolated Europeans will not find the provinces safely tenable–as heretofore.' He realized that it would be political suicide to attempt to govern India if its inhabitants were treated 'with sweeping contempt and hatred.' Thus he concluded that 'it will be a bad day for us when the word "nigger" becomes naturalized in India.'[10]

Canning's successful advocacy of clemency did not, however, alter the fact that the racial warfare and virulent animosities of the mutiny had permanently changed the position of the British in India. No amount of clemency could undo the disillusionment and distrust which the mutiny had produced. Nor could it cover up again the stark necessities of Britain's military and political position. The atmosphere of trust and confidence in the Indian within which the pre-mutiny reformers operated had completely disappeared and could not be recovered. W.H. Russell, *The Times* correspondent in India, saw this clearly during his visit in 1858:

> The mutinies have produced too much hatred and ill feeling between the two races to render any mere change of the name of the rulers a remedy for the evils which affect India, of which those angry sentiments are the most serious exposition ... Many years must elapse before the evil passions excited by these disturbances expire; *perhaps confidence will never be restored;* and if so, our reign in India will be maintained at a cost of suffering which is fearful to contemplate.[11]

The disillusionment and distrust engendered by the mutiny shattered the reforming optimism so characteristic of the pre-mutiny decades. It was impossible to work up any enthusiasm for reform in an atmosphere embittered by memories of race war and indiscriminate vengeance. As Trevelyan commented, 'who can wonder that among a generation which has gone through such a crisis philanthropy is somewhat at a discount.' He pointed out that 'men who have lost their fortunes and friends and health in the desperate struggle' could hardly be expected 'to set to work ... promoting plans for the benefit of their conquered foe.'[12] The net result was, as Bartle Frere remarked in 1861, that :

> In these five years we have changed from an aggressive and advancing power to a stationary one; the sympathy which Englishmen ... felt for the natives has changed to a general feeling of repugnance if not of antipathy; instead of a general feeling of content with their Indian lot ... the English here are, almost generally, openly discontented, disinclined to remain here, or to care for India, and disposed to look at things in any but an Indian light.[13]

But the British government did not abdicate its moral responsibilities to the people of India after the mutiny. Neither Canning nor the generality of civil servants were willing to join the English settlers in indiscriminate vengeance and proscription. Still the experience of the mutiny affected the attitude of the civil servant. The dissolution of trust and confidence did not stop him from doing his duty by the native population, but 'that duty is no longer a labour of love.' In *The Competition Wallah* , G.O. Trevelyan saw this aspect of the mutiny experience with remarkable clarity :

> It is greatly to the credit of the civilians that they have harkened to the voice of humanity and equity. The natives cannot accuse their governors of neglect or injustice ... But the new order of things is not as the old. The children of the soil are no longer regarded with the lively interest, the credulous partiality of yore ... Men cannot at will cast aside the recollection of those times when all was doubt and confusion and dismay: when a great fear was their companion, day and night ... The distrust and dislike engendered by such an experience are too deeply rooted to be plucked out by an act of volition.[14]

The negative after-effects of the mutiny not only destroyed all reforming zeal, it brought Britain's position as an imperial and ruling power into the open. Henceforth military defence and political stability had to be subjects of overriding concern. 'That struggle irresistibly reminded us that we were an imperial race, holding our own on a conquered soil by dint of valour and foresight,'[15] Trevelyan remarked. Britain saw that it could no longer trust the natives to support the government, and that imperial rule could only be maintained by taking those military precautions which political security dictated in a conquered and unfriendly land. In the Army this meant reduction of native troops and the concentration of all artillery in English hands; in general it meant that attention must be given to building up a purely English position in India for defence against future revolt. A dispatch of March 9, 1858 from the Secret Committee to the Governor General forthrightly stated the policy enforced by the mutiny :

> The principle, if such it can be called upon which all our civil and military measures have for many years rested, has been that of implicit confidence in the natives. There seems to have been one universal belief that no danger could ever approach us ...
>
> That feeling of confidence has passed away; and for the erroneous principle upon which we have of late acted,—we deeply regret to admit it,—must be substituted to one of general distrust.
>
> The direction of roads, the selection of points at which rivers are to be bridged, the placing of cantonments, and even of civil stations, must be decided on military grounds.

> We must look back rather to the time of the Romans, and take lessons from them in the military occupation of conquered countries ... We are to become the possessors of one of the noblest Empires the World ever saw; and it would be to our eternal disgrace, if we omitted any measure of military precaution by which it might be preserved.[16]

In this post mutiny atmosphere now flourished a new and more pessimistic attitude which was totally without reforming zeal and laid great emphasis on the military basis of British power. Maintenance of their Indian Empire was henceforth Britain's primary concern, so consideration of political security and stability had consistently to take precedence over plans of moral and social reform. There now bred an avowed authoritarianism, which abandoned the radical hopes for Indian regeneration and accepted without moral qualms, permanent British rule based on force. The Indian could neither be trusted nor reformed, so he must be ruled; this was one of the great lessons of the mutiny. Britain believed that its moral duty would be fulfilled by providing a framework of law and order; further reform must be left to fend for itself on a laissez-faire basis.

Pessimism, conservatism, authoritarianism: these were the hallmarks of the British attitude to India in the post-mutiny years and soon permeated all fields of British Indian policy. Pessimism and conservatism made themselves felt in a cautious attitude toward questions of social reform and in a talukdar settlement for Oudh. Authoritarianism made itself felt in Britain's pre-eminent concern for military and political security, and in the refusal to place Indians in positions of governmental responsibility.

Yet the lessons of the mutiny and the necessities of the post-revolt political situation cannot alone account for the ready acceptance by liberals of this shift from optimism to pessimism, from reforming zeal to stern authoritarianism. England during the 1860's was rapidly becoming democratic under the leadership of Gladstone. In the eyes of educated liberals, Gladstone's variety of liberalism, with its appeal to a popular electorate, seemed to pose a threat to property and to an efficient well-run government. The more democratic England became, the more apparent its evils to the liberal intellectuals. They soon lost all faith in the educatability of the people and viewed the masses with pessimistic distrust, an attitude of mind which, when turned to India, reinforced the lessons of the mutiny.

To counter the chaos of democracy the intellectual liberals relied on authoritarian rule by an educated elite. Not popularly elected officials but competitively chosen administrators were to be placed in power and allowed to govern efficiently, protecting property and enforcing law impartially. This concept in turn, when applied to Indian affairs, resulted in the idealization of the Indian Civil Service and ready acceptance of a permanent authoritarian rule over the uneducated masses by the British. Thus the pessimism and authoritarianism produced by the revolt were both reinforced and justified by a simultaneous disillusionment among English liberals as to the value of democracy.

The two greatest exponents of disillusioned liberalism, both in England and in India, were James Fitzjames Stephen and Sir Henry Maine. As political philosophers they formulated this concept of liberalism in a logical philosophical fashion; and at the same time as Indian officials they gave post-revolt policy the impress of their thought. Both Stephen and Maine were Law Members of the Viceroy's Council;[17] both men extolled the merits of the autocratic Government of India; and both detested the liberalism of Gladstone and J.S. Mill, which they felt had an unwarrantedly optimistic faith in human nature and in liberty.

In order to analyze the imperial attitudes of these disillusioned liberals, it is first necessary to understand the basic political and social theories they developed. A term to describe these men is in itself hard to come by. Liberalism is far too vague and inclusive, but it is what they called themselves, at least until they became Liberal Unionists in the 1880's. They were nevertheless harshly critical of Gladstonian liberalism, with its sentimentality and democratic leanings. Their liberalism was that of an intellecutal and propertied elite, who were primarily concerned for administrative and legal reform so as to produce efficient economical government. In a sense they can be called old liberals or utilitarians; because they held to the Benthamite principles of an active government wielded by disinterested intelligence. They followed Bentham in his Hobbesian insistence on law and order, enforced by the sanction of a powerful legislator. For Stephen as for Bentham happiness and not liberty was the end of government. Stephen illustrates that authoritarian element in utilitarianism which traced its ancestry to Bentham, as opposed to the sentimental libertarianism represented in Gladstone and J.S. Mill.[18]

These intellectual liberals did not, however, share Bentham's optimistic view that the masses would be able to pursue their own rational self-interest, once trained by good government and education, and that they could thus be trusted to implement the greatest happiness principle in a democratic government. Men like Stephen and Maine had become disillusioned as to the possibility of an enlightened popular electorate and so clung to the ideal of scientific government by experts. In England they attempted to preserve the privileges of property from the onslaught of a levelling mob, enfranchised and manipulated by wire-pullers and parties. In India they had their doubts regarding the intellect of the masses and so affirmed the necessity of permanent British rule. They did not possess the optimistic vision of Macaulay and Charles Trevelyan, who trusted the Indian educated classes and worked with them as partners in the great civilizing process. The ultimate measure of their separation from the earlier utilitarians is indeed seen in their stress on authoritarian imperialism in contrast with the willingness of Macaulay and Trevelyan to grant India eventual self-government. So, inspite of the fact that these liberal intellectuals accepted the Benthamite concept of government as a powerful and efficient machine, they lacked the optimistic reforming zeal of a true utilitarian.[19] Their disillusionment and pessimism define a distinctive brand of liberalism and one which was to be dominant in India during the post-mutiny decades.

One of the ablest parliamentary champions of this group was Robert Lowe, whose residence in Australia had rendered him particularly suspicious of democracy. Leading the small band of Liberal Adullamites against the Reform Bills of 1866 and 1867, Lowe forthrightly stated the political convictions of these intellectual liberals:

> Because I am a liberal, and know that by pure and clear intelligence alone can the cause of true progress be promoted, I regard as one of the greatest dangers with which this country can be threatened a proposal to subvert the existing order of things, and to transfer power from the hands of property and intelligence to the hands of men whose daily life is necessarily occupied in daily struggle for existence.[20]

Such apprehensions of impending doom formed a basic motif in disillusioned liberal thought. In a sense, fear of a forthcoming social revolution provided the emotional underpinning for their otherwise highly intellectualized liberalism; as Stephen noted in 1886:

> The old maxims of government, the old liberalism in which I used to believe ... have been and are being given utterlyup, and in their place is being erected a tyrannical democracy, which will change the whole face of society, and destroy all that I love or respect in our institutions ... It is the story of the Paradise Lost of Liberalism.[21]

The two main targets against whom Stephen and his associates levelled their fire were Gladstone and J.S. Mill, both representative of the popular liberalism they detested. Gladstone—The People's William—was to them the archetype of a demagogue, kowtowing to King Mob. His brand of liberalism, Stephen felt, had thrown over the necessary discipline and sense of obedience, and had taught the people that there was no such thing anywhere as legitimate authority. Gladstone's exaggerated principles of abstract justice and international morality likewise found little sympathy among these intellectual liberals, who were more moved by considerations of national interest and patriotism. Stephen dismissed the Midlothian campaign as 'Gladstone's spouting' and wrote to Lytton on February 23, 1885 that 'England seems to have become one huge Gladstone with a conscience like the liver of a Strasburg goose.[22]

Inspite of these divergences from the spirit of Gladstonian liberalism, many of these old liberals maintained their affiliation with the Liberal Party for a surprisingly long time, often until the Home Rule crisis. Robert Lowe was Chancellor of the Exchequer in Gladstone's 1868–74 government, while Stephen stood for the parliamentary constituency of Dundee in 1874. By this time, however, his alienation from liberalism was so complete that Leslie Stephen, his brother, remarked that had he won, 'he would have been comically inappropriate as a Gladstone supporter.'

Stephen reserved his main fire for J.S. Mill. To demolish Mill's philosophy of liberalism was Stephen's avowed purpose in writing *Liberty, Equality, Fraternity* in 1873. Through this attack on Mill, Stephen's own political philosophy found its fullest expression. But beyond that, the controversy between Mill and Stephen is significant because of its repercussions in Indian policy. Not only Mill and Stephen were political opponents in England, but each represented a corresponding school of thought on Indian matters as well. Generally speaking, Mill was a member of that optimistic reforming group dominant before the mutiny who hoped to remodel India in England's image even down to representative government and who saw in the peasants instruments of social revolution. Mill had an optimistic faith in the potentialities of human nature, very much like that of his father and Bentham. Stephen, on the other hand, believed that most men are ineducable and require permanent authoritarian rule. He thus had much less faith in the possibilities of social reform. To a large extent therefore, the differences between the general political thought of Mill and that of Stephen greatly illuminate the similar changes in mid-century liberal attitudes towards India.

Stephen's mental outlook is largely constructed out of an intellecutal affinity to Benthamism, a Puritan evangelical belief in the depravity of human nature, and experience of a well-run despotism in India. Certain of his Benthamite affinities have already been noted, among them a hatred of sentimentalism, and an attempt to judge things by the utilitarian touchstone. 'In a certain sense I am myself a utilitarian, with happiness as an external standard. Expediency is the footing for the value of a moral rule.'[23] And of course, in Benthamite fashion, it was not each individual's own happiness, but the greatest happiness of the greatest number, at which the moralist and legislator was to aim. In clear distinction to Mill's assertion of the intrinsic values of individual liberty, Stephen did not hesitate to state that 'the object is to get the people to accept the legislator and moralist's view of happiness, not to make people happy in their own way'–a version of Bentham's belief in the artificial identification of interests through the coercive sanctions of a despot.

Stephen even found common ground with Mill insofar as both were strict utilitarians. He always adhered to the philosophical and ethical principles expressed in Mill's *Logic* and even regretted that Mill in his later years appeared to have abandoned these principles for 'sentimental' ones: 'I am calling foul of John Mill in his modern and more humane mood–or rather I should say in his sentimental mood–which always makes me feel that he is a deserter from the proper principles of rigidity and ferocity in which he was brought up.'[24] Stephen's decisive break with Mill dates from 1867, when Mill headed the Jamaica Committee investigating Governor Eyre's heavy-handed suppression of Negro revolt. Mill denounced Eyre for his 'revolting excesses of authority' and government of military license,[25] while Stephen extended sympathy to Eyre in his energetic defence of order.

Alienation from Mill combined with his evangelical background to bring Stephen into close personal friendship with Thomas Carlyle, a man temperamentally Stephen's exact opposite; for Stephen never ceased to be logical and practical, while Carlyle was a mystical and intuitionist thinker. Nevertheless Stephen and Carlyle alike detested the small shopkeeper mentality of the Manchester School, with its middle class materialism; and both took a patriotic pride in Britain and the Empire, as against the anti-imperial free trade philosophy of most liberals. These men, despite their temperamental differences, were drawn together by a common contempt for slovenly, haphazard, hand-to-mouth legislation and by a love of vigorous personal administration. And both came to despise the British constitution and the parliamentary system.[26]

In India Stephen found his ideal realized : strong autocratic government by experts, who acted on their convictions and did not 'have to trim their sails to catch the gusts of sentiment in a half-educated community.' It is indeed remarkable how much of Stephen's philosophy has its roots in his experience in India during his years as law member of the Council (1869–72). As a ruling body, the Indian Civil Service, with its elitist spirit and administrative efficiency, excited Stephen's enthusiasm; 'I never saw anything to equal their general level of zeal, intelligence, public service, and vigour.'[27] The Anglo-Indian Government he considered 'the best corrective in existence to the fundamental fallacies of liberalism ... the only government under English control still worth caring about.'[28] In fact Stephen found in the British method of governing India a political ideal applicable elesewhere–even in England; and this ideal was of course in marked contrast with that of those democratic liberals who demanded the exportation of British representative institutions to India. Stephen explicitly acknowledged the debt the political ideas of liberty, equality, fraternity owed to his Indian experience, calling the work 'little more than the turning of an Indian 'lantern' on European problems.'[29] He stressed further this connection of his Indian experience and his political theory in a foreword dedicated to Sir John Strachey, a close friend and member of the Indian Civil Service :

> My Indian experience strongly confirmed the reflections which the book contains, and which had been taking shape gradually in my mind for many years. The commonplaces and the vein of sentiment at which it is levelled appeared peculiarly false and poor as I read the European newspapers of 1870–71 at the headquarters of the Government of India.

The book was planned in India, and partly written on the voyage home.[30] *Liberty, equality, fraternity* is, then, compounded out of Stephen's Indian experience and his dislike of Mill in his later 'sentimental' libertarian stage. In improving morality, Mill considered liberty essential, with coercion restricted to the protection of society from physical harm. Any system of morality based on coercion could easily perpetuate wrong or inadequate morality, since it stifled the discussion which alone produced improvement. Freedom of discussion and action, even various experiments in living, were therefore essential for moral progress. Although Mill claimed to be a utilitarian, he did in fact go beyond it and exalt individual liberty above coercive sanctions as an intrinsic good; for moral improvement could only be accomplished by free discussion and persuasion, not by coercion.[31] Mill thus claimed, in his 'self-regarding principle', that there should be a sphere of activity within which the individual should be sovereign and free from all external interference.[32]

Fitzjames Stephen, on the other hand, saw that in a utilitarian society individual liberty must be subordinated to such systems of morality and religion as are seen to be good for mankind. If morality is socially desirable, which Stephen thought then the only way by which it is practically possible to act upon them at all is by compulsion or restraint. The utmost conceivable liberty which could be bestowed upon them would not in the least degree tend to improve them.[33]

> The great defect of Mr. Mill's later writings seems to me to be that he has formed too favourable an estimate of human nature ... tacit assumption that the removal of restraints tends to invigorate character. Surely the very opposite of this is the truth. Restraint and coercion in one form or another is the great stimulus to exertion. Almost every human being requires more or less of coercion and restraint as astringents to give him the maximum of power which he is capable of attaining.[34]

Since society is shot through and through with coercion, governments ought not hesitate to apply force in pursuit of moral aims. Certainly there is no other way of improving ignorant masses:

> I think that governments ought to take the responsibility of acting upon such principles, religious, political, or moral, as they may from time to time regard as most likely to be true, and this they

> cannot do without exercising a very considerable degree of coercion.[35]

Stephen posits a utilitarian society of people seeking their individual self-interest, but so hopelessly ill-informed that a Benthamite government of the enlightened few, through positive sanctions of law and morality, must force them to a recognition of the greatest happiness. He challenges liberal belief in democratic government by discussion with the assertion that the strong will always rule, inspite of democratic forms.[36] In fact Stephen positively exalts war, conflict, and discipline as beneficial forces in society and as productive of progress: a doctrine abhorrent to Mill and his supporters. Concurrent with this is a natural respect for Hobbes doctrine that order and security, not liberty and equality, are the primary functions of the state, which require a singly ultimate sovereign capable of imposing discipline. It must not be supposed that Stephen, in emphasizing the fabric of coercion underlying society or the values of obedience to a superior, intended to justify tyranny. He always considered the ruler to be restrained by a strong sense of moral duty, but there is no doubt that he effectively defined liberty away.

This concept of a state unashamedly built on force, engaged in applying the moral ideals of its rulers to ignorant masses, was realized by the British rule in India. The Government of India did not hesitate to enforce what it believed right (e.g., religious toleration, suppression of *Sati*), and in so doing it was representative of belligerent civilization, secure in its moral supremacy.

> They (the British in India) found, as everyone who has to do with legislation must find, that laws must be based upon principles, and it is impossible to lay down any principles of legislation at all unless you are prepared to say, I am right, and you are wrong, and your view shall give way to mine, quietly, gradually, and peaceably; but one of us must rule and the other must obey and I mean to rule.[37]

Stephen's conviction that it is the duty of government to enforce order and its views of what is morally valuable, in preference to any abstract notion of religious liberty, evoked a comparison of the British Empire with the Pax Romana of the first century. In particular, Stephen attempted to justify Pilate's crucifixion of Jesus, insofar as Pilate conceived it necessary for the maintenance of the peace of Palestine:

> The position of Pontius Pilate was not very unlike that of an English lieutenant governor of the Punjab. It would not be difficult, nor would it be altogether fanciful, to trace a resemblance between the manner in which the Jews would strike Pilate and the manner in which the Afghans or the Sikhs strike us ...
>
> If it is said that Pilate ought to have respected the principle of religious liberty as propounded by Mill, the answer is that if he had done so, he would have run the risk of setting the whole province in a blaze. No British officer could possibly consider supporting a religious reformer—a Guru or Imam—in India, instead of maintaining British authority.[38]

In contrast to India, Stephen saw in England an unwillingness among liberals to admit such a potent fact of human nature as permanent inequalities of mankind, arising out of the relative illiteracy of the lower classes. Recognition of this fundamental inequality of men should produce not a doctrine of universal suffrage but a 'social hierarchy corresponding as nearly as possible to the real distinctions between men.' Stephen cites approvingly the Indian caste system, which 'though possessed of considerable power of assimilating new ideas, is stable and conservative to a degree utterly unknown in Europe.'[39] Such an ideal is, he concedes, unattainable, for universal suffrage cannot be stopped. Still there is 'no need to praise it as we go'; instead one must start erecting bulwarks against its effects. The party system and parliamentary omnicompetence are the main instruments of democratic government, and it is their waste and inefficiency which must be checked. Stephen is appalled by the way party government wastes talent and destroys any approach to permanence, continuity, or system in the management of public affairs. As for the value of self-government through parliament, Stephen sees no 'moral effect of habitually doing things ill'; for such a system gives power to incompetent electioneering ministers rather than skilled specialitsts. To obtain a more vigorous and efficient central control, Stephen would set up a powerful and independent executive composed of professional administrators and severed from party struggles. In fact 'to give the country really efficient government would require us to restore a considerable degree of real power to the king.'[40] But Stephen would be content with simply an infusion of bureaucratic specialization and discretionary authority, on the order of the Indian Civil Service, into a government still under the general control of parliament.

Stephen's political theory was throughout that of the intellectual liberal; his aim was not to increase the democratic element in government, as the people were incapable of performing duties requiring skill and intelligence, but rather to increase the bureaucratic element, which could alone operate government efficiently. Idealization of the government of India stemmed directly from its operation on these principles. Administrative reform, not political reform, was the goal of Stephen, Lowe, and Maine.

Sir Henry Maine reached many of the same conclusions as J.F. Stephen, but he used a different method–a historical method of political science. Applying the doctrine of evolution to human institutions, Maine traced the society of industrial England from its origins in primitive Aryan village communities through the slow growth of custom. That institutions grow and are not made by the fiat of a legislator was the tenor of his historical theory; and it enjoined acquiescence in things as they are–a conservative suspicion of legislative change and rapid progress. He thus came to find himself in agreement with Stephen in disliking popular government, even though Stephen bases his attitude on a Benthamite theory of strong efficient government, while Maine developed it from a historical consideration of aristocratic progress and democratic despotism.

Maine's theory of history is ultimately based on the same pessimistic view of the potentialities of human nature that motivates Stephen. Most men dislike change; whatever progress has taken place, has been the work of aristocratic minorities. Democracy is not feasible, certainly it is not the irresistible force in history which the radicals claim. If popular government were instituted it would produce a tyranny of mediocrity and ignorance, whose only action would be an anarchic attack on property and privilege. Maine was vehement in his denunciation of democratic Benthamism with its optimistic view of human capability:

> Bentham's theory implied that the truths he saw could be seen by all. In fact they are visible only to the few–the intellectual aristocracy. By his rule we ought to have a perfect system of government; but taking it in connection with the fact that the multitudes include too much ignorance to be capable of understanding their own interest, it furnishes the principal argument against democracy–that it is not conducive to progress; minorities alone have a desire for real change.[41]

Indeed, it is to aristocracy that we must look, for 'from that form of political and social ascendancy all improvement has hitherto sprung.'[42] In this respect Maine was even more conservative than Stephen, for he believed that a hereditary aristocracy could be the enlightened ruling class, whereas Stephen's ideal was the competitively-selected bureaucracy of the Indian Civil Service.

Maine was more motivated by fear of socialism than was Stephen, a fact partly accounted for by the decade which separates their political writings,[43] but which certainly warps his theory of history with its scientific pretensions. To attack the socialists Maine is constrained to find in freedom of contract and several, as opposed to joint property the ultimate key to progress and civilization. His earliest work, *Ancient Law*, (1861), develops the theory that 'the movement of progressive societies has hitherto been a movement *from status to contract*.'[44] Or, as he forthrightly stated in a speech on an Indian Contract bill of December 17, 1862: 'All modern progress seems to be intimately connected with the complete freedom of contract and in some way mysteriously dependent on it.'[45] As Grane Brinton pungently comments, 'History taught Maine what reason had taught Bentham.'[46]

This victory of contract over status, of the free individual over customary obedience, goes hand in hand with the victory of property in severalty over joint property. Man's earliest social organization, Maine claims, was the village community, with property held in common and divided equally. As evidence of its survival to the present, Maine points to the village communities of North-West India and to the Hindu joint family. In the progressive societies of the West, however, joint property has been superseded by property in severalty, 'a more modern institution.' Maine attempted, of course, to justify private property as the culmination of civilization by reference to his scientific historical laws–a kind of Marxism in reverse–but the result shows only too clearly his stake in the established order:

> It is not the business of the scientific historical enquirer to assert good or evil of any particular institution. He deals with its existence and development, not with its expediency. But one conclusion he may draw properly from the facts bearing on the subject before us. Nobody is at liberty to attack several property and to say at the same time that he values civilization. The history of the two cannot be disentangled.[47]

Thus Maine was led to an attack on the democracy which spawned socialism, and to a position alongside J.F. Stephen. The masses are so ignorant and disorderly that they cannot be trusted with political power. 'When a multitudinous majority is called to the government for the purpose of promoting its own happiness, it now becomes evident that ... there is no security that the multitude will know what its own happiness is, or how it can be promoted.'[48] If political power were cut up into small pieces, they would be swept into the hands of the wire-puller and party caucus. *Popular government,* like liberty, equality, fraternity, is permeated with this fear of a democratic future; it is a *cri de coeur* for efficient government by a responsible minority.[49] Unlike Stephen, Maine also saw in constitutional checks and balances, a way of moderating democratic despotism. The House of Lords and the United States Constitution drew praise from Maine, which Stephen, an advocate of more direct power in the hands of a few, did not so readily accord.

Maine's sojourn in India as law member of the Council

(1862–68) provided experiences which buttressed, and often shaped, his political and historical theories. As with Stephen, the example of administrative efficiency set by the Indian Civil Service was congenial to Maine's temperament. In fact, when combined with his insight into the horrors of English democracy, his vision of the virtues of the Indian Government practically drove him into Toryism:

> If there were an ideal Toryism I should probably be a Tory. But I should not find it easy to say which party I should wish to win now ... The truth is, India and the Indian Office make one judge public men by standards which have little to do with public opinion.

As Lord Morley commented :

> Scientific lawyers have seldom been very favourable to popular government, and when the scientific lawyer is doubled with the Indian bureaucrat, we are pretty sure beforehand that in such a tribunal it will go hard with democracy.[50]

In India, moreover, Maine saw 'the great repository of verifiable phenomena of ancient usage and ancient jurisdical thought, which Roman law connects with the legal ideas of our own day.'[51] Maine had adopted the new Aryan philology, which through Sanskrit linked up the Indo-European languages and peoples. Thus he considered it legitimate to cite from Indian as well as Teutonic sources in building up his theory of historical progress in western society. India was indeed a part of this society, but a singularly retarded section, whose institutions–particularly the village community–therefore threw much light on the institutions of the West before it had been imbued with the spirit of progress : 'It [India] is a barbarism which contains a great part of our own civilization with its elements as yet inseparate and not unfolded.'[52] Although India offers potentialities for progress, it is still a primitive and conservative society.

India confirmed his belief that most men are conservative and that innovation must be handled with caution. Attacking the optimistic hopes of English radicals, Maine claimed that progress was no more inevitable than democracy, for 'vast populations, some of them with a civilization considerable but peculiar, detest that which in the language of the West would be called reform ... the Mohammedans, the Chinese ... the enormous mass of the Indian population. Enthusiasm for change is both rare and modern.'[53]

Holding such a view of the conservatism of human nature, Maine was not likely to take up optimistic plans for rapid social reform in India. It was a primitive society and a stable one, which could not readily be made over in a Western image. Macaulay's view of Indian intellect and education were different from Maine's. Benthamite reforms could not be facilely applied to an organic Indian society, whose customary bonds had not yet dissolved into contractual relationships. The force of tradition must be reckoned with in legislating for a primitive society. Maine was a caustic critic of the value of that deductive jurisprudence which made English theories of right and sanction a model for the Indian social system. As he remarked with regard to a proposed codification of the substantive civil law in India, in a speech of December 14, 1866 :

> This law is an excellent and equitable piece of legislation. But it could not be applied to the intestate succession of Hindus, Mohammedans, and Buddhists. It was as much as the empire was worth to impose a uniform law of succession on the country; each sect was entitled to its own law ...
>
> This was then a case in which the strong feeling of the people had compelled the Legislature to maintain a most complex system of law. The people of the country are wedded by custom and religious feeling to complex systems of law and they prided themselves on their usages in proportion to the complexity of those usages. If this were so, the foundation of Bentham's doctrine collapsed, and the doctrine itself had no application in India. The Legislature was estopped, by the conditions of our tenure of the country, from so simplifying the law.[54]

Maine did believe in the civilizing influence of codified law, and more generally in England's moral duty to bring progress to India. Progress as discovered by the Greeks, had invigorated Western society, and 'we Englishmen are now communicating it to India.'[55] But this vague sense of moral duty is common to all Victorians who considered England's role in India. Of much greater significance here is Maine's stress on the historical origins of society and on the stability and conservatism of human nature. A perception of the ignorant, perhaps destructive, character of the masses rather than a belief in mankind's inherent potentialities motivated Maine's political thought–a disillusionment and pessimism which flowered both in *popular government* and in his Indian policy. The contagion of progress was indeed to be injected into India, but slowly and under firm English direction.

The application of this new attitude towards Indian affairs in its most thorough fashion is the work of James Fitzjames Stephen. He developed theoretical foundations for much that was implicit in post-mutiny Indian policy by uniting the political ideals of intellectual liberalism and the facts of Anglo-Indian existence in a consistent theory. Their influences were felt in Indian policy for many decades. Based as always on England's conscious obligation to bring civilization to India by governing on European principles, Stephen's theory nevertheless accepts completely, without any moral qualms, the validity of an Empire founded on force and conquest. At the same time, he never hesitated to defend and justify the present value and future permanence of the British Government of India. For the moralizing of Burke, Macaulay, and Bright he had nothing but contempt; in the liberalism of Ripon and the Ilbert Bill he saw disaster.

Bright echoed much liberal sentiment when he denounced the Indian Empire, because of its foundation on conquest and ambition, as a blot on the English conscience. Since England had criminally conquered India by force, radicals claimed that British rule could only be justified by the assumption of a civilizing trust, owed to the natives by virtue of this conquest, and which must be discharged by educating the natives on self-governance.[56] Against all this Stephen protested vigorously, exalting the positive virtues of conquest and empire. In a letter of January 4, 1878 to *The Times*.

His [Bright's] hatred of military power, his fanaticism in favour

> of popular institutions incapacitate him from doing justice to the Indian Empire or to the men who administer it ... Bright's speech is not that of a fairminded opponent to a great institution; he heaps on what he hates reproaches which are utterly false...
>
> We, the English nation, can hardly degrade ourselves more deeply than by repudiating the achievements of our ancestors, apologizing for acts of which we ought to feel proud, and evading like cowards and sluggards the arduous responsibilities which have devolved upon us. Let us acknowledge them with pride.
>
> I deny that ambition and conquest are crimes; I say that ambition is the great incentive to every manly virute, and that conquest is the process by which every great state in the world (the United States) has been built up.

In a later article, Stephen reaffirmed his belief that 'there is no transaction in the history of England of which we have more just cause to be proud, or which anyone who cares for the reputation of England ought to be more anxious to perpetuate and carry out to a good end, than the establishment of the Indian Empire.'[57]

As an ardent imperialists, Stephen was naturally anxious to rehabilitate the eighteenth century founders of the Indian Empire. He wrote *The Impeachment of Elijah Impey* as an introductory essay on the subject in 1885; in it, with thorough and painstaking care, he showed how extravagantly inaccurate was the picture Macaulay had painted of Impey as a judicial murderer in his *Essay on Hastings*. Stephen intended to follow up the *Impey* with a new history of British India, in which he could properly extricate Hastings and Clive from the mire of crimes in which Macaulay and Mill, following Burke, had sunk them. But this dream was never realized. In any case Stephen's attacks on Macaulay were never so vitriolic as his denunciation of Bright, for Macaulay had the redeeming virtue of patriotism. Stephen appreciated the fact that Macaulay had cited Hastings, inspite of his crimes, as performing a useful and necessary role in the foundation of the Indian Empire.

Stephen rose to defend the character of the Government of India most vigorously during the controversy sparked by the Ilbert Bill in 1883. Seeing in the Ilbert Bill 'a determination to try to govern India upon principles inconsistent with the foundations on which British power rests', Stephen expressed his own views of the nature of the Government of India in a letter of March 1, 1883 to *The Times* :

> The Government of India is essentially an absolute government founded not on consent but on conquest. It does not represent the native principles of government, nor can it do so until it represents heathenism and barbarism. It represents a belligerent civilization, and no anomaly can be so striking or so dangerous as its administration by men, who at the head of a government founded on conquest, implying at every point the superiority of the conquering race ... and having no justification for its existence except that superiority, shrink from the open, uncompromising, straightforward, assertion of it.

Defence of Indian autocracy flows naturally from Stephen's general political principles, that 'men in general are extremely ignorant, and thus are likely to put political power to bad uses unless they submit to the guidance of those who know better than themselves.'[58] Absolute government, based on force not consent, is therefore essential if Britain is to perform its moral duty of introducing civilization into India. Such a moral duty implied, as Stephen readily acknowledged, 'an assertion of superiority' by the English–in much the same way that he asserted the superiority of the intellectual elite at home. Admittedly the Radicals were equally convinced of English moral superiority and of the need for an absolute government in nineteenth century India. But in the permanence of the absolutism and in the type of civilization it is to foster, the great gap separating democratic liberalism and Stephen's intellecutal liberalism becomes clear.

Stephen conceived that autocratic rule in Oriental States, 'where the natives are used to absolutism, are ignorant and under grovelling superstition', had an intrinsic validity which allowed England to maintain permanently an absolutist government in India.

> Absolute government has its own merits and conveniences; it is, so to speak, as legitimate a form of government as any other; if it exists, if it is well and successfully administered, and if it is

> suited to the circumstances and tastes of those amongst whom it exists, there is no reason why those who administer it should seek to substitue for it a representative government, or should feel in any respect ashamed of their position as absolute rulers, or desirous to lay it down. Much of the language used about the British Government in India implies ... the doctrine of the Divine Right of Representative Institutions, or of the Sovereignty of the People; it seems to assume that the exercise of absolute power can never be justified except as a temporary expedient used for the purpose of superseding itself, and as a means of educating those whom it affects into a fitness for parliamentary institutions ... I do not in any degree share in this view ... I do not think that the permanent existence of such a government as ours in India must in itself be a bad thing.[59]

How could Stephen reconcile this permanent absolutism with the educative duties of a belligerent civilization? He certainly has as glorious a conception of Britain's moral mission as might be desired. For instance, in his letter of January 4, 1878 to *The Times* :

> India is not simply a Campus Martius for Englishmen. The British power in India is like a vast bridge over which an enormous multitude of human beings are passing, and will (I trust) for ages to come continue to pass, from a dreary land of brute violence, ghastly superstition ... on the way to a country which is at least orderly, peaceful, and industrious ... and may be the cradle of changes comparable to those of the Roman Empire.

He stresses continually that the benefits England derives from India are not those of exploitation, but 'flow from the honourable enterprise of substituting civilization for barbarism throughout a great empire.' Yet the European principles which motivate this civilizing duty are singularly limited in scope. Although the earlier radicals were conscious of the moral value of codifying law, Stephen envisages England's duty as almost exclusively restricted to law and order. He even grows almost rhapsodic over the benefits conferred on India through government by law:

> The establishment of a system of law which regulates the most

> important parts of the daily life of the people, constitutes in itself a moral conquest more striking, more durable, and far more solid than the physical conquest which renders it possible. It exercises an influence over the minds of the people in many ways comparable to that of a new religion ... Our law is in fact the sum and substance of what we have to teach them. It is, so to speak, the gospel of the English, and it is a compulsory gospel which admits of no dissent and no disobedience.[60]

This preoccupation with the legal, perhaps also the economic blessings of Western civilization is in fact so great that Stephen only grudgingly makes room in his scheme for any general popular education at all :

> The task of the English in India is the welfare of the community, promoted by the introduction of the essential parts of European civilization into a country densely populated, grossly ignorant, steeped in idolatrous superstition ...
>
> Now the essential parts of European civilization are peace, order, the supremacy of law, the prevention of crime, the redress of wrong, the enforcement of contracts ... construction of public works, collection and expenditure of revenue to promote the public interest, interfering as little as possible with the comfort or wealth of the inhabitants, and the improvement of the people.[61]

If 'improvement of the people' is neglected, political education and self-government are now to be omitted from the programme altogether. In sharp contrast with the hopes of pre-mutiny liberals, Stephen considered such aspirations pointless if not actually dangerous. To the widespread post-mutiny distrust of the Indian, Stephen added his own conviction that government is based on coercion and operated by the enlightened few for the ignorant masses. The result was a drastic contraction in the kind of responsibilities implied by the doctrine of trusteeship. Macaulay and Mill had always viewed the grant of self-government as the culmination of Britain's moral trust in India.[62] Stephen vigorously denies it, affirming that political education is no part of the civilization England will bring to India; 'I do not share in the view that it is a moral duty on the part of the English nation to try to educate the natives of India in English ideas in such a way as to lead them to set up a democratic form of government.' Democracy is most unfortunately making an appearance in England. It must be kept out of India at all costs. This would be relatively easy, for 'the mass of the people are satisfied with our principles of government', were it not for 'the officious interference of English theorists.' He continues :

> If the British Government in India is ever seriously disturbed and ruined, it will be by reason of an agitation set up at the instigation of Englishmen against institutions with which the natives, if left to themselves, are perfectly satisfied, and which have conferred upon them, and will, if left alone, contine to confer upon them, altogether inestimable benefits.[63]

To bring civilization to India, then, is not necessarily to bring political consciousness in its train. The two are separable, and civilization is compatible with, in fact dependent on, continued absolute rule by Great Britain. This is patently untrue,[64] but it follows logically from the basic premises of Stephen's political thought. In attempting to remove political education from the English civilizing programme. Stephen illustrated admirably how widespread that disillusionment had become which had sprung up since the mutiny. The character of Indian Society and the very facts of human nature preclude any government but that of the English as an indispensable basis of improvement for India, not only now but for the foreseeable future, according to Stephen. England's moral duty to India implied not self-government, but permanent English rule—for India's own good.

Furthermore, it was hopless to contemplate any possible result accruing from political education in India except anarchy, a lesson which the impending democracy in England seemed to confirm. 'Democratic representative assemblies throughout India would soon make the country ungovernable and uninhabitable by Europeans without in any way benefitting the natives.'[65]

This conclusion was reinforced by Stephen's belief in the basic utility of force and coercion in society. The mutiny had shown the English that their government rested on military force; Stephen reiterated that 'it will never, in my opinion, be safe for the British Government to forget that it is founded not on consent but on conquest.' And Stephen saw no shame in admitting this fact, for the radical ideal of a government based on consent was quite impossible. There was, therefore, no need to take up the notion of a transient trust, which the earler radicals had felt obliged to do. It was entirely legitimate, indeed to India's advantage for Britain to maintain a permanent and firm dominion there, devoted to diffusing the values of Western civilization, excluding of course political education with its attendant evils.

Stephen was by no means the only spokesman of this post-Mutiny attitude, although he is doubtless the most vociferous. Sir Henry Maine agreed that England had a moral obligation to carry on a civilizing mission in India, and he was likewise certain that English control was essential for Indian well-being. With Stephen he deprecated educating young Indians by means of eighteenth century English literature, saturated as it is with party politics and one-sided discussions of India, since such study tends to raise up excessive and unwarranted political aspirations. However, instead of exalting despotism in Stephen's thorough-going fashion as a desirable form of government, Maine applied his historical method. Citing the disadvantages and drawbacks of representative government, and the caste divisions and despotic past of India, Maine concluded that popular government is impractical in India. He opposed the introduction of municipal self-government into the North-West Provinces as law member of the Council, in a speech on March 13, 1868; and he later wrote that its size disqualified India from working representative institutions successfully :-

> It seems to me that such large terms as self-government and responsible government must be discarded from all future discussions of changes in Indian political institutions. There is no reason to suppose that 200 million or 250 million men could govern themselves or enforce responsibility on the part of those governing them. Human experience affords us no ground at present for supposing that the institutions of popular government which have arisen ... and are still on their trial, are

> capable of being applied at all to numbers expressed by such figures.[66]

Sir John Strachey, a close friend of Stephen and an influentical member of the Indian Civil Service, was equally vehement in his denunciation of those 'sentimental philanthropists' in England and 'political agitators' in India who demanded political enfranchisement. By the time Strachey wrote this (1888), the formation of the Congress had clearly shown that educated Indians would be primarily moved by political aspirations. They refused to conform to the role laid out for them by the British, that of teaching their fellow countrymen to abandon customs and atrocious practices repugnant to civilization, within the framework of a benevolent British government. Strachey was discouraged to discover that :

> These gentlemen are at heart as intensely conservative as the mass of the population. They have no desire for social change. It is much safer to talk about political enfranchisement and it is easy in this way to obtain the applause of Englishmen who know nothing of the facts and difficulties ... but who have an undoubting faith that the so-called popular institutions are good for all men under all circumstances.[67]

Contemptuously dismissing the claims of 'Congress agitators, who pose as representatives of an imaginary Indian nation', Strachey cites approvingly the support offered by Muslim and other minority groups who need Britain to protect them from Hindu and Bengali domination. The improvement of India requires strong British rule, not the gratification of political aspirations:

> Not only in our own interests, but because it is our highest duty to India itself, we intend to maintain our dominion. We cannot forsee the time in which the cessation of our rule would not be the signal for universal anarchy and ruin, and it is clear that the only hope for India is the long continuance of the benevolent but strong government of Englishmen.[68]

In pursuit of the impossible policy of introducing civilization without encouraging political aspirations, Britain was obliged to denounce the products of its own Indian educational system as agitators, and to rely on the backward and communal minorities–a striking reversal of Macaulay's trust in the educated man, and a revealing commentary on the pessimism and disillusionment wrought by the mutiny era.

But these views did not go altogether unchallenged. The pre-mutiny liberal tradition of Macaulay and Trevelyan that Indians were fit for some political benefits was revived in the 1880's, largely under the influence of Lord Ripon, Viceroy during 1880–84. A Gladstonian liberal, Ripon was willing to place confidence in the educated natives : 'We have made them, let us use them for their good and our own.' Admittedly much of Ripon's liberal policy was guided by political considerations : 'how to deal with this newborn spirit of progress ... so as to direct it into the right course ... and prevent its becoming a serious political danger.' But he was aware that the introduction of European civilization would inevitably encourage political aspirations. These he did not wish away or denounce in the fashion of Stephen and Strachey; rather he was anxious 'to provide a legitimate outlet for the ambitions and aspirations which we ourselves have created by the education, civilization, and material progress which we have been the means of introducing into the country.'[69] Much as his policy was concerned with 'making the educated natives the friends, instead of enemies of our rule', Ripon was no advocate of permanent authoritarian rule and did not shrink from the ultimate consequences of trusting the educated native. Democracy, in Ripon's mind, was not the ogre it was for Stephen and Maine. In him certainly persisted much of the radical pre-mutiny attitude of mind, along with the sympathies of Gladstonian liberalism.

Ripon was, however, fighting a losing battle during his Vice-royalty. The forces of distrust and despotism were too strong. Ripon suggested that the local municipalities elect members to the Imperial Legislative Council, but this suggestion was ignored by the Home Department. Maine on the Indian Council thought such a policy was risky and of dubious advantage, while the secretary of state regarded the suggestions as premature.[70] What Ripon had originally regarded as a minor measure of liberalization–the Ilbert Bill–raised an immense storm of protest and had to be withdrawn. Stephen claimed that such a measure was inconsistent with the principles on which British power rests, while the Anglo-Indian Community was literally up in arms. The principles of imperialism and conservatism were triumphant in 1884, not to be challenged again until the twentieth century and certainly not before the Montague-Chelmsford reforms of 1919.[71]

Ironically, while the liberalism of Ripon was going down to defeat in India, its counterpart, the liberalism of Gladstone was completing its victory over the intellecutal liberals at home; for by 1885, the Liberal Pary began to be identified with Irish Home Rule. Though the attitudes of Stephen and Maine were dominant in Indian affairs, they were repudiated by the leadership of the English Liberal Party, thus driving the intellectual liberals into the half-way house of Liberal Unionism. There they joined forces with the old Whigs to defend property and the Empire against what they felt to be a Gladstonian social revolution.

When Stephen and Maine brought their concept of disillusioned liberalism to bear on the central event of nineteenth century British Indian history, the mutiny of 1857, the results were predictably in accord with those of other Indian officials, such as J.W. Kaye, who viewed the mutiny as the result of a too active innovating zeal. J.F. Stephen, in a review of Kaye's *History of the Sepoy War*, asserted that Kaye was 'substantially correct' in denouncing the annexation and peasant policies of Dalhousie :

> Everything like an aristocracy which the country possesses was mowen down with relentless vigour. Mr. Kaye's picture of the general result (of the peasant policy) is a sad and memorable instance of the cruelty of ignorant honesty and zealous philanthropy. The young earnest red-hot revenue officers, full of indignation against shams and imposters, full of zeal for the propagation of all English manners and customs, came down on the face of the country with a determination to purge it thoroughly of its abuses (especially talukdars).
>
> It was because he tried to mitigate the hardships which these various forms of harsh and even cruel, philanthropic reforms

> inflicted on the natives of the Punjab, that Sir Henry Lawrence was removed from power there and the province handed over to his brother.[72]

Collision of English and Indian ideas of religion likewise played a role in rousing the resentment which flowered in the mutiny. Here Stephen felt obliged to stress that the English were 'entirely and emphatically right, if we are to believe that there are such things as right and wrong, good and evil.'[73] Inspite of this quite natural assertion of moral superiority, Stephen, like Kaye, was quick to caution against an excess of zeal. The conservatism of Indian society and its attachment to even superstitious customs prevent England from too rudely 'cutting away old landmarks and pouring over the land a flood of new and dazzling knowledge', for 'we cannot govern 130 million people against their own conscious deliberate will with an army of 60,000 Europeans.'[74]

Sir Henry Maine was even more aware of the intense conservatism of the Indian people than Stephen. Maine saw Indian society as so tenaciously attached to its custom and 'numerous exotic' religions that any appearance of an affront to them, however irrational, could provoke 'an outburst of terrified fanaticism.' He claims that English politicians who try to find a rational cause of the mutiny in maladministration do not understand the operation of the Indian mind, which rose up 'in suspicion and fear of an attack on the institution of caste.'[75] Citing the impossibility of communicating this intense conservatism to the English people'. Maine asserts that :

> It is quite evident that the greatest fact in Anglo-Indian history, the revolt of the mercenary Sepoy Army, is as much a mystery to the average man of the west as are certain colours to the colour-blind; and even historians are compelled to supply wholly or partly fictitious explanations of the events of 1857 to a public which cannot be brought to believe that vast popular uprising was produced by a prejudice about a greased cartridge.[76]

Conclusion

The policies pursued by the Government of India in the post-Mutiny decades were an instinctive reaction to the exigencies of the mutiny period, as reinforced and shaped by the philosophic outlook of such disillusioned liberals as Stephen and Maine. Assertion of English moral superiority, and the consequent duty to bring civilization to India remained throughout as the basis of imperial thought. But the pessimistic conception of human nature as ignorant and largely uneducated seemed to imply permanent English trusteeship and the discouragement of native political aspirations. And at the same time recognition of Indian society as intensely conservative and, though Aryan still primitive, cautioned against reforming zeal or hopes for rapid social regeneration along English lines. The unsettling experience of the mutiny and the philosophy of disillusioned liberalism jointly bequeathed to British Indian policy an attitude of conservatism, admirably summed up by Guy Wint as follows:

> Zeal for innovation was checked, and Indian institutions, while still not regarded with any respect by the great majority of the British officers were recognized as having teeth and a power of self-defence which in the previous time had not been suspected. To assail them too openly was to cause too much danger. From this followed a mixture of toleration and contempt. The British had lost any clear conception of what they wanted to change India into, and as time went on, confined themselves in general to maintaining day-to-day administration.[77]

NOTES AND REFERENCES

1. G.O. Trevelyan. *The Competition Wallah*, 2nd. edn. (London, 1866), pp. 238–41.
2. Ibid, pp. 251–52.
3. Letter from Lawrence to Dalhousie, June 16, 1858, quoted in Bosworth Smith, *Life of Lawrence*, Vol. 2, p. 196.
4. Ibid, p.161.
5. Letter from Canning to the Queen, September 25, 1857, quoted in Arthur C. Benson (ed.) *The Letters of Queen Victoria* (New York, 1907), Vol. 3, p. 318.
6. Trevelyan, *Competition Wallah*, p. 242.
7. Letter of September 19, 1857, quoted in G.O. Trevelyan, *Life and Letters of Lord Macaulay*, Vol. 2, p. 367.

8. Letter from Canning to Granville, December 11, 1857, quoted in Fitzmaurice, *Life of Granville,* Vol. 1, pp. 274–75.
9. *Letters of Queen Victoria,* Vol. 3, p. 319.
10. Letter from Canning to Granville, December 24, 1857, quoted in Fitzmaurice op.cit, Vol. 1, p. 282.
11. W.H. Russell. *My Indian Mutiny Diary,* pp. 197–98.
12. Trevelyan, *Competition Wallah,* p. 258.
13. Letter from Frere to Wood, April 10, 1861, quoted in Martineau, *Life of Bartle Frere,* Vol. 1, p. 337.
14. Trevelyan, *Competition Wallah,* pp. 260–61.
15. Ibid, p. 258.
16. Dispatches to India, Secret Department.
17. Maine was in India as Law Member from 1862 to 1868, and Stephen was his successor 1869–72.
18. For discussion of Stephen's authoritarian Benthamite see stockes—*Utilitarians and India,* Ch. IV. Stokes notes for instance that 'Stephen drew his solution from the philosophy of government to be found in Bentham and Hobbes, where law was conceived in authoritarian terms as the will and command of a sovereign. In such a philosophy there was no place, properly speaking, for any notion of the division of powers ... The State operated by force or the threat of force.' p. 274.
19. Stokes saw this when he noted that Bentham and James Mill 'were both fired by the optimism of the eighteenth century enlightenment', while 'Stephen inclined, however, towards Hobbes's darker view of human nature.' Ibid, p.295. This difference in outlook is also visible in the concept of law reform which Stephen held.' Instead of suggesting an entire reconstruction of the existing structure in the light of certain rigid theoretical principles, as Macaulay had done, Stephen concentrated on mitigating the practical defects of the system as it stood', Ibid, pp. 278–79.
20. Speech in House of Commons, May 23, 1865, quoted in A.P. Martin, *Life and Letters of Robert Lowe, Viscount Sherbrooke* (London, 1893) Vol. 2, p. 263. See also Asa Briggs, *Victorian People,* pp. 244–75 for discussion of Lowe. For instance, Briggs notes that 'He did not attack reform as a whig apologist defending an order, but as an intellectual pleading for government by the educated against government by the masses.'
21. Stephen to Lady Grant Duff, April 30, 1886, quoted in John

Roach, 'Liberalism and the Victorian Intelligentsia', *Cambridge Historical Review*, 13 (1957), p. 60.
22. Ibid, p. 71.
23. J.F. Stephen, *Liberty, Equality, Fraternity* (New York, 1873), p.265.
24. Leslie Stephen. *Life of James Fitzjames Stephen* (London, 1895), p. 308.
25. J.S. Mill, *Autobiography*, pp. 251–53.
26. As Carlyle's imperial views partook more of oracular utterances than of consistent philosophy, and as he was a Tory rather than a Liberal, I only mention his friendship with Stephen to show how a Stephen's repudiation of democracy and laissez faire had carried him.
27. Leslie Stephen, *Life of J.F. Stephen*, p. 243.
28. Roach, loc. cit, p. 64.
29. Ibid, p. 64.
30. J.F. Stephen, *Liberty, Equality, Fraternity*, p. 1.
31. Stokes commented that 'In his essays On *Liberty, Utilitarianism*, and *Representative Government*, J.S. Mill had certainly appeared to lose sight of the utilitarian criterion of the greatest happiness of the greatest number, and to adopt liberty as an ultimate principle and goal.' *Utilitarians and India*, p. 291.It should be borne in mind throughout that Mill's libertarianism here expressed did not figure in his India policy, which was firmly based on the need for benevolent despotism and a strong government. Mill did, however, envision eventual application of his libertarian ideals to India after the people were educated. He was confident that coercion could in time be supplanted by discussion in India as in England and it was this assertion which Stephen so vigorously contested.
32. Stephen, *Liberty, Equality, Fraternity*, (New York, 1873), p. 267.
33. Ibid, pp. 267–68.
34. Ibid, pp. 31, 42–3.
35. Ibid, p. 45.
36. He states, for instance, that 'Rulers owe their power in whatever form is the essential thing.' Even Paliamentary Government 'is simply a mild and disguised form of compulsion', Ibid, p. 28.
37. Ibid, p.57. This doctrine implied for Stephen the intrinsic value of autocratic government as an agency of civilization. See *Infra*, pp. 271–79, for discussion of Stephen's views of Indian Government.
38. Ibid, pp. 91, 94.

39. Ibid, p. 235.
40. J.F. Stephen. 'Parliamentary Government' *Contemporary Review*, No. 23 (1873), p.179. This article contains a complete exposition of Stephen's views on administrative reform.
41. H.S. Maine, *Popular Government* (London, 1885), p. 86.
42. Ibid, p. 189.
43. *Liberty, Equality, Fraternity* was published in 1873; and *Popular Government* in 1885. During the intervening decade the 'Socialist menace' had expanded considerably and brought itself more prominently to public notice.
44. H.S. Maine. *Ancient Law*, (London, 1861), p. 170.
45. Grant Duff. *Life and Speeches of Sir Henry Maine*, p. 91.
46. Crane Brinton. *English Political Thought in the Nineteenth Century*, 2nd. edn., (London, 1949), p. 270.
47. H.S. Maine. *Village Communities in East and West*, 3rd. edn. (New York, 1876), p. 230.
48. Maine, *Popular Government*, p. 166.
49. The *St. James Gazette* neatly summarized these fears in an article of February 1888. 'Maine saw that radicalism, pushed to its logical conclusions, means the rule of ignorance, of charlatanism, of blind rapacity, and the banishment of sober sense and experience' Quoted in Grant Duff, *Life of Maine*, p. 74.
50. Both these quotations are in B.E. Lippincott, *Victorian Critics of Democracy* (Minneapolis, 1938), p. 176.
51. Maine, *Village Communities*, p. 22.
52. Ibid, p. 215.
53. Maine, *Popular Government*, p. 133.
54. Grant Duff, *Life and Speeches of Henry Maine*, p. 251.
55. Maine, Village Communities, p. 239.
56. For discussion of Bright's belief in Britain's moral trusteeship as justification for empire, see references 21 to 23.
57. J.F. Stephen. 'Foundations of the Government of India', *Nineteenth Century*, No. 14 (1883), p. 562.
58. Ibid, p. 542.
59. Ibid, p. 551.
60. J.F. Stephen. 'Indian Legislation', In : W.W. Hunter, *Life of the Earl of Mayo* (London, 1876), Vol. 2, pp. 168–69.
61. Stephen, 'Foundations of the Government of India', loc, cit, p. 554.
62. On self-government as the triumph of England's civilizing mission see references 44 to 50. On the contrast between

Macaulay and Stephen, see Stokes, *Utilitarians and India*, p.283 : 'Macaulay and Trevelyan had looked upon the task of modernization as a co-operative enterprise to be increasingly entrusted to Indian hands. The Indian middle classes were to be interpreters and partners in the great civilizing process ... They did not shrink from proclaiming that in the last resort the process must lead to self-government ...To this argument Strachey and Stephen, and the school of which they were spokesmen, were completely opposed. Liberal in the sense of subscribing to free trade, equality before the law, the lifting of all restraints on individual initiative and enterprise, and a rational system of law and government, their liberalism did not extend to a belief in self-government. The British Government in India rested not on consent but force. Its aim and achievement could be summed up in two pregnant words—law and order.'

63. Stephen, 'Foundations of the Government of India' loc.cit, p.563.
64. The British in the late nineteenth century did, however, accept this theory, and they fostered education in the hope that the interest of the educated Indian could be confined to legal and moral, and not political reform. In so doing they were operating under a grand delusion and unwittingly sponsoring that which would be subversive of their Empire, for an Indian once educated could hardly acquiesce in permanent political subjection. British failure to realize this at first produced contempt for the Anglicized Bengalee Baboo, and then gave way to bitter disillusionment when the power of the Congress become manifest.
65. Stephen, 'Foundations of the Government of India', loc.cit, p. 561
66. H.S. Maine 'India' In : T. Humphry Ward, (ed.), *The Reign of Queen Victoria* (London, 1887), p. 512.
67. Sir John Strachey, *India*, (London, 1888), p. 356.
68. Ibid, p. 360.
69. Minutes of December 25, 1882, quoted in Lucien Wolf, *Life of the First Marquess of Ripon* (London, 1921), Vol. 2, p. 93.
70. Ripon's measures of liberalization, and their cool reception are discussed at length in S. Gopal, *The Viceroyalty of Lord Ripon* (Oxford, 1953) pp. 83–5 and 113 ff.
71. In a sense these principles were never challenged, for the concept of moral duty to India after the mutiny was always

based on ultimate British control. This was the permanent legacy of the mutiny, which vitiated the concept of the trust, and contrasts so strikingly with the optimistic hopes of Macaulay and C.E. Trevelyan. Conscessions granted to the nationalists were invariably extorted by force, not coneeded freely. For instance the Morley-Minto Reforms of 1909 expressly ruled out self-government and were nothing more than concessions to nationalists pressure.

72. J.F. Stephen. 'Kaye's History of the Indian Mutiny', *Frasers Magazine*, No. 70 (1864), p. 764.
73. Ibid, p. 766.
74. Ibid, p. 767.
75. Maine 'India' In : T.H. Ward op.cit, p. 474.
76. Maine, *Popular Government*, p. 133.
77. Guy Wint, *The British in Asia* (London, 1947), p. 54.

Chapter 7

Diplomatic History and International Relations 1871–1920

The study of diplomatic history has its difficulties. Sources are always suspect, and the diplomatic historian (like his colleagues in other forms of history) has to be extremely careful and critical. Our sources are primarily the records which foreign offices keep of their dealings with each other; and the writer who bases himself fully on the archives my deem to possess scholarly virtue. But no foreign minister is an autocrat; foreign policy has to be defined as well as executed; and a great deal of our material comes from this process of preliminary discussion. There are those who speak disparagingly of history based on these records. G.M. Young once described diplomatic history as 'what one clerk said to another clerk'; and Bismarck thought that no historian would ever understand the documents, because he would have little idea of the background of personality and unwritten influence. This is to underestimate our expertise. Historians have penetrated into Bismarck's secrets and unravelled his intrigues more effectively than any contemporary statesman managed to do. The half century following the creation of the German Empire is an ideal field for the diplomatic historian. Full records were kept, without knowing that they would ever be published. it was the great age of writing. Even close colleagues write to each other, and copiously. Bismarck did all his thinking on paper, and he was not alone.[1]

Purely diplomatic approach does not exhaust international history. Policy springs from deep-rooted social, economic, and psychological factors; it is not crudely manufactured in foreign offices. Our historian has taken his profession seriously and has done admirably well. In the following pages is given a critical appreciation of some of the basic and important works dealing with various phases of the subject.

A.J.P. Taylor is our great authority on the Bismarckian era. His *Bismarck; The Man and The Statesman* (New York, 1955) is a brief and lucid narrative of the 'Iron Chancellor.' He has handled the rich material with superb craftsmanship and while some of his judgments about Bismarck as a diplomat are arguable, he has painted a fascinating portrait of one of the most complicated personalities in an age which was filled with gifted and original minds. Taylor represents this unlovely figure, and the remarkable effect he had on history, not only with sound scholarship and rare good sense but with eloquence and wit.

Like Taylor, Gordon Alexander Craig has established himself as an authority on both modern Germany and modern diplomacy. The two lines of his interest merge in the slim volume *From Bismarck to Adenauer; Aspects of German Statecraft* (Baltimore, 1958) which displays a remarkable gift of literary presentation. It traces the history of modern German diplomacy, its successes and failures. The author has explained German foreign policy in terms of the personalities who shaped it. The result is not a diplomatic history, but, more fascinating, an analysis (and semi-psycho-analysis) of the German Chancellors from Bismarck to Adenauer. According to Gordon Craig, Bismarck fulfilled Max Weber's three essentials for a successful statesman: passion (i.e. total commitment), a feeling of responsibility, and a sense of proportion.

Bismarck's successors failed to realize–a fact of which Bismarck was fully aware–that the task of conservation is infinitely more difficult that of creation. By measuring them against Bismarck the author obscures this point. He also diminishes Bismarck's share of the responsibility for the regime of William II.

Few people have been so maligned by history as the German diplomatist Friedrich von Holstein who for a quarter of a century exercised an extraordinary influence in the politics of the German Empire. Norman Rich's biography of him, *Friedrich von Holstein: Politics and Diplomacy in the era of Bismarck and William II* (2 Vols; Cambridge, 1965) is an attempt to discover the real face beneath all the dark shades over the portrait. The record of Holstein's work is clouded with legends and misconceptions, and almost every phase of his political life provokes disagreement and controversy. This book, as the author says, 'will not put an end to disagreement and controversy, but ... will provide a reasonably complete record of the evidence much of which is new, and a detailed analysis of the controversial problems.' (p. 15) This is not a simple biography but a life of Holstein embedded in a history of German domestic and foreign politics.

For a thorough grounding in the last decade of the last century, which saw the height of imperialistic rivalry, William L. Langer's *The Diplomacy of Imperialism 1890–1902* (2 Vols ; New York, 1935) gives the complete story and also provides excellent critical bibliographies. During the Bismarckian period, European international relations were predominantly continental in character, but with the consummation of the Franco-Russian Alliance a new era in European diplomacy may be said to have begun, for the new combination, as Langer says, broke the preponderance of Germany and re-established something like a balance of power on the Continent. With two groups of power fairly matched, the old European issues were reduced to a deadlock. The interests and the energies of most of the great powers were devoted to problems which touched the ends of the earth. Hence, Langer's *Diplomacy of Imperialism* is much more a history of world policy than his earlier work *European Alliances and Alignments, 1870–1890.*

The *Diplomacy of Imperialism,* based upon a meticulous study of first hand sources, is undoubtedly an outstanding contribution to historical scholarship. The critical erudition of the author is matched by his capacity for lucid exposition, and his control of detail by a superb power of synthesis. We may differ from his judgment in some respects, or wish to vary the emphasis, but no writer on the period could fail to find his interpretation instructive and stimulating.

A.J.P. Taylor has written *The Struggle for Mastery in Europe 1848–1918* (Oxford, 1954) which tells the story of the great powers in Europe's last age as the centre of the world. In the words of Hans Kohn : 'Taylor writes with scholarship and wit, a not very frequent combination, which may attract a wider circle of readers to his book. His trend to overstress and overstrain, though it may not always please the critical reader, will certainly not displease the general public.'[2] According to Joachim Remak, Taylor ranges 'from the brilliant to the bizarre.' However, he 'manages to be provocative even in his sophistries, and when he is good, he is very very good, and when he is not, he is seldom dull.'[3] Taylor neither disguises his prejudices (his anti-Germanism for instance) nor does he hesitate to set forth challenging interpretations of a highly controversial nature. He makes an effort to probe the historical meaning of given actions, with the tacit assumption that historical progress is rational. In this manner, Taylor is driven to reinterpretations which often appear to be rationalist reductions of highly complex historical situation.

This is a remarkable book; and on a certain plane the author is capable of brilliant and illuminating generalizations. He treates all the stale themes with freshness and vigour. Not the least stimulating part is the masterly bibliography in which the author is as critical as he has been in his narrative. What makes this the best study of European diplomacy since Langer's volumes on the post-1870 period is Taylor's ability to keep the main theme clearly before his readers, while at the same time providing them with circumstantial and absorbing accounts of the policies and ambitions of individual powers and statesmen, the changing diplomatic patterns and the crises which filled the period. And this is done with great knowledge and readability.

The literature, on the crisis of 1914 and the events leading up to it, is probably more voluminous than on any other period of the past. Most of it, however, suffers from the error of retrospection : the first fourteen years of the twentieth century, and sometimes the last decades of the nineteenth, are too often seen solely as prologues to the First World War. The isolation of events that appeared to be causes of the War and the problems of guilt and vindication 'have frequently converted history from its proper role as an inductively reasoned thesis into the improper one of a prosecutor's brief or a tragedian's diagnosis of impending doom.'[4]

However, works of a high quality are not lacking. Three books form the core of the bibliography of the origin of the First World War : Sidney B. Fay, *The Origin of the World War* (2 Vols ; New York, 1928), Bernadotte E. Schmitt, *The Coming of the War, 1914* (2 Vols : New York, 1930), and Luigi Albertini, *The Origin of the War of 1914* (3 Vols.; London, 1952–1957). Some of the details in Fay and Schmitt are now outdated, but on the whole, both books have stood the test of time remakably well. They have remained indispensable. Even their biases–Fay is prone to exonerate the central powers of the Versailles war-guilt verdict, while Schmitt holds it to be essentially true–have not really belittled their worth. Rather, both have defined and documented scholarly positions that all subsequent historians have had to take into account. The Albertini book is in a somewhat different category. It is a mine of valuable information. His three exhaustive, and sometime exasperating volumes stand as reference works that any serious student of 1914 will have to consult.

Fay's work marked a veritable epoch in the discussion of the greatest controversy of the time. Generations of students have been brought up on Fay, the influence of whom on the American outlook can hardly be exaggerated. His account is written with the same cool detachment with which he might have written about the origin of the Seven Years' War. Yet its very lack of passion, its quiet air of thoughtfulness, and the mass of skilfully arranged evidence gives it an entirely convincing quality. It is a monument to American scholarship, and stands as the first purely scientific treatment of the question based upon adequate source material.

Schmitt's *Coming of the War* manifests a degree of skill, subtlety, comprehensiveness, and erudition which must command the highest respect of all who have done scientific work in the field. However, Schmitt's conclusions would possibly have had more practical value, as well as greater scientific validity, if he had been less concerned with the question, 'Who caused the war?' and more eager to discover 'What caused the war?'

Both works–Fay's and Schmitt's–are reflections of divergent outlooks. It is fitting that perhaps the best analysis of all to date should have issued from a relatively neutral quarter in the form of the masterly work of the Italian Albertini. He not only studied the documents and memoirs–he studied more of them, since they were available (many of these, of course, were not yet available when Fay and Schmitt appeared)–but also interviewed and corresponded with many of the statesmen, asking some probing questions and receiving some revealing answers. The trend of Albertini's conclusions was to some extent in the fashion of the times[5], he found the Germans unquestionably guilty. Not by any means solely guilty or guilty of planning a World War years in advance, but definitely guilty of encouraging Austria to attack Serbia at the obvious risk of a general war. The value of Albertini's immense and imposing work lies in its detail, its consistency, its objectivity.

There is a fourth name that should be mentioned with Fay, Schmitt, and Albertini. It is George Peabody Gooch. It is said that 'What Gladstone did to the House of Commons by his decorum and dignity and by his sustained gravity, Gooch has done to the study, understanding, interpreting and writing of history, particularly diplomatic history.'[6] He has, by his extraordinary learning, stern objectivity and studied impartiality in a measured tone and lucid style, raised the study of diplomatic history to a higher level.

Not going into the details of Gooch's scholarship we limit ourselves to a brief comment on one of his works, *Before the War: Studies in Diplomacy, II : The Coming of the Storm* (London, 1938). Here Gooch has chosen to study the policies of each of the foreign ministers of the great powers—Grey, Poincare, Bethmann Hollweg. Sazonoff and Berchtold–instead of presenting an exposition of international relations before 1914.

Thus apart from the historical value of the work as an account of facts, Gooch has given us an admirable picture of the characters of the men who took decisions in the days immediately preceding the World War. Published at a moment when the story of 1914 threatened to repeat itself, this volume offers a penetrating clinical analysis of the disease from which Europe had been suffering. Gooch was able to approach the subject with detachment and utilize a more extensive body of documentary evidence than was available ten years before.

A recent study of the origin of the war is Laurence Lafore's *The Long Fuse : An Interpretation of the Origin of World War I* (Philadelphia, 1965). An excellent brief history, it is based on a reinterpretation of the literature on the war—origin rather than on a study of the primary sources. This swift, coherent narrative sets sorry tales in reasonable array and explains their importance to the destiny of Europe. Its conclusions are rather more tenable; it sensibly focuses on the southeastern European setting of the conflict. Without concerning himself with the question of war guilt Lafore emphasizes two points : one, that when statesmen and people undertook actions they knew might lead to war, they were not visualizing the catastrophe that the war became but rather a quick and limited war; and, two, that without the conflict of Austria and Serbia there would have been no World War in 1914. Too much preoccupation with the role of Germany on the part of historians has blocked from view what should have been obvious.[7] The point is a valid one, and Lafore gives an excellent analysis thereof. Further, he does well to point to one miscalculation of which nearly all European statesmen were guilty. They imagined that the risks of action were small. In 1914 all the powers, for one reason or the other, expected the yielding to come from the other side.

Another recent work on the same topic is Joachim Remak's *The Origin of World War I 1871–1914* (New York, 1967). It is a probing and stimulating interpretation of the situation. Like Lafore, Remak blames the statesmen for their lack of imagination. But history is so unpredictable. Some errors of judgment, some mishap, some accident, and there comes a war. The world, as it approached 1914, was not in so deplorable a state and with all the inflammable material Europe might not have plunged into war. The utmost one can say is that war was a diplomatic crisis gone astray.

By the same author is the study of the Sarajevo assassination, *Sarajevo : The Story of a Political Murder* (New York, 1959). Remak reconstructs the assassination of the Austrian Archduke Franz Ferdinand and his consort Sophie on June 28, the forces that activated it and its aftermath. It is fine readable stuff with a vivid narrative that carries the reader along in interest and excitement. The Archduke's love story is movingly told and the trial of the assassins dramatically presented. The author has written a straightforward description of the recruiting of the murderers, their training, and the almost accidental success of their preparations. He has formed an amazingly true picture of the combination of dash and sloppiness which characterized the last years of the monarchy. Remak has also made judicious use of sources that are plentiful but not always reliable.

The same story is written by Vladimir Dedijer[8] in *The Road To Sarajevo* (New York, 1966), the story of the young men who killed the Archduke in 1914, triggering World War I. The writing is sometimes tedious and repetitive as Dedijer strives for historical accuracy in all details. But the main subject is revolutionary fervour with all of its psychological and sociological ramifications. The author is by birth a Bosnian Serb, like Gavrilo Princip, and understands the emotional background of the assassins. To him they are heroes who fought for a good cause with the wrong methods. Their experiences were, in his view, similar to the processes of self-determination going on today in many economically backward areas of the world. The book is a scholarly survey of the enormous historical literature that has been used for this study and Dedijer has read many original documents. The whole tangled Balkan-Habsburg-Hungarian-Slavic problem has been presented thoroughly well. He shows clearly how mass grievences become intensely personal, and how desperate individuals influence the course of history. Despite its faults the volume remains an instructive and fascinating work, precisely because it is propaganda at its most subtle.

For a study of Anglo-French relations in the decade prior to the outbreak of World War I, Samuel R Williamson's *The Politics of Grand Strategy : Britain and France Prepare for War, 1904–1914* (Cambridge : Harv. Univ. Press, 1969) is useful. The book is thorough and comprehensive though not brilliant, it is ever sensible and matter of fact : conclusions invariably follow stated evidence. Williamson has written what may be regarded the definitive work on the *Entente Cordiale*. He has explored much archival material hitherto inaccessible. He feels that the co-ordinated planning between the British and French military staffs by 1914 had excelled that between not only Paris and St. Petersburg but also Vienna and Berlin.

The war of 1914 was a manifestation of a developing world situation which we can see today in better perspective, the beginning of the end of the dominance of Western Europe. Michael L.G. Balfour's *The Kaiser and his Times* (London, 1964), written half a century after that event, and so with the advantage of hindsight, is a study of Kaiser William II, that complex and disputed personality who enjoyed a pivotal position on the European scene in the three crucial decades before 1918. The society over which William was called to rule was, as Balfour says, one of glaring contradictions. Balfour's profound knowledge of the period gives him a 'feel' of Wilhelmine Germany which is what is needed. This is a comprehensive and elegantly wirtten book : it is a scholarly and reflective one too. But perhaps there is a little too much emphasis on the Anglo-German problem.

K.H. Jarausch's *The Enigmatic Chancellor* (New Haven, 1973) is the study of the fifth German Chancellor's policy from 1914 to 1917.[9] He is seen as the victim of the imperial system which courted death. Jarausch attempts to solve the riddle of Bethmann Hollweg's personality and politics, since it holds the key to the tragedy of the Wilhelmian Empire. The failure of the fifth chancellor's reforming conservatism exposes, says Jarausch, the structural weakness of Germany to find a place among the European nations and to evolve a liberal constitutional system. The moral ambivalence in the mainstream of German politics of which he was both representative and victim, makes Bethmann's struggle, in Jarausch's view, a paradigm of the fundamental flaw of the German solution to the problems of the present century. (p.9) The author demonstrates excellent mastery of the secondary as well as primary sources.

An exciting book which has provoked much controversy is Fritz Fischer's *Germany's Aims in the First World War* (New York, 1967) with introductions by Hajo Holborn and James Joll. Fischer provides a brief history of the origin of the war, the policies of the German government in the July 1914 crisis, and the attempts of the government to secure their war aims. His thesis is that Germany embarked upon an extensive programme of territorial aggrandizement soon after the outbreak of war and adhered to it with utmost tenacity. Austria-Hungary, he said, was to a large extent pushed into war at German pressure, wildly optimistic as the government was of German chances for victory. The Germans were exploiting the occasion for a 'grab at world power'; they never mistakenly staggered into war but chose the course in full knowledge of the risks involved. When the German edition of this book first appeared in 1961, it occasioned much discussion and some shock in Germany.

Fischer should definitely be commended for his excellent research and analysis of a most controversial topic. Much of the evidence he has produced is an important addition to knowledge. His book will remain one of the most definitive studies on Germany's war aims in the First World War. Still, we must admit that his treatment is very narrowly of the German side of things, and a wider survey indicates clearly that the Germans were by no means the only people who were ready to risk a war and who cherished expansionist ambitions.

In February 1916, the Germans attacked in the Verdun sector, catching the French there thoroughly by surprise. Out of this assault grew what those who took part in it considered to be the grimmest battle in all that grim war, perhaps in history itself. The battle produced probably the highest density of dead per square yard that has ever been known. *The Price of Glory : Verdun 1916* (New York, 1963) by the British journalist Alistair Horne is 'the best and fullest study' of this momentous battle which was a watershed of primary importance in the War. Before it, writes Horne, Germany still had a reasonable chance of winning the war; in the course of the ten months during which the battle raged this chance dwindled away. Verdun was a catastrophe, a turning point in western history. It is the distillation of the heroism, stupidities, and horrors of World War I. At frightening cost, the French held. Horne's story of Verdun is well-written, reflective, dramatic, and thoroughly researched. He has addressed himself to complex tactics, muddled situations, and followed the action day by day, hour by hour, sometimes minute by minute.

Paul Guinn's *British Strategy and Politics 1914 to 1918* (Oxford, 1965) is an interpretation of British grand strategy during the War in the light of war aims, national politics, and tactical developments. It also studies the interaction between war policy and domestic politics. It shows that a strategic policy is the outcome of a multiplicity of political and military pressures, it is in fact the projection of the over-all fabric of national life. The book discusses political conflicts over conscription and economic policy; personal conflict between ministers; conflicts between ministers and generals; and efforts to create an effective machinery of direction. It recognizes British resourcefulness amidst error and indecision. This is an exceedingly subtle analysis of a significant subject presented in a lively style on the basis of exhaustive research.

The student of the Versailles Peace Settlement of 1919–1920 will find an enormous literature on the subject. In fact, more has been written about Versailles than about other historic efforts at international peacemaking. And, no peace settlement in modern times has evoked greater controversy than Versailles and its related treaties. While the controversy over German reparations began in the inner circles of the Paris Peace Conference, it exploded into public view with the publication of John Maynard Keynes' famous book, *The Economic*

Consequences of the Peace (New York, 1920). A brilliant British economist, Keynes charged that the economic features of the German Treaty were so severe that they could not possibly be fulfilled. His book is one of the most penetrating, controversial, and historically influential attacks against the Treaty of Versailles. It in fact, created such a stir that it even influenced official policy in Britain as well as significant sectors of public opinion elsewhere.

This is a great book written with a fullness of knowledge, an incisiveness of judgment, and a keenness of perception of economic intricacies. Many have criticized the remedies that Keynes proposed, but no one can deny that the book is a monument of superb economic exposition. The prime importance of the work lies in its insight of the growing moral and economic solidarity of the world, and particularly of Europe, and its diligent search for a sound economic basis on which alone an enduring peace settlement can be made, in view of that solidarity.

In the foregoing pages has been given a very sketchy survey of some of the outstanding works on the period. 'Public opinion', in its widest sense, has had a great fascination, though with inadequate resutls. Historians have been unable to decide whether newspapers form public opinion or express it. Those well-versed in this curious trade may doubt whether they do either. Another phase which has to be further explored is the influence of strategy. Diplomatic history between Sedan and Versailles, between the creation of the Second Reich and the end of Europe as the centre of the world is still an alluring field wide open to study. 'We must be grateful for what our predecessors did', to conclude with Taylor, 'and try to improve on them.'

NOTES AND REFERENCES

1. 'Now the telephone and the personal meeting leave gaps in our knowledge which can never be filled. While diplomacy has become more formal, the real process of decision escapes us.' : See A.J.P. Taylor, *The Struggle for Mastery in Europe 1848–1918* (Oxford, 1954), pp. 569–75.

2. Hans Kohn. *Annals of the American Academy of Political and Social Sciences*, No. 298 (March, 1955), p. 230.
3. Joachim Remak. *The Origin of World War I, 1871–1914* (New York, 1967), p. 153.
4. Laurence Lafore. *The Long Fuse : An Interpretation of the Origin of World War I*, (New York, 1965), pp. 269–70.
5. With the coming of World War II historians began to apprehend everywhere that there was something deep rooted in the German people and the German State that led them to undertake wars of aggression.
6. A.O. Sarkissian, (ed.). *Studies in Diplomatic History and Historiography in Honour of G.P. Gooch* (New York, 1962), p.6.
7. That without the quarrel between Austria and Serbia there would have been no World War in 1914.
8. A leading communist, Dedijer was a great admirer of Tito whose biography he wrote.
9. With a skethcy account of his previous career.

Chapter 8

Outbreak of the First World War : The Problem of Responsibility

The literature dealing with the problem of responsibility for the First World War has reached vast proportions. During the four war years an unconscionable volume of self-defence and corresponding calumniation poured forth. None of it was accurate, let alone complete. Official publications–the *British Blue Book,* the *French Yellow Book,* the *German White Book,* the *Austrian Red Book* and the *Russian Orange Book*–sought to demonstrate with a careful selection from the archives, the integrity of each nation and its allies and the depravity of the enemy. The selections were by necessity concise, and by reason of their purpose, highly misleading. By falsification and clever suppression of documents, truth, incriminatory to the particular country, was concealed. For every nation the hardships imposed by war had to be justified by belief in the guilt of the enemy for starting it, and the necessary energy had to be ignited by enthusiasm and hatred. Modern wars are fought largely by emotion and by the creative forces that emotion, properly managed, can release; and the degree of emotion required in an age of literate publics and industrial economics was proportionately greater during the First World War than ever before. Leading officials in all countries made war speeches asserting the innocence of their own acts, and throwing the responsibility upon the enemy. The result was that, when the war terminated, a 'Commission on the Responsibility of the Authors of the War', solemnly reported to the Peace Conference:

> The War was premeditated by the central powers together with their allies, Turkey and Bulgaria, and was the result of acts deliberately committed in order to make it unavoidable. Germany, in agreement with Austria-Hungary, deliberately worked to defeat all the many conciliatory proposals made by the Entente Powers.[1]

In the deliberations of this Commission, 'unfortunately no Germans were allowed to take part.' A German delegation, to be sure, was officially allowed to present a *German White Book Concerning the Responsibility of the Authors of the War*. It contained valuable new evidence tending to prove that the charge formulated by the Commission was historically untrue and morally unjustifiable.[2] Inspite of this, the Commission paid virtually no attention to it, and Germany was forced to accept the dictum of the victors in Article 231 of the Treaty of Versailles:

> The Allied and Associated Governments affirm, and Germany accepts, the responsibility of Germany and her allies for causing all the loss and damage to which the Allied and Associated Governments and their nationals have been subjected as a consequence of the war imposed upon them by the aggression of Germany and her allies.

On the basis of this assertion the entente powers specifically and concretely erected their claim to reparations from Germany, and by implication the general nature of the entire treaty. 'Treaties signed at the point of a gun do not necessarily tell the truth or do justice.'[3] Yet they very often produce fateful consequences. Adolf Hitler's promise to free Germany from the punitive restrictions of Versailles paved his way to the Berlin Chancellery. The reaction to the Versailles verdict which occurred in the victorious countries as well as in Germany resulted in an attack upon Article 231 in the name of 'revisionism.' 'War guilt' became a basic issue in international relations between the two world wars. Historians were quick to involve themselves in this controversy and the flow of literature was torrential.

For the historians, the judgment of the peacemakers proved to be a boon because the Germans immediately undertook to refute the charges against their nation by publishing a huge collection of documents from their foreign office archives covering the period from 1871 to 1914. This impelled other governments to do likewise. Never before in history were archives so freely and quickly thrown open by so many great powers; never before had so many statesmen hastened to tell at such length the part they played. Thus, when normally the scholar would have had to wait a long time to get at the secret papers of government offices, he was overwhelmed with the riches of documentary evidence on the background of the First World War ever since it ended.

The revisionists argue that it is criminal to impose a moral judgment upon a whole people. Harry Elmer Barnes set forth the extreme revisionist view. Like so many others he became convinced by the early publication of secret documents and memoirs that a great injustice had been done to Germany by Article 231 of the Versailles Treaty. More than any other work, his presentation, based upon all available sources, awakened a reaction in this country to the wartime propaganda of condemnation and hatred of the enemy.[4]

While revisionist battle was raging and new revelations were ever bursting into print to furnish fresh ammunition to the controversy, Sidney B. Fay set to work quietly and systematically to explore the diplomatic background of the war and to unravel the tangled web of the 1914 crisis. His *Origin of the World War* was a sober analysis of the whole problem, and forthwith put him in the front ranks of moderate revisionists who were now more concerned with critical judgment and detached interpretation than with polemical acumen.

The revisionists were confronted with the so-called 'salvagers'–the Entente apologists. With the same documents as Fay had at hand Bernadotte E. Schmitt in *The Coming of the War, 1914* (1930) comes to opposite conclusions concerning war guilt. However, his later pamphlet on *The Origin of the First World War* (published in 1958) reflects the calmer judgments of recent times as well as the mature approach of many years of study. Here Schmitt emphasizes the drive for self-determination as the most important single underlying cause of the war. In his conclusion, he finds with other recent writers that the issue in 1914 was the 'balance of power', and that the alliance system, planned for defence, transformed 'a local conflict into a general war.'[5] Pierre Renouvin, likewise, despite an anti-revisionist position in his earlier work[6], later presented a better balanced interpretation which emphasizes trends and movements rather than individual or national guilt.

George Peabody Gooch's account of the July crisis was dispassionate and convincing. He was able to approach the subject with detachment and utilize a more extensive body of documentary evidence than was available ten years before.[7]

Since the beginning of World War II, there has been a revival of the German 'war guilt' thesis. A.J.P. Taylor offers some challenging interpretations of German guilt and other aspects of the problem.[8] To L.C.B. Seaman too, the German responsibility is 'basic.'[9] Imanuel Geiss is more emphatic in asserting German guilt.[10] Thus interesting developments in the debate–shrill polemics and more rational elements–have made their appearance.

Raymond Aron well conveys the spirit of recent research into the crisis of 1914. Assessments deflecting in one direction or the other are characteristic of the black-and-white approach of many historians. Aron makes it clear that 1914 and its background is no 'simple picture' but rather one of great complexity from which 'storybook villains' are missing. There was no inevitable trend of events toward war, but rather the acts of sovereign states seeking what seemed to them at the time to be in their best interest. Alliances and armaments, designed for defence, proved to be the means of creating tension. The alliances and alignments betokened that the crisis would occur all over Europe.[11] Aron emphasizes tensions and national interests rather than individual responsibility for the outbreak of war in 1914.

Viewpoints change and with them the questions which historians seek to answer. Article 231 of Versailles focused the gaze of the 1920's upon the question 'Who was guilty?' As the revisionist fight[12] subsided, it became obvious that this was not a proper question for the historians because the answer would scarcely contribute to a better understanding of historical processes; it would be to gamble with semantics and with the philosophy of history. As time went on, therefore, more and more attention was paid to such questions as 'What were the conditions that made war possible?' and 'What was at stake in 1914 when so many earlier crises were adjusted peaceably?' The answer to such questions depend not only upon the bare record of the documents and other contemporary evidence, but also upon an awareness of political, economic, social, intellectual, and military as well as psychological, personal, and historical factors in the formulation of policy and the making of decisions by national governments. It may be more purposeful if we answer such questions: Upon what postulations and within what frames of reference were the statesmen of 1914 making their decisions? What choices they had before them? Why did they act in the manner that they did? Given each nation seeking ultimately its own best interests, could saner judgment, or prompt and candid statements of positions have averted bloodshedding, or was the situation such that war was inevitable? Were there 'villains' after all? Has the crisis to be explained in balance-of-power terminology? And, was the war the child of European anarchy, of the worn-out system of sovereign states? Answers to these questions may give us a better understanding of the dangerladen situation which exploded in what became the First World War.

And yet, the question of responsibility is 'Argument without End?' The victors, in 1919, were very certain of the answer. Thirty-three years later, a committee of French and German historians precluded a premeditated desire on the part of any government or nation for a European war in 1914. And the argument is not over yet. Nor should it be. We are, however, luckily, at a vantage ground, being far enough removed from the time, the place, the passions and the vehemence of these events to reach some plausible and penetrating judgements. In the following pages, then, an attempt has been made to do just that, although throughout, 'it will be well to bear in mind that splendid phrase of the great Dutch historian, Pieter Geyl, about "that argument without end which to ... the west is the study of history." '[13]

II

During the Forty years' Peace after 1815, the great powers were afraid of revolution. During the Forty Years' Peace after 1871, they were afraid of one another. In 1871, a new *status quo* was established. Efforts to revise the existing situation began immediately. It is certainly optimistic to describe Europe in the period after 1890 as in a state of balance between the Triple Alliance and the Franco-Russian Alliance. What Bismarck bequeathed to Europe was not balance but extreme tension and the seeds of lasting bitterness were sown. Irredentism–the war of *revanche*–was forecast.[14] The injustice that the French saw in the situation was something deeper than merely the loss of Alsace-Lorraine. The desire for the recovery of the lost provinces, for all their economic and strategic value, was always symbolic of a larger yearning, which peaceful diplomacy could hardly fulfil, for the restoration of France's lost status as a first class power. In eastern Europe the situation after 1878 was menacing as the Ottoman Empire could no more act as a buffer between Germans and Russians. The simultaneous growth of Pan-Germanism and Pan-Slavism was the necessary consequence of the collapse of the old Holy Alliance. Worse still, the growing restlessness of the Balkan states made them dangerously unamenable to control by the great powers. The international situation from 1871 to 1914 was, thus, one of intense tension. Its two basic problems, Alsace-Lorraine in the west and the Balkans in the east, could well make a solution by diplomacy impossible.

It is not surprising therefore that from about 1880 until the end of the century, diplomacy sought to stimulate the diversion of the aggressive energies of its own age to regions as far removed from the explosive European scene as possible. If only Austria-Hungary had had an extra-European sphere of interest war might have been postponed indefinitely. As it was, she was worse off even than the Italians, who, though without prospects in Europe, had an answer to their problems of expansion, though a somewhat dusty one, in Tripoli, Eritrea, Somaliland and Abyssinia.

The elementary logic of the extra-European expansion of France and Russia was that it would lead them into difficulties with England. It was reasonable to calculate that the chief development for the future would be peace in Europe with Russia and France battling with England in Asia and Africa. The natural repercussions of this on European affairs would be tightening of the existing links between England and the Triple Alliance.

The story of international affairs from 1898 to 1907 is the story of how what actually happend turned out to be the opposite of this. England, France and Russia composed their differences outside Europe. Yet, so far from making for peace, the elimination of these colonial rivalries by that date had made war much more likely. That part of the apparatus of peace which depended on France and Russia being engaged in adventures outside Europe had been destroyed. Yet the crux of the frequently described diplomatic revolution of those years is not England's relations with France and Russia, but her relations with Germany.

Morocco revived Franco-German antagonism; Bosnia revived Austro-Russian antagonism. Anglo-German antagonism caused no diplomatic crises; it was a slow poison. The basic causes of these antagonisms were British satisfaction, and German dissatisfaction, with the existing distribution of power in the world. To preserve the existing conditions, Britain built her fleet and made the Entente with France and Russia. To change the existing conditions, Germany built her fleet, stuck to Austria, and tried to disrupt the Entente. Both governments honestly tried to effect a compromise, but attacked the symptoms of the disorder, not the disease itself.

Britain was satiated. Her empire included about a quarter of the world. Her trade empire was even larger. For protection, she had an invulnerable fleet.[15] Little wonder that Englishmen wished to perpetuate so enviable a situation. 'Englishmen did not stop here; few men do' : to quote Raymond Sontag : 'Nearly all men, and groups of men, assume that what is good for them is good for the world, and that what is bad for them is bad for the world. Englishmen forgot their history and assumed that their supremacy resulted from the operation of a beneficent moral law. To challenge British supremacy, thus, was to challenge moral law.'[16]

'And the principal challenge to the Empire', writes Joachim Remak, 'seemed to come from a nation too newly rich to abide by the rules laid down by British gentlemen, from the Kaiser's Germany. It was a threat to be resisted for moral as well as political reasons.'[17]

Ambition, fear and frustration often produce a psychosis of public opinion, threat and counter threat. Long before 1914, there were Englishmen, like Lord Fisher, who believed that for Britain's safety the German fleet should be 'Copenhagened.'[18] The Germans, on the other hand, felt, in Kaiser's words, that they were ringed with bayonets and reacted with what has been called a wave of 'foaming chauvinism.'

There was very little clear thought of what precisely it was that Germany wanted. How really does one translate *Weltpolitik*? 'Global policy' perhaps, a term as hazy, and at the same time as portentous, as the original. The world, not surprisingly, was puzzled and concerned about the scope of Germany's ambitions. What were the Germans aiming at? Was it colonies, was it a new eminence on the continent, was it, possibly, world domination? We know today that most foreign fears were exaggerated, and that no responsible German statesman before 1914 entertained Napoleonic visions. At the time, the matter was less clear, as Kaiser's indiscreet attempts to make Germany the equal of Great Britain, and above all, his ill-considered speeches[19], allowed the impression to prevail that his country was a menace to peace, security, and a decent society.

Germany's challenge to Britain's supremacy as the world's leading trading and maritime nation and the reaction of Britain to this economic-military-psychological threat were, no doubt, among the major factors which caused the First World War. It is, however, only in retrospect that the Anglo-German friction looks so momentous. Indeed, if some sort of apparatus for the precise measurement of hostility between nations were to be found, Anglo-Russian relations, in the half century or so before 1904, might receive its highest score. At the start of the voyage to the Far East, during the Russo-Japanese War, the Russian Baltic fleet met a fleet of British fishing boats at Dogger Bank in the North Sea. The tremulous admiral mistook the trawlers for Japanese torpedo boats and opened fire, missing many, but managing to sink one. There was a storm of indignation in England and the Dogger Bank incident marked a crucial point in Anglo-Russian relations. Had the British retaliated, as easily they might, there would be many a learned volume now explaining how the great Anglo-Russian War of 1904 was a logical and inevitable development of decades of friction between London and St. Petersburg. But, narrowly or not, war had been avoided, and the two countries found possible to come close. There is thus no rigidity about historical development. An unrelieved recitation of troubles can obscure the amount of goodwill that still did exist between England and Germany.

The Triple Alliance of Germany, Austria-Hungary, and Italy (or rather the Dual Alliance, for Italy's reliability had become dubious) after 1907 found iself placed opposite the Triple *Entente* of France, Great Britain, and Russia. It was the triumph of France; it was now Germany's turn to feel nervous. The Germans, confronted with the *Entente,* blenched: the ring was complete. There were no great powers upon whose neutrality–if worst should come to worst–Germany could count. And this fact in turn had profound repercussions : it led the Germans to adventurous investigations of an understanding with Turkey; it frightened German government and public opinion and provided cause for grievance and arguments that the ring must be broken, the anti-German conspiracy demolished; and it made it incumbent for Germany to bolster up the might of Austria-Hungary and its prestige and posture as a great power. The sinister phrase began now to appear with deadly regularity in the German documents as well as in public statements: The Habsburg Monarchy has to be preserved as a great power. If Austria goes, Germany is lost.

Before long, the consequences of this belief were to make themselves felt. 'To the Near Eastern Question, still not worth the bones of a Pomeranian grenadier so far as any of Germany's national or world interests went, the German Empire was becoming shackled by the chains of circumstances.'[20]

The circumstances which preceded the outbreak of the First World War—the changing balance of military power in Europe, the growing social tensions within European nations, the shrillness of chauvinists, a growing arsenal of arms and a press out for blood, nationalism, economic imperialism, conflict overseas and conflict at home—all these have been studied and restudied. All of them were cause of what became the First World War. But the war, that vast phenomenon, 'grew out', to quote Laurence Lafore, 'of a single international event, which was the conflict between the Habsburg monarchy and the kingdom of Serbia.' Had the Danubian monarchy been differently constituted, had the Balkan State posed a less lethal threat to it, there would have been no Austro-Serbian war in 1914; and if a general war had come later, it would have been fought with different stakes and taken different forms. It was the system of alliances and the changing balance of military power in Europe that transformed a Balkan dispute into a world war.[21]

Therefore, it seems plausible to examine the outbreak of the 1914 war with principal focus on South-Eastern Europe. For a very long time, Europe, the prosperous and stable Europe of the west and the north, suffered from the complexities of the lands and peoples of the south-east, whose difficulties, serving as a magnet enticed the major European governments. Here are crystallized, in a sort of gigantic microcosm, the problems of sprouting and conflicting nationalisms, the problems of economic and political unpreparedness, the problems of devising solutions by means that worked in the West, but which everyone realized were unsatisfactory elsewhere. There were deep and abiding sources of conflict in the rest of Europe. But to an astonishing degree they were intertwined with the turmoil and hodgepodge of the nationalities in Austria-Hungary and the Balkans. No solution of Balkan problems can be imagined that would have pleased everyone concerned and that would not have contained some seeds of future eruption. Each of the rival aspirations–Bulgaria's, Serbia's, Montenegro's, Rumania's, Greece's, even Turkey's–had its historic or ethnic justification. Claims and rights were so contradictory and so entangled that the wisest and most disinterested of judges imaginable could never establish one side's justice except at the cost of another's injustice.[22] Tragedy, in the Hegelian aphorism, is the conflict not of right with wrong, but of right with right.[23] This, indeed, was one of the basic aspects of Southeastern Europe's tragedy.

Rivalry in the Balkans combined with accumulating rivalries elsewhere to make the international situation extremely perilous. Recurrent crises in Morocco, as well as in the Near East, were costing every great power some measure of prestige. Germany had been outplayed in the Moroccan crises by France and Great Britain. Yet France had been forced to cede African territory to Germany, and Great Britain to yield predominance in the Ottoman Empire. Russia had been out-played in the successive Near Eastern crises by Austria-Hungary and Germany. Yet Austria-Hungary had been flouted by Serbia and held in leash by Italy, and Germany had to face the fact that instead of exercising a hegemony in Europe, it was now 'encircled' by a ring of potentially hostile powers.

In an atmosphere less conciliatory, the current winds were more gale-like than ever. Nationalism, in an aggravated form, was everywhere rampant; it was dictating to governments an emotional, rather than a reasoned, behaviour; and quite triumphant now in the Balkans, it threatened to spread across east and central Europe, immediately menacing the Habsburg Empire.

No Power ever wants to yield on a matter of prestige, but the Balkan situation made an additional reason why neither France, Russia, Germany nor Austria was at first willling to yield in the Austro-Serbian concflict of July, 1914–it might have a determining effect on the posture of states like Bulgaria and Rumania who were pursuing opportunist policies, and were ready to side with whichever group of the Great Powers seemed likely to prove the stronger and offered better prospects and gains. For several years it had been recognized that a strong Balkan bloc would have an influence in a general European war almost equal to that of Great Power. Hence, in the spring of 1914, Russia was seeking to win Rumania and build up such a bloc including Serbia and Greece, while Austria in turn was trying to erect a counter-bloc with Bulgaria and Turkey.[24] Such was the situation when the shots at Sarajevo precipitated the Austro-Serbian tussle and caused a crisis involving the prestige and power of the Triple Alliance and Triple *Entente*.

III

The killing of the Archduke Franz Ferdinand Von Osterreich-Este, heir apparent to the Habsburg Empire, by a Bosnian student named Gavrilo Princip led to the outbreak of the First World War[25] by a series of quick and irreversible steps–the Austrian ultimatum to Serbia on July 23, her declaration of war on July 28, Russian mobilization on July 30, Germany's declaration of war on Russia on August 1, and French and British declarations of war against Germany on August 3 and 4, 1914. A multitude of books and commentaries have attempted to explain the crucial week following the Austrian ultimatum. Archives have been exhausted, responsible leaders have published their memoirs, and historians have reconstituted the conversations, negotiations, and interviews that had taken place in Vienna, Berlin, St. Petersburg, and Paris. But the very accumulation of documents seemed to result in confusion.

Not going into the detailed maze of the controversy, it would do well to analyze broadly the main actions of the Powers and statesmen which rendered war not only possible, but probable, and finally inevitable; and to explain the intentions of those responsible for them.

It is obvious, as Sidney Fay observes, that 'Austria was more responsible for the immediate origin of the war than any other power.'[26] No one denies that it was the Austrian ultimatum of July 23, that introduced the possibility not only of war, but of general war. What an appalling document it was–and designed to be rejected. The statesmen at Vienna were aware of the risk involved. Russia, who regarded herself as protectress of the Balkan Slavs, would not allow Serbia to be crushed or converted into a sort of protectorate of the dual monarchy and so the Austrian ultimatum was a challenge for her.[27] All Europe realized that the initiative, heavy with menace, had come from Vienna, and that it could not have been taken without the promise of support given in Berlin.

The Serbian reply was conciliatory in its tone, though it rejected the proposal that Austrian officials participate in an inquiry. If we add to the ultimatum the refusal to accept Serbia's reply, and then the severance of diplomatic relations and the bombardment of Belgrade, we have a succession of acts for which Austrian diplomacy (and indirectly German diplomacy) may be held responsible.

Controversy has centred largely on the legitimacy of the Austrian policy. To what extent did the conduct of the Serbian government justify what were exorbitant demands under international law?[28] The facts known at the time gave no ground for Serbia's complicity in the Sarajevo outrage, and consequently gave the Vienna government no authority to make demands incompatible with Serbian sovereignty. Since the Austrian diplomats neither desired nor expected a simple acceptance of their ultimatum, they accepted the possible consequences, including general war.

Why was Austria so intransigent? Was it really driven by a 'vital' necessity to undertake such action, and in such a way? Count Berchtold, the Austro-Hungarian Minister for Foreign Affairs, believed so, and with good reason. The dual monarchy was hovering on the very brink of disintegration, and the corroding Greater Serbia and Yugoslav agitation was nothing less than a menace to her existene. In 1859, the Habsburgs had faced the question of Italian unification, and had been driven out of Italy; in 1866 they faced the same problem in Germany, and with the same result. After the bloody palace revolution at Belgrade in 1903–which supplanted the pro-Austrian King Alexander with the pro-Russian King Peter, making Serbian nationalism intensely Slavophile and bellicose–they were confronted with the Yugoslav problem. And one of the two things seemed likely to happen : either Austria-Hungary must bring the Yugoslavs outside the monarchy (those in Serbia, Montenegro and Turkey) under Habsburg rule, or the Serbs, the most energetic group among the Yugoslavs, would seduce their kinsmen from Habsburg rule and set up a unified indepnedent Yugoslav state. If Habsburg's experience with the Italians and the Germans provided any guide, the second contingency was the more likely.[29]

Naturally those at the helm of affairs in Austria-Hungary favoured the first course. The murder of the Archduke made them adopt brusque methods, to act forcefully and, if need be, by violence. 'That the dual monarchy had the right to take strong action', observes L.C.B. Seaman, 'is sometimes overlooked in the understandable hurry to condemn to action that was in fact taken.'[30] Nor does the view that the Serbs inside the dual monarchy had a right, if they so wished, to join with the free Serbs to build a Great Serb State justify an assumption that the first duty of the Habsburg monarchy was to give its Slav provinces away. 'No amount of righteous anger' about their responsibility in rendering war probable should obscure the difficulty of the dual monarchy's position in 1914.[31]

Yet the choice was not between survival by destroying Serbia or committing suicide after failing to do so. The choice in 1914 was between moderation and death. The fundamental character of the problem. as a clash of German against Slav, race against race, demanded that it be handled with superlative delicacy and restraint. In failing to display either quality, the dual monarchy was guilty of a fatal error of judgment.

It is very questionable whether Berchtold's resolute determination to eliminate Serbia as a factor of political importance was, after all, the right method, even if he had succeeded in keeping the war 'localized' and in temporarily improving the Austrian monarchy. If Russia in 1914, because of military unpreparedness or lack of support, had tolerated the execution of Berchtold's designs, it is quite certain that within the next two or three years she would have taken steps to wipe out this second humiliation, which was so much more damaging to her prestige than that of 1908–9. Berchtold's plan could not be a final solution of the Austro-Serbian antagonism. Franz Ferdinand and many others recognized the delicacy of this situation. 'It was the tragic fate of Austria that the only man who might have had the power and ability to develop Austria along sound lines became the innocent victim of the crime which was the occasion of the World War and so of her ultimate disruption.'[32] For Franz Ferdinand had the reputation of wanting to reconstruct the dual monarchy into a trialism, with the south Slav nationalities as the third pillar, thereby saving the situation and 'taking the wind out of the sails of south Slav nationalism.'[33] The Government did not have the courage to try out such a thoroughgoing solution of the problem as the Archduke had proposed and which would perhaps have led to the assimilation of the south Slavs. It, therefore found itself in a constant struggle with this spirit of irredentism, and did not feel strong enough to succeed in overcoming that spirit by peaceful methods.[34]

The Danube monarchy was an 'anachronism', an 'anomaly' in a continent of virile nations. It had had to contend with the problem of the emergent nations, in one form or another, throughout the nineteenth century. As the successor to the Holy Roman Empire of the German nation on southern European soil, the Habsburg monarchy had never been able to come to terms with a modern world of heterogeneous nationalities all agitating for emancipation. For decades it had been content with a system of 'muddling through' which had led to a state of complete political paralysis. As a result of her anachronistic structure and concomitant stagnation, she had from the turn of the century drifted helplessly into the maelstrom of the Slav nationalist movement. 'In a deeper sense', Imanuel Geiss states, 'the ultimate responsibility (for the Sarajevo affair) falls on the ruling class in Austria-Hungary, less because it sent Franz Ferdinand into an "alley of bomb throwers"[35] than on account of its inability to satisfy the legitimate struggle of their various nationalities for freedom, equality and social justice.'[36]

Men who shape history are admittedly rare. Yet the absence of genius at this fatal moment in Austria-Hungary's history is unfortunate. Count Berchtold found himself in a difficult position. Although not in the least bellingerent by temperament[37] , he saw the dangers for the Danube monarchy. Evidence or not, he was bent on humiliating Serbia[38], as an unrestrained Serbia, he felt, posed a vital threat to the Habsburg monarchy, no matter who had sent Princip to the Bosnian capital. Austria's intransigence after Sarajevo, which surprised and shocked the world, is only intelligible in the light of her experiences and emotions since 1908. At the close of the Bosnian crisis, Serbia had promised to be a good neighbour, but she had not kept her word and her intimacy with Russia was notorious.[39] For Austria to sit with folded arms and await dismemberment at the hands of her enemies was to proclaim her impotence and invite attack. The carefully organised murder of the heir to the throne appeared to demand some striking vindication of the authority of the state. It must boldly come forward as a great power, or it would sink in prestige and hasten its own downfall. Berchtold hurriedly declared war against Serbia in order to forestall all efforts at mediation. The Austrian demands would have to be accepted *en bloc* and must not be discussed. In such cases the powers always tried to water down demands. To Berchtold and his colleagues the mere thought of a renewal of the Ambassadors' Conference of 1912–13 was o'dious. The matter must be settled directly between the two parties immediately concerned. It was purely an Austro-Serb feud.[40] A more perceptive statesman than Berchtold, and one with a clearer vision of the future, might have formulated concrete demands for Serbia that would secure Austria's ends without leaving so much scope for uncertainty about what really was intended as an objective.

Austria's policy of July, 1914 can be explained, but hardly forgiven. 'Austria, in 1914', to quote Joachim Remak, 'had very much of a premeditated desire for a small Balkan war. Did it want that war to spread? No, but the truth was that the reckless and inadequate people who were deciding policy in Vienna did not really care.'[41]

Serbia represented the very antithesis of Austria. If the Habsburg monarhcy entered the twentieth century as an archaic institution, Serbia entered it full of dynamism and ambition. The accession of Peter Karageorgevic resulted in a reorientation of Serbian policy. He aspired to be a second Victor Emmanuel–to liberate the South Slavs and unite them into a strong nation. Peter helped gradually to disperse the cloud of dishonour which had been hovering over the country during the reigns of his predecessors; 'but far more important in rehabilitating Serbia in the eyes of Europe than any question of personalities was its sudden accidental elevation to a central area of conflict between the two rival groups of the Triple Alliance and Triple *Entente*.'[42] 'Little Serbia stood', as G.Lowes Dickinson observes, 'on the verge of satisfying her national ambitions at the cost of the peoples and civilizations of three continents.'[43]

It was natural that Serbia should aspire to unite under her sceptre the discontented southern slav subjects of her neighbour, should use their rankling grievances to foster the Pan-Serb idea, and look to Russia for assistance as in similar circumstances Cavour had looked to France. It was equally natural that Austria, who coveted no man's territory, and who, alone of the eight great powers of the world possessed no colonies, should be determined to oppose energetically the openly proclaimed ambition to rob her of provinces which she had held for centuries.[44] The concept of a unified south Slav state was fully as defensible as was Austria-Hungary's right to survival.

'Tragedy', in the Hegelian definition, 'is the conflict not of right with wrong, but of right with right.' But the Serbians set about achieving their goal with a truly frightening disregard of the consequences. Serbian nationalism was a savage thing, born of centuries of oppression, and therefore ugly with accumulated hatred and suppressed ambitions. The assassination at Sarajevo was its brutal consequence.[45]

In the words of Joachim Remak :

> Without Sarajevo, Europe might have remained at peace for no one can say how many years to come. 1914 was not 1939. Too much was right with Europe then. The world had weathered (and would again weather) considerably worse periods of crisis without recourse to global conflict. History resists prediction; alliances, attitudes, conditions, constellations of power, all change in the normal course of events, often rapidly so. How they had changed between the 1880s and the turn of the century, for instance, and how, with Franz Ferdinand alive, they might have changed once more![46]

Sarajevo, then, was a major cause of the war, not merely its occasion. It was this occurrence as well as the errors of fact and judgement that took place in its aftermath that 'gave all the various elements of friction their unique opportunity of coalescing.'[47] It cannot be denied, observes Edith Durham, 'that the power or powers that wantonly threw the first spark upon the tinder and so precipitated the catastrophe was guilty of a grave crime.'[48]

For nearly a decade the truth about the Sarajevo plot remained shrouded in mystery. The official Austrian version of the conspiracy, which laid the blame largely on the Serbian agitation for a 'Greater Serbia',[49] did not inspire much confidence–to put it mildly–among most people in the *Entente* or neutral countries. Serbian writers, on the other hand, were careful to publish nothing in conflict with the attitude of injured innocence which their governemnt had assumed in 1914. Yet the fact is, as Sidney Fay affirms, that Austria's charges in 1914 'are really an understatement, rather than an overstatement of Serbia's responsibility.'[50] We now know that the assassins of the Archduke, though natives of Bosnia and subjects of the Habsburg Empire, were members of the Serbian secret society of the 'Black Hand', that they obtained their weapons and training in Belgrade, and that they planned and executed their crime with the assistance of several high officers in the Serbian army. Also, we have ground for believing that Nicholas Pashitch, the Prime Minister of Serbia, had foreknowledge of the conspiracy and yet gave the Austrian government no adequate warning, and, after the assassination, took no steps to discover and bring to justice Serbians in Belgrade, who had been implicated in the plot. In fact Serbian police officials appear to have actually aided one of them, Ciganovitch, conveniently to escape. Pashitch waited to see what evidence the Austrian authorites could find. To have attempted to arrest Ciganovitch, who was a member of the Black Hand, and to have divulged the part played by such prominent members of it as Dimitrijevitch and Tankositch, would have still further intensified the opposition which had already rocked the government. Clearly Pashitch did not dare to take action against the leaders of such a powerful organization–a step which would certainly have endangered his own life–and therefore, he adopted a purely quiescent attitude hoping that Austria and Europe would not learn the truth.[51]

In the opinion of R.W. Seton-Watson : Energetic action by Pashitch 'during the week or even fortnight following the murder' would have 'increased the chances of friendly mediation from outside. To this extent, then, the Pashitch Cabinet must share the responsibility for what befell.' This omission is only very partially explained by absorption in the electoral campaign. But, continues Seton-Watson, 'a true grasp of European realities should have shown that infinitely more was at stake. Yet Pashitch remained passive, took no steps to put himself in the right at Vienna ... It convicts him of great remissness and lack of judgement.'[52] 'The three precious weeks', says Edith Durham, 'during which the criminals could have been brought to book and Europe purged of danger were allowed to pass by ... Serbia preferred to risk war rather than risk exposure.'[53]

Did Serbia 'warn' Austria? This question is exceedingly important in apportioning the blame. The 'warning' was given in the most general terms; it contained no hint of the possibility of assassination by civilian conspirators or of any plot such as was actually on foot. It referred only to the possible danger of disloyalty among the troops. It is, therefore, small wonder that so little attention was paid to it. Nor does it in any way relieve the Serbian government of the guilt of withholding information concerning a plot to commit murder, connived at by its own officers.[54]

A truly unenviable dilemma confronted Pashitch. If, as Joachim Remak observes, 'he revealed the plot to the Austrians, he might well find himself the next victim marked for assassination by the Black Hand.' In the opinion of Remak, Pashitch was no coward, but there were other dangers involved as well : 'Telling the Austrians the facts would mean admitting the extent to which the Serbian government was aware of, and had tolerated those subversive activities which it had always disclaimed.'[55] The relationship between Serbia and Austria was awfully delicate. Pashitch decided to give a sort of cryptic warning which would be neither formal nor specific.

The crime of Sarajevo, in the opinion of Seton-Watson, remains 'an indelible blot upon the movement for Yugoslav Unity.'[56] If the Serbian government had knowledge, however vague, of the conspiracy against the Archduke Franz Ferdinand, 'it must be charged with a serious dereliction of duty in not conveying a warning (in the true sense) to the Austro-Hungarian authorities. Its negligence may be explained by 'the peculiar character of Austro-Serbian relations' and by its internal political difficulties, but hardly excused.'[57]

On the other hand, it is necessary to consider that by its rigid adherence to outdated political and social conceptions the traditional Austrian Empire left no room for the political agitations of the young South Slav intelligentsia who, in their desperation, were finally driven to the crime of political murder. When the young Bosnians murdered the Austrian heir, it was a whole political system which they were overthrowing, or thought they were overthrowing.

The Serbian government found itself in a difficult situation when faced with the Austrian ultimatum. Pashitch and his colleagues had instantly decided that 'no Serbian government could accept the Austrian demands in their entirety.' Such being the case, and since Austria would evidently reject any reply which did not yield on all points, they could afford to give their reply a very conciliatory form, apparently yielding on many points. This kind of a conciliatory reply was more of a diplomatic gesture than a serious effort to satisfy Austria; it would help win the sympathy and protection of the powers[58], and tend to place Austria in the wrong when she rejected it. It is significant that two or three hours before the reply was given, the Serbian government had already ordered the general mobilization of the army. If war was inevitable, Serbia would carry it on.[59]

Germany was at this moment, according to a German historian, passing through 'a crisis in her position as a world power'[60], and she was irritated and disturbed by Austria's weakness. In her own interest, she felt the necessity of buoying up her ally. If Austria was broken up, Germany would stand alone in Europe (since Italy and Rumania were allies in nothing but name), wedged in between a hostile Russia and a France bent on revenge. Bethmann-Hollweg, Chancellor of the German empire, regarded immediate action as the best solution of Austria's difficulties in the Balkans, and from an international standpoint he considered the present moment more favourable than later.[61] It was regarded as Austria's last chance to reestablish her claim as a great power. It was not only the right but the duty of the dual monarchy to take action against the great Serbian movement which menaced its existence; and it was in Germany's interest that Austria should not stagger before the southern Slavs, over whom Russia aspired to play the part of protector. If the Austrian empire were destroyed, the roots of the German empire would be impaired. Therefore, the German government felt bound to accede to Berchtold's request for support and gave him a free hand to deal with Serbia; it also hoped and expected to 'localize' the Austro-Serbian conflict.[62] The mistake that Berlin committed was not in promising aid but in allowing Berchtold alone to steer the ship. On entering such a perilous course, where the existence of the German nation was at stake, the

Wilhelmstrasse should have insisted on consultation throughout.

Germany was the victim of her alliance with Austria and of her own folly. Bethmann was soon to learn that after promising unconditional support, Germany's influence at Vienna had virtully ceased to count. He confessed that he considered the ultimatum too sharp, and it was precisely on the contents of that document that the destiny of the world was to turn.[63]

Germany's great initial blunder, according to M.P. Price, was that she refused to regard the Austro-Serbian dispute as one that concerned any other but those two countries, and would not recognize the claim of Russia to be consulted about the fate of Serbia.[64] There is every reason to think that the central powers 'would have been satisfied with only a limited degree of success', which would have strengthened their position and reestablished their prestige. But they did demand that Europe should keep her hands off, that she should stand by and watch Serbia being crushed. Was this probable or even possible with Russia so openly hostile? It was unthinkable that she should abandon the Balkan Slavs, who were her special proteges. The great question was whether the St. Petersburg government would limit itself to a diplomatic protest, or whether it would resort to armed intervention. Bethmann-Hollweg recalled that Russia had been satisfied with mere threats on two occasions already. She might easily withdraw a third time.[65] 'That it was psychologically impossible for resurgent Russia', says G.P. Gooch, 'to watch unmoved the chastisement of her protege was hidden from the eyes of Berlin.'[66]

That it must stand by its ally on a vital issue seemed clear. Yet, while steadfastly championing Austrian policy in public declarations, the Chancellor privately preached moderation at Vienna. Austria had announced that she did not want any territorial aggrandizement in Serbia; but she had not explained her aims to her ally. Serbia's reply had gone so far to meet her demands that it created a favourable impression on the Chancelleries of Europe. If Austria remained adamant, opinion would gradually turn against her throughout the continent. The German Ambassador at Vienna had to handle the situation dextrously. It was a question of combining the suppression of Pan-Serb propaganda with the avoidance of a world war. If Russia were convinced that the occupation of portions of Serbian territory would be purely temporary, she might be induced to accept the situation. If war came, the responsibility must be recognized to fall on her shoulders. Nor was Bethmann any better pleased with Berchtold's attitude to Rome. Relations between Austria and Italy were anything but cordial. The coming war was contrary to Italian interests, since in the event of success, Austrian power in the Balkans would be increased. To her demand for compensation under Article 7 of the Triple Alliance, Berchtold had replied that territorial acquisitions were not contemplated, and that it would be time to discuss it if they were made. It was arranged that, if Italy fulfilled her duty as an ally, she might have Valona, in which case Austria would hold North Albania under control.[67] The clumsiness of Austrian diplomacy with regard to Italy irritated the Kaiser and the Chancellor. Her declaration that, in the event of permanent occupation of Serbian territory, she would consult Italy, falsified her assurance to Russia of territorial disinterestedness and would inevitably be known in St. Petersburg. Germany should not tolerate a double policy. Besides, if on the eve of a possible European conflagration Austria threatened to disrupt the Triple Alliance, the whole structure would become unstable.[68]

When Bethmann realized that Russia was likely to intervene, that England might not remain neutral, and that there was danger of a World War of which Germany andAustria would appear to be the instigators, he made a genuine effort to call a halt on Austria, but it was too late. He pressed mediation proposals on Vienna, but Berchtold was insensible to the pressure.[69] On July 30, Bethmann sent a pathetically urgent appeal to Vienna : 'If Austria rejects all mediation, we are faced with a conflagration in which England is against us, Italy and Rumania in all probability are not with us, and we should be two great powers to four.'

Owing to England's hostility, Germany would bear the brunt. 'Under these circumstances we must urge the Vienna cabinet to accept mediation for honourable conditions.' Bethmann also sent a grim warning to Vienna that the refusal of any discussion with St. Petersburg would be a grave error, for it would actually provoke Russia to intervene, which was in Austria's interest to avoid. Conscious of 'our duty as allies ... we must (yet) decline to be dragged into a world conflagration by Vienna, wantonly and in neglect of our advice.' The effect of the Chancellor's exhortations was diminshed by a telegram from Moltke[70] to Conrad[71] urging instant mobilization against Russia, and adding that Germany would follow suit.[72] The German Chancellor was fighting a losing battle, and he knew it. And the military pressure was beginning to tell on him.

Russia's general mobilization produced the same effect in Germany as the German violation of Belgian neutrality was to produce in England, for no better cry could rally the nation than the threat of a Russian invasion. The provocation of mobilizing against Germany while she was mediating in Vienna at Russia's request was so vehement that there was a clamour for sharp measures.[73] In the opinion of Sidney Fay : 'It was the hasty Russian general mobilization, assented to on July 29 and ordered on July 30, while Germany was still trying to bring Austria to accept mediation proposals, which finally rendered the European war inevitable.[74]

Germany's geographical position between France and Russia, and her inferiority in number of troops, had made it necessary for her to crush the French army quickly at first and then turn against Russia. This could only be done, according to her strategists, by marching through Belgium, as it was generally anticipated by military men that she would do in case of a European war. On July 29, after Austria had declared war on Serbia, Bethmann sent to the German minister in Brussels a sealed envelope which the latter was not to open except on further instructions. It contained the demand for the passage of the German army through Belgium. 'This does not mean, however, that Germany had decided for war.' In fact, Bethmann was one of the last of the statesmen to abandon hope of peace[75], but he was an amateur in diplomacy and was never master in his own house. 'In fact to accuse Germany of having consciously planned and provoked the outbreak of war in August, 1914', wites A.J.P. Taylor, 'is to credit Germany with more direction than she possessed.' Berchtold, overwhelmed in July, 1914 with contradictory telegrams from Bethmann and Moltke, passed the best verdict on German politics : 'What a joke! Who does rule in Berlin then?'[76]

With the tightening of the Triple *Entente*, Germany was forced to lean ever more heavily on her sole dependable ally, who turned the altered relationship to account. The paradox that the tougher partner should be taken in tow by the weaker was the product of the blunders which left Germany without other powerful friends. During the July crisis the policy of Berlin, as of Paris and London, was governed by the nightmare of isolation. It would be too much to expect a Bismarck in every generation. But at this time a statesman of the highest calibre was needed perhaps more than ever. In the Bulgarian crisis of the eighties, Bismarck had told his ally point-blank that he would not fight for her Balkan ambitions; but at that time the wire to St. Petersburg was intact and he possessed the friendship of England, which his bungling successors had lost.

Benthmann declares that the decision whether there was to be a world war rested with Russia, and the blame was hers. He failed to see that she had no real choice. The situation had changed much in the last few years and the smooth triumphs of the Bosnian crisis were no more possible. True, Russia lacked Austria's excuse of struggling for mere existence; but from the standpoint of international diplomacy there is not much difference in such terms as self-preservation, prestige, honour, or 'the best interest' of a nation. The failure of Berlin, once it had become plain that an Austro-Serbian war was likely to become European in scope, to search for a compromise by straining every nerve, is unpardonable. There is little excuse for the panicky and pernicious decisions that Berlin made during tne July crisis, and for stumbling into an undesired conflict when the best cards were in the hands of the enemy. 'Every war is a gamble, and the conflagration implicit in the German response to Austria's appeal was among the most desperate ventures in history.'[77] German policy during the crucial weeks preceding the outbreak of World War I can justly be accused of shortsightedness, vacillation, lack of method, want of forethought and an understanding of the psychology of other peoples. 'But no one can maintain with any show of reason that, says Erich Brandenburg, 'she either wished for war or strove to bring it about.'[78] And she made genuine, though too belated efforts to avert one.

Russia was partly responsible for the Austro-Serbian conflict because of the repeated encouragement which she had given at Belgrade, that Serbian national unity would be ultimately achieved with Russian aid at Austrian expense. This had emboldened the Belgrade cabinet to hope for Russian support in case of a war with Austria, and the hope did not prove vain in July, 1914.

Russia's defeat in the Far East had thrown her back on Europe, and it was obvious that as soon as she recovered her breath she would, in conformity with tradition, pursue her historic ambitions in the turbulent Near East. Her inability to take up the challenge in 1909 was a bitter memory, and no one had a right to expect that she would submit to such humiliation again. Indeed, the Bosnian crisis was not only a stimulant to Yugoslav nationalism, it deepened Habsburg fears of the disruption of their polyglot empire.[79] The Russian press took up the cry that the Slavic brothers in the Balkans must be liberated, and that war between Slavdom and Teutondom was inevitable. Thus, apart from diplomacy, the clash had a deeper cause in the movement of ideas and passions. For two supranational empires still existed in an age of nationalism. The Ottoman Empire had not yet been liquidated, and already diplomats were anxiously looking forward to the time when they would be confronted with the problem of the successsion to Austria-Hungary.[80] With such hopes Russian military preparations went forward briskly. By 1914 her armaments, though not yet completed, had made such progress that her military were confident of success, if they had French and British support.

Both Russia, assured of her strength, and Austria, driven by desperate fear, were determined not to yield an inch in the next Balkan crisis. If either received a setback her rival would capture Balkan leadership. As Berchtold saw the long arm of Russia in the Sarajevo murder, so the Russian foreign minister envisaged the Austrian ultimatum as a blow at Nicholas II not less than at Peter Karageorgevitch. Though bound by no treaty obligation to intervene, Russia could not forfeit her historic claim to be the champion of the Slav races. The same instinctive pride of a great power 'which prompted Vienna to throw down the glove compelled St. Petersburg to pick it up.' It is true that, while Austria fought for national existence and self-preservation, Russia, whom nobody threatened, marched out to battle in the name of prestige. But, as said earlier, in the accepted scale of national values, prestige, honour and security are motive forces of approximately the same weight. Russia's championship of Pan-Serb ambitions was Austria's chief anxiety. yet the ultimate cause of the conflagration was the rivalry of two proud empires, which was far older than the Austro-Serb feud.[81] Thus when the hour of reckoning came, neither side cared or dared to draw back. It was doubly tragic that the fate of the Balkans rested largely with Sazonoff and Berchtold, two clumsy and impetuous statesmen prone to dash headlong into sudden and dangerous action.

Sazonoff had feared that some sudden stroke might be attempted by Austria, which would humiliate Serbia directly, and thereby Russia indirectly. He was always apprehensive lest Germany or Austria might do something to damage Russia's prestige in the Balkans and in Europe. It was a point on which he was very sensitive, particularly in view of the strong Pan-Slav sentiment of the Russian press and the militarists, who were not wholly friendly to him, and who might drive him from office if he suffered a diplomatic rebuff.[82]

Austria's promise of 'territorial disinterestedness', which held good only for the time being, did not imply that the balance of power in the Balkans would be maintained.[83] Even if he did not suspect the sincerity of this 'disinterestedness', the Russian minister for foreign affairs felt that the Austrian demands would reduce Serbia to the level of a vassal state, and would be an overwhelming blow to the prestige of Russia. He was strongly encouraged by the French ambassador to stand firm in protecting Serbia and in checking Austria. French President Poincare's visit fired the Russian militarists with new zeal and hope, and even stirred the Czar. It is, therefore, hardly surprising that Sazonoff should have wished to block Austria's path, and that he should have rejected outright the idea of localization. Knowing of the Austrian ultimatum, he had decided to take the side of Serbia, if necessary, even if it should involve war.[84] He adopted the plan of 'partial mobilization' which was a dangerous method of exerting diplomatic pressure. The Russian foreign minister thought that Austria could be checked by a firm stand just as Russia had been checked in 1908–1909, and the Czar, in an exalted mood, hoped for the best.

If the announcement of partial mobilization should not succeed in restraining Austria, it could at least be used conveniently to explain and screen the measures of the 'period preparatory to war', which it was decided were to take place over the whole empire and which would greatly facilitate the general mobilization against Germany as well as against Austria, if eventually necessary. Sazonoff believed that he now had the trump cards in his hand. He could continue to negotiate, and he was armed with the threat of force to fortify his bluff; but at the same time military preparations would be going on preparatory to a general mobilization if his bluff of partial mobilization was called.[85]

There seems little doubt, however, that the partial mobilization plan was seriously regarded by Sazonoff and the Czar, if not by the general staff, as a good means of checking Austria without provoking Germany. And if it provoked Germany, Russia would wait for it to declare war or attack first, and thus be branded before the world as the initiator. There seems equally little doubt that between July, 26 and 28 Sazonoff honestly carried on diplomatic negotiations with the optimistic hope, not shared by the Russian military authorities, of achieving a peaceful solution satisfactory to Russia.[86]

What thus began auspiciously, ended direfully. The news of Austria's declaration of war on Serbia put an abrupt end to Sazonoff's optimism and gave a new and fatal turn to Russian danger. Had Russia mobilized her forces against Austria only, a negotiated peace, giving due recognition to both Russia's and Austria's legitimate interests, might still have been possible. But the decision to proceed with partial mobilization was followed (on the afternoon of July 30) by the orders for general mobilization. This was a much more serious step to take. Here we come to, what Joachim Remak feels, 'Russia's quite staggering responsibility for World War I.' The reasons for general mobilization were technical rather than political; honest error and the absence of flexible military planning rather than premeditated design accounted for the Czar's decision.[87] Russian mobilization was a much slower affair than German mobilization, and if there were really no hope of maintaining peace, it was in Russia's interest to begin as soon as possible to summon her reservists and to arrange for the transportation of troops. Furthermore, the plans of the Russian general staff had not admitted the possibility of partial mobilization which might seriously damage the whole technical military machinery.[88] But no amount of explaining can alter the fact that by ordering general mobilization Russia had taken the step 'which military men everywhere clearly understood almost certainly meant war.' Partial mobilization might be undertaken by a great power without leading to war, as had happened on several occasions in Russia and Austria in the preceding years. But general mobilization by a great power was normally undersood to mean that it had only resorted to this final step of putting the great military machine in motion when it had finally concluded that war could no longer be avoided. 'The choice of the moment is influenced by a complex of varied political causes.' But once the moment has been fixed, there is no going back; 'it determines mechanically the beginning of war.'[89]

Russia's responsibility for the catastrophe was greater than

Sazonoff was prepared to admit. A less volatile and more judicious statesman than Sazonoff, and one surer of his ground, might not have reacted with so much emotion and so little regard for political realities as he did on hearing of the Austrian ultimatum. A smaller concern for Russia's prestige and his own might have prevented his urging the Serbs to reject the ultimatum (as he did) and it might have delayed the period preparatory to war and given time for fruitful negotiation. Like the foreign ministers in the other capitals, he was convinced that he had no alternative. All of them wanted peace, but they desired other things still more. He also distrusted German influence in the Ottoman Empire, and believed, like his predecessor that 'the way to Constantinople lies through Berlin.'[90] The story of Germany's 'blank check' to Austria is well known, but the Russians were doing no better at Counselling caution to Belgrade. The essence of the whole matter of Russian responsibility for the outbreak of the First World War is stated by William L. Langer in his review of Sazonoff's *Fatefull Years* : 'Sazonoff wholeheartedly supported the military men in the demand for general mobilization ... (he) did nothing to avert the catastrophe, but backed the Serbs to the limit and allowed things to take their course.'[91]

As for the French Government, it had no eagerness for war, though it had a morbid fear lest France should lose an ally and the alliance should lose its prestige; and if, peradventure, general war should come, it might have the advantage of enabling France to undo the defeat of 1870.

France had never abandoned the hope of recovering the Rhine provinces, and for that reason could not be included among the satiated powers who at any given moment are the most effective champions of peace. Poincare and his friends were still pursuing what Boulanger had, except that they were doing so with greater intelligence, tact, patience, and skill and, hence, with greater effectiveness. The desire to undo the settlement of 1871 was as powerful a motive force in France's system of alliances as any. Yet, all speculations about France's ultimate objectives have about them a degree of uncertainty. Perhaps France would, some day, have fought to avenge Sedan, perhaps she would not. We will never know.

We know that France was striving for the balance of power, that master principle which incited treaties, crystallized *Ententes*, and guided the Chancelleries of Europe on their perilous course. Raymond Poincare's accession to office[92] had opened a new phase in French foreign policy, when the French Government felt the need to revive intimacy with Russia. The experience of the Agadir crisis had shown what a bitter memory Russian statesmen retained of the attitude of France in the Bosnian crisis. If fresh Franco-German difficulties arose, was it not prudent to count on stronger Russian support? And if reciprocity was to be assured, was it not necessary to evince a greater interest in Russia's Balkan policy? This was the probable explanation of the new tendencies revealed in the application of the alliance in 1912, when Poincare, in view of a possible Austro-Russian friction about a Serb port, adopted a more decided attitude.

Thus, under the stress of events, a broader interpretation of the partnership was pursued. The probability of a general conflict augmented with the Agadir crisis and increased still further with the Balkan struggle. England offered no such support as the French longed for. Russia alone could be counted on in case of need, just as Germany and Austria formed a solid phalanx.[93]

'Sazonoff must be firm, and we must support him' : these words sum up better than anything else the significance of Poincare's visit to Russia in July, 1914. He was conscious of Sazonoff's vacillating and mercurial temperament, of his fervent Russian nationalism, alternating, however, with a genuine desire for peace and a certain timidity which made him recoil at crucial moments from supporting the Serbians to the point of bayonet. Which is why Poincare wanted to stiffen Sazonoff's attitude toward Austria. He wanted him to warn Austria against making impossible demands on Serbia, and to prevent him, in case of need, from accepting any compromise which might be regarded as a diplomatic defeat for the Triple *Entente* at the hands of the central powers.[94] He gave a grim warning to Count Szapary, the Austro-Hungarian ambassador at St. Petersburg : 'With a little goodwill, this Serbian affair is easy to settle. But it is easy also for it to become envenomed. Serbia has very warm friends in the Russian people. And Russia has an ally, France. What complications are to be feared here!'[95] Poincare virtually gave Russia carte blanche in the Balkans.

The position of the French ambassador at St. Petersburg, Maurice Paleologue, was very influential. He went 'far beyond the terms of the alliance, beyond the need to show diplomatic solidarity, beyond the limits of previous French policy.'[96] 'A different ambassador might well have altered the course of events.'[97]

France clung steadfastly to her ally : a devation from this course might have been detrimental, so she thought, to her prestige; it would have increased the contempt for a 'decadent power' entertained in German circles, and left her defenceless against the victorious Teuton.

President Poincare made no attempt to restrain Russia from military measures which he knew would call forth German counter-measures and cause war. If he had expressed himself forcefully and unmistakably to Russia : 'Do not order general mobilization for the present while diplomatic negotiations are going on'–if he had even spoken as vigorously as Bethmann was speaking to Vienna–there was a possibility that war might still have been avoided.[98] Nor did he keep his government promptly and fully informed of the military steps which were being taken at St. Petersburg.

He was by now more concerned in procuring England's aid and in taking military precautions in France, than in holding back Russia. Upon his return to France, Poincare made efforts for peace, but his great preoccupation was to minimize French and Russian preparatory measurs and emphasize those of Germany, in order to secure the certainty of British support in a struggle which he now regarded as inevitable.[99] And this conflict between efforts to satisfy strategic and diplomatic interests was the origin of the famous '10-kilometer withdrawal.'

There was no line drawn exactly ten kilometers from the frontier everywhere. At numerous points it was only four or five kilometers. Nevertheless, the fact that the French Government did hold back its covering troops a few kilometers from the frontier was a wise measure. It did tend to prevent unfortunate 'incidents' which might have precipitated a war. But it would be wrong to ascribe it to Poincare's love of peace. Rather it was a measure essentially calculated to win British approbation and military support, and to diminish the importance of the military measures France was undertaking preparatory to war.[100]

Sir Edward Grey's first peace proposal for 'direct conversations' between Vienna and St. Petersburg fell flat, owing to Poincare's strong disapproval and desire to substitute in its place Triple *Entente* pressure at Vienna.[101] The direct conversations to which Sazonoff agreed later, July 26-28, after Poincare had left Russia and no longer exercised such an immediate influence on the Russian foreign minister, were owing to the initiative, not of Grey, but of the German ambassador in St. Petersburg.[102]

In most of the peace proposals, England was generally recognized as holding the key to the situation, for several reasons. Her direct interests in the Balkans were less than those of the other great powers. Just as during the Balkan Wars, so in July 1914, the British secretary for foreign affairs was looked to as the man most impartial and best able to take steps toward calling an international conference or providing some other means of preventing the two groups of great powers from colliding. Besides, England was not bound by any formal alliance with either group. And finally, it was realized that with her great sea power she was in a position to exert a decisive pressure both upon Franco-Russian and Austro-German policy.

Nobody knew precisely what action enigmatic England with her powerful navy would take in case of war. In the dramatic week of July 25–August 1, Grey persistently used his influence to preserve peace. Yet his policy was not clear, nor his conviction definite. On the one hand he affirmed that England was still free to choose her course, on the other he had consented to secret Anglo-French military and naval conversations and had privately assured France that England would doubtless support her if attacked by Germany. Grey seemed to drift with the tide, turning this way and that, and leading both groups of powers 'to gamble, the one on British neutrality, the other on British support.'[103] Towards the end of the fatal week, Grey was urgently pressed by France and Russia to announce England's solidarity with the *Entente*, in order to make Germany cautious and force the Triple Alliance to become conciliatory. But Grey refused to take this advice, partly because he was warned by his ambassadors at Paris and St. Petersburg that a blanket endorsement of the *Entente* would play into the hands of the French and Russian war mongers, and partly because he had a cabinet nearly evenly divided. Consequently, he moved cautiously, may be overcautiously.

Historians have argued that if Grey had candidly committed England to either neutrality or belligerency, the war might have been averted or at least postponed. If the Germans had been told, early and with conviction, that Britain would take part in the war, they would very probably have prevented instead of encouraging the Austrian ultimatum and declaration of war. There is strong evidence for this. 'A less fastidious, conciliatory, and correct statesman', writes Laurence Lafore, 'might have acted more effectively. A modest measure of duplicity, such as many diplomats regard as a proper tool of their trade, would have permitted him to make much stronger representations much sooner than he did.' No absolute commitment was necessary; he could have pointed out to both Lichnowsky, the German ambassador, and William Goschen, his own ambassador at Berlin, that Great Britain did regard the Austro-Sebrian problem as one of European and British concern (that would have been a matter of judgement, not of propriety) and that if war broke out, Great Britain would almost certainly join it. This would have been tricky, but seasoned diplomats of the utmost rectitude like Arthur Nicolson and Eyre Crowe were pressing for something like it. 'Sir Edward suffered', Lafore observes, 'from an excess of scruples and perhaps an insufficiency of grasp; his case is a demonstration for the argument that there is at times nothing so dangerous as pacific punctilio.'[104] No serious student of history has ever questioned Grey's personal intentions, but doubts lurk as to his political determination and diplomatic skill.

The violation of Belgian neutrality roused the country to righteous anger, but it was an occasion rather than the cause of England's entry into the war.[105] *The Times* was right when it wrote, on December 4, 1914, 'We have always fought for the balance of power. We are fighting for it today.'[106] Fear of isolation if France and Russia were crushed, and the German menace intensified, impelled Great Britain, much against her will, to enter the conflict. Before the guns had been moved into position, however, it can scarcely be said that the British did much better in restraining the Eastern member of theTriple *Entente* than they would accuse the Germans of doing vis-a-vis Vienna. George MacMunn has aptly remarked : 'it is a matter of history that our Liberal Governments have usually been those to have war on their hands.'[107] An examination of the actions of different governments and their statesmen makes it clear that the verdict of the Versailles Treaty that Germany and her allies were responsible for the war is historically unsound.[108] The European scene was not occupied by 'sheep and wolf' states, but by sovereign states equally determined to maintain their power and prestige. No nation willed the war, and statesmen blundered into it rather than sought it. Nor is there any scientific way of apportioning blame for it among the various sovereigns and diplomats who have been referred to in the preceding pages. They would have been quite unable to precipitate a world war, had they not been equally with millions of common people, the more or less willing agents of immense forces, which for a generation had been predisposing the civilized world to mortal combat.

In the forty years following the Franco-Prussian War there developed a system of alliances which divided Europe into two hostile groups. This hostility was accentuated by the increase of armaments, national antagonisms and ambitions, militarism, economic rivalry, and newspaper incitement. But it is very doubtful whether all these dangerous tendencies would have actually led to war, had it not been for the assassination of Franz Ferdinand. The shots in Sarajevo brought all the gathering tensions in the world, on the continent and in the Balkans in particular, into sudden eruption.

Ridden by dissident and hostile minorities, Austria-Hungary believed that only strong measures could save the venerable monarchy from disintegration. The Sarajevo crime brought out the Vienna plan for a final reckoning with Serbia whose ambitions for a Greater Serbia could not be harmonized with the interests and territorial integrity of Austria-Hungary. Russia knew that if she showed vacillation the loyalty of her proteges would waver. Therefore, no yielding. Vienna and St. Petersburg were both firmly resolved. Unfortunately, neither saw clearly the resolution of the other.

Germany felt that she must heed the call of her last dependable ally, and hoped by the old threatening attitude to prevent Russia from intervening. She underestimated the dangers of that policy, and had a feeling that if the great reckoning must come, it was perhaps as well it should come now than later when both Russia and France would be better prepared militarily. She would not agree to bring her ally before a European tribunal in which she had little faith. William II and Bethmann had imagined that they could 'localize' the Austro-Serbian conflict, but the determined attitude of Russia filled them with consternation. So, somewhat tardily, the Chancellor pressed Austria to negotiate directly with Russia, but Berchtold was impassive to the pressure, and the *Entente* Powers did not believe in the sincerity of his pressure, especially as it produced no results.

That Bismarck's successors would not be his equals might have been expected; that quite so much would divide them from him was another matter. It was foolish to gamble on the belief that Russia might abstain from action; that Italy might, despite all indications, prove loyal to its allies; that France might prove disloyal to its ally; or that British neutrality could be counted on. If the principle of nationality remained the foundation of European states, the anachronistic states belonging to an earlier generation had to be broken up and removed. When Germany, not realizing this position, bound up her destiny with that of Austria-Hungary, she committed a gross and disastrous mistake from the point of view of historical development, and was thereby involved in its ruin.

Repulsed by Japan in the Far East, Russia looked for compensation in the Near East. With the consummation of the Anglo-Russian *Entente* her old desire to possess the Straits welled up again. From this vantage point she could exercise hegemony over the Balkans and possibly penetrate Asia Minor. The crisis of 1908 drew Russia and Serbia closer. The Balkan Wars exacerbated both nationalism and international rivalry. In the clash of petty nationalisms, Russia found inevitably that Austria's idea of a solution of the Balkan problem was the precise opposite of Russia's. She could not allow Austria to crush Serbia and become the predominant power in Balkans, and, secure of support from France, she would force all the risks of war.

France believed that she must support Russia or risk the danger of isolation. She had no immediate stakes either in Serbia or in Austria-Hungary, but as an ally of Russia she might readily become embroiled in a general war. Poincare unconditionally promised Russia French assistance and urged her to take an uncompromising stand.[109] A diplomatic defeat for Russia would weaken the *Entente*. A political realist, Poincare seems to have regarded war as inevitable, and as the Austro-Serbian crisis developed, he devoted his time chiefly in bringing Britain into the conflict. He incited the British by calling attention to Germany's military manoeuvres while preventing them from learning of similar action by France and Russia. In line with this strategy, the Russians were cautioned to keep their military moves secret, and the French army was withdrawn from the frontier.

England did not consider it compatible with her interests that France should be defeated a second time. The alternatives to war, in the innocent summer of 1914, looked bleak, much worse than war itself. The Austrians dreaded that if they did not march forthwith, they might forfeit the final opportunity to save their empire. The Russians felt that if they recoiled, that would irreparably damage their prestige. The feeling of insecurity in a hostile world, among the German, French, and English diplomats, tended the hand of Mars. The British did not see how they could acquiesce in German control of the channel ports, let alone in German dominance over Europe. None of these fears were baseless, but war was about as good an answer to them as suicide is to the fear of death. The statesmen were thinking of the defence of visible interests that seemed vital; they failed to discern that invisible and much larger interests were involved in their decisions. Though they may be acquitted of the crime of deliberately starting the avalanche, they must jointly bear the reproach of having chosen the path which led to the abyss. In this sense, 'all the European countries, in a greater or lesser degree, were responsible' for war.[110] But leaders thereof never envisaged four years of horror; nor the social revolutions and the collapse of Europe.[111]

A word may be said of the more than occasional preponderance of military over political considerations. The Germans and the Russian were the biggest, though not the only, culprits here. Instead of serving policy, the preparations of Russian and German military authorities–general mobilization and Schlieffen Plan–decided policy in the event, with disastrous effects.

NOTES AND REFERENCES

1. Sidney Bradshaw Fay. *The Origin of the World War*-2 Vols., 2nd. rev. edn. (New York: The Macmillan Co., 1949), Vol. I, p.7, first published 1928.
2. Ibid, pp. 7–8.
3. Elbridge Colby, cited by Harry Elmer Barnes, *The Genesis of the World War : An Introduction to the Problem of War Guilt*, rev. edn. (New York : Alfred A Knopf, 1929), p. 35, first published 1926.
4. Barnes, *The Genesis of the World War*. For some particulars on 'authorities on war guilt and the revisionist position' pp. 662–84.
5. B.E., Schmitt. 'The Origin of the First World War', In : *The*

Outbreak of the First World War, who was responsible, Dwight E. Lee (ed.) rev. edn., (Boston : D.C. Heath and Co.,1963), p. 79.

6. P. Renouvin. *The Immediate Origin of the War*, (June 28–August 4, 1914), trans. Theodore Carswell Hume (New Haven : Yale Univ. Press, 1928).
7. G.P. Gooch. *Before the War : Studies in Diplomacy, The Coming of the Storm* (London : Longman Green and Co., 1938), Vol. 2; G.P. Gooch, *Recent Revelations of European Diplomacy*, 4th rev. enl. edn. (London: Longman Green and Co., 1940).
8. A.J.P. Taylor. *The Struggle for Mastery in Europe 1848–1918* (Oxford : Clarendon Press, 1954), pp. 511–31.
9. L.C.B. Seaman. *From Vienna to Versailles* (New York : Harper and Row Publishers, 1963), p. 178.
10. I. Geiss writes : 'There are hardly any more doubts possible about the overall share of Germany in causing the First World War' : *July, 1914 : The Outbreak of the First World War: Selected Documents*, I. Geiss (ed.) (New York, 1967), p. 365.
11. Raymond Aron, 'Causes and Responsibilities', In : *Outbreak of the First World War*, Lee (ed.), pp. 62–72.
12. A vivid illustraion of this fight is M.H. Cochran, *Germany not Guilty in 1914* (Examining a Much Prized Book), with a foreward by H.E. Barnes (Boston : Stratford Co., 1931). It is an indictment of B.E. Schmitt, *The Coming of the War, 1914*.
13. Joachim Remak. *The Origin of World War I, 1871–1914* (New York: Holt, Rinehart and Winston, 1967), pp. 132–33.
14. Moltke, the Elder, who humbled France in the Franco-German War, warned : 'What our sword has won in half a year, our sword must guard for half a century', quoted in Hanson W. Baldwin, *World War I, An Outline History* (New York : Harper and Row Publishers, 1962), p. 3.
15. A great armada stood watch in the North Sea; in 1906 Britain launched a new type of battleship, the *Dreadnaught*, more powerful by far from any thing else afloat.
16. Raymond James Sontag, *European Diplomatic History 1871–1932* (New York : The Century Co., 1933), pp. 125–26.
17. Remak, *Origin of World war I*, p. 74.
18. Destroyed, as Nelson destroyed the Danish fleet at Copenhagen.
19. Few half-truths have caused as much misery in the world as these.
20. Laurence Lafore. *The Long Fuse : An Interpretation of the Origin of World war I* (New York : J.B. Lippincott Co., 1965), p.140. In a typical instruction of the mid-eighties, Bismarck wrote to

the German ambassador at Vienna that Germany ought never to encourage 'the temptations to which the Austrians are prone ... If Austria should ever be a victim of Russian attack, German aid would freely be given 'but an attack on Russia is something we will not engage in, nor will we, in case Austria should undertake it, consider the alliance to be operative ... For us, Balkan question can never be motive for war' ... Remak, *Origin of World War I*, p. 14. Much water had flowed under the bridges since Bismarck gave these instructions.

21. Lafore, *Long Fuse*, pp. 16–17.
22. Sidney B. Fay is quite ready to admit that, 'of all the major conflicts of interest which have been alleged as making it (the World War, 1914–18) 'inevitable', the Balkan problems were those most nearly incapable of a peaceful solution. *Origin.* Vol. 1. p. 546.
23. Remak, *Origins*, p. 55, G.P. Gooch *Recent Revelations*, p. 465.
24. Fay, *Origins, I*, p.546.
25. 'Gavrilo Princep fired his pistol not only at Archduke, but also at the facade of a quiet, apparently stable world': Vladimir Dedijer, *The Road to Sarajevo* (New York : Simon and Schuster, 1966), p.18. Edmond Taylor writes : 'In five minutes Franz Ferdinand and Sophie (his wife) will be lying unconscious in their speeding car bleeding to death from an assassin's bullets : an ancient dynasty and with it a whole way of life—will start to topple; then another and another and another. Close to nine million men fell in World War I as a direct result of those two shots fired in a dusty Balkan town roughly half a century ago; then 15,000,000 more in second, greater conflict implicit in the ending of the first one. The visit that the Habsburg heir and his wife paid to Sarajevo lasted only a little more than an hour–not quite the length of a normal feature film–but the drama of those sixty of seventy minutes has literally revolutionised the whole course of modern history; reconstructing it helps to understanad many of the tragic dramas that humanity has witnessed since': *The Fall of Dynasties : The Collapse of the Old Order* (New York : Doubleday and Co. Inc., Garden City, 1963), pp. 1–2.
26. Fay, *Origins, II*, p. 550.
27. And Russia was in a position to accept the challenge, having recovered from the consequences of the war against Japan.
28. Edward Grey, British Secretary of State for Foreign Affairs, described the Austrian ultimatum of July 23, as 'the most

formidable document ever presented to an independent state': G.P. Gooch, *Before the War : Studies in Diplomacy*, Vol. II, *The Coming of the Storm* (London : Longman Green and Co., 1938), p. 440.

29. Bernadotte E. Schmitt, 'The Origin of the First World War', In: *The Outbreak*, Lee (ed.), 73.
30. Seaman, *Vienna to Versailles*, pp. 177–78.
31. Ibid, p. 178.
32. Fay, *Origins, II*, pp. 551–52.
33. Geiss, *July 1914*, p. 51, 'In the light of this the choice of the heir apparent as the victim of the assassination was" says Imanuel Geiss', certainly no coincidence, the less so since Franz Ferdinand made his entry into Sarajevo at ... the anniversay of the Battle of Kasovo in 1389' (when the Serbian army was defeated by the Turks and the medieval Serbian state overthrown, and so a day of national mourning) : Ibid, Whether Franz Ferdinand would have been able to accomplish his objective is anybody's guess. He was a rather hot-headed, bigoted, difficult man who was heartily disliked by the great majority of his people.
34. Renouvin, *Immediate Origins*, p. 334.
35. As a matter of fact the Austro-Hungarian authorities were so neglectful of precautionary measures for the protection of the Archduke at Sarajevo that Wickham Steed (*Through Thirty Years*, 1892–1922, (New York, 1924, Vol. I, pp.393–4) insinuates foul play on the part of the Austrian government. Certainly, however, the evidence is not sufficient to prove such an assumption.
36. Geiss, *July 1914*, p. 53.
37. Ibid, p. 57.
38. And was determined to use the crime as a good excuse for clearing up the unsatisfactory situation and for putting an end once and for all to danger to the Austrian monarchy from the greater Serbia agitation and the Russian intrigues against Austrian influence in the Balkans : Fay, *Origins*, II. p. 183.
39. Berchtold and others did not believe that Serbia, flushed with victory over Turks and Bulgars and encouraged by promises of Russian support, would remain content with the frontiers of 1913.
40. Gooch, *Before War, II* : *Coming Storm*, pp. 444 and 272.
41. Remak, *Origins*, p. 314.
42. Ferdinand Schevill. *The History of the Balkan Peninsula* (New York, 1933), p. 458.

43. G. Lowes Dickinson. *The International Anarchy, 1904–1914* (New York, 1926), p. 429.
44. 'So just was the cause of Austria held to be', reported Sir Maurice de Bunsen, the British ambassador, 'that it seemed to her people inconceivable that any country should place itself in her path, or that questions of mere policy or prestige should be regarded anywhere as superseding the necessity which had arisen to exact summary vengeance for the crime of Sarajevo' : quoted in Gooch, *Before the War II, Coming Storm*, p. 445–46.
45. Seaman, *Vienna to Versailles*, p. 177.
46. Remak, *Origins*, p. 169.
47. Ibid, p. 149.
48. Edith, M. Durham. *The Sarajevo Crime* (London, 1925), p. 9.
49. Austria's ultimatum to Serbia and the *dossier* offered to the Powers put the blame on the subversive activities of the Serbian patriotic association known as the 'Narodna Odbrana', : *Austrian Red Book* of 1914, nos. 7–9, 19.
50. Fay, *Origins, II*, p. 57.
51. Ibid, p. 146.
52. R.W. Seton-Watson. *Sarajevo : A Study in the Origin of the Great War* (London, 1925), pp. 134, 136–37.
53. Durham, *Sarajevo Crime*, pp. 12–13, In the words of Hermann Wendel : 'In the decisive weeks the Serbian Government was undoubtedly inspired by a certain passivity and an oriental indolence. Passive and indolent it was in every respect.' Durham, *Sarajevo*, p. 125.
54. Fay, *Origins, II*, p. 166.
55. Beside, a parliamentary election was due in Serbia that summer. 'Many Serbian voters would consider the assassins heroes not murderers. Should it ever become known that Pashitch had delivered these youths and their Bosnian helpers to the Austrian police, he might just as soon announce his retirement from politics and save himself the bother of an election campaign', J. Remak, *Sarajevo : The Story of a Political Murder* (New York, 1959), pp. 72–73.
56. Seton-Watson, *Sarajevo*, p. 155.
57. Bernadotte E. Schmitt, *The Coming of the War 1914*, (New York, 1966), Vol. I, pp. 247–48, (originally published in 1930).
58. The Serbian reply not only won the approval and sympathy of all the Powers except Austria, it also commanded the admiration of the man who framed the Austrian ultimatum

itself. (i.e. of Berchtold), 'as the most brilliant example of diplomatic skill which I have ever known' : Fay, *The Origins*, II, p. 340.

59. Ibid, pp. 340–41.
60. Renouvin, *Immediate Origins*, pp. 334–35.
61. When Russia's strategic railways on the Polish front would be complete and the Three Years Service in France in full operation.
62. Fay, *Origins, II*, p. 552.
63. Gooch, *Before the War*, Vol. II : *Coming Storm*, p. 271.
64. M. Philips Price (ed). *The Diplomatic History of the War : The Texts of the Official Documents of the Various Governments* ... (New York, 1914), p. 7.
65. However, there were others in Berlin like Ambassador Lichnowsky who were convinced that the Czar's Government could not help intervening in an Austro-Serb war; in his opinion, the whole idea of localization was 'an idle fancy' : Renouvin, *Immediate Origins*, p. 336.
66. Gooch, *Before War, II* : *Coming Storm*, p. 277.
67. Ibid, p. 445.
68. Ibid, p. 278.
69. Fay, *Origins, II*, p. 553.
70. Chief of the German General Staff.
71. Austro-Hungarian Chief of the General Staff.
72. Gooch, *Before War, II* : *Coming Storm*, pp. 279–80.
73. Ibid, p. 281.
74. Fay, *Origins*, p. 554.
75. Ibid, p. 553.
76. According to Taylor : 'Bethmann did not want a war at all, nor even the advance of German supremacy; the German masses wanted a glorious Germany, but without war or even military domination; the great industrialists wished to advance their economic domination over north-eastern France and Southern Russia, but could do it better and more certainly without war; the Junkers wanted a militarist Germany to preserve their social position, but not a war of conquest which would ruin it; the generals wanted a victorious war, but as an academic exercise and without the slightest idea what they would do with their victory when they had won it' : *The Course of German History : A Survey of the Development of Germany Since 1815*, new edn., (New York : Coward McCann, Inc., 1951), pp. 163–64.

77. Gooch, *Before War II : Coming Storm*, pp. 284–86.
78. Erich Brandenburg, 'Conclusion : The Causes of the War', In : *The Outbreak*, Lee (ed.), p.8.
79. Although on the surface Austria had won a brilliant diplomatic victory and gained a large slice of territory.
80. Raymond Aron, 'Causes and Responsibilities, '*The Outbreak*' Lee (ed.), p. 71.
81. Gooch, *Before the War II : Coming Storm*, pp. 369–70.
82. Fay, *Origins, II*, pp. 276–77.
83. 'As a matter of fact, Austria was secretly intending to hand out strips of Serbia to Bulgaria and to Albania. An imprudent remark by one of her diplomats in Rome or London had doubtless been picked up by the representatives of the *Entente*, and it is quite likely that its echoes had already reached the ears of Sazonoff', Renouvin, *Immediate Origins*, pp. 339–40.
84. Fay, *Origins, II*, p. 326.
85. Ibid, p. 308.
86. Ibid, p. 322.
87. Remak, *Origins*, pp. 136–37.
88. From a strategic point of view the partial mobilization was simply a folly. It was the intention to mobilize four Military Districts—Kiev, Odessa, Moscow and Kazan with thirteen army corps, against Austria. But to strike at Austria effectively from the east and north, it was necessary that some troops advance through the Warsaw Distt. Yet in order not to alarm Germany the Warsaw Distt. was to remain untouched! And if no preparations were made in the Warsaw Distt., the part of it which bordered Austria would remain uncovered and unprotected. It would then be impossible to have a successful blow against Austria, and a wholly new scheme of campaign would have to be suddenly improvised. Worst of all, if a general mobilization should eventually follow a partial mobilization, the confusion would be intolerable, in as much as the Warsaw Distt. had to draw some of its reservists from the four Distts. already dislocated by partial mobilization. Fay, *Origins*, II, pp. 294, 450–51.
89. Ibid, pp. 479, 481.
90. 'Izvolski became convinced that the Straits could only be secured by a European war ... the road to Constantinople is through Berlin ... and he set about it so to manipulate the European situation that when the time came Russia would be in a position where victory would be probable' : Barnes, *Genesis*

of the War, p. 147.
91. Ibid, p. 376.
92. Poincare, French Premier, January 1912 to February 1913; President of the French Republic, February 1913 to 1920.
93. Gooch, *Before the War II* : *Coming Storm*, pp. 198–99.
94. Fay, *Origins, II*, p. 282.
95. Ibid, p. 281.
96. It may be added : 'His actions and influences offer a precise counterpart to those of Tschirschky (German Ambassador to Austria-Hungary) in Vienna', Lafore, *Long Fuse*, p. 265.
97. Ibid, p. 266.
98. Fay, *Origins, II*, p. 486.
99. Ibid, pp. 555–56.
100. Ibid, pp. 491–92, See also Ibid, p. 489.
101. The 'direct conversations' suggestion of Sir Edward Grey was an excellent one, but it met with instant and emphatic condemnation from President Poincare who said it would be 'very dangerous' very dangerous to have Austria and Russia converse with a view to coming to a friendly and peaceful solution of the Austro-Serbian conflict? One is amazed. Very dangerous to what? Certainly not to the peace of Europe. But perhaps to Poincare's policy of having the Triple *Entente* stand as a solid block in opposition to Germany and Austria. For more than two years he had sought to prevent separate understanding by any one of its members with Germany or Austria. Ibid, p. 366.
102. Ibid, pp. 368–69.
103. B.E. Schmitt 'Triple Alliance and Triple Entente, 1902–14', *American Historical Review* (April, 1924), p. 466.
104. Lafore, *Long Fuse*, pp. 265–66.
105. Only by being directed to the Belgian issue could the English people be made to understand what was at stake; just as in 1701 they could be persuaded that Louis XIV's Spanish policy was a threat to them only when they had been told that he had recognized the old Pretender as James III.
106. The *Times* insisted on this point repeatedly. See K. Zilliacus 'Economic and Social Causes', *The Outbreak*, Lee (ed.), p. 45.
107. George MacMunn, *The Crimea in Perspective* (London, 1935), p.10.
108. H.E. Barnes emphatically asserts : 'There is no authoritative and informed historian in any country who has studied the problem of the genesis of the World War in a thorough fashion

who does not regard the theory of war guilt held in Articles 227 and 231 of the Versailles Treaty to be wholly false, misleading and unjust' : *Genesis*, p. 684.

109. In the fourth volume of his memoirs Poincare has made 'a skilful and elaborate plea, to prove '*La France Innocente* : But he is not convincing' Fay, *Origins, II*, p. 555.

110. Ibid, p. 548.

111. Or at least, very few of them did. One of the few, curiously, was the German Chief of Staff, von, Moltke, who, allegedly, feared that a general war would mean the annihilation of the civilization of Europe for decades to come. He was approximately correct; still, he was urging measures that would bring general war. He believed that the soldier's job was to make sure that war was fought on favourable terms; he was obeying the imperatives of his position. Lafore *Long Fuse*, pp. 22–23.

Chapter 9

Foreign Political Ideas : The German Resistance Movement

Introduction

German foreign policy after the First World War was staggering. It had to choose between a policy of fulfilment with international understanding as the basis for loyal cooperation, and a policy of national isolation accompanied possibly by orientation towards the East. It was a rocky road towards fulfilment; the harsh terms of the Versailles Treaty left little scope for hope. Furthermore, the two Anglo-Saxon great powers retracted from continental politics and left the task of building up a new order to France, a country which had been seriously affected by the war. France's intransigent attitude, which constituted a threat to the removal of old antagonisms, kept Germany in a state of ferment. Against this background, German foreign policy up to the fall of the Bruning–including even its attempts to obtain a revision of the Treaty–may be looked upon as a series of efforts towards fulfilment and understanding. Unfortunately, however, other countries underestimated the difficulties with which the new government had to cope and were too late in recognizing that it was in the interests of Europe and of democracy for the new democratic Germany to achieve success in its foreign policy.

The national socialist foreign policy included both nationalist and imperialist tendencies. The call of *Heim ins Reich**

* Home to the Reich

was a nationalist slogan, but its logical development into the policy of 'living room' went further. The *Drang nach Osten* (pressure to the east) was the consequence of an expansionist policy–the 'seizure of power outside the Reich.' Germany's break with the League of Nations signified that she ceased to take part in international cooperation. The national socialist aggressive policy involved a breach with continuity, and in the end it embroiled the country and the continent into a catastrophe of unprecedented dimensions.

On the other hand, Carl Friedrich Goerdeler–the civilian leader of the opposition–himself advocated a foreign policy which, although less expansionist than Hitler's hardly seemed congruous with the reconciliation between Germany and Europe.[1] At the beginning of 1940, after the German Army's startling victories, other opponents of Hitler in Germany harboured ambitions of German leadership in Europe. Later, when the changed war situation had obliterated all dreams of German hegemony. Ulrich Von Hassell noted that the overthrow of Hitler was becoming more urgent by the day : but the reason for this was to save at least a vestige of the Bismarckian empire.[2]

There have been many erroneous conceptions among historians about the foreign political views of the German opposition.[3] According to Wilhelm Von Schramm : 'The main object of the German revival, as seen by Beck, Goerdeler and their political friends, was the federation of the countries of Europe. This had remained their aim since the years when they had gone on their political travels.'[4] By contrast, George K. Romoser roundly disputes the political viability of the Oppositions's projected foreign policy :

> The political hopes of the conspirators in regard to foreign policy were to a considerable extent unrealistic fantasies. This term can be applied, above all, to their territorial aims. Many of the conspirators were preoccupied ... with questions of national interest. One need only read the memoranda of Carl Goerdeler, Ulrich Von Hassell, or even Adam Von Trott zu Solz to discern the existence of vague and unrealistic foreign policy views.[5]

Assessments such as these, each deflecting in one direction or the other, are characteristic of the black and white approach of many historians. Such commentators necessarily overlook the fact that ideas of the German resistance evolved: from its internal strains and dissensions there eventually emerged a movement towards a changed Europe. Opposition should not be viewed as a monolithic and static entity, with notions on foreign policy as proof of either rabid nationalism or devotion to the European ideal. These conceptions have to be studied in relation, not merely to the Nazi dictator, but to the changed realities in Europe at that time.

The Conservatives

General Ludwig Beck and Carl Goerdeler, the principal animators of the military and civilian oppositon in the Third Reich, became the twin pillars of the National Conservatives, the group which, between 1938 and 1942, was to determine the typical form of the Opposition's potentially activist section. 'At the outset, however, this group's views on foreign policy were still completely dominated', states Hermann Graml, 'by the outlook of a Europe which had once regarded herself as the centre of the universe.'[6] The concepts of inter-European power politics and the claim to have control over the Afro-Asian world were the natural bequest of the members of this group. 'In such men, the western democratic leaders saw, or thought they saw', as Margret Boveri observes, 'the traditional ruling class of Germany returning to power after a period of mob madness.'[7] They belonged to a generation and a class which had experienced and revelled in Germany's entry into world politics.

Europe as a whole did not initially hold the prominent place in the foreign policy ideas of this group. Their thoughts were focused upon Bismarck's German Reich, a Reich which would be complemented by acquisitions along greater German lines from the inheritance of the dying Habsburg Empire and become the core of a solid central European structure; while colonial policy would provide an assurance of Germany's world standing. In essence their outlook combined the idea of a nation state with a 'reasonable' imperialism by which

Germany's smaller neighbours might in some measure benefit.[8]

Although disillusioning, the crucial events of 1918 did not bring about any fundamental change in their ideas. By applying a cautious and patient policy, it would still be possible to set up in central Europe the requisite preconditions for the Greater German Reich. Between the two World Wars, this group's thinking with regard to foreign policy was concerned solely with healing the wounds inflicted upon the German national consciousness and stabilizing and expanding Germany's position. Hence they believed in and advocated the revision of Versailles. Goerdeler prepared a list of 'vital German questions' (*deutsche Lebensfragen*) which formulated the concrete demands of this programme, and which no doubt represented the national sentiments of a great majority of the German people. These were : union with Austria and the Sudeten areas; the elimination of the 'Polish Corridor'; and the acquisition of colonies.[9] Yet the circle round Goerdeler and Beck was unanimous in condemning war as an instrument of foreign policy. They never for a moment doubted that a war instigated by Germany would end in defeat. The feared, moreover, that war would precipitate unwholesome economic or social processes. A lost war might entail a peace far harsher than that of Versailles; it might also mean a revolution that Germany had narrowly escaped at the end of the First World War. The Goerdeler group had seen Red mutineers in the streets of Berlin, a sight which they never wanted to behold again.

Trevor-Roper suggests that '1940/41 saw a parting of the ways in Germany'[10]; that is the parting occurred after Hitler had completed the revisionist phase of his foreign policy. However, Trevor-Roper is wrong and the parting of the ways between the National Conservatives and Hitler took place, as Hermann Graml rightly observes, 'as early as 1938 during the Sudeten crisis with Hitler's decision to back up his revisionist policy by force of arms, and hence must be seen as due to that revisionist policy itself.'[11] Indeed the fact that Goerdeler and his friends advocated a revisionist foreign policy in opposition to Hitler symbolizes a basic position of the resistance : in changing circumstances and in the face of perilous situations, men like Beck, Hassell and Goerdeler felt themselves to be the custodians of the 'true national interests' of Germany, which were being staked by an unscrupulous adventurer and his megalomania. On March 22, 1939, Hassell wrote in his diary; 'The point at which Talleyrand left Napoleon has certainly been passed.'[12]

During his travels abroad, Goerdeler had noticed an increasing tendency, markedly in Britain, to straighten the Versailles system and to satisfy German claims. He got this impression, that there were no longer any insuperable impediments to the revision of Versailles, although this would require patient negotiation. Hence he was horrified to realize during the course of 1938 that Hitler, who was also aware of the British attitude but had reached different conclusions from that knowledge, was determined to attack Czechoslovakia. Indeed, as he candidly said, a short war would be enough to turn world opinion against Germany, so that her 'vital questions' would remain unsolved. Thus, war must be prevented at all costs, and to this end he developed a plan for a *putsch* which postulated British support.[13]

Goerdeler's criticism of Britain's appeasement policy was not levelled at its underlying principle, but at the fact that London was negotiating with the wrong partner; and the alternative he suggested to Britain was not a different policy, but a different partner. He tried to get Paris and London to take a strong stand against Hitler.

Hitler's brutal invasion of the 'rump' of Czechoslovakia (March 15–16) created a completely new atmosphere for future planning. The shock to the Western cabinets, and especially to British policy, is well known.[14] In his memorandum of this period, Goerdeler stated that a neutralized Czechoslovakia should be restored under international guarantee within the frontiers agreed at Munich. And further : 'The independence of the states of Europe would be guaranteed except in so far as it was considered reasonable to impose certain limitations on their sovereignty.' The memorandum adds : 'Because of its history, Germany must always have special interest in the approaches to her eastern frontiers. This must be expressed in terms of a reasonable balance of power.'[15]

Gerhard Ritter, the devoted biographer of Carl Goerdeler, in his commentary on these ideas, writes that Goerdeler 'thought of the Reich of the future ... as a genuine peace power embedded in a European community of a cooperative character.'[16] This statement has to be accepted with reserve. What Goerdeler envisaged was no doubt a pacified Europe*, resulting from the satisfaction of German claims, but it was not a united Europe. What he in fact proposed was reverting by a government liberated from Hitler to the policy of Locarno, provided the German demands in the east were acquiesced in. This policy was in line with that pursued by Stresemann. But Goerdeler as a direct consequence of Germany's recent expansion of power, was casting covetous glances on regions which had been far beyond Stresemann's field of vision.[17] Had Goerdeler become Chancellor at this time, as a result of a *coup d'etat* effected without foreign aid, the realization of his proposed foreign policy as well as the consolidation of Hitler's gains would have been altogether feasible, especially since Goerdeler was sincere in declaring that Germany would be satiated by the solution of the vital German question : his promise that Germany would participate in an international peace front, was equally genuine.

Nevertheless, such thoughts, as Graml observes, could not serve as a basis either for an alternative to Hitler that would be enduring and progressive, or for an alliance aimed at his overthrow between the opposition and the British Government. Apart from the question of whether success for the opposition was possible, Goerdeler's thinking was far too much imbued with German interests : indeed, there seemed little difference between Nazi and opposition policy. Goerdeler's views were conditioned largely by the psychological necessities of the internal situation in Germany, for the only antidote to Hitler's political successes seemed to lie in the opposition taking the credit for those successes. This

* Goerdeler had proposed a close alliance between Great Britain, France and Germany, and in addition Germany's return into a reformed League of Nations.

would have proved no argument in the international sphere, so long as the necessity to fight the Germany Hitler was leading, had not been proved beyond doubt. Besides, the realization of Goerdeler's concept would not have meant progress for Europe, for the heart of Europe would have contained a National Conservative bloc obstructing any closer federation within the continent.[18]

A new feature was added into this situation, not by Hitler's attack on Poland, but by his pact with the Soviet Union. The alliance had a truly stimulating effect on the group round Hassell, Goerdeler and Beck. For the manner of Moscow's re-entry into European politics was regarded menacing, and not as the restoration of normal Soviet-German relations. Hassell noted in his memoirs : 'About the Russian pact, Hitler said that he was in no way altering his fundamental anti-Bolshevist policies ... all means were justified in dealing with the Soviets, even such a pact as this. This is a typical example of his conception of 'Realpolitik.'[19] According to Goerdeler, 'Hitler is himself creating the conditions which will bring about his downfall.'[20] It was regarded that Germany, by linking herself with Russia, 'had now irrevocably become England's mortal foe', and was moving towards 'separation from Europe', and more than ever before stood alone. In view of the Conservative Opposition, Germany's isolation rendered her dependent on the Soviet Union to an extent which could hardly fail to produce fatal internal repurcussions.[21]

According to Hans Mommsen, the opposition looked upon the Bolshevist system as 'the expression of total dehumanization in all social and human relations.' It used the term Bolshevism as a synonym for 'complete and anarchic stereotyping' and depravity. The conspirators soon recognized the similarity between the national socialist and Soviet dictatorship.[22] They grossly overrated the true political significance of the Nazi-Soviet pact and painted a gloomy picture of a Bolshevist Germany.

Now that Hitler had lightly thrown aside that tool of German foreign policy which had proved so useful at Munich–the British dread of Bolshevism–the opposition was in a position to turn the dread to its own account. Between the time of the Sudeten crisis and the outbreak of war, the opposition had no such diplomatic lever. The feeling was that Great Britain–and also France–would, in the event of a revision of Russo-German policy, 'pay a good price for Germany's reversion to Europe and to the European community of nations.' 'Indeed', says Hermann Graml, 'the consolidation of all Hitler's conquests–excluding the General government in occupied Poland and the open "protectorate" in Bohemia–as also of Germany's position of unchallenged hegemony in Central Europe was now regarded by the group round Hassell and Goerdeler as both desirable and feasible–provided Hitler was overthrown.'[23]

While the claims of the 'representatives of the true national interest' had grown, their path was steadily diverging from Hitler's. Yet this divergence did not bring the opposition any closer to Europe. In two respects it had perhaps assumed too much, overestimating not only Britain's apprehension of Russia, but also her consequent willingness to concede the position attained by Germany. It is true that the West looked upon Moscow with consternation, but at the moment Germany's menacing superiority on the continent constituted the greater threat to England and more especially to France. Even a 'sane and liberal' German government would probably have had to be content with the pre-Munich *status quo*.

The unparalleled victories of the German army in Holland, Belgium and France made the position of the opposition entirely hopeless. Yet it says much for the genuineness of the convictions which sustained the opposition that on nearly all of them the victory had a shattering effect, making them see the future with despair rather than hope.[24] Their antipathy to the Fuhrer and his regime never for a moment wavered.

Induced by what they now deemed to be Germany's assured and expanded imperial position, Goerdeler, Hassell and Johannes Popitz developed their idea of German leadership in central Europe to an idea of German leadership of the whole of Europe; there floated through their mind the seductive vision of a Germany Reich of medieval dimensions, Prussian and conservative in character. 'The German concept of *Ehre* (honour), like the French of *gloire*, was the enemy of rational analysis,[25] observes Prittie.

Hassell was more balanced about the political forms of German leadership. His *Grossraum* (greater area) too extended far across central Europe, but he constantly reiterated that such a *Grossraum* could only survive if leadership by the central state did not involve the others in servitude. On the other hand Goerdeler now turned his gaze to the 'national' complements to the German nucleus which had been unattainable before 1940; that is to say to Alsace-Lorraine and to the South Tyrol.[26]

The spirit inspiring these ambitions was certainly not identical either with the theory and practice of Hitlerian supremacy, or with the concepts then being expounded by the more extreme official national socialist Reich theorists who put empahsis upon German supremacy and the subordination of non-German sections of the Reich.[27] Yet there is an undeniable similarity in the ideas of the National Conservative Opposition and those of the Third Reich official theorists. The significant distinction between the terms 'leadership' and 'supremacy' the latter being peculiar to national socialism–was pointed out.[28] However, it is evident that these men of the opposition had nothing to offer to save the national principle and a conservative outlook–that is, German leadership and an illeberal order. Characteristic is the role which Bismarck now began to assume in the thoughts of men like Goerdeler and Hassell.[29] They were incapable of envisaging the unification of Europe in any form other than that taken by the unification of the Reich under Prussia.

The revival of the imperial concept would have been repugnant to Europe; its individual flaws, such as the undefined position of France in the new scenario, were of as little importance, in view of the concepts of basic invalidity, as the fact that there was never the slightest chance of making peace with western powers on such a basis.[30] Never was the National Conservative Opposition so remote from the rest of Europe as when it began to think in European terms.

The events of June 22, 1941, put new vigour into the

National conservative opposition, however much they deplored Hitler's action on military and ethical grounds. Hassell expressed the feeling that it might now be possible to rally the European public behind Germany under the anti-Bolshevist banner, and begin the resetting of Europe unencumbered by considerations of a Britain now rendered powerless. This in turn postulated the early fall of Hitler.

Goerdeler also perceived the supposed opporunity. He had always been particularly sensitive to the conflict, in his eyes almost insoluble, between the theory of a *Grossraum* under German leadership and the reality of a Europe comprising national states.[31] But now, sustained by, what appeared to him, the possibility of a European crusade against Bolshevism, he believed that the hour had come for reconciliation between the 'concept of national states and the need for a *Grossraum*.' This conviction was responsible for his long memorandum, *Das Ziel* (The Goal) which must have been written somewhere during the latter half of 1941 and the early months of the following year, and which marks the climax of the hopes and aspirations of the National Conservative Opposition. There could still be a European federation of states under German leadership within ten or twenty years, with timely action, that is the cessation of war in favour of a sensible political system. But if the propitious moment was allowed to pass 'it would be a long time before even the idea of German leadership could be envisaged.'[32]

A change began to take place in the thinking of the National Conservative Opposition after the end of 1941, leading to the gradual cooling down of the demand for German leadership in Europe, though not of the idea of European federation. This could not be attributed solely or even mainly to developments in the war situation. The entry of Russia and America into the war, and the consequent definitive realization of the change in world politics, profoundly influenced political thought. The recurrence of 1917, which this time was to have lasting repurcussions, inaugurated ideological, political and military conflicts of global dimensions, and Europe became aware that she was only one continent among several. The opposition could not fail to perceive the change. There was an intensification of the feeling of European solidarity, and at the same time the tussle over the hegemony in Europe suddenly dwindled into background.[33]

The age of colonialism, Hassell said, was approaching its end. The European's intellectual and economic supremacy throughout the world had disintegrated. National and social independence movements, in the Afro-Asian world, were on foot which, whatever the outcome of the war, could not and should not be checked. It was imperative that Europe seek a new relationship with these emergent powers and make them feel that the European was not inimical to natural development. An insight of this kind necessarily induced a lasting change of approach to internal European problems. Aside from this, however, the opposition found itself increasingly confronted with the fact that the imperial concept was slowly being disintegrated, 'corroded and destroyed by its own parasitic hypertrophy'; for if, within German shphere of influence, horrible atrocities were daily being committed under the aegis of that Reich which the opposition desired to present to Europe as pacific and benign, how could these men put forth their own claim to German leadership with a clear conscience.[34] 'It is Hitler's achievement', wrote Hassell later, 'that the German has become the most loathed animal in the whole world.'[35]

But the end of 1941 and the beginning of 1942 saw not least the beginning of the serious dialogue with a wholly divergent resistance group, the Kreisau Circle, and this interaction, coalesced with the changing political situation, reoriented in certain important respects the political thinking of the National Conservative Opposition.

The Kreisau Circle

The members of the Kreisau Circle numbered amongst themselves 'socialists, land owners, Jesuits, left-wing intellectuals, Protestant clergymen, right-wing politicians, economists and diplomats—in fact cross-section of what should have been the German ruling class.' They set out to devise among themselves 'the fundamental principles', writes Constantine FitzGibbon, 'on which a moral and cultural renaissance might, once the nightmare was over, be founded.'[36] They went further, and in broad outline traced the form that the future German and European society should follow.

This fascinating group of highly unorthodox Christian socialists, socialist Christians and Christian socialist aristocrats was distinguishable from the National conservative notables, especially in foreign policy, by the fact that nationalism was for them no longer the determining motive of political action. They believed that mankind would in due course destroy itself unless national sovereignty could be transcended and the establishment of an effective supra-national authority put in hand. They were abreast if not ahead of the resistance groups in German-occupied countries in planning how post-war Europe could be integrated and organized.[37]

To these men, too, Versailles was distasteful, not least because it had wounded their patriotism and harmed their country. 'Yet they criticized Versailles even more harshly', says Graml, 'for being simply a product of nationalism regardless of whose nationalism benefited and whose suffered.' The spirit of Versailles could not cure Europe's 'sickness.' 'Thus the core of their thinking was', Graml continues, 'not the revision but the overcoming of Versailles.'[38] It was not by the shifting of frontiers that Europe could be wriggled out of 'the anarchy of Versailles', but only by a new order based upon genuine understanding.[39]

In this conception there was no room for the idea of a central European *Grossraum*, a new concept brilliantly expressed in 1938 by Hermann Brill.[40] Either France could rule over a fragmented Germany–which had been the Napoleonic solution–or Germany could dominate central Europe in order to weaken France–which had been Bismarck's solution. 'Both were nationalistic. Both failed ... But there is also a European solution ... "[41] The central idea was the rationalization of European foreign policy so that Europe might become 'a community of pluralistic states prepared to settle conflicts in a rational spirit, instead of a collection of powers whose arbitrary moral standards could only lead to irresponsible action.'[42] According to Zeller, the Kreisau Circle 'laid the basis for a community to cope with the future emergency.'[43]

The documents make it clear that the foreign policy proposals of the Kreisau Circle were based upon a fundamental belief in a Europe integrated into a federal state. It need hardly be said that these ideas had nothing in common with the Nazi new order, and were the exact antithesis of the foreign policy of Hitler's Germany which was both nationalist and imperialist.[44]

One important motive behind the stress on European cooperation was the desire to achieve a settlement of the minorities problem, not only for German minorities but for the entire central and eastern Europe. Another was the intertwining of the separate national economies which would accelerate the post-war work of reconstruction and remove the threat of a new war.[45]

In the words of Ger van Roon :[46]

> The Circle believed that efforts should be made to establish new forms of cooperation and that the idea of Russia as the arch enemy–which had made peaceful cooperation impossible from the outset–had to be avoided. They believed ... that it was totally wrong to identify the people of a country with the regime or political system, because they discovered the detrimental effects of such an attitude in their own experience.[47]

Social democrats such as Julius Leber and Theo Haubach were representative of the marked progressive elements in the Kreisau group. But the other members of the group, bourgeois in the widest sense of the term, too had, even before the Second World War, evolved conceptions no longer dominated by 'vital national questions', but by one 'vital international question'–how to discover the ground for and the means to accomplish rational European cooperation.[48]

There were no doubt differences. Count von Moltke had thrown off all nationalism and denied the 'idol of the state.' Adam von Trott, certainly no nationalist himself in the true sense of the word, nevertheless had a deep-rooted national feeling and a high sense of the special contribution, both spiritual and political, which his people and fatherland could and should make to the general culture of Europe.

He now believed, however, that the age of unrestricted

national sovereignty had run its course and must come to an end, since the existence of non-restricted states would inevitably lead to war and to the self-annihilation of nations. For their own protection, he maintained, the peoples and states must renounce full sovereignty.[49] Trott suggested that there should be a 'Pan-European civic status, and a common supreme court of law, as well as communal European fighting forces.' His formulation was based on the postulation of unavoidable German defeat, and his admonitions against a 'super Versailles' after the war are poignant. A harsh peace would only intensify the German 'persecution complex', provide fertile ground for demagogues, and obstruct the assimilation of Germany into a new Europe; there was even the danger of the mortified Germans seeking refuge in Bolshevism or 'National Bolshevism.' Thus, he emphasized the necessity of announcing moderate war aims well in advance : the Allies must give assurance to Germany that she would be guaranteed an 'equitable basis for national existence.'[50] Trott[51] himself was not interested in territorial goals and suggested the German frontiers of 1933.

The question of whether Trott's programme[52] as a whole was realistic is difficult to answer. Whereas the ideas enunciated by the National Conservative Opposition would not only have retarded Europe's progress in political and spiritual matters, but would indeed have meant retrogression, Trott's ideas were remote from the reality of Europe, probably because they were too much ahead of their time. Moltke's ideas, too, were utopian. In 1914, he described his concept of 'a Pan-European state divided into smaller, non-sovereign state structures which presented few real possibilities for Europe. But what is valuable in these European plans is not this or that fantastic detail : their significance lies in the recognition that 'in Europe the end of the politics of force, of nationalism and of the concept of race if it had not already arrived, must be induced, and that, to make European federation possible, the "preponderance of the former major states of Germany and France must be abolished".[53] These men had thus discerned the basis of Europe's perplexities at that time.

Future Plans of Germany and Europe

With the beginning of 1942, the impact of the Kreisau Circle upon the Conservative Opposition did much to mould the thinking–especially on foreign policy–of the latter group. A conspicuous instance of this development is Goerdeler. Whereas in the spring of 1941, he was still asking of the British government the virtual recognition of German leadership on the continent. In the middle of 1943, he wrote that the peoples of Europe must 'find their way freely and independently towards a lasting, peaceful federation in which neither Germany nor any other state would claim supremacy.'[54]

However, as can be understood, the prominent National Conservatives were not wholehearted converts to the Kreisau viewpoint, and beneath their concurrence there was a certain uneasiness. It was psychologically difficult for the old National Conservative, Goerdeler, to change the life-long ideas-pertaining to the sovereign German nation state–emanating from the national claims of 1848 and Bismarckian era. It apparently never occurred to him that his reason and justice were oriented solely towards German interests, and that it was German wounds alone that he sought to heal. Indeed, he never quite got over the sense of power Germany had attained between 1939 and 1942.[55] Yet it may be assumed that as Chancellor in 1943 or 1944, Goerdeler would not have allowed this or that territorial claim to impede and delay peace negotiations and international harmony. With Hassell, to preserve the Reich, even in truncated form was the main concern.[56]

The tactics by which Goerdeler and Hassell sought to salvage the Reich from the crisis of war on two fronts were those of the traditional diplomatic manoeuverings. What could be more natural than to assume that with every fresh Soviet victory, London's disquietude would increase as did that of Germany? Was not the survival of Germany as a viable country, if not as an ally, of supreme importance to Great Britain? The Goerdeler-Hassell group recalled the British policy of appeasement, which partially aimed at the exclusion of Russia from Europe, and also the fact that during the 1920s, Britain had tried to prevent France from inflicting too great a hardship on Germany. Now the situation was far more dangerous and Germany's collapse would involve catastrophic consequences; so, they protested, and the chances of cooperation were proportionately increased. Further, Poland, on whose behalf Great Britain had after all entered the war, was more exposed than any other country to Russian expansionism. Yet Britain was not in a position to protect her, and only the German army stood between Moscow and Warsaw. It is ironical historically that the very country through which Hitler had plunged Germany into hostilities was now to be used by the opposition as a lever to extricate the Reich from that same war.

Hassell argued that a strong and healthy nucleus would be needed to maintain a balance in Europe. Germany with unimpaired powers would be the only antidote to a Europe falling progressively in Russian clutches : conversely a strong and healthy Germany would be for Russia the only effective antidote to Anglo-American preponderance. He writes : 'Germany, situated in the middle of Europe, is the heart of Europe. Europe cannot live without a sound, strong heart.'[57]

On August 15, 1943 Hassell wrote : 'In this game (*Muhlespiel* : being on good terms with both sides) I prefer the western orientation, but if need be I would also consider an agreement with Russia. Trott agrees with me entirely; the others are doubtful for theoretical and moral reasons, which I understand. But they are gradually coming around.'[58] By the spring of 1944, Beck and Goerdeler had realized that they could no longer reckon without Moscow, and had become resigned to the view that after the *coup d'etat* they would have to begin negotiations both with the West and with the East.

Thus, their main concern now was salvaging the German state. That was natural and was neither morally nor politically unjustifiable. No nation is expected to commit political suicide, even if its name is heavily laden with guilt. Yet in the meantime, there had taken place a fundamental change in their concept of Germany's relationship towards other countries and towards Europe. It was not only that, as from the beginning of 1942, they retracted the claim they had laid to the leadership of central, if not the whole of Europe. But alongwith this return to the normality of pre-war European politics, we perceive a new forward-looking idea. Whether as a greater or lesser Germany, they are now willing to incorporate the Reich into one great entity, the community of the states of Europe. Goerdeler had stuck steadfastly to the imperial concept and to the boundaries of 1914, but once having grasped the concept of European federation in which Germany, abandoning all claims, would be absorbed, he clung to it with no less persistence. Hence, the change denoted not merely a return to the earlier European normality, but at the same time entry into the normality of a future, then still hypothetical, Europe.[59]

This is a clear indication, states Graml, of the Kreisau influx. On the other hand, the members of that circle were also effected by the thinking of the National Conservative Opposition. The ideology of the Kreisau Circle acquired, as it were, some of the nationalist semblance. Trott was most receptive to these ideas. He had come to adopt Goerdeler's claim to the Sudeten areas and to at least some parts of west Prussia. He too was brooding over ways, not only of salvaging Germany's existence as a nation, but also of avoiding unconditional surrender.[60] Thus, he found himself toying with the antithesis between the western powers and the Soviet Union–and that in a manner similar to that of Hassell and Goerdeler. Yet he had never, and indeed never, could have, considered what might be called an 'eastern solution.'[61]

The feeling of affinity with the West was altogher genuine. In so far as disagreement existed on the East-West problem, it was never a queston of either/or. The disagreement lay between those who thought only in terms of negotiations with the West and those who, while acknowledging the primacy of agreement with the West, considered it vital to come to an understanding with Russia as well.[62] Trott's attitude toward Russia has often been debated; what he was trying to convey was that the German resistance movement, in order to avert the exigency of an 'eastern solution', must effect a shift to the left. In his secret talks in Stockholm and Geneva, Trott pointed out that the only constructive ideas for the rebuilding of post-war Germany were coming from Russia, while the western democracies appeared to have slammed all the doors on the resistance. The German social democrats pleaded with the western leaders to do something to fill the vacuum. Stalin's famous words, 'Hitlers come and Hitlers go, the German people are eternal', were actively used by the communist underground to win approval and sympathy. The West offered the Morgenthau Plan and it was against the negation in western attitude that Klaus Stauffenberg, Trott and Leber struggled.[63]

The radical members of the Kreisau group, being more interested in the direction of social policy, were less touchy to the cession of external powers and to losses of territory, and hence were earlier resigned to their inevitability. Julius Leber said that Goerdeler was a visionary in foreign affairs : he himself showed little patience with discussions about the Sudeten territories and the eastern frontier of 1914. Further, the Kreisau Circle, with its dominant Christian outlook, was susceptible to the vision of the theologian Dietrich Bonhoeffer : the tremendous guilt accruing to Germany no longer admitted of 'foreign-policy solutions', ... that action by the resistance should be seen as an 'act of repentance', and that 'it is only through defeat that we shall atone for our terrible crimes against Europe and the world.'[64] Those who could not comprehend this concept and who, in fact, resorted to 'foreign-policy solutions', were not in a position to understand that they were repudiating the only attitude that betokened any prospect of success in foreign affairs.[65]

It was at any rate, plain to Leber as well as to Moltke very early that Germany, even with a resistance government, would be confronted with unconditional surrender and considerable territorial sacrifices. Not that this attitude indicated passivity in regard to foreign affairs. Moltke held 'an unequivocal military defeat of Germany and her subsequent occupation to be absolutely essential on moral and political grounds' ; and so he considered the Allied demand for total surrender to be justified. Since he and his friends were convinced that they were fundamentally in concord with the West on spiritual and political matters, especially with reference to the future of Europe and Germany, future collaboration was assured more explicitly than by formal guarantees (which, in the then circumstances, could in any case not be made).[66]

Kreisau's image of Europe, then, was the Europe of the future. The roots of the National Conservative leaders were undoubtedly inculcated in the old Europe. They had started as champions of a natural and inevitable nationalist revisionist policy but, their aspirations having been complied with (by the dictator), they did in fact revert to a pattern of power politics which, to say the least, had become outdated. Dazed by the unleashing power of Germany, they visualized the Reich for a brief instant of time as the power that would lead and direct Europe, and in this they were confusing Germany with Prussia and Europe with Germany. But even before the last phase of the war, they had become conscious of their error; their tragedy lay in the fact that at the precise moment when they sought a *rapprochement* with Europe, Europe shrank from them, while they in turn believed that they could not act without Europe's help. Thus these men could not save the Reich from the accursed tyrant whom they looked upon as an alien, a mere parasite. But they had already been able to associate their own values and their own world to the concepts and ideology of a new epoch which found its most cogent manifestation in the Kreisau group. Thus, in the final analysis, whether their *putsch* succeeded or failed,[67] they were not without hope for a new Germany in a new Europe. They testifiied that 'Europe is something far deeper and more living than an ethnic or aesthetic dream image, and her spirit will emerge all the more clearly for her crushing self-surrender.'[68] In mounting the gallows ignominiously, they pointed the way for the best of the Germans of the present generation to liberty, to Christian civilization, to the Europe of tomorrow : they put the nation, so brilliantly efficient, so talented, and yet so lacking in the power of self-examination, on the right road to finding its own soul.

NOTES AND REFERENCES

1. Goerdeler insisted that Germany must retain her 1914 eastern frontier as well as Austria and the Sudeten areas, gain the South Tyrol and have her share of European colonial possessions overseas. Even in the long months in prison 'there is no real variation' in the contents of his programme : Gerhard Ritter, *The German Resistance : Carl Goerdeler's Struggle against Tyranny,* trans. R.T. Clark (New York : Frederick A. Praeger, 1958), p.226;
2. Ulrich Von Hassell. *The Von Hassell Diaries 1938–1944.* The story of the forces against Hitler inside Germany. (New York : Doubleday and Co, Inc., 1947), pp.286, 318.
3. The German opposition to Hitler, according to Hans Rothfels, moved through 'various stages of nonconformity : from antagonism muted by prison walls and the silence of a potential opposition, from humanitarian protest and clandestine aid to victims of persecution, to sabotage by the illegals and their subversive activities, to spiritual attack upon the very essence of totalitarianism, to active planning and political resistance. In addition, it can be stated that the German opposition reached definite form long before the war, and that it reached its first climax in an attempt to prevent war. It was not the threat of defeat which made the opposition articulate; on the contrary, some of its leading elements were convinced that Hitler's victory would be the greatest of all possible catastrophies–a victory of "the arch enemy of the whole world" of the Antichrist; they worked against this danger at a time when German military victory still seemed probable': Hans Rothfels, *The German Opposition to Hitler : An Appraisal* (Illinois : Henry Regnery Co., 1948), p. 159.
4. Hermann Graml. 'Resistance Thinking on Foreign Policy' *The German Resistance to Hitler* (Berkeley : University of California Press, 1970), p. 2.
5. George K. Romoser. 'The Politics of uncertainty : The German Resistance Movement' *Social Research,* 1964, Vol. 3, p. 79.
6. Graml, *German Resist,* p. 4.
7. Margret Boveri. *Treason in the Twentieth Century,* trans. Jonathan Steinberg (London : Macdonald, 1961), p. 225.
8. Graml, *Ger. Resist,* p. 5.
9. Ibid, pp. 5–7.
10. Ibid, p. 7.

11. Ibid, p. 8.
12. Hassell, *Diaries*, p. 38.
13. 'Why was the September 1938 *coup* never carried out? German historians have given two main reasons. The first is that the Western Powers—in particular the British—failed to give the generals clear enough indications of their determination to fight if Hitler marched into Czechoslovakia. The second reason given is that the signing of the Munich agreement on September 29, 1938, by the Western Powers cut the ground from under the generals' feet. How could they overthrow Hitler when he had achieved a bloodless victory by uniting the Germans of the Sudetenland with the Reich' Terence Prittie, *Germans against Hitler* (London, 1964), p. 63.
14. J.W. Wheeler-Bennett. *Munich* (London, 1948), p. 352, for a full account of the effects of Prague.
15. Ritter, *Goerdeler*, p. 125.
16. Ibid, p.126.
17. Graml, *Ger. Resist*, p. 11. Goerdeler's allusion to the reasonable limitations of the sovereignty of European states cannot, in view of the political developments at that time, possibly be interpreted as an attempt to keep margin for any larger Pan-European Federations. A statement of this nature, coming from a German at the end of March, 1939, could only signify a demand for the recognition of Germany's protectorate over Prague and Bratislava, and such no doubt was its real import.
18. Ibid, pp. 13-14.
19. Hassell, *Diaries*, p. 67.
20. Ritter, *Goerdeler*, p. 136.
21. Graml. *Ger. Resist*, pp. 15–16.
22. Hans Mommsen, 'Social Views and Constitutional Plans of the Resistance' *The German Resistance*, Graml. p. 73.
23. Graml, *Think. For. Pol.* Ibid, pp. 17-19.
24. During the last week of May 1940, Hassell noted in his diary : 'Since National Socialism, as it has now developed, is completely soulless, its intrinsic creed being power, we shall get a godless nature, a dehumanized, cultureless Germany, and perhaps a Europe conscienceless and brutal' : Hassell, *Diaries*, p.139. In his memorandum of July 1, 1940, Goerdeler expresses his views thus: 'War is never an end in itself; its aim can be nothing but a happy and lasting peace'. 'From such a peace we are farther away than ever–this war serves the ends, not of constructive design, but of fantastic scheming such as

once before we saw in the Napoleonic era' ... It will not be possible before history to throw the responsibility for this war on others : ... A tyrant can never create anything but a tyranny; each fresh success makes him not wise and moderate but always more ambitious, more brutal, more filled with the lust of conquest. Goerdeler painted a horrible picture of Europe's future under Hitler' Ritter, *Goerdeler*, p. 171.

25. Prittie, *Ger. Hitler*, p. 30.
26. Graml, *Ger. Resist*, pp. 22–23.
27. Ibid, p. 23.
28. Helmut Rumpf., *Mitteleuropa*, Ibid, p. 23.
29. Nothing could be more natural, especially for men confronted with the Fuhrer, than to long for a man like Bismarck, admirably versed in the art of diplomacy, a man of moderation in whom they could place their trust. In the words of Hassell : 'In his own way he (Bismarck) knew how to win confidence in the world; exactly the reverse of what is done today. In truth, the highest diplomacy and great moderation were his real gifts.' Hassell, *Diaries*, p. 353.
30. H. Graml./H.Krausnick. 'The German Resistance and the Allies' Jacobson, July 20, 1944 : *The German Opposition to Hitler* as viewed by Foreign Historians–An Anthology (Bonn, 1969), p. 281.
31. In the words of Graml : 'Students of the German Resistance ... have found it difficult to reconcile the opposition's apparently universal, or at least supranational outlook on the one hand, and their advocacy of a policy of strength and national interests on the other; generally the contradiction remains unsolved'. Graml, *Ger. Resist*, p. 2.
32. Ibid, p. 26–27.
33. Ibid, pp. 27–28.
34. Ibid, p. 28.
35. Hassell, *Diaries*, p. 303.
36. 'Thus their thought was ethical, philosophical, theological' : Constantine FitzGibbon, *20 July* (New York : W.W. Norton and Co. Inc., 1956), p. 84.
37. M.L.G. Balfour. 'Introduction', *German Resistance to Hitler : Count von Moltke and the Kreisau Circle,* Ger. Van Roon, trans. Peter Ludlow (London : Van Nostrand Reinhold Co. 1971), p. 7.
38. Graml, *Ger. Resist*, p.30. Somewhat unrealistic notions.
39. 'Theo Haubach "Foundations of a Socialists Policy in Europe" Ibid, p. 31.

40. Though not a member of the Kreisau Circle, Hermann Brill formulated the programme and aims of the socialist group, the 'German Popular Front' which differed very little from the foreign aims of the Kreisau Socialists : Ibid, pp. 30–31.
41. Ibid, p. 31.
42. Ibid, p. 32.
43. Eberhard Zeller. *The Flame of Freedom : The German Struggle against Hitler* (University of Miami Press, 1969), p. 95.
44. Roon, *Gerr. Resist*, p. 256.
45. Ibid, pp. 257–58.
46. Dr. Van Roon's diligent researches have explored almost every significant aspect of the Circle's origins, its activities and the lives of its members. As the Circle was one of the main groups in Germany working against Hitler and the Third Reich, Roon's work–*German Resistance to Hitler : Count von Moltke and the Kreisau Circle*– is valuable and important to all interested in the history of the period.
47. Roon, *Ger. Resist*, p. 265.
48. Graml, *Ger. Resist*, p. 35.
49. Ibid, pp. 35–36.
50. Ibid, pp. 39–40.
51. Adam von Trott Zu Zolz had become the chief foreign policy expert of the Kreisau Circle.
52. In 1939 Trott had put forward a clearly defined European concept : he pleaded Anglo-American politicians for cooperation 'for a constructive European future', and it is significant that in this memorandum he ascribed to the German working classes a special aptitude for politics within the total framework of Europe. Trott's idea of Europe's interest would approximate to 'the example of the United States of America whose common national frontier and whose customs and currency union have *prima facie* excluded the possibility of internal armed conflict.' He was fully aware of the problem inherent in the superior German industrial system and, to relieve the resultant stresses, he proposed 'common European action for economic development' Graml., *Ger. Resist*, p. 39.
53. Ibid, pp. 40–41.
54. Ibid, pp. 41–42.
55. Significantly, Goerdeler never desired a German-Polish agreement regarding the eastern frontier; rather he sought to negotiate an understanding with the British government 'over' Poland. Ibid, p. 43.

56. Hassell, *Diaries*, p. 318, vide supra p. 2.
57. Ibid, p. 353.
58. Ibid, p. 316. 'Von Trott travelled to Switzerland to contact British and American agents, and to urge them to offer a "fair" peace to a non-Nazi Germany–ostensibly in order to discourage the opposition from "turning East". In addition, Trott wanted the cessation as a gesture, of all allied bombing of Berlin' Prittie, *Ger. Hit*, p. 235.
59. Graml, *Ger. Resist*, p. 49.
60. 'By the principle of unconditional surrender they (Britain and the United States) wished to reassure the free peoples and bring home to them the need for, and devotion, to the war effort. At the time all applauded the Casablanca decision. It reinvigorated the fighting spirit of the regular army and the clandestine forces. 'It was not till long afterwards that several British and American historians–Chester Wilmot, J.F.C. Fuller, Hanson Baldwin and Liddell Hart—singled out unconditional surrender as one of the biggest mistakes of the war'; H. Bernard: 'The German Resistance against Hitler' *July 20*, 1944, Jacobson p. 37.
61. Graml, *Ger. Resist*, p. 50.
62. Boveri, *Treason*, p. 307. The Stauffenberg group envisaged the 'East-West solution', a Germany occupying a mediatory position between two worlds, and not the "West solution" and nothing but the "west" ' M. Baumont 'General Ludwig Beck', *July 20*, Jacobson, p. 183.
63. Boveri, *Treason*, p. 309.
64. Bernard, *Ger. Resist*, *July 20*, Jacobson, p. 15.
65. Graml, *Ger. Resist*, p. 52.
66. Ibid, p. 52.
67. Von Tresckow said about the *putsch* 'The attempt must be made whatever the cost ... For now it is no longer the practical purpose that counts, but the fact that before history and the world, the German Resistance has chanced its decisive throw. Nothing else signifies', cited by Ernst Wolf, 'Political and Moral Motives behind the Resistance,' Graml, *Ger. Resist*, p. 233.
68. Trott, cited by Graml, Ibid, p. 54.

Chapter 10

The Treaty of Rapallo

That the Allies had evinced a woeful lack of foresight in attempting to impose a punitive peace on Germany by means of the Treaty of Versailles, to which one of Germany's great neighbours remained uncommitted and unfavourably inclined, is a common place. By doing so, they impelled Germany to seek in the development of her relations with this one uncommitted neighbour, a path of escape from the strictures of the treaty. On the other hand, it provided the Bolsheviks with the much desired opportunity to rend their capitalist adversaries, and to deal with them separately.

The logic of this situation found no more vivid illustration than in the circumstances around the conclusion of the Treaty of Rapallo between Germany and Soviet Russia on Easter Sunday, 1922.

The name Rapallo–actually that of the Italian seashore resort where the treaty was signed—has come down through subsequent decades as a symbol of sorts, implying different things to different people. To western liberals it has been a symbol of the sinister German-Soviet plot against the liberties of the West. To the defeated Germans, it has marked the starting point of an independent German foreign policy–policy of manoeuvre between East and West, as the alternative to melancholy and frustration. To Soviet ideologists, it has appeared as an advantageous pact with a bourgeois state, an agreement which afforded to Moscow all the benefits of smooth diplomatic and commercial intercourse without hampering its freedom to attack the political system of the country in question.

The Rapallo Treaty was a turning point in the foreign policies both of Germany and of Soviet Russia, and the most conspicuous landmark in European diplomacy between Versailles and Locarno.[1] The process of building up normal state relations between the German bourgeois republic and the Russian Soviet republic was slow and gradual. It was not till the beginning of 1921, when most Germans became convinced for the first time that the Soviet regime in Russia had come to stay and when thoughts on the Russian side were beginning to concentrate on projects less ambitious than world revolution that the negotiations which led to the Rapallo Treaty were first brewed.[2]

Throughout 1919, Soviet Russia was completely isolated. After the Versailles treaty, the Allied powers even established a 'blockade' of Russia, and in October, 1919 invited Germany to join in it, but Germany refused. The refusal was put on the ground that Germany was herself still being subjected to an Allied blockade and that joining presupposed a recognition of equality of rights. But it was nonetheless significant that the first occasion since Versailles on which the German Government had ventured openly and flatly to reject an Allied demand, was on a Russian issue.[3]

As the Soviet leaders turned to the task of the revival of trade with the West, their attention focused on Germany, the leading industrial power on the continent. She was admirably placed to provide the things Russia needed. Besides, with Germany less trouble was to be expected on the subject of debts and claims. She scarcely figured in the pre-war debt, and in the war debt, of course, not at all. Her property claims were inconsequential in comparison to those of some of the Allied powers. And she was now so humiliated, so crushed, so without alternatives, that she could be expected to be less adhesive about such problems and more interested in getting trade started at once, without formalities or preconditions.[4] By the beginning of 1922, there was a definite move in Germany toward an eastern orientation of German foreign policy. 'But the fort of loyalty to the West', says G.F. Kennan, 'continued, for the moment, to be tenuously held by President

Ebert and by the new Foreign Minister, Walther Rathenau, who believed deeply in the necessity for a general accommodation with the West.'[5]

In the winter of 1921–22, the idea prevailed in Europe that an international conference be convened to bring about the rebuilding of the European economy. To many it appeared expedient to organize some great collaborative efforts if recovery from the shackles of war was to be effected. Lloyd George, the British prime minister, made himself an enthusiastic exponent of this suggestion. It was decided to call a general European conference at Genoa, in April, 1922. Here, for the first time since Versailles, both the Russians and the Germans–the two bad boys of the European family–were to be invited.[6]

Initially the two main items of discussion at Genoa were to be : first, the inclusion of Russia in Europe's economic orbit as it was believed that European rehabilitation was closely linked with the reintegration of the Russian economy into that of the continent as a whole; and second, the problem of German reparations and war debts. The Entente Powers knew that ostracizing Russia would cut off their goods from vast markets. 'The British, admirably realists in international politics', observes H.A. Gibbons, 'were first to grasp the cutting-off-the-nose-to-spite-the-face danger of keeping Russia in coventry.'[7] They were also eager for sympathetic treatment with Germany. Lloyd George, influenced by Keynes' indictment of Versailles in his *The Economic Consequences of the Peace,* appeared to show some understanding of Germany's problems. The European countries were seemingly unable to recover, by their own individual efforts, from the economic effects of the war. In the opinion of Kennan, the situation was not dissimilar to that which preceded the launching of the Marshall Plan in 1947.[8]

The attitude of the French Government, however, was less congenial. The question of the enormous debt of the Czarist regime, made it extremely difficult for the government to renew relations with Russia. Further Poincare, who was in power in France, would not allow the problem of German reparations to be placed on the agenda. The Germans, he was adamant, were not to be given the chance of expressing their grievances on this issue before a European forum. Thus Poincare dealt the Conference its death blow before it even started.[9]

The Soviet leaders welcomed the possibility of Russia's economic collaboration with the West but they regarded askance their seemingly 'ulterior' motives. Georgi Chicherin, the Soviet foreign commissar, expressed these fears as follows :

> We want economic collaboration and they want it, but we will fight against such economic collaboration taking the form of economic domination over Russia ... We are about to have our wishes satisfied, but we are also about to meet the new and serious danger of an attempt to unite all economic interests for the purpose of turning economic collaboration with us into our economic enslavement. It is precisely this which we would fight.[10]

The Soviet diplomats were especially apprehensive of the danger of being confronted at Genoa with a united front of their capitalist creditors. It appeared almost certain that the western governments would raise the question of debts and claims, and would make satisfaction on this score a requisite for any renewal of commercial contact with Russia.[11] So the Soviet leaders desperately tried to pressurize Berlin to conclude a special treaty whereby mutual claims would be annulled and full diplomatic relations would be restored. And here the Russians had a terrific weapon which lay at the core of the whole Rapallo episode. What was that? It was Article 116 of the Versailles Peace Treaty, which had been inserted under French influence. It stated : 'The Allied and assorted powers formally reserve the rights of Russia to obtain from 'Germany' restitution and reparation based on the principles of the present treaty.'[12]

So Russia could chop off her pound of flesh out of the Germans, who were regarded as fit for any amount of this sort of exploitation. The Allies could start putting pressure on Moscow to pay the Czarist debts and the Soviets could decide to reimburse themselves at German expense. And so Article 116 hung over the German head like the sword of Damocles.[13]

Something had to be done or the Genoa Conference might bring this sword down. The refusal of the French to permit reparations to be discussed at Genoa came as a cruel blow to the Germans. It seemed to cut off the last chance of relief from the reparations burden. Worse still, there was no guarantee that new reparations would not be added on the basis of Article 116.

These, then, were the circumstances in which the Genoa Conference convened on April 10, 1922. It was not exactly a happy congregation. Lord Curzon's words were prophetic indeed : 'I can feel no certainty that we may not find ourselves committed to something pregnant with political disaster here.'[14] Lloyd George headed the British delegation, Barthour–the French, Chicherin and Trakowsky–the Russian, while the Germans were led by Chancellor Wirth and Rathenau. Twenty-nine European states were represented at the conference, including neutrals and ex-enemies.[15]

In the words of H.G. Daniels :

> It (the Conference) led to the ventilation of a great mass of pious opinion on peace, while really achieving nothing applicable to the immediate problems. Its programme, the economic reconstruction of credit throughout the world for the purpose of creating purchasing power for the benefit of industry, was conceived on the purely capitalist basis of adequate material security as the indispensable condition for loan or credit. The wording of the agenda appeared, and was interpreted, to be directed against Russia.[16]

It was obvious that Germany, in view of her geographical position 'could not participate in any political movement that might expose her to ultimate reprisals from her eastern neighbour.' says Daniels. Two, possibly three other motives actuated the German delegation in rejecting any policy directed against the Bolsheviks : the Germans believed in self-help as the basis of European reconstruction : 'they regarded themselves as the nation pre-eminently destined to form the economic link between Russia and western Europe'; German military thinkers entertained hopes that cooperation between German military science and Russian military resources might be turned to the advantage of Germany's liberation. The geographical position had led Germany to avoid at all cost 'being drawn into either the western or eastern European orbit. This policy had never been dictated by any consideration of the claims of western civilization, but solely by Germany's material interests. Moreover, Germany had held a predominant position in the past as the intermediary between the Russian purchaser and the European market.'[17]

Daniels, reasoning explains only partly the background for the pact with the Bolsheviks. In the words of Viscount D'Abernon :

> Evidence continues to accumulate to the effect that the Germans were jumped at Rapallo, Berlin, May 3, 1922. Many diplomatists thought and think that Maltzen was working for a signature at any price ... But a good witness, who saw Maltzen and his assistants on the day they left for Genoa, is pretty certain they were then against concluding anything ... Maltzen, on the same day, said that, while he was anxious to make an agreement with the Bolsheviks, he was altogether against recognizing them officially before Genoa. 'What do we get by official recognition? ... We shall get no concessions from the Russians for recognition, unless we add cash to the recognition. That is what they are really after. From the German point of view, the only reason for hurry is Article 116.'[18]

'Rathenau', states Kennan, 'still desperately hoped that Germany's policies, both vis-a-vis Russia and with regard to European reconstruction generally, could somehow be merged with those of the Western community on the basis of the agreement to be reached at Genoa, and that Germany would thus be spared the necessity of a bilateral deal of this sort with Moscow.'[19]

For the first time the vanquished and the Russians met together with the victors when delegates from all the European countries assembled at Genoa. This factor seemed to auger well for the success of the conference. Upto this time, the Entente Powers had failed to re-establish peace in Europe because they had outlawed half of it. Whether Germany and Russia deserved to be put in coventry was not the point. No one disputed the justice of insisting that Germany live upto the obligations she had assumed in order to escape the overrunning of her territory and the disagreeable consequences of defeat in a war in which she had been the challenger. Neither was anyone inclined to receive Soviet Russia with open arms into the councils of the nations of whose political and social institutions she was the outspoken enemy.[20] The Russians resented the effort to make them appear at Genoa, as the Germans had been made to appear at Versailles, as criminals and debtors. The Entente Powers had no idea of admitting reciprocity. The assumption was that Great Britain and France had the right to do what they denied to Germany and Russia. Germany was a defeated nation and Russia was an outlawed nation. But the purpose for which the conference had been called could not succeed without the cooperation of these two. The statesmen of the Entente Powers could not hope to ameliorate economic and political conditions in Europe unless they possessed and were willing to use the means of coercing Germany and Russia or unless they intended to treat these two on the basis of give and take, as they treated one another.

Because none of the above alternatives were considered, the Genoa Conference was a complete failure.[21] The Entente Powers began all wrong. They held a preliminary meeting to decide upon their programme, assuming that the role of the German and Russian delegations would be simply that of acquiescence. And 'the two outcast powers retaliated in a startling way. They signed a treaty at Rapallo ... The Treaty of Rapallo torpedoed the conference.'[22]

The Rapallo treaty was of considerable value to both states. It contained a sweeping mutual renunciation of all financial claims of every sort, thus relieving the Germans of the nightmare of Article 116. Article (Ia) of the treaty provided that :

> The German Reich and the Russian Socialist Federal Soviet Republic mutually agree to waive their claims for compensation for expenditure incurred on account of the war, and also for war damages, that is to say, any damages which may have been suffered by them and by their nationals in war zones on account

> of military measures, including all requisitions in enemy country. Both parties likewise agree to forego compensation for any civilian damages, which may have been suffered by the nationals of the one party on account of so-called exceptional war measures or on account of emergency measures carried out by the other party.[23]

Louis Fischer observes :

> Both delegations attached to the treaty tremendous significance. It was significant, first, as an unspoken protest of the anti-Versailles powers against the Versailles powers–and herein lies one explanation of the storm which the treaty loosed against Germany ... The treaty robbed the Entente of one of its most effective weapons against Moscow and Berlin : pressure by isolation ... That move interfered with the Allies' plans with respect to Russia, a Russia befriended by Germany.[24]

'The fact of signature', so says E.H. Carr, 'was more important than the formal contents of the treaty.'[25]

By this agreement, Germany and Russia, at one stroke, cleaned the slate covered with claims and counter-claims accumulated in previous years. They renounced all compensation for damages caused by war, intervention and occupation, and for civil damages caused by Soviet measures of nationalization (Article 1). Thus the Damoclean sword of Article 116, was no longer hung over the heads of the German Government. Article 2 gave Germany the right to bring up the question of Russian debts for re-examination in case the Soviet Government satisfied similar claims of other states. This safety clause assured the Germans that they were not voluntarily incurring a decided disadvantage; on the other hand, it served to discourage severely any potential Soviet intentions to settle the debt question with other countries at Germany's expense. The treaty provided for the resumption of full diplomatic and consular relations (Article 3). In Article 4 both countries granted each other the most favoured nation status. Finally, in Article 5, the German Government promised to help private firms in the extension of their contracts with the Soviet Government.[26]

In the words of Hilger and Meyer :

> This was not a Grand alliance nor an aggressive treaty; it was not even a treaty of non-aggression or even neutrality. Its principal aim was the removal of impediments to mutual understanding and goodwill created by the war and the revolution, thus making future friendly relations possible.[27]

The anger with which the Rapallo treaty was received by the Allies was a key to its importance. Lloyd George not very convincingly demanded the unconditional withdrawal of the treaty which was refused with equal charge by both Germany and Russia. Later, it was reported that the Prime Minister had been filly aware of Russia-German negotiations there while the 'gentleman' in Paris' as Lloyd called Poincare was instructing his representative in Genoa urging him to take forceful action. Its effect on the diplomatic map of Europe was quite incalculable. Soviet Russia had regained a foothold in the capitalist world with pretensions to resume the rank and status of a great power. 'The policy of strangling Germany', said Radek at the fourth congress of Comintern in November 1922, 'implied in fact the destruction of Russia as a great power; for, no matter how Russia is governed, it is always to her interest that Germany should exist ... A Russia weakened to the utmost by the war, could neither have remained a great power nor acquired the economic and technical means for her industrial reconstruction, unless she had in the existence of Germany, a counter-weight to the preponderance of the Allies.'[28]

The German Government was less assured in what it had done. Daniels is sceptical of the good the treaty could do to Germany. He observes : 'It may be doubted whether this instrument was the means of fulfilling even a small proportion of Germany's hopes. The pursuit of Russian *ignis fatuus* had led Germans on a sorry dance through a maze of illusions ever since the Peace of Brest-Litovsk ... It was discovered that the new Russia was but the old Russia under a different sign ... As for the prospect of colonizing Russia with the expert German technician, the Soviet Government soon showed that it had no intention of tolerating anything of the kind. Russia was still in the shadows. The spirit of the age required, not that Germany or any other country should break in, but that Russia should break out.'[29]

Yet the treaty established a balance. The German government could manoeuvre freely between east and west, playing off the two rivals against each other, disclaiming any irrevocable commitment to either, extorting concessions from one by threatening to fall into the arms of the other, and always keeping its own choice open. This was the policy which was to serve Germany in good stead for the next seven years. In reality, however, Rapallo represented no reorientation of Germany's foreign policy. 'But the position' as D'Abernon observes, 'is not immutable; extreme pressure or extreme distress is likely to convince the Germans that a change in their policy is necessary. If any such change occurs, the main responsibility will rest on French extremists, who are doing their utmost to bring about what they and we have most to fear.'[30]

The scope and meaning of Rapallo were far exaggerated by its critics. Further, there have been sweeping accusations that Rapallo ran counter to 'international morality.' 'International morality' to quote Hilger and Meyer, 'is a most elusive concept, and even if it were better defined it would be difficult to brand the settling of mutual debts as "immoral" especially after the repeated efforts on the part of the Allies to free Russia of its debts to Germany unilaterally.'[31] It was said that Rapallo meant a return to old-fashioned "secret diplomacy", and that Germany had violated the principle of mutual collaboration and consultation. This principle had, clearly been violated first by the western diplomats who kept the German delegation at the Genoa conference in utter isolation and the reproach of secrecy also boomeranged, for it is well-established that Rathenau made repeated but unsuccessful attempts to get in touch with Lloyd George. The Germans had reason to complain of the Allies' attempt to reach an agreement with Soviet Russia independently of Germany and to her probable detriment.[32]

Lord D'Abernon holds that Rapallo had been brought about by a series of accidents and blunders. It was not the result of a pre-arranged plot. The news came as no less of a surprise to the government in Berlin than to the governments in London and Paris.

The British Ambassador states :

> My opinion has always been that the signature of the Rapallo Treaty was not the result of any serious faith in a policy of lasting cooperation; it was more of the nature of a provocative demonstration. A strange element of mockery if often evident in the proceedings of the Soviet Government; they delight to play a trick on capitalistic powers, even though the trick mars the success of their own policy. I doubt if they regard the Germans as possible collaborators in their scheme for reforming the world.[33]

For Chicherin, Rapallo was one of the main pillars of Soviet foreign policy, a spiritual need, and the concept of *Schicksalsgemein schaft* was no empty phrase for him.[34] His counterpart in Germany was less jubilant. Rathenau's tragic last days were a melancholic evidence of the callousness with which the western democracies treated the moderate and well-disposed elements in the Weimar Republic; how vindictive anti-Germanism toyed into the hands of Soviet diplomatists.

The treaty as such was innocuous. It was in no sense a precedent for the Nazi-Soviet Pact of 1939. For the West, Rapallo signified the loss of Germany as a possible partner in a western approach to the problem of Russian communism. Thus, Rapallo could justly be described as the first great victory for Soviet diplomacy. According to the Soviet comment on the Rapallo Pact : 'The diplomacy of the *entente*, hoping to force Soviet Russia to its knees ... suffered a complete defeat. To both of the participants, on the other hand, the Rapallo Treaty brought serious political advantages ... the ring of economic blockade against Soviet Russia was broken. On the other hand, Germany, too, gained the possibility of widening her trade.'[35] The Soviet claim, evidently, has to be accepted with reserve.[36]

That Chicherin and his coadjutors deserve much credit for Rapallo, on the basis of their dexterous handling of the situation that developed at Genoa, cannot be confuted. But it seems clear that the most important determining factor in this transaction was the deficient diplomacy of the western democracies. To this must be added the downright and inexcusable American refusal to participate in the crucial conference. This was not the last time in history when an astonishing Soviet diplomatic triumph resulted partly by Soviet contrivance and tenacity of purpose, but more by naivete, complacency and discord on part of the West.

Appendix

TREATY OF RAPALLO

(Translation*)

No. 498–German-Russian Agreement, Signed at Rapallo, April 16, 1922.**

The German Government, represented by Dr. Walther Rathenau, Minister of State, and The Government of the Russian Socialist Federal Soviet Republic, represented by M. Chicherin, People's commissary, have agreed upon the following provisions :

Article I

The two Governments have agreed that the arrangements arrived at between the German Reich and the Russian Socialist Federal Soviet Republic, with regard to questions dating from the period of the war between Germany and Russia, shall be definitely settled upon the following basis :

(a) The German Reich and the Russian Socialist Federal Soviet Republic mutually agree to waive their claims for compensation for expenditure incurred on account of the war, and also for war damages, that is to say, any damages

---

* Translated by the Secretariat of the League of Nations. Text done in French and English, only English translation given here.

** *League of Nations Treaty Series*. (1923). Germany and Russian Soviet Republic, Agreement signed at Rapallo, April 16, 1922, Vol. 19, (No. 1, 2 and 3), pp. 250–52.

which may have been suffered by them and by their nationals in war zones on account of military measures, including all requisitions in enemy country. Both parties likewise agree to forego compensation for any civilian damages, which may have been suffered by the nationals of the one Party on account of so-called exceptional war measures or on account of emergency measures carried out by the other Party.

(b) Legal relations in public and private matters arising out of the state of war, including the question of the treatment of trading vessels which have fallen into the hands of either Party, shall be settled on a basis of reciprocity.

(c) Germany and Russia mutually agree to waive their claims for compensation for expenditure incurred by either Party on behalf of prisoners of war. Furthermore, the German Government agrees to forego compensation with regard to the expenditure incurred by it on behalf of members of the Red Army interned in Germany. The Russian Government agrees to forego the restitution of the proceeds of the sale carried out in Germany of the army stores brought into Germany by the interned members of the Red Army mentioned above.

Arctilce 2

Germany waives all claims against Russia which may have arisen through the application, up to the present, of the laws and measures of the Russian Socialist Federal Soviet Republic to German nationals on their private rights and the rights of the German Reich and States, and also claims which may have arisen owing to any other measures taken by the Russian Socialist Federal Soviet Republic or by their agents against German nationals or their private rights, on condition that the Government of the Russian Socialist Federal Soviet Republic does not satisfy claims for compensation of a similar nature made by a third Party.

Article 3

Diplomatic and consular relations between the German Reich and the Russian Socialist Federal Soviet Republic shall be resumed immediately. The conditions for the admission of the consuls of both Parties shall be determined by means of a special agreement.

Article 4

Both Governments have furthermore agreed that the establishment of the legal status of those nationals of the one Party, which live within the territory of the other Party, and the general regulation of mutual, commercial and economic relations, shall be effected on the principle of the most favoured nation. This principle shall, however, not apply to the privileges and facilities which the Russian Socialist Federal Soviet Republic may grant to a Soviet Republic or to any state which in the past formed part of the former Russian empire.

Article 5

The two Governments shall cooperate in a spirit of mutual goodwill in meeting the economic needs of both countries. In the event of a fundamental settlement of the above question on an international basis, an exchange of opinions shall previously take place between the two Governments. The German Government, having lately been informed of the proposed agreements of private firms, declares its readiness to give all possible support to these arrangements and to facilitate their being carried into effect.

Article 6

Articles 1 (b) and 4 of this Agreement shall come into force on the day of ratification, and the remaining provisions shall come into force immediately.

Original text done in duplicate* at Rapallo on April 16, 1922.

(Signed) RATHENAU.

(Signed) CHICHERIN.

* French and English : Only English translation given here.

NOTES AND REFERENCES

1. Carr., Edward Hallett. *German-Soviet Relations Between The Two*

World Wars(Baltimore : The John Hopkins Press, 1951), p. 67.
2. Ibid, p. 49.
3. Ibid, p. 50.
4. Kennan, George F. *Russia And The West Under Lenin And Stalin* (Boston : Little, Brown and Co., 1961), p. 209.
5. Ibid, p. 211.
6. Ibid, p. 212.
7. Gibbons, Herbert Adams, *Europe Since 1918* (New York : The Century Co., 1923), pp. 191–92.
8. Kennan, op.cit, p. 211.
9. Kessler, Count Harry. *Walther Rathenau : His Life and Work* (New York : Harcourt, Brace and Co., 1930), p. 304.
10. Degras, Jane (ed.), *Soviet Documents on Foreign Policy 1917–1924* (London : Oxford University Press, 1951), p. 291 : extract from Chicherin's report to the Central Executive Committee on the invitation to the Genoa Conference, January 27, 1922.
11. Kennan, op.cit, p. 212.
12. *The Treaty of Peace Between the Allied and Associated Powers and Germany signed at Versailles June 28, 1919* (London : H.M. Stationary Office, Imperial House Kingsway, 1919), Section 14: Russia and Russian States, Article 116, p. 67.
13. Kennan, op.cit, p. 213.
14. Curzon, Harold Nicholson. *The Last Phase 1919–1925—A Study in Post-War Diplomacy* (New York : Harcourt, Brace and Co., 1929), p. 245.
15. D'Abernon Viscount, *Versailles To Rapallo 1920–1922*—The Diary of an Ambassador (New York : Doubleday, Doran and Co., Inc., 1929), p. 305.
16. Daniels, H.G. *The Rise of the German Republic* (New York : Charles Scribner's Sons, 1928), p. 184.
17. Ibid, pp. 184–85.
18. D'Abernon Viscount. *An Ambassador of Peace*, 3 Vols. (London : Hodder and Stoughton, 1929), Vol. I, pp. 305–6.
19. Kennan, op.cit, p. 214.
20. Gibbons, op.cit, pp. 534–35.
21. Ibid, p. 535.
22. Ibid, p. 536.
23. *Leagues of Nations Treaty Series* (1923), Vol. 19 (Nos. 1, 2 and 3), 'Germany and Russian Soviet Repbulic, Agreement signed at Rapallo, April 16, 1922', p. 250 : for full text of the treaty see appendix.
24. Fischer, Louis. *The Soviets In World Affairs* (New York : Jonathan

Cape and Harrison Smith, 1930), Vol. I, pp. 342–43.

25. Carr., op.cit, p. 64.
26. Hilger, Gustav and Meyer, Alfred G. *The Incompatible allies* A memoir history of German-Soviet relations 1918–1941 (New York : Macmillan Co., 1953), pp. 78–79.
27. Ibid, p. 79.
28. Carr, op.cit, p. 65.
29. Daniels, op.cit, pp. 185–86.
30. D'Abernon, *An Ambassador of Peace,* op.cit, pp. 303.
31. Hilger and Meyer, op.cit, p. 79.
32. D'Abernon, *An Ambassador of Peace* op.cit, p. 293.
33. Ibid, p. 311.
34. Hilger and Meyer, op.cit, p. 111. Chicherin assured the French that 'The treaty of Rapallo has no other object than the settlement of questions which have accumulated between two States which were at war with one another and which feel the mutual necessity of re-establishing peaceful relations, in their own interests and in the interests of mankind ... Far from being directed against France or any other Power ... these treaties should serve as the basis for pacification and stability throughout the world'. Degras, op.cit, 'Letter from Chicherin to the French foreign minister on the Treaty of Rapallo, April 29, 1922', p. 304.
35. Kennan, George F. *Soviet Foreign Policy 1917–1941*, Snyder, Louis L. (gen. ed.), (New Jersey : Princeton, 1960), Part II, Doc. No. 14, p. 142.
36. According to Kennan : 'That the "ring of economic blockade around Soviet Russia" was broken by Rapallo is a bit of inaccurate boasting. The Allied blockade of Russia had been removed by the Supreme Allied Council two years earlier. Rapallo itself changed little in the condition surrounding Soviet trade with western countries. What was broken at Rapallo was Russia's political isolation', Ibid, pp. 141–42.

Chapter 11

Yalta : German Questions

The wartime military alliance between the United States, the Soviet Union, and Great Britain posed formidable political problems for them in the event of an Axis defeat. Allied wartime unity was primarily based on the commitment to defeat the Axis Powers and not on common objectives or mutual trust, major and potentially divisive differences among these Allies persisted. If left unresolved, these differences could thwart attempts to attain a durable peace enabling Germany or Japan to exploit these dissensions to regain power and influence. Further, from the U.S. standpoint, postponing political and military considerations till a regular peace conference and thereby allowing the military situation to determine post-war developments was strategically indiscreet. Such actions would surely permit the development of spheres of influence.[1]

In part, the desire to avoid the post-World War I experience instigated Roosevelt, Churchill, and Stalin to support summit diplomacy. Thus, the Big Three, at times only Two, met occassionally, at Casablanca, Moscow, Quebec, and Tehran, to coordinate military strategy and delineate areas of agreement towards future wartime and post-war developments in Germany, eastern Europe, the Balkans, and the Far East. However, they avoided binding commitments, except on pressing military issues.[2] Any discussions involving their conflicting political objectives and policy differences were kept in abeyance. But by 1944, with the successful establishment of the Second Front and the continuous military reversals suffered by Germany and Japan, this procedure was no longer feasible. The certainty of military victory made it incumbent upon the wartime Allies to reach an agreement on peace aims and post-war objectives.

The Conference held by President Roosevelt, Prime Minister Churchill and Marshal Stalin, accompanied by their respective advisers at Yalta in Crimea from February 4 to 12, 1945, was thus, in the nature of a preliminary peace Conference.[3] It was designed to coordinate policy and strategy as the war entered its closing phase. The paradox of the Yalta Conference was that it was convened at a time when the Allies were on the verge of military victory, but had resolved little else through diplomatic negotiation.[4]

In the words of Stettinius, Secretary of State :

> The Yalta Conference 'was the most important wartime meeting of the leaders of Great Britain, the Soviet Union, and the United States. It was not only the longest meeting of President Roosevelt with Prime Minister Churchill and Marshal Stalin; it was also for the first time that the three great leaders reached fundamental agreements on post-war problems as distinct from mere statements of aims and purposes.'[5] The Conference marked the high tide of British, Russian, and American cooperation on the war and on the post-war settlement.[6]

For the Soviet Union, the future of Germany was the central and most critical political issue for the Allies to decide during the war. Obviously Nazi Germany was doomed but 'the Germans, clinging to their malignant leadership were fighting on and would continue, it seemed, until the very earth fell away from them or they were buried in it. They had survived great defeats in the past and would survive this one.'[7] Stalin had told the West that Soviet Union could not be expected to fight Germany once every generation.[8] Typical of his frequently expressed concern were his words to Tito : 'They will recover.' Give them twelve to fifteen years and they'll be on their feet again.'[9]

All three Heads of state at Yalta professed that their only goals were to end the war and to create a stable peace. They were unanimously determined that Hitler, his accomplices and his system must be crushed. They all felt justified in demanding the punishment of the war criminals and the payment of reparations.[10] 'Yet, at Yalta, the West was shying away from a harsh policy against post-war Germany and moving toward the idea of reconstructing Germany on pre-war lines–minus, of course, the Nazi hierarchy.'[11] The Allies feared the disastrous effect the dismemberment of Germany might have on western trade. Members of the British Government were in doubt whether a post-war Anglo-Soviet alliance would be more advantageous or an Anglo-German one.[12]

President Roosevelt opened the second plenary meeting* announcing that the agenda was 'Political Aspects of the Future Treatment of Germany.' He said that the first question was that of the zones of occupation, which he understood had been agreed upon in the European Advisory Commision. He said there was one question still open and that was the desire of France to have a zone of occupation and French participation in the control machinery of Germany.[13] He emphasized that the question of zones did not relate to the permanent treatment of Germany.

Then the President handed a map[14] of the agreed tripartite zones to Marshal Stalin, pointing out that although these zones had been agreed upon in the European Advisory Commission, they had not yet been signed by the three governments.[15]

Marshal Stalin said that in the discussion on Germany he would like to include the following points :

1. The question of dismemberment of Germany–a definite decision should be made on whether to dismember Germany and if so, what form of dismemberment should be considered.
2. Would it be better to give Germany a central government set up by the Big Three, or simply an administration? More specifically, if the country was dismembered, would each section have a government? Or would it have only an administration?

---

* Discussions on Germany which started on February 5th and continued sporadically until the final protocol was approved by the Heads of the governments on February 11th, have been given in a concise and consolidated form. No dates have been specified.

3. The conditions of Germany's surrender were also to be decided. Would the Allies preserve the Hitler government if it surrendered unconditionally? Keeping in mind the precedent of Allied support of pro-Fascist factions in Italy after the invasion. In Italy, 'unconditional' surrender did in fact have conditions. Therefore, Germany, like Italy, should have specific terms spelled out.[16] Suppose, for example, a German group had declared that they had overthrown Hitler and accepted unconditional surrender, would the three governments deals with such a group as with Badoglio in Italy?[17]
4. Whether Germany should pay reparations, and, if so, what should be the amount?[18]

A quick agreement on the instrument of surrender was signed by the three powers at Yalta. Churchill read Artilce 12 (a) of the surrender terms agreed on by the European Advisory Commission : it stated–

> The United States of America, the United Kingdom and the Union of Soviet Socialist Republics shall possess supreme authority with respect to Germany. In the exercise of such authority they will take such steps, including the complete disarmament and demilitarization of Germany, as they deem requisite for future peace and security.[19]

Germany was to accept unconditional surrender. In doing so, it was to submit to the orders in all spheres of the United Nations. The whole German military establishment was to be disbanded with utmost speed and thoroughness, and all German arms were to be delivered to the Allies or destroyed, National socialism in every phase was to be extinguished. The German people were required to accept all possible measures for the redirection of their life.[20]

Stalin once again insisted upon an immediate settlement of dismemberment, claiming it was a primary question that had never really been settled. He repeated Roosevelt's Tehran proposal to divide Germany into five parts. He recalled how Churchill had agreed to the principle of dismemberment and reminded him that in their October conversation in Moscow, the prime minister had produced a plan for dividing Germany into two States Prussia and Bavaria, with the Ruhr and

Westphalia under international control. Stalin asserted they would have adopted this proposal had the President been there.[21] But he created a situation that made it difficult for the British and Americans to retreat from their own plans.

'Dismemberment', declared Stalin, 'was not an additional demand; it was an integral part of the terms of surrender. Therefore, a clause with no details, should be added to the terms, stating that Germany would be dismembered. Churchill agreed that this was important, but insisted it was not the main consideration.[22]

Roosevelt, like Stalin, felt dismemberment was an essential condition of surrender rather than a detail. He declared that it would be advisable to present the Germans with terms of surrender including the Allied intention to dismember.[23] He thought it was very risky to follow the plan of the prime minister and say nothing to the German people about dismemberment by the Allies. Instead by stating it in advance, Stalin said, the German people would know what was in store for them.[24] Roosevelt shared this view. Churchill also agreed finally, but stressed that he did so on his own and without the explicit approval of the war cabinet.[25]

> Supreme authority in Germany was to be exercised by the American, British, and Soviet commanders-in-chief, each in his own zone of occupation, and also jointly in matters affecting Germany as a whole. They were to act together as members of a top organ called the Control Council. This Council, among its other functions, was to
> 1. insure uniformity of action in the respective zones ;
> 2. make plans and decisions affecting Germany as a whole, on the basis of instructions received by each Commander from his government;
> 3. control the German central administration; and
> 4. direct the administration of Greater Berlin. Thus if the governments of the members could not agree on any main matter of policy, the Council would not be able to act, and the decision would rest with the separate zone commanders.[26]

George Crocker's comment on German dismemberment, by no means favourable, has some justification. He observes :

> The German nation was to be dismembered. The details were referred to a committee, but this much was settled : a huge chunk was to be torn off and given to Poland as a sop for the mayhem to be performed on that unhappy country; some choice morsels, such as the city of Konigsberg, were to be donated to the Soviet Union outright; and the rest of Eastern Germany was to be spread-eagled for forced communization by Russian masters, since occupation by the Red Army meant nothing less than that. How and when this nightmare would ever end was too unpleasant a subject to be faced at Yalta ...Ten million Germans were doomed to be turned out of their homes and set out on the roads to flee westward ... What followed Yalta was a mass expulsion which Churchill himself was impelled to allude to as 'tragedy on a prodigious scale.' Actually, never in history, even in the worst of pagan times, has there been such a millionfold uprooting of human beings.[27]

The recent addition of France to the European Advisory Commission and to the proposed Security Council of the United Nations raised the question of French participation in the occupation of Germany. This question had two parts–a French zone of occupation and a French seat on the Allied Control Commission. The British were keen to gain agreement on both. They strongly felt that the rehabilitation of France was necessary for filling the power vacuum which would follow the defeat of Germany.[28] France was not only the nearest neighbour of Germany in the West but the only ally of any consequence without which Britain would be left alone to contain the might of Russia, as Churchill put it. Eden concluded : 'Europe expects us to have a European policy of our own, and to state it ... we are likely to work more closely with France even than with the United States.'[29]

It was understood that the Soviet zone was not to be cut down; and any zone for the French would be formed out of the American and British areas as already delineated.[30] All that the prime minister sought was that the Soviet government would agree that the British and American Governments should have the right to work out with the French a zone of occupation which would not in any way affect the proposed Soviet zone.[31] Churchill pointed out that France had had a long experience in dealing with the Germans.[32]

Stalin had no real interest in France's formal status in the Inter-Allied machinery. Consequently he followed Roosevelt's lead. Further appealing to Stalin on a very sensitive point, Churchill compared Britain's need of France with the Soviet dependence upon the Poles for support against Germany.[33] Churchill's parallel of the French and Polish roles vis-a-vis Germany was not wasted on Stalin. A 'friendly' Poland would serve Russia against Germany just as a 'friendly' France would with Britain. Stalin dropped his antipathy and admitted the necessity of a strong France.[34] It was resolved that France should have a zone. Further, they agreed that it would be a mistake to bring in any other nations.[35]

But French representation on the Allied control machinery to oversee the occupation of Germany was another question, at least for Stalin who insisted that the peace must be protected only by those nations which had made the greatest sacrifice and contribution to winning the war. Stalin lamented that he could not alter the facts, which were that France had contributed little to the war and had opened her gates to the enemy.[36] The Allied Control Council must reflect this. If France were given a place in the Control Council that, he foresaw, would make it much harder for the Council to conduct its business; France would want to make bargains for its own benefit.

Churchill ignored Stalin's criterion; he repeated that the question was one of the future role of France. He argued that temporary conditions did not determine the greatness of a power and that France would take her place in the world again. Churchill and Eden added that France could cause more trouble off the Council than on it. Roosevelt explained that if France was awarded both a zone and participation in the Council, it would be easier to get de Gaulle to go alongwith other agreements that had been reached at Yalta, for example, to join in the Declaration on Liberated Europe. Stalin having procured very much of what he wished concerning Poland, gave in.[37] Great Britain now had finally succeeded in gaining for France a position which would enable her to help defend herself against German aggression and this Churchill hoped, would strengthen Britain in Europe.[38]

Stalin then said that he would like to discuss the question of German reparations. 'This was one of the most controversial issues at the conference.' says Stettinius.[39] The differences of attitude and interest became focused on the issue of what reparations Germany should be required to make. The Soviet government sought very great reparations. It not only wanted them but was determined to have them. Even so–it emphatically asserted–what could be procured from Germany would fall immensely short of the damage that Germany had done to the Soviet Union and her people.[40] The recovery of Soviet Russia from the destruction of war would depend to a large extent upon the material compensation the Kremlin could extract from the remains of the Nazi empire.[41] By Yalta, Churchill was firmly opposed to reparations in any form and he labelled the Soviet reparations plan as 'madness.'[42]

All the three powers, however, agreed that the reparation question needed more specialized and thorough study than could be done during the brief meeting at Yalta. Churchill had said that they were dealing with the fate of eighty million people and that required more than eighty minutes to consider.[43] It was arranged that this should be conducted by a Reparations Commission that would start work in Moscow as soon as possible. And so the argument that ensued at Yalta dealt with the definition of the principle by which this Commission was to be guided in its work and conclusions.[44]

The Soviet Government proposed that Germany should be required to make reparations not in money but in kind, and in addition to labour, services to be rendered by the Germans. In part the payment was to be made from the finances obtained from factories, machinery, ships, rail equipment, powerplants which would be removed from Germany and shipped to the recipient countries. These were to be selected with two purposes in mind : to eliminate industries primarily useful for military purposes and to reduce other German heavy industries to about 1/5 of their previous capacity. These removals were to be accomplished within two years after the end of the war. The rest of the reparations were to be paid by the delivery of the goods currently produced in Germany, during a period of ten years. The Soviet plan contemplated Anglo-American-Soviet control over the German economy, and more directly over those enterprises that were producing for reparations.[45]

The Soviets also suggested that the total amount to be demanded in these two forms should be set at twenty billion dollars, and of this Soviet Union should be given half. It also required German labour and truck services within the Soviet Union to reconstruct the devastated regions. Churchill and Eden protested that this sum was excessive and could not be collected.[46] They opposed the Kremlin's fixing an exact amount, and forecast that if an attempt was made to enforce the Soviet plan, the United States and Great Britain would again, as after the last war, have to provide the means for the Germans to live; it would mean that other countries would be paying German reparations to the Russians.[47] They urged that no decision should be made at Yalta as to the total reparations to be demanded, and also that the period of payment should be shortened.[48]

Stalin asserted that the Germans would be able to pay what the Soviet Union was asking and still live as well as the countries east of them. He suspected that Britain really wanted Germany to be left strong after the war. He went on to insist that the conference decide that the Moscow Commission should fix the amount considering what he called the American-Soviet proposal that there should be twenty billion dollars of reparations, with fifty per cent to the Soviet Union.[49]

In the end, Roosevelt assented to this broad formula : possibly because he believed that it left the question sufficiently open to further examination. The Soviets were happy to have American support concretely formulated. This American proposal, therefore, became the basic document upon which final agreement was reached at the Yalta Conference.[50] However, the plan met with serious opposition from the British. The Soviet and British delegations clashed over the amount of reparations. Churchill admitted that in principle the Soviet Union should receive compensation from Germany, but he refused to agree to any specifics.[51] Eden too continued to demand prior study by the Commission. The ministers finally recorded that two of the Allies had agreed to consider the Soviet sum, with British dissenting.[52] (Soviet minutes record Churchill's acceptance—Soviet Crimea Documents, 6, p. 101–but the American minutes do not record Churchill-Stalin interchange in detail).

Stalin suggested that the Yalta Conference affirm the principle that Germany must pay reparations, and that the Moscow Commission would set the amount of payment. The Soviet-American proposal of twenty billion dollars with fifty per cent for Russia should be the Commission's basic document.[53] The final protocol was prepared by Molotov and it reflected the Allies' agreement and disagreement.[54]

Once they left Yalta, the three heads of state could feel that they had done what was imminently necessary for dealing with Germany during the period of surrender and control. Stalin would have been happier if they had etched their imprint more deeply and permanently upon that ill-fated country. But this was against Churchill's instinct. The cold and rigid determination to enforce a programme upon the hidden future was not for him.[55] In the words of Crocker :

> It was in this war that Roosevelt refused to man the ramparts, leaving Churchill a lonely figure, impotent to act alone. Thus the paradox : the moment of 'Victory' was for Churchill a 'most unhappy time.' Veiled by the temperence of his words is a branding accusation which history will not overlook.[56]

Roosevelt's responses give the impression that he was fatigued by the weight of the problem. Crocker's censure however, is scathing : 'Mesmerized from the start, Roosevelt presented a spectacle that can only be described as pitiful–this fading president, floating slowly out of this life, outmatched and outwitted at every point, mouthing meaningless cliches, and dripping with flummery in the presence of the dictator.'[57] To him Yalta was 'Stalin's show.'[58]

Perhaps, as Stettinius has observed, 'the Yalta Conference was the culmination ... of long patient efforts ... to find some basis for a new international understanding with Russia.'[59] But 'Stalin had dishonoured his Yalta promises before the ink was dry, and the black shadow of a new and ghastly tyranny had descended over eastern Europe.'[60]

According to Feis : the accord reached at Yalta served the Big Three's most immediate purposes well–to sustain the concert of military action against Germany until that war was won and to manage German surrender smoothly. Whether thereafter the three great victorious powers would really observe common policy that would fulfill the aims of each remained dubious.[61]

NOTES AND REFERENCES

1. Theoharis, Athan G. *The Yalta Myths*, An Issue in US Politics, 1945–55. (Missouri, 1970), p. 10.
2. Ibid, p. 12.
3. Dean, Vera Micheles. *The Four Cornerstones of Peace*, (New York, 1946), p. 25.
4. Clemens, Diane Shaver. *Yalta*, (New York, 1970), p. 8.
5. Stettinius, Edward R. Jr. *Roosevelt and the Russians*–The Yalta Conferece, Johnson, Walter (ed.), (New York, 1949), p. 3.
6. Ibid, p. 4.
7. Feis, Herbert. *Churchill-Roosevelt-Stalin*, The war they waged and the peace they sought, (Princeton : New Jersey, 1957), p. 530.
8. Clemens, op.cit, p. 137.
9. Djiles, Milovan. *Conversations with Stalin*, (New York, 1962), pp. 114–15.
10. Feis, op.cit, p. 530.
11. Clemens, op.cit, p. 137.
12. Moran, Lord Charles, *Churchill* : Taken from the Diaries of Lord Moran Boston, 1966, p. 152.
13. *Foreign Relations of the United States, Diplomatic Papers*. The confernece at Malta and Yalta 1945, (Washington D.C., 1955), Bohlen Minutes, p. 611.
14. Ibid, A reproduction of this map faces page 612.
15. Ibid, p. 611.
16. Clemens, op.cit, p. 141.
17. *Yalta Documents*, Bohlen, p. 613.
18. *Yal. Doc.*, Bohlen, p. 611, *Yal. Doc.*, Mathews, p.624. Soviet

Crimea Documents U.S.S.R. *'Documents : The Crimea and Potsdam Conferences of the Leaders of the Three Great Powers'*, International Affairs, (Moscow, 1965), No. 6, p. 67.

19. *Yalta Documents*, op.cit, p. 117, see also Bohlen Minutes, p. 615.
20. Feis, op.cit, p. 530.
21. Bohlen, op.cit, p. 612. Clemens, op.cit, p. 142.
22. Ibid, Bohlen, pp. 614–15, Ibid, Clemens, p. 144.
23. Ibid, Bohlen, p. 615. Ibid, Clemens, p. 145.
24. Ibid, Bohlen, p. 615.
25. Ibid, p. 660.
26. Feis, op.cit, pp. 530–31.
27. Crocker, George N. *Roosevelt's Road to Russia*, (Chicago, 1959), pp. 255–56.
28. Moran, op.cit, p. 241.
29. Eden, Anthony. *The Reckoning*, (Boston, 1965), p. 461.
30. Feis, op.cit, p. 531.
31. *Yal. Doc.* Bohlen, op.cit, p. 616; Ibid, Mathews, op.cit, p. 628.
32. Ibid, Bohlen, op.cit, p. 617; Ibid, Mathews, p. 629.
33. Ibid, Bohlen, p. 617.
34. Ibid, Bohlen, 618, Clemens, op.cit, p. 152.
35. Ibid, Bohlen, Clemens, Ibid.
36. Ibid, Bohlen, *Yal. Doc.* Mathews, op.cit, p. 629.
37. Ibid, Bohlen, pp. 899–900. Feis, op.cit, p. 532.
38. Clemens, op.cit, p. 158.
39. Stettinius, op.cit, p. 299.
40. Feis, op.cit, pp. 534–535.
41. Clemens, op.cit, p. 159.
42. Ibid, p. 139.
43. *Yal. Doc.* Bohlen, op.cit, p. 614.
44. Feis, op.cit, p. 535.
45. Ibid.
46. Ibid.
47. Ibid.
48. Ibid.
49. *Yalta Documents*, Bohlen Minutes, op.cit, p. 901.
50. Clemens, op.cit, p. 165.
51. Ibid, p. 166.
52. *Yal. Doc. Page Minutes*, pp. 807–9. *Yal. Doc.* Hiss, p. 812. Setttinius, op.cit, pp. 230–32.
53. Clemens, op.cit, p. 169.
54. Ibid, p. 172.
55. Feis, op.cit, p. 540.

56. Crocker, op.cit, p. 262.
57. Ibid, p. 252.
58. Ibid, p. 251.
59. Stettinius, op.cit, p. 6.
60. Crocker, op.cit, pp. 248–49.
61. Feis, op.cit, p. 540.

Chapter 12

Towards Sarajevo

In the last week of June 1914, Archduke Franz Ferdinand, heir to the Austro-Hungarian throne of the Habsburgs, was making an official trip to the Bosnian town Sarajevo, accompanied by his wife, Sophia Chotek, Duchess of Hohenbeg. As the party was leaving the City Hall, a young Bosnian, Princip, lying in ambush, leapt out and fired a revolver at point-blank range, at the Archduke and his wife. They both died within a few minutes. It was about 11.30 a.m., St. Vitus's Day, Sunday, June 28, 1914. This was the spark that set Europe and the world ablaze!

Background of the Murder

That Europe in 1914 was divided into two hostile armed camps is common place. The diplomatic atmosphere was charged with electricity. It therefore, cannot be denied that the power or powers that wantonly threw the first spark upon the powder magazine thereby precipitating the catastrophe called World War I was guilty of a heinous crime.

What were the true details of the Sarajevo plot? What were the motives of the assassin? Who were his instigators or accomplices? Whose was the brain behind the gruesome network? These are stark questions which have remained more baffling than most of the problems pertaining to the immediate causes of the war, information from the Serbian side was not only scanty, it was contradictory. The official Austrian version of the conspiracy which laid the entire blame on the door of Serbia[1] on its turbulence for a 'Greater Serbia' failed to convince–to put it mildly–most people in the entente[2] or neutral countries.

The whole murder mystery was associated with many factors–the 'Slav' factor[3] being the most prominent. It was also interlinked with radicals like men of May 29.[4] It was also said to be the handiwork of organizations like the 'Black Hand' which had suicidal troops which were symbol of escutcheon.[5] The killing was also associated with Komitaji.[6]

Under all these various versions, the Sarajevo plot remained shrouded in mystery. People prejudiced against the central powers were prone to discredit the Austrian evidence as fabricated accusations. Serbian writers, on the other hand, were careful to publish nothing in conflict with the attitude of injured innocence which their government had assumed in 1914.[7]

In the words of Joachim Remak :

> Nearly five decades after Sarajevo, some of the details surrounding the crime that set off the First World War are still obscure, and are likely to remain so ... some of the participants have been prevented from talking, while others have voluntarily kept silent; some have deliberately lied about the roles they played, while others have attested to facts of which in reality they had little or no knowledge.

Yet; Remak continues :

> A time has now arrived when enough evidence is available to separate truth from falsehood with some degree of accuracy, and to reconstruct the story of the plot that should be substantially correct.[8]

Since 1923 came numerous Serb disclosures, whose authors were motivated by different factors : simply to establish the truth so that justice should replace injustice; to indulge in party politics; or, curiously enough, to claim the doubtful honour of being among those who by scheming the murder of the Archduke indirectly led to the establishment of the glorious Yugoslav kingdom.[9]

In order to appreciate the true nature of the crime, and to understand the omnious deed in its proper perspective, one must make a proper evaluation of Austro-Serbian politics at the time when it was committed. This would necessitate a scrutiny of Austro-Serbian relations from the last quarter of the nineteenth century.

THE AUSTRO-SERBIAN CONFLICT

The murder of the Archduke Franz Ferdinand and his wife on the streets of Sarajevo was merely the flash that fired the powder magazine of Europe. But the 'Southern Slav Question' of which it was a manifestation, was one of the most fiery of the pre-war problmes. It was far from being a new problem. 'Indeed, its origin and explanation are to be sought' states Seton-Watson, 'as far back as the Turkish conquest of Serbia and Hungary, which arrested the political development and the culture of the southern Slavs, and was followed by the long struggle of Habsburg imperialism to eject the infidel invaders from its dominions, to win back south-eastern Europe for Christendom, and at the same time to establish German-Habsburg hegemony over the Balkan Peninsula.'[10]

In the nineteenth century the growth of national feeling in Europe transformed the relations between Austria and the southern Slavs, a majority of whom were actually living on Habsburg territory even before the occupation of Bosnia. Serbia started from very modest beginning as a vassal peasant state, but with each new generation tended more and more to become a centre of national culture, and also a point of attraction for her kinsmen under alien rule.

It was not, however, till the great Eastern crisis of 1875–78 that Austria-Hungary became irrevocably involved in a real conflict of principle with Serbia. Though Serbia and Montenegro received certain extensions of territory, they were thwarted in their main aim of union with Bosnia-Herzegovina and had to look on in impotent rage, while the diplomatists of Europe, assembled at the Congress of Berlin in 1878, gave to Austria-Hungary a mandate for the occupation of the two coveted provinces. 'It was a decision typical of diplomatic mentality, since it frankly set aside the claims of nationalism in favour of the expansion of a great power.'[11] states Schevill.

Thus two Serbian provinces had been added to the Habsburg dominions, which now held nearly twice as many Yugoslavs as outside them. Worse still, Russia had definitely abandoned Serbia as an Austrian sphere of influence and was concentrating her own efforts upon Bulgaria.[12]

The decades immediately following the Congress of Berlin constitute a very depressing chapter of Serb history.[13] True, Serbia had not been wholly neglected at Berlin, for, in addition to a slight territorial increase, she had been relieved of the last bonds tying her to Turkey. But her guidance under Milan Obrenovic was peculiarly unfortunate. The looseness of his private morals 'became one of the chief and most succulent subjects of contemporary European scandal.'[14] By a secret political treaty concluded in 1881, Serbia became the vassal of Austria-Hungary.[15] Unable to withstand the opprobrium visited upon him, Milan Obrenovic resigned in 1889 in favour of his son Alexander. This however, did not lead to any essential change of regime, for the new king perpetuated the personal scandals of his father's court, and worse still, his arbitrary tendencies. All this and fierce party dissensions kept Serbia in turmoil till, in 1903, she was rid of her impossible king and queen by a brutal palace assassination which set a precedent for military interference in politics.[16]

The removal of the Obrenovic dynasty, however, revolting the circumstances under which it was accomplished, leads to a very general improvement. It 'brought acceleration of nationalistic activities at home and abroad and gave vent to rapidly growing Yugoslavism,[17] states Vucinich.

The new sovereign Peter I was a reputable man, who helped gradually to disperse the cloud of dishonour which had been hovering over the country during the reigns of Milan and Alexander; 'but far more important in rehabilitating Serbia in the eyes of Europe than any question of personalities was its sudden accidental elevation to a central area of conflict between the two rival groups of the Triple Alliance and Triple *Entente*.'[18]

'From the beginning of the reign of King Peter', says

Temperley, 'Austria-Hungary showed further unfriendliness towards the little state. It is certain that the Austrian General Staff came to the well-warranted historical conclusion that the true military road to Salonica (*Drang nach Sudosten*) was up the valley of the Morava.'[19] The perfectly technical military opinion had an important influence on Austrian policy : an advance through Novibazar could be made along purely Turkish territory, and Serbian opposition could easily be brushed aside.[20] 'The annihilation of Serbian independece', Temperley continues, 'in one form or another, was therefore, indispensable if Salonica ... was ever to be reached. Military opinion in Austria-Hungary therefore weighed the scales in the direction of hostility towards Serbia.'[21]

Austrian ministers observed with dismay the growth of Serbian nationalism. It meant that the kingdom of Serbia would act as a dangerous magnet, drawing away Austria's Serbs within her fold. In view of this danger, Austrian officials began to adopt measures to stifle the growing movement in Serbia for political and economic independence from Habsburg influence.[22] Serbia having no direct outlet to sea, had been virtually dependent upon Austria-Hungary for a market for her agricultural products. In 1906 when the Austro-Serbian tariff treaty expired, tension between both countries ran so high that it was not renewed. As a consequence a bitter tariff war–the so-called Pig-War ensued, 'in which the last remnant of decent neighbourly feeling received its death blow.'[23] It complicated their relations and convinced Serbia that Austria-Hungary could not be trusted.[24] In the desert, says an Arab proverb, 'no man meets a friend'; in the Balkans no people trusts its neighbour.[25]

'The Pig War', says Vucinich, 'stimulated industrial development in Serbia.'[26] Austria's attempt at economic intimidation far from compelling Serbia to return to an Austrophile policy, had just the opposite effect. It drove her more than ever into the open arms of Russia and made her realize more clearly her need for a direct economic outlet to the sea.[27]

As this war synchronized with the German-Baghdad

concession[28] and the formation of the Triple entente, one can understand how this narrowly circumscribed economic conflict came to be raised to the level of an international issue. Russia had encouraged Serbia's resistance to Austrian demands, while Russia's associates France and Britain, stood by as silent aiders and abettors. Little Belgrade had, with bewildering suddenness, become a leading diplomatic centre of contentious Europe.[29]

In the words of Ferdinand Schevill :

> Since the city was the natural gateway from Europe to Balkania, Austro-German plans, looking to ascendancy in the Near East, would, if blocked at this point, become paralyzed. Not only Berlin and Vienna were aware of this, but in no less degree St. Petersburg, London, and Paris. So at this vital crossroads the great counter-currents of European ambition came together and, amidst a loud roar, flung out a cloud of spray, in which Serbia, a pigmy among giants, was practically buried from sight.[30]

Into a situation already strained to the breaking point, Austria in October, 1908, flung the annexation of Bosnia releasing a commotion which shook Europe like an earthquake.[31] It was chiefly this *'acte brutale'* which, as Schevill observes, 'made Europe rock with a crisis, which afterwards was correctly recognized to have been in effect a rehearsal for the fateful drama of July and August, 1914.'[32]

Serbia, deeply wounded, rose to protest against Austria, fortifying her position in a land which, although technically lost to her, she still claimed on the score of nationality. She had lived thirty years in the fond illusion that the occupation of the two provinces in 1878 was not necessarily more than a passing phase, and now saw the erection of a permanent obstacle to her national and her economic expansion.[33] As Austria had committed an undeniable breach of the treaty of Berlin, the cabinets of St. Petersburg, Paris and London could take good legal ground in frowning upon Austria's annexation. But as she in her turn, had the backing of her ally, Germany, she felt encouraged to maintain her stand.

> The result was that an immense agitation seized alike upon governments and peoples in Europe threatening from moment

> to moment to precipitate that general war of which everybody had for years been talking and which everybody professed to abhor. It was a bitterly tense season, the winger of 1908–9, but in the end war was avoided.[34]

Baron Aehrenthal, Austrian foreign minister, calculated that Russia could not fight a great war so soon after the conflict with Japan, and he judged rightly. Russia's surrender brought with it the humiliation of Serbia.

'The events of 1908–9', says Temperley, 'made a permanent impression on Serbia. The annexation passed, the danger and the desire for vengeance remained.'[35] In the words of Seton-Watson :

> The Bosnian crisis converted the Southern Slav Question and the relations between Austria-Hungary and Serbia into an international problem of the first rank.

The Austro-Hungarian Empire had been virtually divided into two separate states. Austria was trying to give some seats to poor classes and minorities in its lower house. But Hungary ignored them. It was by and large a feudal state dominated by Magyar aristocracy with a Magyarizahai policy. Hungary had to face the problem created by Croats who looked towards Serbia for a Yugoslav or South Slav federation. Bosnia and Herzegovinia were also inhabited by southern Slavs, and a new problem started. The heir to Austro-Hungarian states, the Austrian, Crown Prince, Archduke Francis Ferdinand started favouring reforms, which would ultimately give equal rights to Slavs under dual monarchy just liked German Magyars. This was against Hungary's policies which liked to rule Slavs and Serbia wanted to lure them against Hungary and Austria.

Archduke Franz Ferdinand, was not a popular figure. He was a rather hot-tempered, bigoted, difficult man who was thoroughly disliked by the great majority of his subjects. But his gruesome murder at the hands of a man of Serbian race (who, however, was a Habsburg subject) gave the forward party an excuse for action against Serbia. The cabinet in Vienna promptly decided that the heaven-sent opportunity for settling scores with Serbia should not be lost.

The full details of the crime at Sarajevo have never been unearthed. Yet we may outline briefly the main threads of the assassination plot and the three factors which largely contributed to it : *the Narodna Odbrana*, the Black Hand, and the Revolutionary Movement in Bosnia.

In the sixties and seventies of the nineteenth century, many Serbian revolutionaries gathered in Switzerland and came under the spell of Russian terrorists and anarchists. They imbibed a revolutionary programme which was to be accomplished by deeds of terrorism. But not all the young Serbians studying in Switzerland adopted this creed. Among the latter was Nikola Pasic. He founded in Serbia in 1881 the Radical Party whose programme was people's uplift and freedom at home, and the country's unification with other parts of Serbdom abroad. The party aimed at keeping aflame this discontent in the Serb regions of the Turkish and Habsburg empires until the future war should merge them into a Greater Serbia. These two political ideals, individual acts of assassination practiced by reckless, raw students and by military cliques on the one hand, and national unification by a well-organized movement as preached by the Radical Party, dominated Serb politics until the success of the latter in the World War. This dualism of ideals provides the clue to the complex problem of the origin and relations of the *Narodna Odbrana* and the Black Hand.

The annexation of Bosnia-Herzegovina was proclaimed on October 6, 1908. Next day a meetnig of the influential Serbians was held to consider the future course of action to abate public resentment at the Austrian 'misdemeanour.' It was proposed to form a society to be called *Narodna Odbrana* (national defence) which should protect and promote Serb interests in the annexed provinces. This was agreed to, and the society was duly organized. It was to enrol and train volunteers and fortify Serbia for an armed struggle.

The great indignation in Serbia at Austria's flouting of the Berlin Treaty brought together prominent representatives of both the dualistic tendencies mentioned above. Thus at its inception the *Narodna Odbrana* membership included important members of Radical Party and representatives of the army comprising the awesome personalities, Dragutin Dimitrijevic and Voja Tankovic, who had taken part in the palace assassination of 1903.

After the annexation crisis had subsided, the Serbian Government withdrew its official support, but the society continued to exist, thanks to a nationwide organization that was being built up. The society did not restrict its operation to Serbia, but was active in Bosnia as well.

The Austro-Hungarian Government maintained that the *Narodna Odbrana* was not so innocuous an organization as it was commonly represented. After the adjustment of the annexation crisis in March 1909, when Serbia had to give an assurance to refrain from her subversive agitation, the *Narodna Odbrana* made a show of transforming itself into a purely 'cultural' organization. However, it never became so completely 'innocent' and cultural as was often claimed.

On the other hand, it is true that the direct involvement of the *Narodna Odbrana* in the Sarajevo conspiracy was overstated in the Austrian ultimatum and dossier. As the founding of the *Narodna Odbrana* was public and that of the Black Hand was secret, it is not surprising that abroad and especially in Austria, the two societies were believed to be one and the same. However, it cannot be doubted that the *Narodna* secretly maintained 'tunnels' and smuggled revolutionary literature from Belgrade into Bosnia. It helped Bosnian emigrates into Belgrade and was thus instrumental in abetting the revolutionary movement in Bosnia and preparing the ground for the Sarajevo crime. We now turn to the other organization–the Black Hand–more directly implicated in the Sarajevo affair.

By 1911, the old rift between the Radicals and the more hot-headed, zealotical military clique became more marked. The latter who had machinated the palace revolution of 1903 were impatient of the moderate radical policy. They yearned for 'deeds', *Narodna Odbrana* did not satisfy the Men of May 29, 'who had tasted blood. Accordingly on May 22, 1911, a secret revolutionary known in its statutes as *Ujedinjenje ili Smrt* (union or death) but commonly called as the Black Hand, was founded. At its head stood Colonel Dragutin Dimitrijevic, a man of boundless energy, resourcefulness and intense patriotism.

The aim of the Black Hand was : fulfillment of the national ideal, the union of all Serbs. It preferred terrorist action to intellecutal propaganda, unlike the *Narodna* and therefore, had to be kept strictly secret from non-members. It organized revolutionary activity in all the lands peopled by the Serbs. The execution of more extensive revolutionary programme had to have the prior approval of the central committee at Belgrade, the chief executive body.

The conditions of membership were such as to deter all but the most resolute. A member 'forfeits his own personality' and 'is bound to absolute obedience' to his committee; he might never withdraw from the organization. It is by his acts that the member harmed the organization, he was liable to death penalty. Well did the society deserve the name 'Black Hand' given to it in Serbian popular parlance!

To terrorism was added mystery. Members were not known to each other personally. They were designated by numbers. The initiation ceremony was quite melodramatic: 'The candidate had to appear in a darkened room before a table draped in black, and take a high-sounding oath by the sun and earth, by God, honour and life.' The seal of the Black Hand with ominous significance bore a muscular hand with bent fingers, grasping an unfurled flag : on the flag as escutcheon a death's head with cross-bones, and beside the flag, a dagger, a bomb and poison.'

Dragutin Dimitrijevic, although at first lukewarm, soon perceived the potentialities of the organization and did not take long in becoming the life and soul of this society. He was in every respect a superb organizer; considerations of what was possible and what was not did not exist for him. He was described as Mazzini and Garibaldi joined in one person.

Dimitrijevic was head of the espionage department of the Serbian General Staff. His chief aid was Major Voja Tankovic who had organized a *komitaji* school in which he trained Bosnian emigrants who came to Belgrade. Another important member of the Black Hand, more mysterious and enigmatic, was Milan Ciganovic. According to Sidney B. Fay,. Tankovic and Ciganovic were the two men who directly helped in preparing the assassination plot in Belgrade, giving the three youths who were to murder the Archduke, bombs, Browning pistols and poison to be swallowed as soon as their deed was done.

The Black Hand organization seemed to represent the spirit of the sixteenth rather that of the twentieth century. As for the *Narodna Odbrana*, it was not so divorced from the Black Hand as was often averred. As a matter of fact the two societies had the same ultimate goal, with many members in common.

The facts that are linked with the ghastly Sarajevo affair as cause and effect are : Firstly, Serbia could not swallow the Austrian annexation of Bosnia and Herzegovina which it regarded as downright robbery, and declined to accept it as a finally accomplished fact. Secondly, the Bosnians themselves struggled hard for union with Serbia and remained sullenly unreconciled to Austrian subjection.

With the moral backing of Serbia, a good amount of unrest developed in Bosnia. The agitation took two main forms. One was to use existing legal organizations as covers for illegal undertakings. The other was to work through an underground organization called *mlada Bosna*–Young Bosnia–patronized by the Black Hand. Its members were impatient and 'desperate.' They laid emphasis on the 'cult of the individual deed' as a short-term method to prepare the ground for a new 'Yugoslav' nationalism. Deeds of terrorism served a double purpose : they created panic among the ruling classes : and they heightened the moral of the masses.

The first important mainfestation of this new fad was the 'deed' of Bogdan Zewrajic, a Herzegovinian Serb, who fired five shots at the Governor General Vareshanin. Zewrajic forthwith committed suicide on the spot. Promptly he was hailed as a hero and 'first martyr' by the Serbs of Bosnia and Serbia. His grave became a spot of pilgrimage for young

Bosnians filled with nationalistic fervour and inspired to copy his example. Thus Princip, the evening before he fired at the Archduke, is said to have put flowers on Zewrajic's grave and to have sworn by it that his hand should not miss his target the next day. The poor and insecure Bosnian youths were prone to be the psychological victims of such perverted idealism.

The guiding spirit behind *Mlada Bosna* was Vladimir Cacinovic. He was a great admirer, of Bakunin, the Russian anarchist, who exhorted that the way to achieve a free and happy society was to assassinate the proper number of kings, presidents, grand dukes and other celebrities. The tense and explosive atmosphere of the province fitted well with a born agitator as Gavinovic. He wrote a great eulogy. 'The Death of a Hero' on the murderer Zewrajic and had urged young Serbs to avenge Zewrajic's death. Finding the *Narodna Odbrana* too mild, he joined in 1912 the newly incepted Black Hand. He also came into direct touch with various Russian revolutionists, including Trotsky. '

The revolutionary ferment of the period showed itself in the widespread practice of youthful Bosnians moving back and forth between Serbia and their own land. These emigres enjoyed escaping from the stifling atmosphere of Habsburg authority and breathe the fresh and bracing air of Belgrade which was of course eager to receive them. The Serbian government officially did not approve of the Black Hand activities in Bosnia, but at the same time it did nothing to prevent them.

Life was nevertheless, arduous for those Bosnians for they had little money. Poor food, and lodging impaired their health, made them neurotic; the company they moved in was not of the type to inspire respect for authority. Among them could be found men ready for any kind of desperate action; chiefly, the three youths Gavrilo Princip, Nedjelko Cabrinovic and Trifko Grabezh who executed the plot at Sarajevo on June 28, 1914.

It is assumed that Glorinovic[36] was an agent of the Austrian secret police. According to Seton-Watson :

> Cabrinovic was the son of a notorious Austrian police confidant–a fact which is known to have had a decisive influece upon his own psychology. He bitterly resented his father's role and at one time thought of changing his name ... to one of his intimates he admitted that the main motive of his terrorist activity was to wash himself free from the stain and in a sense to atone for his father.[37]

But another hypothesis has also been put forward : that Cabrinovic was himself an Austrian secret agent and a plot was concoted by which he should make a pseudo-attempt on the Archduke Franz Ferdinand, in order to provide the Austro-Hungarian Government with an excuse for intervention in Serbia; it was only in the spring of 1914, after talks with Princip, that Cabrinovic decided to make a real attempt to murder Franz Ferdinand.'[38]

'Obviously, this theory', Schmitt correctly states, 'has to be treated with the greatest possible circumspection, for it sounds inherently impossible.'[39] This seems almost certain that he was wavering in his murderous attempt on the Archduke.

The third member of the student trio was Trifko Grabezh. He was expelled from the gymnasium at Tuzla for having boxed his teacher on the ear during the fall of 1912. He proceeded towards Belgrade to finish his studies where he met Princip and other emigres, and became fired with Serbian nationalism and an ardour to take part in political assassination.

This brief recital of the careers of these three men is bound to create a most unfavourable impression of them, for in western Europe and America, terrorism and murder are not considered as proper methods for deciding political issues. It is obvious that the real initiative in the Southern Slav Question was rapidly passing from the hands of statesmen and politicians alike into those of raw and hare-brained youths who stuck at nothing, and whom not even the direct consequences could deter. Yet something may be said in extenuation. All three were mere youngsters, hardly out of their teens, and they suffered from ill health; they grew up in atmosphere charged with discontent and unrest; and they were actuated not by selfish motives, but by the conviction that desperate measures were necessary to relieve their people of the repulsive Austrian tutelage. It is not at all surprising that they lent themselves to infernal suggestions.

The various factors in a complicated situation have been explained and the leading personalities described. We may now examine the preparations for the plot to murder the Archduke.

PREPARATIONS FOR THE ASSASSINATION PLOT

In December, 1913, according to the testimony of Mustapha Golubic and Paul Bastaic, members of the Black Hand,[40] Tankovic in the autumn of 1913 instructed Gacinovic, then in Lausanne, to assemble the leaders of *Mlada Bosna* in Touluse to plan the assassination of the Archduke Franz Ferdinand and other important Austrian officials, in order to rouse the Slav elements in the Habsburg lands. The meeting was held in January, 1914 where only three persons appeared—Gacinovic, Golubic, and a Mohammedan Serb, Mohammed Mehmedbashic. Gacinovic insisted on the assassination of the Archduke, which he thought would stimulate the Austrian Slavs and even lead to a European war, and evidently this was agreed to in principle.[41] But it was decided first of all to finish with General Potiorek, who was held directly responsible for the existing regime in Bosnia. This latter scheme however fizzled out.

Mustapha Golubic and Paul Bastaic also revealed that–Gacinovic had written to Princip, then in Sarajevo, that he and Ilic should come to Lausanne to discuss the details of the assassination plan. Ilic, however, first sent Princip to Belgrade to consult Tankosic, who said the journey to Lausanne was not necessary, as it had already been decided at Belgrade that the Archduke should be murdered. Princip was kept in Belgrade till the end of May, and trained in revolver shooting by Milan Ciganovic.[42] Informed of the change of plan, Ilic himself went to Belgrade a few days before the murder, met Tankovic and Dimitrijevic, and received final instructions. Upon his return to Sarajevo, he, Mehmedbashic, and Princip sent a postcard to Gacinovic bearing the words 'Revolutionary greetings', as well as a letter informing him of their plans.[43]

According to Seton-Watson, the initiative for the assassination plot 'came from Bosnia, not Serbia', and Danilo Ilic and Gacinovic took prominent part in it.[44] Fay, however, finds it difficult to accept this view. Relying on the evidence of M. Bogicevic–which is based on the testimony of Golubic and Bastaic—he observes : 'There seems to be no doubt that the effective impulse to the plot came from Princip at Belgrade and not from Ilic at Sarajevo.' It is likely that Princip had already, as he said, 'formed the determination' to kill the Archduke before his trip to Bosnia was announced. It is probable that he was supported in this, if indeed, it was not suggested to him by Ciganovic in Belgrade, the intimate associate of Tankovic, and who later secured from Tankovic the Browning revolvers to be used against the Archduke. It would have been quite in conformity with the character of Major Tankovic, continues Sidney B. Fay, as well as in keeping with the purposes and methods of the Black Hand, that the idea should have originated with Tankovic or with Ciganovic; but, the same authority concludes, 'whether it really did originate with Tankovic, as asserted by M. Bogicevic's two informants, may be regarded as uncertain until further evidence confirms their assertion.[45]

In March, 1914, the Zagreb newspaper *Srbobran* published an announcement that Austrian army would hold summer manoeuvres in Bosnia and that the Archduke Franz Ferdinand would be in command. From the political point of view it was highly desirable that a member of the imperial family should show himself in the recently annexed provinces. Among the impressionable simple peasant population, nothing was better calculated to stimulate and strengthen the feeling of personal and traditional loyalty than such official visits of princes. They flattered local pride. The simple peasant liked the pageantry of princes and liked to see his ruler, and find in him a flesh and blood human being like himself. Merely to see him or hear him speak was to renew the human bond of common understanding. Such a visit would strengthen the Roman

Catholic and other royal elements[46] and might counteract Yugoslav revolutionary propaganda and the Serb agitation for a 'Greater Serbia.' This was the political aspect of the trip, and it partly explains that Archduke did not wish to be protected by heavy guards of soldiers and secret police, but preferred to ride about freely in an open automobile.

The main object of the trip, however, was that the Archduke might attend the manoeuvres of the XVth and XVIth Army Corps, which were regularly stationed in Bosnia. As Inspector-in-Chief of the Army, he had in recent years regularly represented the Emperor at such manoeuvres.[47]

It was also announced that the Archduke would visit Sarajevo on June 28, which was the anniversary of the battle of Kossovo in 1389, when the medieval Serbian state had been overthrown.[48] The revolutionary group in Sarajevo was at first greatly disturbed by this news. It feared that his visit would deal a blow to Yugoslav aspirations for national unity and independence. But the alarm of Kruzhoc members was only momentary. They at once saw that here was the opportunity for the best possible political assassination of the kind Gacinovic had long been preaching. But they did not have the nerve to think of planning to commit the murder themselves. Instead, the chance could be best utilized by the more venturesome and fanatical Bosnian emigres at Belgrade with their Komitaji friends in Serbia. So one member of the group, Michael Pushara, cut the announcement from the *Srbobran* and sent it, without any comment save the word 'Greetings', to Cabrinovic in Belgrade.

When Cabrinovic received the newspaper clipping from Sarajevo, he showed it to his friend Princip, and they began to discuss the murder of the Archduke. As they lacked the necessary weapons, they turned to their friend Ciganovic, who promised to provide what was necessary and to take them to Bosnia through a 'tunnel'. Meanwhile, Grabezh came to Belgrade, and was asked to join the conspiracy. Ciganovic had a private supply of bombs, but for revolvers he had to go to Tankosic, who got from Dimitrijevic the money with which to buy them. At the suggestion of Tankosic, who wanted to make sure that there would be no failure, Ciganovic also gave the students lessons in shooting. He finally handed over to the three young men six bombs, four Browning pistols, 130 dinars, some cyanide of potassium, and a road map of Bosnia, at the same time instructing them that they should avoid the civil authorities.[49]

During the preparations, it was Ciganovic with whom the students dealt chiefly, but he evidently was acting with the sanction of Tankosic and Dimitrijevic, leading members of the Supreme Central Committee of the Black Hand. Tankosic however, kept himself for the most part in the background. This was confirmed by Grabezh who declared that Major Tankosic was a side figure. Dimitrijevic kept himself even more completely in the background. At their trial, the accused never mentioned his name, so it is not clear whether they were even aware of his existence. The conspirators left Belgrade at the end of May, so that they might reach Sarajevo long enough before the visit of the Archduke to avoid rousing suspicions of the local authorities.

Meanwhile at Sarajevo, Ilic who had been in correspondence with Princip, was making the necessary local arrangements : he enlisted three more young men as 'reserves.' Thus was the plan laid for the tragic events of June 28, 1914.

THE RESPONSIBILITY FOR THE SARAJEVO ASSASSINATION

Later Revelations

A decade or so after the crime, there came numerous Serb revelations, whose authors were motivated by several factors: simply to tell the truth and see that justice should replace injustice; to play party politics; or, curiously enough, to claim the dubious honour of being among those who by contriving the death of the Archduke, were instrumental in the eventual establishment of the glorious Yugoslav kingdom.[50]

The first of these disclosures to attract attention beyond the frontiers of Serbia came through the writings of a very reputed professor of history at Belgrade, Stanoje Stanojevic. He does not mention his authorities, but says in his preface that he gathered much of his information at first hand from surviving Serb conspirators with whom he was personally acquainted.[51] In his attempt to minimize the responsibility of the *Narodna Odbrana*, he throws the blame on the leader of the Black Hand whose architects had played a sinister role in Serbian politics since 1903. Its moving spirit in 1914, as we have said earlier, was no less a person than the Chief of the Intelligence Department of the Serbian General Staff, Dragutin Dimitrijevic. Stanojevic goes on to describe in detail how he helped organize the plot in Belgrade.[52]

Some months after Stanojevic made these admissions which went far beyond the Austrian charges of 1914, a Yugoslav journalist, Borivoje Jevtic came forward with an interesting pamphlet. It minimizes the influence of Serbia, and narrates the elaboration of the plot in Sarajevo. He even gives a vivid description of how he spent Saturday night, the eve of the crime, in company with Princip, who fired the fatal shots next morning. He says that there were no less than ten conspirators waylaying for the Archduke that day; that had he escaped Princip's bullet in the same way as Cabrinovic's bomb, so many others were prepared to assault him that he could scarcely have left Sarajevo alive.[53]

The most sensational revelation, important because it was made by a prominent Serbian official who was minister of education in the Pasic Cabinet in July, 1914, was that of Ljuba Jovanovic. To celebrate the tenth anniversary of the outbreak of war, a Russian journalist published an 'almanac' entitled *Krv Slovenstva* ('Blood of Slavdom'); the opening article was written by Ljuba Jovanovic, 'which pulled down the house of cards.'[54] He states :

> I do not remember whether it was at the end of May or the beginning of June, when one day M. Pasic said to us ... that there were people who were preparing to go to Sarajevo to kill Franz Ferdinand, who was to go there to be solemnly received on Vidov Dan ... M. Pasic and the rest of us said and Stojan agreed ... that he should issue instructions to the frontier authorities on the

> Drina to prevent the crossing over of the youths who had already set out from Belgrade for that purpose. But the frontier authorities themselves belonged to the organization, and did not carry Stojan's (minister of the interior) instructions, but reported to him (as he afterwards told us) that the instructions had reached them too late, because the youths had already crossed over.[55]

It was certainly definite enough. But was it true? Stojan Protic was dead, but Pasic was very much alive; in fact he was at the head of theYugoslav Government. yet he said not a word, and it was easy to conclude that there was nothing he could say.[56] From this it appears that members of the Serbian cabinet were cognisant of the plot a month or so before the murder took place, but took no effective measures to forestall it. The Serbian Government was thus criminally negligent, to say the least. Not having nipped the plot in the bud when it was brewed in their capital by one of their own general staff officers, and not having prevented the youths from crossing over into Bosnia, the Serbian Government should atonce have notified the Austrian government, giving the names of the criminals and all other details which might have led to their arrest before their execution of the plot. But Pasic and his cabinet did nothing of the sort.[57] Furthermore, after the foul deed was done, they should have made a thorough inquiry into the secret organizations in Serbia, and arrested all the accomplices involved in the plot. Instead, as we shall see, they sought to conceal every trace of it, and denied all knowledge of it in the hope 'that Vienna would be unsuccessful in establishing any connection between official Serbia and the deed on the Miljacka.'[58]

Jovanovic's essay first aroused attention in England in December, 1924 when Edith Durham liberally quoted from it. Great prominence was also given to Jovanovic's admissions by Sidney B. Fay. Seton-Watson, the prolific writer on the Balkans, and long a vigorous champion of the Yugoslavs, was much disturbed at Jovanovic's confessions but could not persuade himself to accept them as trustworthy or true. he declared : 'The whole article (of Jovanovic) is written in a careless, naive and reminiscent vein, and its author seems to be blissfully unaware how damning are his admissions, if they are to be taken literally'... [59] Seton-Watson however, believes that 'Jovanovic for reasons of his own has misrepresented the true facts.' and that 'he is one of those politicians who like to exaggerate their own importance ... ' Since the war the Radical Party had strained every nerve to gain control of Bosnia-Herzegovina, but with no great success. The younger generation in these provinces regarded the revolutionary movement of 1913–1914 with feelings of admiration and looked upon Princip and his associates as martyrs. So, in the opinion of the British writer, it occurred to Jovanovic to make a bid for the support of the Bosnian youth by showing that the pre-war government in Serbia, which was thoroughly radical, had sympathized with the revolutionary movement : if he were successful, he would have a powerful lever in his tussle with Pasic for the control of the Radical Party. The crafty Pasic, on his part, preferred 'to use the incident to isolate a dangerous competitor for the party leadership than to clear the honour of his country.' A friend wrote to Watson, 'there would seem to be no other example in the history of a government which is accused of grave offences remaining obstinately silent for eleven years, despite all appeals from friend and foe, and simply snapping its fingers at the opinion of the civilized world.[60] He (Pasic) was reluctant, so Seton-Watson complained,

> to stand up before his countrymen and to produce the proofs (which I have reason to believe him to possess) that he, as leader of the nation in 1914, was ignorant, and even disapproved of an underground movement which some admire as having led directly to national unity.[61]

These arguments, in the opinion of Schmitt, are not very convincing. If Jovanovic had been bidding for the support of the Bosnian youth, as Seton-Watson would have us believe, he would certainly have chosen a more impressive and spectacular manner of making his revelation than by writing an article in an obscure publication. Secondly, when Pasic did finally 'stand up before his countrymen', he did not produce the proofs which Seton-Watson believed him to possess; he did not deny the charges of his adversary with definiteness and firmness, at least he did not say categorically that he knew nothing of the plot.'[62]

Fay rightly observes that 'there is no good reason to doubt the accuracy of M. Ljuba Jovanovic's revelations of 1924.' Seton-Watson's argument, that they were written in a 'careless, naive, reminiscent vein, is indeed a reasoning for their genuineness. Jovanovic evidently made no effort to embellish them carefully as a political pamphlet to win adherents or to show his own personal importance.[63]

The testimony of an Italian writer Magrini also supports the story of Jovanovic and weakens the denials of Pasic.[64] It may, however, be worthwhile to remark that, however exact the knowledge of the Serbian government may have been, it is not suggested by any of the evidence that the government approved of the plot or assisted in its preparation.[65]

Motives of The Assassins

A man's motives are usually jumbled and often not clear even to himself. This is especially true in the case of a political murderer, who has every reason to expect that one of the consequences of his acts will be his own death. This is in fact the case with the half dozen youths who conspired against the life of the Archduke Franz Ferdinand. The best materials for judging their motives are their statements after their arrest and at their trial, if due allowance is made for the fact that they were speaking as prisoners under indictment for murder and treason, and were trying to shield one another and their accomplices in Serbia. Making allowance for this tendency in their statements, one may say that the motives of Princip and Cabrinovic were mainly of three kinds.

Firstly, there was a personal motive–frustration in their own lives and a desire to be national martyrs and heroes like Zewrajic. Both Princip and Cabrinovic had been unhappy at home. Both, but especially Cabrinovic, suffered from ill health and lack of proper food, and were probably already consumptive. Life seemed to hold out little for either of them; then why not achieve the honour of a martyr's crown by treading on the footsteps of Zewrajic. Both youths were thus clearly psychopathic, maladjusted by personal suffering, and therefore prone to malign influences.

A second motive was to take vengeance on Austria for the severe regime in Bosnia, stimulate opposition to it and engender a revolution which should put an end to it. 'The main motive which guided me, in my deed', said Princip, 'was the avenging of the Serbian people.' 'I killed him', he declared, 'and I am not sorry. I knew that he was an enemy of the Slavs[66]... Cabrinovic also asserted, 'I hated him because he was an enemy of Serbia.'

A third motive was to kindle further opposition towards the Habsburg regime, and so prepare the ground for tearing the two provinces—Bosnia-Herzegovina—away from the dual monarchy uniting them with Serbia in some kind of a national South Slav State, and thus reviving the empire of Stephen Dushan.[67]

Such were the three chief motives of the two principal plotters. But which was the strongest of the three—their personal psychopathic condition, or their desire for vengeance on Austria, or their Serb nationalism—would be difficult to say. Yugoslav writers and sympathizers[68], as Sidney Fay observes, assert Yugoslav nationalism as the main motive. But in 1914, the accused themselves hardly knew.[69] Moreover, it has to be admitted that the assassins were misguided youngsters, raw and unseasoned; and the real scrutiny ought to be done of the men behind them–designers who incited them to do the deed.

It is suggested in extenuation of the crime that it was a wanton provocation on the Archduke's part to hold manoeuvres in Bosnia, as the Serbs dreaded he meant to attack Serbia, and that they further resented his visiting Sarajevo precisely on a Serb national anniversary like Vidov Dan, a day of mourning, that the aggrieved Bosnians regarded it a deliberate insult. The latter view is absolutely unwarranted, the former untenable. Princip and Cabrinovic had in fact begun to organize their plot, as Fay rightly observes, when they heard of the Archduke's impending trip to Bosnia but before they were aware that he would visit Sarajevo on Vidov Dan. 'They had decided to assassinate him in Bosnia, not because they resented the visit or feared an attack on Serbia, but because his presence in Bosnia afforded an excellent opportunity[70] for giving effect to their motives.'

Pasic, The *Narodna Odbrana* And The Black Hand

Some mention has already been made of the activity of the *Narodna Odbrana* and the Black Hand, and of the probable cognizance of a plot on the part of Pasic and some members of his cabinet. But to understand more appropriately the responsibility of Serbia some more light has to be thrown on the relations between these two Serbian organizations to the Serbian government.

Though the *Narodna Odbrana* probably had no official knowledge of the plot to assassinate Franz Ferdinand, its network of 'confidential men' and its 'tunnel' for secret communications between Serbia and Bosnia were certainly used by the Black Hand officials and the three youths who travelled from Belgrade to Sarajevo to commit the act. This overlapping activity of the two Serbian societies, which apparently had somewhat different aims and were not altogether friendly, was simplified by the fact that the secretary of the *Narodna Odbrana*, Milan Vasic, and other members were also members of the Black Hand.[71] Thus the Serbian government may be regarded as responsible for an organization whose secret agents in Bosnia were planning the disruption of Austria-Hungary.

The relations between the Serbian Government and the Black Hand were quite different. The government was well aware of the existence of this organization, which was a matter of common knowledge in Belgrade and was discussed in the newspapers, but probably did not know in any detail about its membership and its subterranean activities. To begin with, the relations between the government and the Black Hand leaders were tolerably smooth, but friction developed over the so-called 'priority-question'[72] which arose after the Balkan Wars leading to a party conflict between the Pasic radicals and the Black Hand military officers. This internal tension is often cited as proof that Dimitrijevic and the Sarajevo assassins could not be in league with the Serbian Government. This is possibly true. It is also perfectly certain that Pasic and his cabinet had nothing to do with the originating of the assassination.[73] It was hatched behind their backs and they probably had no inkling of it until the preparations were fairly complete and the youths were on the verge of leaving for Sarajevo.

The Austrian Negligence

As a matter of fact, the attitude and conduct of the Austro-Hungarian authorities offers a problem that is not easily resolved; it was indeed so strange that connivance with the plot, on part of Austria-Hungary, had been charged. Wickham Steed insinuates foul play on part of Austrian authorities. He states :

> To me who had been present at the Emperor Franz Joseph's visit to Sarajevo in 1910, it seemed remarkable that the Archduke should have been assassinated there, for I had rarely seen a town that lent itself better to the police precautions usually taken in Austria-Hungary in such circumstances. And when it transpired, on the morrow, that the Sarajevo police had received orders to take no special measures for the protection of the Archduke ... my suspicion of foul play hardened into something like certainty.[74]

Certainly the evidence is not sufficient to prove the connivance of the Austrian authorities with the assassination. To quote Schmitt :

> Recent disclosures dispel much of the mystery, and the theory of complicity (on the part of Austria-Hungary) has been generally abandoned.[75]

In the opinion of Schmitt, it might have been felt that drastic measures of precaution would reflect both on the courage of Franz Ferdinand and on the strength of the government, but still, as Schmitt affirms, Potiorek cannot escape the blame for what happened as a result of his carelessness.[76]

The Serbian Neglect to Arrest The Accomplices

Even if the Serbian Government was at first ignorant of the assassination plot, there are two serious charges against Pasic : his failure to give any definite warning to the Austrian authorities after he had learnt that the assassins had gone to Sarajevo, and his sluggishness after the murder in failing to search for and arrest the accomplices-in-crime in Belgrade.

In fact Serbian police officials appear to have actually aided one of them, Ciganovic, in his escape. To have attempted to arrest him, and to have divulged the part played by such prominent members of the Black Hand as Dimitrijevic[77] and Tankosic, would have still further intensified the opposition which had already caused the temporary setback of the cabinet. Clearly Pasic did not dare to take action against the leaders of such a powerful organization–a step which would certainly have endangered his own life–and, therefore, he adopted a purely quiescent attitude hoping that Austria and Europe would not learn the truth.[78]

In the opinion of Seton-Watson : Energetic action by Pasic 'during the week or even the fortnight following the murder' would have 'increased the chances of friendly mediation from the outside. To this extent, then, the Pasic cabinet must share the responsibility for what befell.' This omission is only very partially explained by absorption in the electoral campaign. 'But', continues Watson, 'a true grasp of European realities should have shown that infinitely more was at stake. Yet Pasic remained passive, took no steps to put himself in the right at Vienna ... it convicts him of great remissness and lack of judgement.'[79] 'The three precious weeks', says Edith Durham, 'during which the criminals could have been brought to book and Europe purged of danger were allowed to pass by ... Serbia preferred to risk war rather than risk exposure.[80]

AN INADEQUATE WARNING

Did Serbia 'warn' Austria? This question is exceedingly important. If the Serbian Government did honestly try to inform the Austro-Hungarian government of the plot, having failed to intercept the conspirators in their journey from Belgrade to Sarajevo, its responsibility for the murders at Sarajevo would be sensibly diminished. It is hardly surprising that in this connection a good deal of conflicting evidence has been brought forward. Without going into the details, let us focus the attention especially upon three points : (*i*) To whom was the warning given, if given at all? (*ii*) Was it given on his own initiative and unofficially by Jovanovic, the Serbian minister in Vienna, or officially upon instructions from Belgrade? (*iii*) Did it contain any hint of a definite plot, or was it merely a vague general statement about the undesirability of the Archduke's visit to a disturbed province?

Jovan Jovanovic came to Vienna as 'Serbian minister at the end of December, 1912, to replace Dr. Simic, an elderly, experienced diplomat of tact and dignity. Even in normal times the position of the Serbian representative in Vienna was no easy one after 1903. At the moment when Jovanovic arrived in 1912 the situation was particularly delicate and tense on account of the commotion let loose by the First Balkan War and the Austrian efforts in the London Confernece to deprive the Serbians of the fruits of their victories. Jovanovic, in contrast to his predecessor, was a young man of hardly forty. In Vienna, people accused him of fomenting trouble in 1908 against thc annexation of Bosnia and Herzegovina. His reception there was far from cordial. When he was presented to Franz Joseph, the emperor is said merely to have bowed to him, instead of the customary handshake on such occasions. The Archdukes would not see him at all. Count Berchtold[81], the Austrian foreign minister, was frigid, and would not go beyond official contact.[82] In this galling atmosphere, Jovanovic appreciated his cordial relations with von Bilinski, who, being recently appointed joint finance minister, had charge of the civil administration in Bosnia and Herzegovina, and so had much in common with the Serbian minister.

In fact, it was soon approved by Franz Joseph and Berchtold, that Bilinski should manage diplomatic dealings with the Serbian minister, and then report upon them to Berchtold.[83] This was, of course, wholly anamalous and irregular. But further reasons for it are to be found in Berchtold's natural indolence, and in Bilinski's ambition to increase his own importance. It elucidates, however, why in June, 1914, Jovanovic should prefer to choose Bilinski, rather than Berchtold or anyone in the Austrian ministry of foreign affairs, as the person to whom to make his delicate suggestion that it might be hazardous for Archduke Franz Ferdinand to go to Bosnia.

In the words of Jovanovic himself :

> I am glad to give you an authentic account of the warning given to the Archduke which came from me and arose from my own initiative ... I learned that the heir to the throne intended to be present at *manoeuvres* in Bosnia ... I resolved to visit Dr. Von Bilinski ... So far as I remember, my visit took place about June 5– thus 23 days before the assassination. I explained quite openly to the minister... it will arouse the greatest discontent among the Serbs who must regard this as an act of provocation. Manoeuvres under such circumstances are dangerous. Among the Serb youths there may be one who will put a ball-cartridge, and he may fire it, and the bullet might strike the man giving the provocation. Therefore, it would be good and reasonable that the Archduke should not go to Sarajevo; that the *manoeuvres* should not be held on Vidov Dan; and they should not be held in Bosnia.

Jovanovic further says :

> To these clear words, Dr. Von Bilinski replied that he took note of them, and would inform me what result they had with the Archduke, although he himself could not believe in any such result of the manoeuvres as I foresaw; and that moreover, he was in possession of information that Bosnia was completely quiet. A few days later I again called on Von Bilinski about this matter. But nevertheless had shortly to learn that the original programme would be followed and nothing changed inspite of my warning. The Archduke was certainly informed, but would heed none but himself.[84]

This account of Jovanovic appears to be, in the opinion of Fay, 'the closest approximation to the truth hitherto made from the Serbian side.' Thus there was a warning, but of a peculiar kind!

A truly unenviable dilemma now confronted Pasic. If, as Remak observes, 'he revealed the plot to the Austrians, he might well find himself the next victim marked for assassination by the Black Hand.' In the opinion of Remak, Pasic was no coward, but there were other dangers involved as well. 'Telling the Austrians the facts would mean admitting the extent to which the Serbian Government was aware of, and had tolerated, those subversive activities which it always disclaimed. Besides ... should it ever become known that Pasic had delivered these youths and their Bosnian helpers to the Austrian police, he might just as soon announce his retirement from politics.'[85]

Finding himself in this quandary, Pasic chose a peculiar course of action. He decided to warn the Austrians but to make the warning neither formal nor specific. This form of warning, if extremely well-handled, had the advantage that, without giving too many of the facts away, it might be sufficient to absolve him from any further responsibility for what would happen to the Archduke and the would-be-assassins. The trouble with it was that it probably was too clever by far, and that it definitely was badly handled. Pasic's instruction to alert the Austrians, and yet to do so in an innocuous manner, severely taxed Jovanovic's diplomatic ingenuity. He could not afford to create the impression that his government was trying to intimidate the Austrians to the point of making Archduke Franz Ferdinand abandon his Bosnian trip.

Is it possible that Jovanovic, as he himself alleges, made his communication 'on his own initiative?' The statement made by Jovanovic to Bilinski, as Schmitt correctly states, 'was so unusual that only an instruction from Belgrade offers a reasonable explanation.'[86]

The use of the phrase 'personal initiative' is a time-honoured and useful diplomatic practice. Translated into non-diplomatic language, its meaning is roughly that the person using it is speaking in the name of his government—no diplomat who wishes to remain one ever makes truly private suggestions involving policy to a foreign government, especially regarding Austria and Serbia where the relationship was awfully delicate–but that, if so desired, no official cognisance need be taken of his words. In this fashion, should his proposals be accepted, nothing will be lost. Should they be disregarded, the rejection will cause the home government no loss of prestige, since for the record, they had never been made in the first place. Bilinski, presumably unfamiliar with the meaning of the phrase 'personal initiative', and far from guessing that he was being warned about an actual assassination plot, tried to reassure Jovanovic, who confessed that he was worried. Bilinski had not seemed at all impressed by his cryptic warning, but despite his misgivings, Jovanovic did not take the matter up again in more explicit terms either with Bilinski or with any one else in Vienna.[87] Europe was, thus, a very large step closer to the World War.

It would be interesting to hear what the person who received the 'warning' has to say about it. But curiously enough, Bilinski's two volumes of memoirs, say nothing of this.[88] During the war he told an Austrian historian that he 'wished to draw the veil of oblivion' over the Sarajevo plot.[89] Some writers assert that he never received any warning, or else he would have surely mentioned it because of its crucial interest.[90] This argument does not seem tenable. Rather Fay's reasoning is sound and convincing :

> ... more probably he avoided recalling the painful fact that he did not dissuade the Archduke from his fatal trip, or that at least, as the minister officially responsible for the administration of Bosnia, did not make sure that adequate arrangements were made for his protection ... In view of the terrible consequences to Austria and the world, this neglect must have haunted him as the most dreadful nightmare of his life.[91]

That is why he 'wished to draw the veil of oblivion' over the Sarajevo affair. He would gladly talk about every other aspect of this sad episode, except precisely this point which he wished to bury in the debris of history.

To sum up : If the Serbian government had knowledge, however vague, of the conspiracy against the Archduke Franz Ferdinand, it must be charged with a serious dereliction of duty in not conveying a warning (in the true sense) to the

Austro-Hungarian authorities. Its negligence may be explained by what Jovanovic called 'the peculiar character of Austro-Serbian relations' and by its internal political difficulties, but hardly excused.[92]

Conclusion

There is enough evidence to show that the theory of direct complicity on the part of the Serbian government in this unfortunate occurrence, is presposterous and illogical.

Bernadott Schmitt sums up the situation as follows :

> I have no desire to defend the methods by which the Serbian propaganda in Bosnia-Herzegovina was carried on; but equally I cannot defend the methods by which Austria persecuted Serbia for a generation. In this case of 'dog eat dog', the provocations invaribaly, as it seems to me, began with Austrian action. It was the Austrians who proposed to construct a railway that would encircle Serbia. It was the Austrians who annexed Bosnia in contravention of the Berlin Treaty. It was the Austrians who tried to keep the Serbs from an Adriatic port. The only thing that the Serbs did in answer to all that was propaganda, until ultimately a group of somewhat irresponsible Serbs killed the Archduke.

He continues :

> There was a clear issue between the idea of Yugoslav nationalism on the one hand and a highly conservative government on the other. The conflict between them was probably inevitable, and by the force of circumstances, that conflict could not be fought out alone. It had become a matter of European politics in which every state in Europe was more or less interested.[93]

'The crime of Sarajevo', states Seton-Watson, 'is an indelible blot upon the movement for Yugoslav Unity.[94] but Austria-Hungary', he continues, 'by a policy of repression at home and aggression abroad, had antagonized all sections of the Yugoslav race. Murder or no murder, the seething pot would have continued to boil until Austria-Hungary could evolve a policy compatible with Yugoslav interests, or, alternatively, until the Yugoslavs could shake off.'

NOTES AND REFERENCES

1. A small state in South Eastern Europe now once again it was in the limelight after the fall of U.S.S.R.
2. The alliance between France, Great Britain and Russia.
3. A race spread over most of South Eastern Europe like Serbs, Croats, Bulgars, Slovenes, Slavonians etc.
4. The Gang of Regicides is usually referred to in Serb documents as the Men of May Twenty-Nine, the date of murder of King Alexander and Queen Draga.
5. Shield with a coat of arms on it.
6. Member of band of irregular soldiery in the Balkans, or any Balkan guerrillero.
7. Fay, Sidney B. *The Origin of the World War,* (New York, 1956), p. 57.
8. Remak, Joachim, *Sarajevo,* The Story of a Political Murder, (New York, 1959), p. 7.
9. Fay, op.cit, Vol. 2, p. 57.
10. Seton-Watson, R.W. *Sarajevo* A Study in the Origin of the Great War, (London, 1925), p. 15.
11. Schevill, Ferdinand. *The History of the Balkan Peninsula,* (New York, 1933), p. 457.
12. Seton-Watson, op.cit, pp. 21–22.
13. Schevill, op.cit, p. 457.
14. Ibid, p. 457.
15. Seton-Watson, op.cit, p. 22.
16. Ibid, p. 23.
17. Vucinich, Wayne S. *Serbia Between East and West,* The Events of 1903–1908, (Stanford: California, 1954), p. 234.
18. Schevill, op.cit, p. 458.
19. Temperley, Harold W.V. *History of Serbia,* (New York, 1969), p.288.
20. In 1878, the Austrians had thought the road lay through the mountainous defiles of Novibazar, but at some date before the end of 1908 they recognized that the Sanjak would be a death-trap to an invading army. The way was not through Novibazar at all, but along the old rod trodden by Byzantine, Bulgarian, Hungarian and Turkish armies from Belgrade to Nish, and from Nish to the coveted harbour of Salonica ... But an advance through Belgrade could only be made if Serbia was absolutely dependent or utterly crushed by brute force. Ibid, p. 288.
21. Ibid, pp. 288–89.
22. Fay, op.cit, Vol. 1, pp. 358–59.

23. Schevill, op.cit, p. 460.
24. Temperley, op.cit, p. 293.
25. Ibid, p. 293.
26. Vucinich, op.cit, p. 235.
27. Fay, op.cit, p. 360.
28. German railway enterprise culminates in the Baghdad line. For Baghdad project, Schevill, op.cit, pp. 446–68.
29. Ibid, p. 460.
30. Ibid, p. 460.
31. Ibid, p. 460–61.
32. Ibid, p. 456.
33. Seton-Watson, op.cit, p. 32.
34. Schevill, op.cit, p. 461.
35. Temperley, op.cit, p. 305.
36. Seton-Watson, op.cit, p. 32.
37. Seton-Watson op.cit, p. 113.
38. Dushen Tovdoreka, cited in Schmitt, op.cit, 213.
39. Ibid, p. 213–14.
40. M. Bogitchevitch, cited in Fay, op.cit, p.105; Schmitt, op.cit, p. 225.
41. Schmitt, op.cit, pp. 225–26.
42. Ciganovic came from Bosnia in 1908, and secured a post on the Serbian state railways. During the Balkan wars he belonged to the Komitaji of Major Voja Tankosic, and became a well-known character. He joined the Black Hand supposedly at the instigation of Tankosic although, according to one account, it was at the suggestion of Pasic, who wished to have an agent in the organization. Whether he was or was not a spy upon the Black Hand is a matter of great importance, for if he was, then Pasic would be kept informed of its activities. But if he was, it is remarkable that he was not known to government circles. There is no doubt that at a later date he was the agent of Pasic, as the Salonica trial showed; but it is not known when he assumed this role, Ibid, pp. 218–19.
43. Ibid, p. 226.
44. Seton-Watson, op.cit, p. 78.
45. Fay, op.cit, pp. 110–12.
46. In Bosnia and Herzegovina, according to the census of 1910, the population consisted of Greek Orthodox, Mohammedans and Roman Catholics, approximately in the proportion of 4, 3 and 2. Generally speaking, the Greek Othodox sympathized with the Serbians in the neighbouring kingdom; the Roman

Catholics were divided between loyalty to Austria on the one hand, and on the other, their nationalistic desires for a national Serb-Croat Union, either as a self-governing unit in a federalized 'trialistic' Habsburg state, or as part of a 'greater Serbia' or of an independent Yugoslav Federation; the Mohammedans were generally loyal to the Habsburg Monarchy. Ibid, pp. 93–94.

47. Ibid, p. 45.
48. Saint Vitus's Day, June 28, 1389 : The Turks after a murderous battle defeated the Serbian army at Kossovo, or Blackbird's Field, in the plains of Southern Serbia. Henceforth, Serbia became a vassal state of Turkey. A whole cycle of legends, folk songs, and ballads gathered around the battle, and each year, the Serbs commemorated June 28 as a day of national mourning. Remak, op.cit, p. 113.
49. Ibid, pp. 227–28.
50. Fay, op.cit, p. 57.
51. Ibid, pp. 57–58.
52. Ibid, pp. 58–59.
53. Ibid, pp. 60–61.
54. Schmitt, op.cit, p. 230; Fay, op.cit, p. 61.
55. Fay, op.cit, p. 62.
56. Schmitt, op.cit, p. 231.
57. Fay, op.cit, p. 63.
58. The river flowing through Sarajevo near which the Archduke was murdered. Ibid, p.65. In her 'The Reminiscences of Ljuba Jovanovitch', Edith Durham quotes him, it is recognized that the Government did not fail to do everything possible to show their friends and the rest of the world how far removed we were from the Sarajevo conspirators. Referring to Ljuba's later fluctuations Durham states 'Ljuba's struggles only plunge him deeper in the mire', Durham, op.cit, p. 147.
59. Seton-Watson, op.cit, p. 153.
60. Ibid, pp. 157–59.
61. Ibid, p. 159.
62. Schmitt, op.cit, p. 235.
63. Fay, op.cit, p. 74.
64. Schmitt, op.cit, p. 236.
65. Ibid, p. 236.
66. Pharos, p. 36. cited in Fay, op.cit, p. 132.
67. This is the period of the greatest bloom of the Serb state, a period (1331–55) which modern Serbs still look upon with

passionate pride. Schevill, op.cit, p. 152.

68. Like Jevtic and Seton-Watson.
69. Fay, op.cit, p. 134.
70. Ibid, p. 135.
71. Ibid, p. 141.
72. This 'priority question' arose out of a dispute between the military and civillian officials concerning the government of the territories which Serbia had conquered from Turkey. In this conflict the military officers were supported by the opposition political groups who demanded the resignation of the Pasic Cabinet. Pasic thereupon actually did resign. However, under Russian pressure, King Peter, on June 11, 1914, had to restore Pasic to power, Ibid, p. 44.
73 Ibid, p. 45.
74. Steed, Henry Wickham. *Through Thirty Years*, (New York, 1924), Vol. 1, pp. 393–94.
75. Schmitt, op.cit, p. 248.
76. Ibid, p. 253.
77. Popularly called 'Apis.'
78. Fay, op.cit, p. 146.
79. Seton-Watson, op.cit, pp. 134, 136–37.
80. Durham, op.cit, pp. 12–13.
81. According to Sidney B. Fay, Berchtold more than anyone else was responsible for the World War, Fay, op.cit, Vol. 1, p. 18.
82. Ibid, Vol. 2, p. 156.
83. Ibid, p. 157.
84. Neues Wiener Tageblatt, No. 177, June 28, 1924 : Ibid, pp. 158–59.
85. Remak, op.cit, pp. 72–73.
86. Schmitt, op.cit, p. 246.
87. Remak, op.cit, p. 76–77.
88. Fay, op.cit, p. 161; Schmitt, op.cit, p. 247.
89. Schmitt, op.cit, p. 247.
90. Fay, op.cit, p. 161.
91. Fay, op.cit, p. 161.
92. Schmitt, op.cit, p. 247. In the words of Hermann Wendel : 'In the decisive weeks the Serbian Government was undoubtedly inspired by a certain passivity and an Oriental indolence. Passive and indolent it was in every respect. Cited in Durham, op.cit, p. 125.
93. Schmitt and Barnes, 1926, op.cit, p. 35.
94. Seton-Watson, Ibid, p. 15.

Chapter 13

British Radio and the Danish Resistance Movement, 1940–1945

The use of some form of propaganda in wartime is nothing new. Even in the Middle Ages, scrolls wrapped around arrows were shot into besieged castles. During the First World War, propaganda pamphlets urging the enemy to surrender were carried across No Man's Land by little free balloons, fired from trench mortars, or dropped from bombing planes.[1] But it was not until the development of radio that propaganda became a strategic weapon of first-rate importace; all the mediums previously used had been in some way or other unsatisfactory.[2] The radio, through which–its originators had piously hoped–nation would 'speak peace unto nation'[3] the propagandist at last found an almost ideal vehicle for his aims. It was every man's friend. He turned to it instinctively for news, comfort, and diversion. Radio recognized no barriers. 'Bans on listening, even if enforced by a vigilant Gestapo and backed by dire penalties', says Charles J. Rolo, 'have proved ineffective.'[4]

'Propaganda', according to Daniel Lerner, 'is conceived as an instrument of policy in the competition for political power, and psychological warfare is the form propaganda takes when this competition becomes violent.'[5] It takes on the character of a struggle for the attention, beliefs, and loyalties of whole populations. In this sense, psychological warfare is, as Lerner observes, the invention, and the destiny, of the twentieth century.[6] Hans Speier writes :

The distinctly new feature of modern war propaganda is its

> extension to non-combatants ... to bolster up the material spirit, or at least the will to resistance, among the millions of workers and farmers, men and women and children, is a phenomenon unknown to earlier centuries of modern history ... Thus under the conditions created by these three factors–the development of technology, mass participation in war, and nationalism–the morale of the nation itself becomes of decisive *military* importance. A major war assumes the character of siege warfare on a huge scale, with economic and symbolic war supplementing the strictly military effort.[7]

At the outbreak of the Second World War in 1939, Denmark declared her neutrality. It was hoped that the country–as in 1914-18—would keep out of war. Things, however, turned out differently.[8] On April 9, 1940, 'Denmark lost, for the time being her thousand-year-old independence and liberty; and the oldest kingdom in Europe, whose rulers are so closely related to the English royal family, is now obliged to submit to every humiliation that Nazi-German despotism may care to impose upon it,'[9] reveals Paul Palmer. Yet, as T.M. Terkelsen observes :

> When future historians survey the vast field of Europe under the Nazis, they will ponder over the strange case of Denmark. They will find nothing with which to compare it. Everything went according to rules different from those valid in other occupied countries–even down to the Germans trying to behave as gentlemen, though admittedly feeling uncomfortable in the new part. Here was an occupied country with a government, a parliament and a king, all trying to fulfil their normal functions in internal matters. This was the country where the Germans permitted a general election, the main result of which was to show that less than two per cent of the electorate sympathized with the Nazis. Here, also, the king visited the synagogue, and a German spokesman for the extermination of nations pursued a policy of appeasement. And here lived a traditionally peaceful people, who in twelve months were transformed into some of the most efficient saboteurs of Europe. Denmark with its four million inhabitants topped the list of sabotage in European countries, despite its Lilliputian size ... it may be thought that the Danes, who were allowed more liberties, more independence, and more food than any other occupied country had reached

> the conclusion that there is no *ersatz* for freedom. This view approaches the kernel of the truth.[10]

It was the British Broadcasting Corporation (B.B.C.) which motivated and inspired the Danes during the dismal war years.

II

The first B.B.C. broadcast in Danish was on April 9, 1940–the day of the German invasion of Denmark.[11] The B.B.C. became, and remained throughout the war, Denmark's main contact with the free world. According to the *Citizen* newspaper, 'Inspite of German jamming, wartime listening to the B.B.C. was probably more intensive in Denmark than in any other country.[12] Travellers from Denmark testified 'that almost every household tunes in regularly to England.[13] German jamming apparatus was made largely ineffective by Danish sabotage actions.[14]

It was not prohibited in Denmark to listen to foreign broadcasts as it was in Norway and other German-occupied countries. This was a real benefit of Hitler's moderate policy towards Denmark. A large percentage of the Danish population were also radio owners. From the beginning the B.B.C. therefore had an advantage.[15]

The objectives of the B.B.C. were two fold. First, and foremost the broadcasts aimed at providing a comprehensive news service to Danish listeners. News was what the Danish listeners wished to hear to keep hope alive in 1940. It was during 1940 that the news service began to build up its great reputation in Denmark for objectivity, because it did not attempt to disguise the gravity of the situation in Europe. Secondly, the broadcasts to Denmark were political, aimed at influencing and moulding the thinking of the Danish people. Throughout the war the Danish section of the B.B.C. European Service was effectively the major instrument of British political propagands in Denmark.[16]

Britain did not indulge in the same kind of propaganda as Goebbels. Reliability and accuracy were considered more valuable here than extravagant promises. 'The B.B.C. was proud of the standards of truth, honesty, and good taste it had striven to maintain' : observes Charles J. Rolo. And further : 'In its code of ethics, it worked out a more realistic policy.'[17] This subtle type of propagands was far more effective[18] in Denmark than the German form of propaganda. The Nazis' increasing concern over 'Churchillism', says C.J. Rolo, 'is just one proof' of the success of the B.B.C.[19]

In April 1940, when the Germans overran Denmark, the B.B.C. European services were only in a rudimentary stage. However, the importance of the services to Europe had been recognized, and their broad principles laid down. These were to be, as stated above, truth, news and objectivity. The latter was important, for the main difference between German and British propaganda became strikingly conspicuous. The British principle in the darkest days of the war was, and could only be, an attitude of waiting. In 1940, the broadcasts from London were in character with the 'blood, toil, tears and sweat' attitude of Winston Churchill.

In contrast, German propaganda assured a quick victory, and the more it was delayed the less convincing became German protestations. For Britain this was a position of vantage from which to work. Evidently from the allied side there could be no rash promises of an early British victory, when most of Europe was occupied by the enemy, and Britain itself was threatened. Although the B.B.C.'s objective approach was a policy, it was also a necessity.

This policy did pay dividends. Broadcasts from Britain were considered more reliable than the German, especially as a German victory became less and less likely. The Nazi periodical, *Kritisk Uqerevue*, complained in September 1941, that 'all Danish homes that listen to the British radio are convinced that only there can they hear the truth, and that the German announce-ments are only propaganda which is being forced upon Denmark.'[20]

According to Robert Jorgensen : 'The news is the fundamental factor of Danish transmissions.'[21] The desire for news explained the great wartime popularity of the B.B.C. and also demonstrated the deep psychological need of the peoples in the German-occupied countries. The B.B.C. broadcasts convinced their listeners that all hope was not lost, and that events were not really as bad as they often appeared to be from the German-controlled state radio and from the censored newspapers. London was the last remaining stronghold which had not fallen to the Germans, and therefore its voice carried great prestige. The broadcasters were constantly aware that across that short intervening space of water their most zealous adherents were risking torture and death to hear the news and pass it on.[22] M. Leon Blum, a captive throughout the war in the hands of the Germans, 'has told us that he found the words of B.B.C. 'as beautiful as Beethoven symphony' ... In a world of poison, the B.B.C. became the great antiseptic.[23]

During April and May 1940, when the Danish section of the broadcasting service was being organized, British public opinion on Denmark was not favourable. Both the public and the press were not sympathetic to Denmark's fate, and there was little understanding of why it had not resisted the German invasion. During the spring and summer of 1940, the British press did not know whether to treat Denmark as a friend or a foe. The formal status of Denmark after the April decision was thus, hard to define. 'From abroad, Denmark's position was variously defined, or rather : it was never clearly defined at all.' observes Joerge Haestrup. Few in Britain in April 1940, showed much optimism about the fate of Denmark. The British were disgusted at the familiar story that the German troops came as 'friends' and would 'protect' the country against imminent invasion from the Western powers.[24]

However, Britain was not in a position to criticize Denmark for failure to resist the colossal Panzer forces which were suddenly thrown against her, as she herself had refused to offer her assistance in the event of invasion. At the time, nevertheless, Denmark was being compared with Norway, and received little British sympathy. Later, when it was seen how easily the German armies overpowered France and the low countries, Denmark's surrender seemed more understandable.

It was in these inauspicious circumstances that the B.B.C. began its broadcasts in Danish. The vital question during the latter part of 1940 was what policy the broadcasts should follow. Policy making was a more difficult problem for the Danish section than for any other foreign section because of the complex status of Denmark after the invasion. This country had never declared war on Germany, and the Danish King ramained in Denmark after the German occupation. It was truly embarrassing for the Danish section of the B.B.C., therefore, to make its broadcasts effective, when it seemed that the Danish people were satisfied with the position of their government under occupation. The speakers of the Danish section from the beginning, were unable to openly encourage the Danish people to resist the enemy, because of the position of the government acting as a barrier between the Germans and the Danish people. The Danish section had, to begin with, to broadcast to a country with a national government which had undertaken to govern democratically inspite of the presence of the Germans. The situation was delicate and needed careful diplomatic handling. Those who criticized the Danish section for having no clear and definite policy for the first two years of the war, tended to ignore this crucial problem.[25]

After a period of apparent indecision until about the middle of 1941, the broadcasts began to crystallize into an attack against certain Danish personalities, followed by an attempt to create discontentment in Denmark with the policy of the government. The aim of the section was to force a rupture between the Danes and the Germans by showing on all possible occasions that the so-called Danish National Government could not, and did not, act in Danish interests because it was constantly under heavy German pressure. As more and more concessions were made to the demands of the Germans, the Danes eventually realized that they could no longer trust their government to protect their interests. The B.B.C. thus, succeeded in trying to show Denmark how helpless its government really was under Nazi occupation.[26]

The method adopted by the news service was to attack the Danish Government's policy of negotiation with the

Germans. However, it had to exercise some restraint until about November 1941. The section was cautious in mounting its propaganda offensive against the policy of the government. The editor[27] of the Danish section had to find out what the official British view on Denmark was, so that the broadcasts did not follow an entirely different policy. Several of the Danish section speakers wished to give broadcasts that would encourage unrest and sabotage in Denmark, but they had to co-ordinate with the broadcasting Director's[28] and the Special Operations Executives' (S.O.E.) policies.

Jeremy Bennett states:

> The policies of the S.O.E. and the B.B.C. Danish section were similar–to force a break between the Germans and the Danish government, and to bring Denmark into line with the rest of enemy-occupied Europe. The Danish section of the B.B.C. had, however, to wait until S.O.E. was ready for operations in Denmark. There was no possible use in encouraging premature revolt. S.O.E., in turn, had to wait for the foreign office to decide upon action, and this explains the lack of consistent aggressive policy in the broadcasts of the Danish section of the B.B.C. in the first two years of the war.[29]

The broadcasts from Britain during the first few months following the German occupation of Denmark were, therefore, deliberately uncontroversial and were based mainly on general war news. The most that the section could do, was to explore the possibility of Denmark eventually taking an active line against the Germans. This was done discreetly and intelligently by emphasizing the pro-allied activities of Danes abroad, particularly of Danish seamen.[30] Stories about other European Resistance Movements were also frequently broadcast in the first year of the war.[31] With the formation of the Danish Council in London (October 9, 1940) this policy of broadcasting news of Danish activity in Britain took concrete shape. 'In the Danish Council, the B.B.C. found its first propaganda weapon', writes Bennett, 'and upon it built its first policy.'[32] It was, as one B.B.C. commentator said, 'to stir the consciences of Danes at home by telling them what Danes abroad were doing towards the common fight.'[33]

'Relations were of necessity close', states Bennett, 'between the Danish section of the B.B.C. and the Danish Council, as one needed the other for its work–the B.B.C. needed the Council to show Denmark that Danes abroad were behind Britain, and the Council needed the B.B.C. to enable its members to speak to Denmark.'[34]

The Danish journalist Emil Blytgen-Petersen said on January 23, 1941:

> We free Danes believe–as you no doubt do yourself–that the liberation of Denmark depends on the victory of the Allies, and that it is our duty to aid Great Britain in her struggle, and we believe that by doing so, we shall also be saving Denmark.[35]

The B.B.C. thus gradually built up a firm anti-German and anti-collaborationist policy in its Danish broadcasts. However, by August 1941, it was definitely felt in the B.B.C. that the Danish section had reached a 'saturation point in the first stage of its policy of emphasizing the activities and views of the Danish Council and the Free Danish movement.'[36] There was also a dissatisfaction in the intelligence section of the B.B.C. with regard to this. Moreover, from the summer of 1941, a more positive and activist line was demanded from the Danish section.[37]

Gradually, from the latter half of 1941, the broadcasts to Denmark became stiffer in tone with a more open attitude. Against a background of increasing attacks from Britain against the Danish government, the Danish 'V' campaign was launched.

The famous 'V' sign was a brain child of the Belgian section of the B.B.C. European Service and caught the imagination of the whole of Europe with its symbol of European solidarity and cooperation.[38] On July 20, 1941, Winston Churchill sent this message to the people of Europe.

> The V sign is the symbol of the unconquerable will of the people of the occupied territories and a portent of the fate awaiting Nazi Germany. So long as the people of Europe continue to refuse all collaboration with the invader, it is sure that his cause will perish and that Europe will be liberated.[39]

The V sign caught on quickly in Denmark[40] as it came at a very appropriate time, when the Danish section of the B.B.C. was about to take a much stronger line towards Denmark and when, as an instrument of propagands, the Danish Council was becoming less effective. 'The V campaign, launched in the summer of 1941', says Bennett, 'was Britain's first concrete contribution to the rise of the Danish resistance movement.'[41] Perhaps the British had learnt from the Nazi 'swastika' that a symbol was an essential psychological weapon.[42] The V, therefore, became the sign of the 'unofficial Denmark' which, against the orders of its government, treated the Germans as enemies. It was the symbol of an attitude, action and in this may be traced the beginning of the Danish resistance movement, encouraged by the British Government.[43]

The Danes had to be made to feel that if they remained inactive throughout the occupation, Denmark would receive little support after the war ended. However, the phrase, 'there is a chair waiting for Denmark at the allied council table', used over the B.B.C. was indicative of the promise of British support if Denmark asserted herself. It was clear that this chair 'has to be earned. It can be earned only by deeds.'[44]

The news service attacked the Danish Government and individual members like Stauning and Scavenius by name throughout 1941 and in the summer of that year, the B.B.C. tried to turn Danish public opinion against the government's policy of negotiation with the Germans, without directly encouraging sabotage.[45]

In June 1941, the Russians entered the war and this gave the British propaganda food for thought. The Danish listener was to be warned by the B.B.C. that this was a Baltic war which could have deep effect on the Danes. The regional aspect, from the Danish viewpoint, was to be stressed.[46] By this time reports too began to come in from Stockholm that the B.B.C. broadcasts were becoming highly popular in Denmark and that Danes, who understood English listened to the B.B.C. Home Service, as they felt it was less biased and less exaggerated. This was encouraging for the B.B.C.

During the month of November, the Anti-Comintern Pact

(November 25, 1941), evoked most protest. It was supported by the Prime Minister Stauning and prominent government member Scavenius and his ally Gunnar Larsen. 'The surrender ... induced a deep sense of humiliation in the Danish people', states Viscount Chilston, 'and caused demonstrations in Copenhagen for several days.'[47] The pact placed official Denmark squarely on the side of Germany against the Russians and therefore the Allies. In the words of Jeremy Bennett : 'This gave the Danish section of the B.B.C. its first real opportunity since the occupation of exploiting a dangerous situation in Denmark.'[48] For large sections of the Danish population the pact was clearly a move in the wrong direction and the serious rioting in Copenhagen was the spontaneous outburst for which the B.B.C. had been hoping and working since the early summer of 1941.

Bennett states :

> To what extent the rioting was directly or indirectly influenced by the B.B.C. broadcasts cannot of course be assessed. However, it is probable that the feelings of the population on this sensitive issue were inflamed by the B.B.C. broadcasts. At least the intelligence section of the B.B.C. considered that the riots following the signing of the pact were 'the most striking single proof yet received of the power of the B.B.C.'[49] Radio propaganda was not the direct cause of the outburst, but in giving wide publicity to events at this time, the B.B.C. showed the Danish population that its spontaneous outburst was encouraged from Britain, and this was the kind of reaction to German pressure which Britain expected of the Danish people as a whole.[50]

III

In the spring of 1942, there occurred an unexpected switch in British policy towards Denmark. The leaders of the intelligence section of the Danish army, who were referred to as the 'League', suggested to the S.O.E. that the *status quo* should be respected in Denmark while the Danish army officers put the so-called P-plan into operation. This was to form illegal military groups of trained personnel throughout the country, so that they could be mobilized at any suitable moment. In the meantime, the vital intelligence information which the League had been sending regularly to Britain through Sweden was to be continued, and if possible increased. Sabotage was to be avoided at all cost, as it would only serve to make the task of the League more difficult. This proposal was accepted by the British authorities. S.O.E. now had to curb its activities.

The policy of the B.B.C. was thus forced to stalemate, and the success which it had achieved in November, 1941 could not now be consolidated with further assaults against the Danish government.[51]

The relations of the Danish government and the Germans were now deteriorating and this led to the Danish crisis of October, 1942 cuased by the King's curt acknowledgement of Hitler's telegram of congratulations for the King's 72nd birthday.[52] This precipitated Hitler's demand for 30,000 Danish volunteers, for a change in the government, and the consequent emergence of foreign minister Erik Scavenius as Prime Minister.

The directives from the Director of European broadcasts between October 7 and 13, encouraged the B.B.C. to take the strongest line possible. It was hoped that the crisis would not subside. If it did, it would only mean that the Danish government had sold itself completely to the Germans.

The Political Warfare Executive (P.W.E.) directive of October 10, was considerably milder in tone than that of the B.B.C. and the attitude was strikingly different. The B.B.C. was only too eager to exploit the crisis. It hoped that the government would stand out against the German demands, and as a result the Germans would be forced to assume control and Denmark would at least be brought in harmony with the other enemy-occupied countries of Europe. This, as mentioned earlier, had been the aim of the Danish section since April, 1940–to encourage the Danish home front as much as possible, so that a situation should develop which might make the functioning of the national government impossible.

P.W.E. on the other hand held a more moderate view of the crisis. Their policy was to await events, rather than to forestall them.[53] Subsequent events proved that they were correct, as the final crisis for the Danish government did not come until August 1943. Denmark was not prepared to carry things to the extreme and the October crisis was averted.

It was not until the late spring and early summer of 1943, when negotiations between S.O.E. and the League had broken down and when in the general election in March, the Danish people expressed their opinion of Nazism and collaboration in Denmark, that all groups in Britain concerned with Denmark policy united. The October affair had shown how confusing it was for an editor when his advisers disagreed, and how warily he had to tread when opinions clashed.[54]

IV

The year 1943, a critical year in the history of German-occupied Denmark, opened with the familiar ... theme of B.B.C. on Scavenius and the Germans. The charge that Scavenius was, in fact, advancing the German and strangling the Danish interests was elaborated further. It was recounted how Scavenius and Dr. Werner Best, the German plenipotentiary in Denmark, were not only working together against Danish patriots, but were undermining the authority of the king. 'This was a clever approach', as Bennett observes. Since the invasion the king had become more and more a symbol of pride and unity to his people. As German pressure grew in Denmark, King Christian, as the father of his people, became more important. Any suffering people cling to a straw, and King Christian served this purpose. This was part of the B.B.C.'s policy to rouse Danish national consciousness and patriotism.[55] Throughout 1943, King Christian was continually mentioned by the B.B.C.

A direct propaganda such as this was superimposed on the general war perspective. The purpose was to show that the German grip on Europe was gradually loosening, and that any adherence to Nazi ideals at this stage of the war would be disastrous for Denmark. 'The entire attitude taken by official Denmark may prove fatal for its future position in post-war Europe.'[56] The feeling of impending doom for pro-German element in Denmark was encouraged too by the mention of 'blacklists' being drawn up in Britain of Danish collaborators. In fact, little became of these blacklists after the war, yet they had a definite propaganda value. The fear of 'backing the wrong horse' must have been very real in early 1943 for many Danish industrialists.

By April 1943, it was becoming apparent to S.O.E. that there was no possibility of building up active resistance in Denmark with the help of the army officers. It appeared no longer necessary for British foreign policy to respect the League's demand for the maintenance of *status quo* in Denmark. In the words of J.Bennett : 'The change to an active anti-Danish government policy from Britain began some time during the spring of 1943.'[57] The Danish section of the B.B.C. projected this change in its broadcasts. The problem now was how to bring the population to express, and not only to think and feel, its protests and this policy was what the Danish section followed during April 1943.

Several factors worked to the success of the B.B.C.'s objectives. War situation had changed for the better. Britain was psychologically and materially in a far better position to sustain active resistance in German-occupied countries. The principle that there was to be no strong propaganda offensive over the radio to encourage unrest in Denmark, until Britain was in a position to back it by material support, had been followed. Further, the general election held in Denmark in March 1943 and the breakup of S.O.E.'s negotiations with the League, contributed greatly to the British decision to encourage sabotage openly in that country.[58]

The propanagda value of the elections to the Germans was evident. The whole world was to see that if Denmark was allowed to hold a general election, then it was not in reality writhing under the tutelage of German occupation. The Danish section was quick to point this out. T.M. Terkelsen in a broadcast on March 11, warned his listeners of the true import of these elections. The Germans wanted to give 'a proof of the incredible freedom to move, which Denmark enjoys inside the walls of the prison.'[59] In this broadcast the Danes were also encouraged to show by their voting what they really felt.

The result of these elections was clearly very important for British policy. The Danish section of the B.B.C., until April 1943, had had the formidable task of avoiding two extremes. On the one hand, the section was unable, and in fact unwilling, to broadcast openly for sabotage, and the destruction of the coalition government. The other extreme which had to be avoided was that of giving the impression that Britain was satisfied with Denmark, that Denmark could not help the events of April 9, and that Denmark should be quiet under German occupation. This had to be avoided at all costs.

During this long period of three years the Danish section 'steered, as it had to, a middle course veering towards an active line at particular times ... The B.B.C. attempted to destroy the myth that coalition government helped the Danish cause.' This is why at times the Danish broadcasts were a list of the promises which the Germans had violated since April 9, 1940.[60] The aim of the section had always been that Denmark should enter the fight on the side of the Allies, but that the Danish people would have to show their readiness to do this by spontaneous action in Denmark. A general and widespread indication of the earnestness had to be made, before the final assault against the Danish Government began from Britain.

In the words of Bennett :

> So the elections were very important both to the Danish section of the B.B.C. and to S.O.E. and the foreign office. Best's decision to hold these elections was a massive propaganda gamble, which failed. For just as Best wished to show Berlin the success of his moderate policy in the 'Model Protectorate', Britain hoped that at long last, Denmark would 'show' itself, by the safe yet effective method of voting anti-Scavenius and anti-Nazis.[61]

When the election results became known, they were open to several interpretations. They could be seen as a victory for Scavenius and the policy of negotiation with the Germans. Or, as the B.B.C. interpreted the vote as a triumph for the principle of democracy in an enemy-occupied country.[62] The elections proved once and for all that any attempt at setting up a Danish Nazi Government in Denmark would end in complete failure.

Meanwhile, the decision to try and precipitate action in Denmark had been taken. The Danes were made to realize the necessity of demolishing factories which were manufacturing arms and weapons for the Germans. The B.B.C. began to report sabotage activities in great detail to draw the attention of Danish listeners.

T.M. Terkelsen writes :

> Because sabotage was a new departure in Denmark, people actively engaged in it approached the subject with an unbiased mind. New ideas were tried out, and Danish ingenuity reached record heights. The Germans doubled the guard in front of Gestapo headquarters in Copenhagen and searched people coming in and out. The saboteurs climbed the roof from a neighbouring building and lowered their deadly explosives through the chimneys ... Saboteurs often appeared in Danish police uniforms, or for the sake of the good cause—they would dress themselves in the quisling uniforms of the Danish *Schalburg Korps*. The result was that Denmark became the country in Europe where sabotage most effectively checked the German war effort.[63]

The formation of a corps of Danish sabotage guards for duty in factories was attacked by the Danish section of the B.B.C. Commenting on the setting up of a body of guards of 15,000 men under the Anti-Sabotage Bill, Blytgen-Petersen ended with the words : 'This is becuase the Danes employ this weapon of sabotage with dexterity and common sense ... Sabotage will be one of the most effective weapons against Hitler in 1943.'[64]

Scavenius received the brunt of the B.B.C. attack, and was accused for forming the anti-sabotage corps, so that Danes should do the dirty work of the Germans. During May, Terkelsen elaborated, with more detail, the argument against the sabotage guards. He pointed out that, in effect, Dane was now forced to kill Dane : 'From a safe distance, the Germans can stand and laugh, and smile broadly, becuase they have succeeded in making the wise Danish Government place

Danish men in the most exposed posts.'[65] During June, the Danish section could report with some satisfaction that more and more Danish workers were refusing to serve as factory guards and that the Copenhagen courts were imposing heavier fines on those who refused.[66] This was exactly the situation which the B.B.C. had envisaged : 'British propaganda can fairly claim a share of the credit for the failure of Scavenius' sabotage guard policy.'[67] It was in fact, as Terkelsen hoped, the Danish workers' disinclination that caused the failure of this scheme. Thus, the B.B.C.'s methods of stimulating Danish unrest were both direct and indirect.

The attack on sabotage guards could be classed as part of the indirect attack. Similarly, the argument that sabotage was in the interest of Denmark's economic future after the war was another propaganda attack which could be classed as indirect. Rodney Gallop joined this propaganda attack aimed at appealing to Denmark's economic self-interest. He said that there was a likelihood of the paucity of raw materials after the war, and that nations would receive material aid, and indeed protection, according to whether they had earned it or not. This although effective as propaganda, was a form of economic blackmail.[68]

Another indirect but effective form of attack from Britain was to describe what had happened to the legal system in Denmark since the German occupation. In the words of Sten Gudme :

> Gradually the Germans now began to corrupt the Danish judicial system ...
>
> The first with a civilized country's administration of justice was the enactment of a penal law having retroactive effect ... This was a typical example of the Germans' behaviour in Denmark ... the Germans were ... foisting on the country a law which meant a definite breach of the principles of Danish administration of justice, but which they thought necessary because of the steadily growing resistance and unrest among the people.[69]

A man could, by this law, be imprisoned for acts which when they were committed, were not even crimes. In May 1943, Terkelsen pointed out that nobody should believe the minister of Justice who said : 'We must at all costs keep the administration of Justice in Danish hands.' This was complete fiction.[70]

The propaganda attack by Britain during the first part of 1943 was highly impressive. Further, the B.B.C. broadcasts by giving full publicity to all acts of Danish sabotage, gave the impression that sections of the Danish population had already taken up the battle in earnest. There is great excitement in being noticed, and the B.B.C. made Denmark as a nation, and the world at large, sit up and take notice. Something real was at last happening in Denmark. The eyes of the world were on Denmark. The Danish people were intoxicated, as it were, and contributed still more.[71]

Rodney Gallop warned the more cautious and timid Danes 'to make up their minds now to make all necessary sacrifices at the right moment.'[72] He also reminded listeners of the 'blacklist' of collaborators and traitors.

By August, Britain was in high spirits in the fond hope that Denmark would at last show its hand openly. Gallop explained over the B.B.C. that Britain had of necessity to restrain sabotage in some countries, but that this did not apply to Denmark. His concluding words were : 'This does not mean that we want you to take undue risks, but that we think you can now do more without taking undue risks.'[73]

The amount of unrest that was passing through Denmark could be perceived by the number of sabotage actions, going up to six or seven daily. This unrest passed through the population, and particularly from the factories into the open streets. The German retaliatory measures led to the beginning of a virtual reign of terror.

The mood of the people manifested itself in a number of strikes throughout the country. They served a useful purpose in demonstrating Danish unity and in giving all classes a feeling that in this situation they could depend on one another. A typical case was the general strike in Esbjerg, Jutland's largest west coast port. The general strike was hundred per cent effective. Similar strikes broke out in Aalborg, Odense, Kolding–almost every large town in Denmark had its general strike to protest against some German outrage. When the final German ultimatum was presented on August 28, 'even Scavenius despite his lack of understanding of the mind of the common man, realized that public opinion would not allow him to give in.'[74] In the words of Irving Werstein : 'Instead of truckling further, the government declared itself dissolved and the charade of Danish independence was ended.'[75] T.M. Terkelsen states : 'The Government dispersed, while an ominous silence fell over the town with the night that separated the shattered German illusion of a 'Model Protectorate' from the hard realities of a nation in open conflict.'[76]

On August 29, 1943 listeners to the B.B.C. Home Service heard a detailed report on the three years of German occupation in Denmark. It said : 'After three years of Hitler's new order, the whole of Denmark has today had to be put under a form of martial law by the Germans.[77]

As Jeremy Bennett observes :

> The members of the Danish Section of the B.B.C. could look with satisfaction over their past three years' work. By continual broadcasting, they had helped the Danish population to see that the government stood for nothing. By their emphasis on sabotage and unrest in 1943, they had encouraged the Danish population to force the issue. The result was the collapse of the Danish Government, which was what the section had always hoped for. The broadcasts from London did not, by themselves, force the German ultimatum and the resulting collapse of the government. They had helped to bring the Danish population to such a pitch that the failure of the government and of its policy was the logical conclusion to Danish unrest.[78]

Evidence of the effect of British radio on events in Denmark can be found in the pages of *Faedrelandet*, the Danish Nazi newspaper, during 1943. *Faedrelandet* declared that London was greatly responsible for much of the sabotage carried out in Denmark. 'The true originator (of sabotage) is the London Radio over which Christmas Moeller and other escaped Danes daily say that it is a *Holger Danske*[79] deed to sabotage the Germans to the utmost.'[80] 'Radio has proved a dangerous weapon', wrote *Faedrelandet*.[81] This was the clearest evidence of the success of the B.B.C.'s policy since April 1940. It had become an enemy to be reckoned with.[82]

V

From August 29, onwards the Danish section of the B.B.C. was able to carry the war openly into the enemy's camp without being encumbered with the extreme political difficulties caused by the existence of a Danish government.[83] However, the events of October 1943 also produced a political vacuum in Denmark. The situation was confused in the extreme. The position had simplified somewhat since the fall of the government, but the lack of any kind of leadership clearly worried those concerned with policy towards Denmark.

The answer to the problem of who should lead the Danish resistance was found in the Freedom Council. 'A group of illegal leaders–seven in all–met and constituted the Council, Muus as representative of S.O.E. being a member of the Council, thus forming a link to the Western Allies.'[84] says Haestrup.

Anonymously, the Council appealed to the people, gave general guidance and took upon itself to act as leaders of resistance where all leadership otherwise had come to an end.

The Freedom Council did not receive the support of the B.B.C. until October 31–it was founded on September 16, 1943. For this delay in giving important publicity over the radio to the Freedom Council, the Danish section of the B.B.C. cannot be blamed. This was a major decision of policy which was also the concern of the foreign office and of P.W.E.[85]

Clearly, any new development in Denmark required a certain amount of time for consideration by the foreign office. It was natural for it know what the Freedom Council stood for, before it approved British support over the B.B.C. The foreign office had to think, too, of long-term policy. The Freedom Council had no constitutional right to exercise authority in Denmark. However, very often realities are more important than formalities. Strategic necessity demanded that resistance activities were coordinated, not only inside Denmark but also between Denmark and the Allies.[86]

On October 31, Christmas Moeller was allowed to welcome the setting up of the Freedom Council over the B.B.C.[87] From this time onwards the support of the B.B.C. became a very valuable contribution to the effective control of Danish resistance by the Freedom Council.

In the winter of 1943–44 the question of Denmark's formal position towards the Allies was brought up. It was a Danish wish to be considered and Allied nation. Behind that wish lay interests as well as feelings. However, the question of an acknowledgement of Denmark as an Allied nation was not an easy one. Denmark had never declared war on Germany and no legal body existed which could now take such a step. From a strictly formal point of view, Denmark could hardly be considered an Allied nation.

There is evidence to show that the position of Denmark was being reviewed by the foreign office during November and December 1943. There were strong foreign office reactions to a B.B.C. Danish broadcast on December 7, 1943. The broadcast entitled 'North Sea Powers', began with the words : 'Denmark was today recognized as an Ally in speeches by British ministers of the Crown, and representatives of Norway, Holland and Belgium, at a function held in London ... in honour of King Haakon of Norway and honoured guests from the North Sea Powers, Great Britain, Norway, Denmark, Holland and Belgium.[88]

This statement was incorrect. As a result of this broadcast, the Controller of the B.B.C European Services received a complaint from the foreign office.[89] Despite this reprehension from the foreign office, there was at this time some new consideration of policy towards Denmark. Gradually its position had improved and especially so after August 1943, the Danish contribution to the allied cause was generally acknowledged. Free Danes abroad and resistance at home for a long time, showed that the Danes were practically at war with Germany. The foreign office was convinced that Denmark should be accepted as a fighting ally. In early 1944, the Danish section of S.O.E. worked hard to obtain a solution.[90] It prepared the provisional text for a declaration on Denmark's position by the three powers, Britain, U.S.A. and Russia. It said :

> The Governments of Great Britain, the United States of America and the U.S.S.R. recognize ... that the Danish nation has placed itself side by side with the United Nations and like them, is determined to contribute to the common struggle for Victory over Hitlerism and for the attainment of the aims of the Atlantic Charter.[91]

The declaration avoided using the terms 'associated' or 'allied' about Denmark, yet it was an acceptance by the Allies of the fact that Denmark fought with them against the Germans. Britain and the U.S.A. agreed on the text initially; it only remained for the third party, Russia, to give its approval.[92]

At this point, because of Russian disagreement, the whole scheme fizzled out. Russia was only prepared to acknowledge the resistance movement and the Council as its head and was not inclined to quit the past, 'an attitude which could not be surprising.'[93] The fact that Russia had recognized 'Fighting Denmark' and had received its representative. Thomas Dossing, in Moscow did not mean that the Danish policy of 1941 was forgotten and this answer was final.

There the matter had to rest. Thus, the British-American attempt to solve the Danish problem at one stroke was stranded. So far the two powers restricted themselves to two separate declarations of July 12, 1944, given by the two ministers for foreign affairs. Both declarations emphasized the fact that Danes both at home and abroad now actually fought alongside the people in the United Nations and mentioned the fact that, as there was no Danish Government, the country could not formally enter the United Nations. The British declaration stressed the importance of the Freedom Council and acknowledged expressively its work.[94] The British position, as stated by Anthony Eden in the House of Commons, was somewhere between the position adopted by the Americans and the Russians. There was clearly in his mind, as in the Russians', a sharp division between 'official' Denmark and 'fighting' Denmark. This remained the British attitude throughout the war, and it seems that the Russian posture was responsible for influencing British policy.[95]

In the circumstances, limited recognition was all that Denmark could expect. For both legal and diplomatic reasons, the British government could not recognize the Freedom Council as an allied government.

Formal recognition as an ally had to wait until Denmark was invited to take part in the San Francisco Conference in 1945 where the Allied nations met to constitute the United Nations. On that day was achieved what the resistance had hoped and fought for and what Christmas Moeller had defined as the ultimate goal : To change Denmark's position from that of an occupied to that of an allied nation.

VI

The *Standing Directive for Psychological Warfare*[96] made clear that Sykewar was not confined to 'nothing but' the truth, by restricting its instructions to overt propaganda. The rule of accurate reporting which prohibited deviation from the truth in statements that could be verified, had to be strictly observed in overt or 'white' Sykewar. No such restriction was placed upon the covert 'gray' and 'black' forms of Sykewar output. '"Gray" propaganda, which omitted all mention of source', states Daniel Lerner, 'specialized precisely in *not* telling 'the whole' truth. 'Black' Sykewar, which identified itself by a false source, may be viewed as, in the last analysis, a speciality in telling 'anything but' the truth.' The theory was that by leading this double life, Sykewar could carry on like a wanton woman in covert forms, while protecting the good name of S.H.A.E.F. (Supreme Headquarters of Allied Expeditionary Force) in 'white' output.[97]

Although the B.B.C. was during the war, as it is today, an independent corporate body, it was also in wartime a part of foreign policy. The broadcasts to Denmark–as well as to other European countries–were the chief means of spreading British propaganda abroad. This was recognized by the government.

Yet the fight against the Nazis was partly a fight for the mind. It was also a propaganda war against both the enemy and the neutrals. Psychological warfare was aimed at influencing the mind, and sometimes the nerves. The Nazis used every technique possible in this battle. The British Government felt that it could not adopt similar techniques officially, and yet the realists amongst the British propagandists felt that Britain could not enter the propaganda fight handicapped with one arm bound. The solution was found in black propaganda.

During the war the public was not allowed to know anything about black or gray propananda. Not only was the work secret, it was not even acknowledged by the government. The government was not responsible for it, and yet it was carried out by a government department.

Black propaganda was Britain's unofficial answer to all Goebbels' techniques. It gave more extreme and detailed broadcasts than the B.B.C. could. 'Radio Denmark', as the secret station broadcasting from Britain to Denmark was called, was involved in a lighter shade of black propaganda than, for example, *Soldatensender Calais*.' It, however, interfered in Danish internal politics more than the B.B.C. could, and it spoke with a voice for which the British Government had no official responsibility.[98]

Sefton Delmer, in his book entitled *Black Boomerang*, writes : 'Trickery and deception ... were tasks which lay outside what it was possible or desirable for the B.B.C. to undertake. A new weapon of psychological warfare was needed for this purpose.'[99]

Delmer compared the virtue of black and white propaganda. he wrote this book with particular reference of propaganda to Germany. His view that black propaganda was in many ways more effective than the B.B.C. broadcasts, was not applicable to Denmark. The reason for this was simply that Denmark never became a theatre of war and, therefore, there was never any necessity for propaganda to be coordinated with military operations to such an extent as in France and Germany. In the words of Bennett :

> The B.B.C. provided first and foremost a news service, and news had to be accurate. The B.B.C. could not therefore allow itself to be subjected to the will of a service ministry as a propaganda tool, for some short term advantage, which might in the end prejudice the reputation for accuracy which it had gradually built up.[100]

'In broadcasting to Denmark', continues the same authority, 'the independence of the B.B.C. was the most vitally important factor, and it was in countries such as Denmark and Norway that the B.B.C. made its greatest impact.' From this it follows that the B.B.C. broadcasts were more important to those countries which were not combat areas, because the competition from black propaganda was less, and the B.B.C. was subject to less pressure from Britain's military strategists. B.B.C. broadcasts could be used for operational purposes to a limited extent only. At no time during the war was black propaganda ever as important to Denmark as the B.B.C. broadcasts.[101]

The news service exercised complete control of programme content, but in policy making it was not independent of the foreign office. This control by the foreign office of the Danish section was maintained throughout the war. Policy control of the Danish section was probably greater than over other European sections of the B.B.C., as Bennett observes, because of Denmark's intricate political status after the German occupation. However, a certain amount of flexibility was allowed to the section within the terms of the directives.[102]

It seems that the Danish section of the B.B.C. reflected as correct a picture as it is possible to obtain, of British foreign policy towards Denmark during the Second World War.

At no time during the war could it be claimed that the B.B.C. broadcasts *created* an atmosphere of unrest which directly led to action. Propagnda is rarely the direct cause of action. It is most effective as a probe when events testify that a tense and inflammable situation exists. Denmark was no exception to this general rule.

The B.B.C., nevertheless, can claim that its broadcasts supported active resistance by exciting any unrest that existed.

It put salt into Danish wounds. Referring to the Copenhagen riots of November 1941, Christmas Moeller admitted that, although the outburst was a genuine expression of Danish feelings, the effect of the rioting was augmented by broadcasts from London.

'The broadcasts during the summer of 1943', as Bennett states, 'showed the B.B.C.'s propaganda at its best.'[103] There were several factors involved, but the news service could reasonably claim a share of the credit for encouraging the Danish resistance precipitate the crisis of August 1943.

The B.B.C. could never insist on having played more than a minor role in the success of that enormous organization which was the terrific Danish resistance by 1945. To be a member of that resistance movement required a spontaneous decision on the part of each individual, and that decision meant real sacrifice, possibly death. The Danish section realized that this decision had to be made by each individual. The B.B.C. could not make this decision. It could only foster and fortify it, once it was made.

NOTES AND REFERENCES

1. Edwin Muller, 'Waging War with Words', *Current History*, August, 1939, p.24.
2. Scrolls and pamphlets were easily discovered and confiscated.
3. 'Pre-war motto of the British Broadcasting Corporation': Charles J. Rolo, *Radio Goes to War:The Fourth Front* (New York : G.P. Putnam's Sons, 1942), n. 6, p.33.
4. 'And' it may be added, 'direct interference by "jamming" — that is, broadcasting loud, raucous noises or "artificial static" over the wavelength used by the enemy–though widely resorted to by the Nazis, is at best a makeshift and highly unreliable form of defence against radio propaganda. ... It immobilizes the "jamming" transmitter ... In addition, "jamming" may produce a "dead" zone followed by a zone of normal reception a few hundred feet away.' Broadcast words have further advantages over their printed rivals. Lost in a flash on the ether, they are not subject to reconsideration or critical scrutiny. The can, at will, be used to initiate, supplement, or round up action in other fields.' ... Ibid, p. 34.

5. 'Psychological Warfare is one of the magic phrases in current parlance. A study of its use in World War II is beset by temptations to dramatize, for the subject suggests moods appropriate to Greek tragedy', Daniel Lerner, *Sykewar : Psychological Warfare against Germany, D-Day to VE-Day* (New York : George W. Stewart Publisher, Inc. 1949) pp. 1–2.
6. Ibid, p. 8.
7. Hans Speier, 'Morale and propaganda', In : *War in our Time.* Hans Speier and Alfred Kahler (eds.) (New York : W.W. Norton and Co., Inc. 1939) pp. 300–03.
8. Sten Gudme states : 'During the last war, Scavenius, who was then Foreign Minister also, succeeded, by the exercise of great ingenuity and dexterity in keeping Denmark out–and even then he would not have done so had England not been so long suffering ... "Erick Scavenius, who was of course not Foreign Minister at the beginning of this war, did not judge the situation so optimistically now : difficulties were greater, and Germany even more brutal and inconsiderate than in the last war.' 'Hitler's war against Europe killed the small States', hope that it was enough to be neutral in this world's settlement of life's ideals', Sten Gudme, Denmark : 'Hitler's Model Protectorate', trans. from the Danish by Jan Noble (London : Victor Gollancz Ltd., 1942), pp. 155, 160.
9. Paul Palmer. *Denmark in Nazi Chains* (W.C. 2 : Lindsey Drummond, 1942), p. 13. In the words of Sten Gudme : 'A thousand years of history, sometimes in greatness and splendour, sometimes in poverty and need, but always in freedom, were wiped out in a single night', Gudme, op.cit, p. 7.
10. T.M. Terkelsen. *Front Line in Denmark* (London : Free Danish Publishing Co., 1944), pp. 9–10.
11. It ran thus : 'For the second time Denmark has been brutally invaded by Germany. The British people have received the news with deep indignation and wish to send to the Danish people a message of warm sympathy. This event has strengthened the British resolve to pursue the war until the nations of Europe are liberated from the menace of Prussian aggression' : cited by Jeremy Bennett, *British Broadcasting and the Danish Resistance Movement 1940–1945* (Cambridge University Press, 1966), p. 1.
12. The *Citizen* Newspaper, (Gloucester January 31, 1944) cited by Ibid, n. 2, p. 3.

13. Rolo, op.cit, p. 156.
14. 'The B.B.C. had earlier in the war given instructions to Danish listeners on how to avoid German jamming. They were told to construct aerials of a special type which would defeat German counter-measures. It was reported that as a result 'thousands of Danes can now hear every word' Bennett, op.cit, p. 3.
15. Ibid, p.4; Vide also Palmer, op.cit, p. 88.
16. Bennett, Ibid, pp. 4–5.
17. Rolo, op.cit, p. 158–59. 'In occupied Europe the B.B.C. broke the German blockade on truthful news, and brought new hope and new moral strength to the oppressed nations'. T.O. Beachcroft, *British Broadcasting* (London : Longman Green and Co., 1946), p. 24.
18. Daniel Lerner points out : 'A strategy of truth ... is not synonymous with honesty .... The word to be emphasized, in the first instance is not "truth" but "strategy", for truth in propaganda is a function of effectiveness ... Propagandists do not decide to tell the truth because they personally are honest, any more than they decide to tell lies because they are dishonest. Given a particular audience to be reached with a particular policy, the basis for decision is an estimate of what will work', op.cit, p. 26.
19. Rolo, op.cit, 'The British broadcasts are more deadly than steel', said the German authorities in 1942. Beachcroft, op.cit, p. 8.
20. Palmer, op.cit, p. 88.
21. Bennett, op.cit, n. 1, p. 8.
22. 'Of course there were mistakes, but these were admitted faults and no part of a false intention'. Beachcroft, op.cit, p. 38.
23. Ibid, p. 39. Henning Krabbe writes : 'On leaving Britain to settle in my own country, Denmark, after seven years, I want to express my gratitude to the British Broadcasting Corporation, that great institution where I had the privilege of working during the war. In all occupied Europe the B.B.C. gave hope during the years of tyranny and strengthened resistance to the common enemy. It also gave expression to that common sense, tolerance and humanity which constitute the only hope of the future of mankind' (London : July, 1946) Henning Krabbe (ed.), *Voices from Britain : Broadcast History* (London : George Allen and Unwin Ltd., 1947), p. 200.
24. Joerge Haestrup 'Denmark's Connection with the Allied Powers during the occupation' In : *European Resistance*

Movements 1939–45 (New York : The Macmillan Co., 1964), p. 282.

25. Bennett, op.cit, pp. 11–13.
26. Ibid, p. 25–26. 'In July 1940 ... the notoriously pro-German Scavenius was made Foreign Minister ... Scavenius's first act was to issue immediately (July 8, 1940) a "declaration" in favour of Danish-German collaboration ... a gesture which made later attempts to deny the validity of German claims very much more difficult. "It was not surprising that this should provide the prelude to a series of concessions, which whether major or minor, were none the less damaging to Danish self-esteem" : Viscount Chilston, "The Occupied Countries in Western Europe". In : *Survey of International Affairs 1939–1946 : Hitler's Europe,* Arnold Toynbee and Veronica M. Toynbee (eds.) (London : Oxford Univ. Press, 1954), p. 521.
27. Editor was B.B.C. terminology for the leader of one of the regional sections of the European Service. On May 28, 1940 Robert Jorgensen was appointed editor of the Danish section of the B.B.C. He remained at the head of the Danish section until the end of the war. Bennett. op.cit, p. 9.
28. To maintain contact with all the regional sections, the director of European broadcasts N.F. Newsome, held meetings twice daily ... in his office, where all the editors of the various sections were present. As a result of these meetings, a general directive was issued each day to the editors, giving news of general importance and showing how the news should be treated' : Ibid, p. 27.
29. Ibid, p. 29.
30. Chilston, op.cit, p. 522.
31. Henning Krabbe, a member of the Danish section of the B.B.C., told Jeremy Bennett that 'one of his main tasks in 1940–41 was to assemble material on the activities of other European Resistance Movements, so that stories about them could be broadcast in Danish'. Bennett, op.cit, n. 2, p.31 vide also supra n. 3, p. 7.
32. Confirmed by Robert Jorgensen in an interview with Jeremy Bennett, Ibid, p.31 also n. 3.
33. 'Leif Gundel in an interview' with Bennett : cited by Ibid, p. 32.
34. Ibid, p. 32.
35. 'B.B.C. Archives' cited by Ibid, p. 33.

36. 'This is evident from a report produced every month by the B.B.C. Intelligence section intended as a survey of the European audiences'. Ibid, p. 35.
37. Ibid, pp. 35–37.
38. 'When the history of the war is written it seems likely that the "V" campaign will appear as something more than a propaganda stunt. It has certainly done much to make the people of occupied countries conscious of their national and international solidarity' : Rolo, op.cit, pp. 172–81. Vide Beachcroft. op.cit, pp. 36–37.
39. Krabbe, 'Voices from Britain' op.cit, p. 93.
40. 'On July 14, 1941, it was reported in the *Daily Telegraph* that the Germans were taking stern measures in Denmark to repress the "V" sign'. Bennett, op.cit, n.1, p. 41.
41. Ibid, p. 42.
42. 'The "V" sign was a most dramatic signal that the audience was there, that the battle of ideas had already been partly won in the teeth of German occupation. The Germans, even at the height of their victorious period, were alarmed; so alarmed that they made a determined effort to capture the "V" symbol for themselves. The effort failed'. Beachcroft, op.cit, p. 37.
43. 'If sabotage was called for too early over the Radio, before either S.O.E. was ready to send in equipment and men to help with such operations, then pointless bloodshed and the death of patriots would be the result. There is evidence that the B.B.C. was fully aware of this possible danger, and of the necessity for co-ordinating, its broadcasting policy with that of S.O.E.' Bennett, op.cit, p. 43.
44. Ibid, pp. 47, 49.
45. A general directive to the B.B.C. European Services from the Political Intelligence Department, dated August 13, 1941, headed 'Sabotage' read : 'The Pan-Slav Conference in Moscow has ended with a rousing call to the whole of Europe to indulge in widespred sabotage ... We ourselves are not making appeals for sabotage ... We should be extremely discreet in using anyone else's appeals for sabotage. We should report any event like the Pan-Slav Conference quite objectively and not in a rousing manner. We should report, with discretion, sabotage that is actually taking place. Much hangs on the word, "discretion" but the foregoing will perhaps indicate what is meant. It is important too that we should not give too many details of sabotage that is being carried out' 'Danish

Archives' cited by Ibid, p. 49.
46. Ibid, p. 50.
47. Chilston, op.cit, p. 522.
48. Bennett, op.cit, p. 53.
49. 'Report, January 1942', cited by Ibid, p. 55.
50. This view that the B.B.C. Danish broadcasts had influenced events in Denmark during November was later supported by a report on propaganda. The report dated May 20, 1942 spoke of the November events as : 'At the time of the Anti-Comintern Pact when active propaganda was directed to Denmark from London, the broadcasts may have increased the weight of the demonstrations but they would almost certainly have occurred even if the B.B.C. had been non-existent. But asked whether the transmissions were useful, the reply must be very much so. They supplied the demonstrating youth with ... an encouragement because the youth felt that their actions were being appreciated'. 'Danish Archives' cited by Ibid, p. 55.
51. Ibid, pp. 64–67 : for details vide pp. 58–82.
52. 'To what extent the well-known telegram episode is a frame-up is not yet clear, but dark forces may have been at work'. Terkelsen, op.cit, p. 15.
53. The view to avoid aggressive broadcasting 'was surprisingly supported by the B.B.C. Intelligence section, and it suggests that there were internal conflicts and differences of opinion within the B.B.C. itself'. Ibid, p. 94, for details vide pp. 83–94.
54. Ibid, pp. 83–94.
55. 'Robert Jorgensen confirmed in an interview that it was part of the B.B.C.'s policy to mention the king frequently in broadcasts, in the hope that Danish patriotic feeling would be stirred. For example the general directive from the Director of European Broadcasts for the October 13 read : 'Feature Nazi attacks on King Christian'. Ibid, n. 1, p.96 vide also Gudme, op.cit, pp. 114–20.
56. 'B.B.C. Archives' : talk, January 9, 1943 : cited by Bennett, Ibid, p. 97.
57. Ibid, p. 98.
58. Ibid, p. 102.
59. 'B.B.C. Archives', Ibid, p. 104.
60. Ibid, p. 105.
61. Ibid, p. 106.
62. 'The general directive from the Director of the B.B.C.'s European Broadcasts read, on March 24, 1943 : "In this

connection, too, the Danish Election results, a defeat for the Nazis and the Scavenius collaborationist party, are of great interest-one small state votes against the Statute of Europe". Ibid, n. 5, p. 107.

63. Terkelsen, op.cit, p.18 : 'Danish feelings had hardened to such an extent that the peaceful, freedom–loving population had been transformed into a determined block. A series of general strikes swept the country, and German Government circles in Berlin began to show themselves restive–events in Denmark were heading for a showdown'. Ibid. In the words of Irving Werstein' 'Seldom was any nation so united in its opposition to the enemy', *That Denmark Might Live : The Saga of the Danish Resistance in World War II* (Philadelphia : Macrae Smith Co., 1967), p. 10.
64. 'B.B.C. talk by E. Blytgen–Petersen January 4, 1943. (B.B.C. Archives), Bennett, op.cit., pp. 113–14.
65. B.B.C. talk by T.M. Terkelsen, May 31, 1943 (B.B.C. Archives), Ibid, p. 114.
66. B.B.C. talk by T.M. Terkelsen, June 14, 1943, Ibid, p. 115.
67. Ibid, p. 115.
68. Ibid, p. 116–17.
69. Gudme, op.cit., pp. 64–65 : retroactive law was passed on January 17, 1941.
70. 'B.B.C. talk by T.M. Terkelsen, May 12, 1943 (B.B.C. Archives), Bennett, op.cit., pp. 117–18.
71. Ibid, p. 118.
72. 'B.B.C. talk by Rodney Gallop, June 20, 1943 (B.B.C. Archives), Ibid, p. 120.
73. B.B.C. talk by Rodney Gallop, August 5, 1943, Ibid, p. 121.
74. Terkelsen, op.cit., (Front Line in Denmark), p. 19.
75. Werstein, op.cit., p. 9.
76. Terkelsen, op.cit., p. 20.
77. Bennett, op.cit., pp. 124–25.
78. Ibid, p. 126.
79. 'It was said that Holger the Dane would always rise from the past to help Denmark in its hour of need. 'One well-known resistance group took its name from Holger Danske'. Ibid, n. 1, p. 136.
80. Ibid, p. 137.
81. '*Faedrelandet*, August 23, 1943', cited by Ibid, p. 139.
82. Ibid, p. 139.
83. 'The general directive from the director of the B.B.C.'s European

Broadcasts for September 17, 1943 showed that the B.B.C.'s task was easier now that there was no Danish government'. Ibid, n. 1, p. 127.

84. Haestrup, op.cit., p. 292.
85. Bennett, op.cit., p. 143.
86. Haestrup, op.cit, pp. 292–93.
87. 'B.B.C. talk by Christmas Moeller, December 31, 1943 (B.B.C. Archives and Danish Archives), Bennett, op.cit, p. 145.
88. B.B.C. talk dated December 7, 1943 (Danish Archives) Ibid, p. 149.
89. Ibid, pp. 149–50.
90. Haestrup, op.cit., p. 294.
91. 'Text quoted in Hemmelig Alliance, Vol. 1, Ch. 9, Bennett, op.cit, p. 150.
92. Ibid, pp. 150–51.
93. Haestrup, op.cit., p. 295.
94. Ibid, p. 295.
95. Bennett, op.cit., p. 152.
96. The Standing Directive for Psychological Warfare Against Members of the German Armed Forces (June 1944), 'section 4' : This was the basic statement of Sykewar policy, and is reproduced in full as an appendix to Daniel Lerner's Sykewar, op.cit., pp. 403–17.
97. Ibid, p. 27.
98. Bennett, op.cit., p. 221.
99. Sefton Delmer, *Black Boomerang* (New York : The Viking Press, 1962), p. 32.
100. Bennett, op.cit, p. 245. 'To give hard, correct information was the aim of the B.B.C. broadcasts to Denmark'. Ibid, p. 252.
101. Ibid, pp. 245–46.
102. Ibid, pp. 247–49.
103. Ibid, pp. 253–54.

Chapter 14

The Birth of New Europe*

A STUDY IN EUROPEAN CONSCIOUSNESS : TWO DECADES AFTER THE WAR

Like its predecessor, World War II bequeathed to its survivors more problems than it settled–except that this time there was a quantum jump. Towards the end of the war, Alfred Weber, the eminent German sociologist, finished a work which in its English translation carried the grim title, *Farewell to European History*.[1] He wrote what was in effect Europe's epitaph : Thanks to 'her unique dynamism she has been the mistress of the earth ever since A.D. 1500 and has made it dependent on her–something that Greece was never able to do in the small Mediterranean area.'[2] Weber's principal thesis however, was less gloomy than his title for his concern was largely with the future of European civilization.

The book expressed a sentiment that was increasingly felt after 1945. Europe's persistent refusal to admit the validity of any theory that questioned her capacity to survive with dignity in a world dominated by Soviet and American power, made the earlier alarms about inevitable European decline untenable.[3] Such confidence could not have been possible without definite economic and social gains; these, indeed, came with astonishing frequency after 1950.[4] In almost every phase of life, Europe

* The term 'the New Europe' was made familiar by George Lichtheim, *The New Europe—Today and Tomorrow*. (New York: Praeger, 1963).

manifested a vitality greater than what was once presumed possible. While Europeans remained incredulous of the roseate views of those who prophesied a great new age, they were truly excited by the stirrings within their world and curious about what they might betoken.[5] The immediate postwar pessimism was clearly outmoded; so, also, were the various forms of optimism that unleashed immediately after the liberation.[6] Both were replaced by an absorbing preoccupation with immediate and overwhelming problems. There was little interest or faith in long-range prophecies.

In the general optimism that prevailed it was easy to imagine that Europe was changing so rapidly that she would soon cease to be like her old self. The vocabulary of the twentieth century shows a softness to the idea of 'revolution', with all its promise of new beginnings. Men tended to magnify the importance of individual events, attributing to essentially parochial developments a universal significance.[7] After 1962, when, for example, De Gaulle's actions gave serious cause for offense, an importance was attributed to them which must have puzzled even the French President. He appeared to stand between Europe and the possibility of effective political union. The loss resulting from Great Britain's exclusion from the Common Market was mentioned in bold letters : there was an attempt to keep the illusion that Europe stood at an important crossroad, confronted with major options, on the resolution of which her future depended. This was a time of talk about a so called 'inward-looking Europe', a particularly dangerous possibility at least to those who invented the term.[8]

Luckily, however, it is not the only interpretation of the contemporary European scene. Let us recall the views of the great nineteenth century French historian, Alexis de Tocqueville who argues that change, while always difficult to effect, does in fact occur, but that even in revolutionary situations it is rarely complete. De Tocqueville's method reminds us to beware of thinking too exclusively in terms of 'decline and fall.' Both, no doubt, occur, but less frequently than is sometimes presumed. It is worthwhile not to lose sight of de Tocqueville's approach for our own analysis of contemporary Europe.[9]

The conception of a 'new Europe' cannot be interpreted too literally. It would be preposterous to write about Europe as if her history began at the moment when Hitler lay dead in his Berlin bunker. To shut our eyes to Europe's past and dwell wholly on the present is to believe that change is easy, that Europe is capable to adjust quickly to any form. As a matter of fact, historical changes are evolutionary. Europe is today the product of many influences, not the least significant being those which ensue from experiences having little to do with the twentieth century. To argue this is not to belittle the importance of recent changes.

Europe! The continent of paradox! Her civilization has become the world civilization; at the same time her expansion is over. Her world rule has collapsed, she may be destroyed from the outside; at the same time she is turning inward, confronting herself. She is still the historical continent, her history is the most important part of the history of the world; the states and even the people of Europe may no longer be the principal actors, but Europe still is the principal theatre of history. The centre of the cold war has been Europe and the centre of Europe is Germany. Such a statement does not merely refer to a condition of world strategy: it states a condition whereby, for example, West and East Germany are more important factors in the present history of the world than, say, India or Indonesia–ancient and enormous Asian states ten or twenty times larger than Germany, in size and in population.

> The reasons for this extraordinary condition are complex ones: neither geography nor economics can explain them : they involve phenomena of quality rather than quantity : they are involved with certain qualities which are still attributed to the peoples of Europe : thus they involve the power of prestige even more than the prestige of power, conditions of thinking even more than conditions of productivity ... Conditions of thinking : another reason for Europe being the historical continent par excellence. Europe is the continent of historical consciousness.[10]

Europe is the continent of historical thinking. To be European is inseparable from a historical experience. No definition of Europe will do and it is not merely that the edges are ambiguous. It is that the definition of Europe cannot be stationary. There have been 'successive changes of emphasis in the historical development of the idea of Europe, from a religious through a cultural idea; but the very form of idea is involved with it; the historical development of the idea of Europe is the idea of Europe'[11]

Michelet had observed in 1845 : 'Whatever is the least simple, the least natural, the most artificial, meaning the least fatal, the most human, the freest–that is Europe.'[12]

One hundred years later in 1948, Carlo Morandi said : 'The concept of Europe escapes every definition : Europe is, however, a historical formation, a living expression of spiritual and moral, political and social, realities concentrating there, in different forms, through a long succession of centuries.'[13] Gonzague de Reynold stated in 1951 that 'Europe is a historical organism, which means something that is much more than a continent ... The problem of Europe, for us, is a historical problem.'[14] According to Federico Chabod : It is 'a Europe which we have felt to be distinct from other parts of the globe because of certain definite characteristics of thinking and of action ... through traditions, memories, aspirations... . Europe which forms an entity ... an historical individuality... .'[15] (1961). Otto Brunner has observed : 'The origin of historical thinking is European; it is a western achievement. A very great achievement; but it has its own dangers, too. Yet the great spiritual movements of Europe were never without their dangers. They have been challenged. We cannot avoid them; we must face them.'[16] (1956).

The difference between the first and the last four statements, a century apart, is noteworthy. They mark the evolution of European consciousness in a historical and existential direction.

This historical consciousness produced the recognitions in minds such as Oswald Spengler's[17], or Paul Valery's, in the early decades of the twentieth century. In the gloomy year of

1919, Paul Valery wrote : 'Will Europe become what it is in reality–that is, a little promontory on the continent of Asia? Or will it remain what it seems, that is, the elect portion of the terrestrial globe, the pearl of the sphere, the brain of a vast body?'[18] The 'what it seems' and the 'what it is in reality' are absolutely interchangeable : one could say, with equal reason and justice, that Europe 'seems' to be a little promontory of Asia. Second, if Europe is to survive, her function is no longer that of 'the elect portion of the terrestrial globe', no longer the incaranation of the brain but, rather, of historical thinking which may amount not so much to something old but to something new, to post-scientific thinking.[19]

But will she survive? According to John Lukacs, there are several dangers facing Europe in the foreseeable future :

> First, she may be entirely destroyed at some future date, in a horrible atomic war, provoked by Europeans. Second, she may be destroyed by some new kind of inadvertent pestilence loosened upon the world by science–including the possibility that her air may be poisoned by an atomic war fought by distant world-powers. Third, she may be conquered by Russia. Fourth, she may be subjugated by the masses of Asia, by China. Fifth, her will to live may be fatally affected by the experiences of yet another of her self-imposed tyrannies. I have listed these dangers in what seems to be their decreasing order or probability ... now.[20]
> 'It is, of course, also possible that in the future, "Europe" and "European" may become meaningless attributes, again merely geographical designations–if Europe dissolves, merging into a vast and unitary world civilization. This is what most professional experts on international relations .... now foresee. I believe, instead, that the meaning of "Europe" and of "European" will crystallize further; and I see the prospect of a single, unitary, homogeneous world culture so far away that I cannot visualize it at all, except on a very theoretical and very abstract (and, therefore, unhistorical and unrealistic) plane of my mind.'[21]

What is the relationship of the European mind to the rest of the world now, at the end of a great historical age? Lukacs puts it this way : the European mind has begun to enter a phase which is beyond political and mechanical categories.

In the words of Ernst Haas :

> The New Europe–is the future of that part of history which has also been aptly described as 'the end of ideology.' It owes so little to the visions of the Abbe de Saint-Pierre, of William Penn, of Immanuel Kant and of Victor Hugo that these oft-invoked precursors of the contemporary movement could scarcely be expected to recognize their brainchild.[22]

While many people of Asia and Africa are now only beginning to be acquainted with political ideologies, Europe (and to some extent also the United States) seems to have entered the post-ideological age. This is the existential, and historical, reaction of European peoples to the last wild period of political religiosity, from about 1895 to 1945.[23] In Europe, more than anywhere else, the political 'Isms' (including Communism) are, in reality, 'Wasms.' On both sides of the iron curtain Europe is in the post-communist (and also in the post-Nazi and post-Fascist) stage of her history.[24] She has outlived the phase during which faith in political ideologies replaced faith in religion. Europe has not yet outgrown all, or even most, of the infantile diseases of modernism, but she has survived–although at what cost:–the ravages of political ideologies.[25]

In the second place, the European mind seems to be moving away from the scientific phase of history, of the modern age which the peoples of Asia and Africa are now beginning to enter. Lukacs distinguishes between 'post-scientific' and 'anti-scientific' and insists that large portions of the world–including certain parts, peoples and problems of Europe, and perhaps especially the peoples of Latin America—must live through an 'American' phase before they become European.[26]

If Europe seems to be moving into a post-ideological age, into a post-scientific age, is she too, in the post-religious (and specifically, in the post-Christian) phase of her history? The answer is both in the affirmative and negative. Affirmative, because in Europe, and especially in some of the most advanced nations of Europe, faithful Christians are a small minority now. Negative, because Europe means 'a certain conception of human nature' which has a definite Christian ingredient.[27] In Continental Europe, the old warfare between science and religion is largely over. The inseparable gulf between them belongs to the nineteenth century: a rapport between Christians and atheists is now becoming possible in Europe through some of their common and existential recognitions of human problems and human nature.[28] While in the nineteenth century some of the best philosophers, writers, artists, and scientists of Europe were atheists or agnostics, so to say; by 1940 European anti-clericals such as Benedetto Croce would say : 'We are Christians, and we cannot be otherwise.'[29] Federico Chabod confirmed this and added, 'We cannot be non-Christians, even when we no longer follow the practices of the Christian religion, since Christianity has left ineradicable marks on our ways of feeling and thinking.'[30] Free will and original sin are now recognized by Europeans as undeniable realities of the human condition, and indeed, as part of the European patrimony; and it is exactly these two factors in the concept of human nature that are remote to the Asian mind.[31] The historical connections between European religiosity and European rationality have thus been rediscovered. Belief in freewill involves the quality of our determination to live.[32] The manifestations of this factor transcend religion.

'True culture', said the Hague Congress of European Unity in 1948, 'is not an ornament, not a mere luxury, or an ensemble of unique refinements which do not concern the average man. It is born of a growing awareness of life, of the perpetual need to deepen the meaning of existence and to increase the power of man over things.'[33] The power of man over things! man the measure of things; this conception of human nature is still the rather unique European conception.[34]

If Europe emerged from the war uncertain about the future, the reasons are not hard to find. Certainty in this situation would have been a form of hypocrisy. It was only gradually that the post-war European world began to discern what it might be required to contend with; where it stood. The loss of power was obvious. Just as the war bore only a flimsy similitude to the earlier one, so the post-war period quickly assumed a course quite different from what Europe had known in the 1920's and 1930's. To begin with, there was almost no nostalgia for the immediate past. No one thought of going back to 'the good old days before 1939.' No one deceived himself that they had been good.[35] A consciousness grew that Europe's situation was in certain respects markedly different from any she had known in the past, a fact made poignant by the hovering Soviet and American military forces. Europeans saw the continent riven by new and unnatural boundaries, typifying the accidents of war more than the circumstances of nationality, history or geography.[36] Dependent peoples in Asia and Africa revolted against their European tutelage, or made their intentions so clear that Europeans thought it wiser to quit gracefully. A structure of relations, assiduously built up through the eighteenth and nineteenth centuries seemed to dissolve as if it stood on sand. In this situation, there was sufficient reason for anxiety and even consternation. Curiously enough, neither developed to the extent that might have been predicated. The war itself had purged Europe of all fears, as it were.[37] So much had she suffered that a sort of immunity had emerged. Thus, wasting no time or tears, Europe concentrated on her massive immediate problems. It was as if an entire society wished to skip a generation, forget the shame of two wars, and even more, the disgrace of vacillation and injustice of the inter-war period, the true 'locust years' of the century.[38]

Europe had every reason to despair, but accepted none of them. The concept of a single European society, which had gone out of fashion in the second half of the nineteenth century, revived. But it was difficult to predict how far the resurgence of European sentiment would go, but there was no denying its reality. Economic cooperation might stop with the common market and never lead to political union, but the very fact that it had been raised in serious political debates throughout Europe, and that it had not been dismissed as visionary, is highly significant. Increasingly, the idea of Europe penetrated the rank and file; men might interpret the term differently, criticize it, but they refused to deny it. A consciousness of Europe, once the property of educated men, became a common possession.[39] The nations of western Europe seemed to be acquiring in their status of no longer being the principal actors in historical panorama, they would make their mark on the world by the steadiness and prosperity of their increasingly harmonious institutions. Physical vicinity, which for a long time had seemed the condition of national war and rivalry, emerged as a factor favouring unity. European frontiers, in the West at least, became demilitarized; the Franco-German understanding was certainly as striking a development as any other in a century of diplomatic dealings. Soviet military power, which loomed ominously at times of crisis, appeared scarcely more threatening to Europeans after 1956 than it did to those more protected by distance.[40] Technology had done much to annihilate the barriers of terrestrial space, and Europeans resigned themselves with a certain stoicism to the close proximity of Soviet power. If war did come, Europe would almost certainly suffer deeply, but others might not suffer less. This was evidently no consolation, but Europeans knew they would be almost powerless to prevent the hostilities. The Cuban affair in 1962 gave Europeans a further proof, if one was needed, that on certain issues involving the security of the United States, Europe would be informed after, rather than before, the decision-making process was completed. This indisputable reality remained. With crippled resources, she was incapable of defending herself, this fact could not be ignored. Her dependence on American protection was complete. This situation had no historic precedent.[41]

Further, Europe, for all practical purposes, was barred from the scientific and technological pursuits linked with the exploration of space. For the first time in centuries, sensational discoveries were made wherein Europe had no part, when infact, all the early steps—including the important ones taken during the Second World War—were vastly indebted to European scientific and technological ingenuity. This issue symbolized Europe's dilemma.[42] Michel Crozier opines : 'If one admits that culture is a means, a resource, and not a treasure to be accumulated and kept under lock and key, contemporary Europe is paralyzed by its past successes. Its culture, too prematurely perfected and too advanced, has congealed in the past and finds itself inadequate to the tasks imposed by the modern world.'[43] 'One might conclude' continues Crozier, 'that European inferiority is destined to continue, faced with an America which does not suffer from the same weight of social structure, but this would be to forget that the obstacles of a difficult accomplishment also have their advantages.' He asserts that Europe will overcome many problems only when Europeans understand that they cannot copy America, and that what they can find in America is a stimulus and not a solution.[44]

The opposition to Americanization does not imply underestimating the importance of steel production or the advantages of well-being. Rather it expresses a sense of necessity which Europeans feel, that they must continue to be something which Americans are not. This is a strange reversal of roles: Europe in the twentieth century, is seeking independence from the other, which America so prided itself on securing in the eighteenth.[45] The difficulty of achieving this identity in any meaningful way arises from the fact that there is so little in Europe's recent past that is immediately relevant to the present.[46]

By 1955 most of the ruins in west Europe were gone. yet its newly sprouting materialism was, in itself, one, of a specifically European kind; and, in some places, the restoration of ruined buildings as well as the reconstruction of certain ways of life had something to do with historical consciousness, another of the peculiar qualities of European civilization.[47]

At some point, the economic and the political, the material and the spiritual phases of the story no longer remain separate. During the six years of the common market's period of adolescence, vast changes occurred in the world, affecting the future of Europe. The cold war between America and Russia relaxed giving way to the twilight situation of a cold peace; the spectre of China haunted the Russian rulers from the east, to some extent drawing the Soviets closer to the West. Charles de Gaulle became something like the constable of a new Europe and perhaps even the symbol of a new kind of European consciousness. He decisively affected the two outstanding problems of the common market : the eventual development of its political integration and its relations with the rest of the world (specially with Britain and the United States).[48]

In 1964, twenty years after Anglo-American liberation of western Europe and the Russian subjugation of eastern Europe, the material reconstruction of the former was completed and its economic unification was close to being accomplished; but its political integration had only just begun.[49]

Prophecy with regard to history is difficult in any century; in the twentieth it appeared to be a lost art. European-Soviet and Euroepan-American relations could certainly be modified, partly because of the policies pursued by the great powers and partly because of Europe's own growing consciousness of her own capabilities.[50]

Nonetheless, it would be hazardous to guess what these changes will be. If there is a reluctance to construct new utopias, this need not be interpreted as evidence of fatigue or frustration. Europe definitely shows remarkable vitality and hope. It should not surprise anyone if in the next half century or so, she seeks again, with something akin to her former self-confidence, to be an 'example' to the world.[51] Edward Heath in 1962 observed : 'A new Europe is being created; one which is regaining some of the things which were most valuable in the old and which is hoping to banish the differences which marred and maimed previous centuries.'[52]

Hans Nord concludes thus :

> The essential difficulties in the way are not technical; technically, the thing is complex, that is agreed, but it is not insoluble. The real problem is a human problem. The real problem is whether the Europeans in the twentieth century are still creating enough to add another dimension to their political activity; whether they can create some form of European unity without sacrificing their national diversity ... That is the key to the whole question ... Perhaps we might be guided in this by the appeal of the American President in his inaugural address, which I might be allowed to adapt; 'And so, my fellow Europeans, ask not what Europe can do for you, ask rather what you and country can contribute to Europe.[53]

Will there be a history of 'Europe' in the future? We know, for example, that the history of 'Asia' is a whim. With all of the valid generalizations about the European mind, further crystallization of a European consciousness, is, at best, probable, but by no means certain. In 1962, Walter Hallstein said about the common market :

> The European Community has no emblem, it has no flag, no anthem, it holds no parades and it has no sovereign. It has no instruments of integration which appeal to the senses, to the eyes or to the ear.
>
> This is in keeping with the style of our community, a style of realistic, hard, prosaic work, which even leads to our being criticized for being a technocracy. The basis on which we work is common sense rather than emotion, our strength is reasoned conviction rather than myths, our tactic is discussion rather than the sway of passion.[54]

True, but a post-ideological age does not necessarily imply the termination of politics. There are certain political rather than economic considerations for the further whetting of a European consciousness involving a clarification of Europe's relationship to the rest of the world, and even her assumption of new forms. The successful establishment of a European confederation must, at least to some extent, depend on the realization by other world powers, and specifically by the United States, that such a Europe would be in their interest, too, and the world at large. Yet much water has flowed under the bridges since Oswald Spengler snarling at the prospect of a bourgeois Europe, declared in 1933 that the future of such a Europe would be pitiful,[55] a–*Verschweizerung*, There are many Germans who twelve years later would have given much, if not all, to be able to enjoy some of the respects and benefits of *Verschweizerung*.

It was, in any event, a Swiss high bourgeois, the patrician Burckhardt, a more perceptive historical thinker than Spengler, who wrote, seven decades prior to the fateful year 1945 :

> Is the tendency of Europe now a rising or falling one? That can never be decided through calculations. Its peoples are not yet exhausted in a physical sense, and in a spiritual and moral sense, one must always reckon with the existence of still invisible forces, even now.[56]

NOTES AND REFERENCES

1. Weber, Alfred. *Farewell to European History,* (London, 1947).
2. Ibid, p. 2.
3. Graubard, Stephen, *R.A. New Europe,* Graubard (ed.), (Boston, 1964), p. 632.
4. Ibid, p. 632.
5. Ibid, p. 633.
6. Ibid, Crozier, Michel, *The Cultural Revolution* : Notes on the changes in the intellectual climate of France, pp. 602–630; also Rogers, Earnesto N. *The Phenomenology of European Architecture,* pp. 424–438. The optimism of the immediate postwar years has been too little written about.
7. Ibid, p. 632.
8. Ibid, pp. 632–33.
9. De Tocqueville, Alexis, *The Old Regime And The French Revolution,* trans. Stuart Gilbert, (New York, 1955), pp. 20, 209.
10. Lukacs, John. *Decline And Rise of Europe*—A study in recent history, with particular emphasis on the development of a European consciousness, (New York, 1965), p. 256.
11. Ibid, p. 257.
12. Michelet, Ibid, p. 257f.
13. Carlo Morandi, Ibid.
14. Gonzague de Reynold, Ibid.
15. Federico Chabod, Ibid, p. 258f.
16. Otto Brunner, Ibid.
17. Spengler, Oswald. *The Decline of the West,* 2 Vol. (New York, 1926–28).
18. Valery, Paul, cited in Lukacs, op.cit, p. 260.
19. Lukacs, op.cit, p. 260.
20. Ibid, p. 260.
21. Ibid, pp. 260–61.
22. Haas, Ernst B. *Technocracy, Pluralism and the New Europe,* Graubard, (ed.), op.cit, p. 62.
23. Lukacs, op.cit, p. 261.
24. Ibid.
25. Ibid.
26. Ibid, p. 269.
27. Ibid.
28. Ibid, p. 270.
29. Benedetto Croce, cited in Ibid.
30. Chabod, cited in Ibid.

31. Ibid, pp. 270–71.
32. Ibid, p. 272.
33. Ibid, p. 273.
34. Ibid.
35. Graubard, op.cit, p. 647.
36. Ibid.
37. Ibid.
38. Ibid, pp. 647–48.
39. Ibid, p. 648.
40. Ibid, p 648–49.
41. Ibid, pp. 649.
42. Ibid, pp. 649–50.
43. Crozier, op.cit, p. 629.
44. Ibid, pp. 629–30.
45. Graubard, op.cit, p. 650.
46. Ibid.
47. Lukacs, op.cit, p. 59.
48. Ibid, p. 83.
49. Ibid, p. 87.
50. Graubard, op.cit, p. 652.
51. Ibid, p. 653.
52. Heath, Edward. *Introduction, The New Europe,* Oxford Lectures, Conservative Political Centre, (London, 1962), p. 5.
53. Ibid, Nord, Hans, *The European Idea,* p. 16.
54. Lukacs, op.cit, p. 275.
55. *Jahre der Entscheidung : Deutschland und die weltgeschichtliche Entwicklung* (Munich, 1933) : translated by Charles Francis Atkinson as *The Hour of Decision* : Part I : Germany and World-Historical Evolution (New York, 1934), cited by Oswald, Spengler.
56. Burckhardt, Jakob, Historische Fragments cited in Lukacs, op.cit, p. 278.

Bibliography

Albertini, Luigi. *The Origins of the War of 1914*, trans. ed., Isabella M. Massey. Vol. 1 : *European Relations from the Congress of Berlin to the Eve of the Sarajevo Murder*. London : Oxford University Press, 1952.

Albertini, Luigi. *The Origins of the War of 1914*, trans. ed., Isabella M. Massey. Vol. 2 : *The Crisis of July 1914. From the Sarajevo Outrage to the Austro-Hungarian General Mobilization*. London : Oxford University Press, 1952.

Albrecht-Carrie, Rene. *A Diplomatic History of Europe Since the Congress of Vienna*. rev. edn., New York : Harper and Row Publishers, 1973.

Aron, Raymond. 'Causes and Responsibilities.' *The Outbreak of the First World War : Who was Responsible*? rev. edn., Dwight E. Lee. (ed.), Boston : D.C. Heath and Co., 1963.

Aubry, Octave. *The Second Empire*. Philadelphia : J.B. Lippincott Co., 1940.

Bagley, J.M. *Life in Medieval England*. London : B.T. Batsford Ltd., 1960.

Baldwin, Hanson W. *World War I, An Outline History*. New York : Harper and Row Publishers, 1962.

Bapst, Edmond. *Les Origines de la Guerre Crimea : La France et la Russia de 1848–1854*. Paris : C. Delagrave, 1912.

Barie, Ottavio. 'Cavour, Napoleon III and the Unification of Italy.' Napoleon III and Europe. Bibliographical Studies. Oxford : Pergamon Press, 1965.

Barker, A.J. *The War against Russia 1854–1856*. New York : Holt Rinehart and Winston, 1970.

Barnes, Harry Elmer. *An Economic History of the Western World*. New York : Harcourt, Brace and Co., 1940.

Barnes, Harry Elmer. *The Genesis of the World War* : An Introduction to the Problem of War Guilt. rev. edn., New York : Alfred A. Knopf, 1929.

Baron, Hans. *Burckhardt's Civilization of the Renaissance*—a century after its publication–*Renaissance News*, Vol. 13, 1960.

Baron, Hans. *From Petrarch to Leonardo Bruni*. Chicago, 1968.

Baron, Hans. *The Crises of the Early Italian Renaissance*, Vols. 1 and 2, Princeton: New Jersey, 1955.

Bateman, Somerset. *Simon de Montfort*–His Life and Work. Birmingham : Cornish Brothers Ltd., 1923.

Beachcroft, T.O. *British Broadcasting*. London : Longman Green and Co., 1946.

Beck, James M. *The Evidence in the Case : A Discussion of the Moral Responsibility for the War of 1914, as Disclosed by the Diplomatic Records of England, Germany, Russia, France, Austria, Italy and Belgium*. rev. edn., New York : G.P. Putnam's Sons, 1915.

Becker, Marvin B. *Florence in Transition*, Baltimore, 1968.

Bemont, Charles. *Simon de Montfort Earl of Leicester 1208–1265*. A new edn., trans. E.F. Jacob, Oxford : Clarendon Press, 1930.

Bennett, Jeremy. *British Broadcasting and the Danish Resistance Movement 1940–1945* : A Study of the wartime broadcasts of the B.B.C. Danish Service. London : Cambridge University Press, 1966.

Berry, W. Grinton. *France Since Waterloo*. New York : Charles Scribner's Sons, 1909.

Binkley, Robert C. 'Realism and Nationalism 1852–1871.' *The Rise of Modern Europe*. Vol. 16. William L. Langer, (ed.) New York : Harper and Brothers, 1935.

Blake, R.L.V. French. *The Crimean War*. Connecticut : Archon Books, 1972.

Bloch, Camille. *The Causes of the World War : An Historical Summery*. trans. Jane Soames, New York : Howard Fertig, 1968. (First published in English in 1935).

Boveri, Margret, *Treason in the Twentieth Century*. trans. Jonathan Steinberg. London : Macdonald, 1961.

Bowden, Witt; Karpovich, Michael; and Usher, Abbott Payson. *An Economic History of Europe since 1750*. New York : American Book Co., 1937.

Brandenburg, Erich. 'Conclusion : The Causes of the War.' *The*

Outbreak. Lee (ed). Boston : D.C. Health and Co., 1963.

Brucker, Gene. *Renaissance Florence*, New York, 1969.

Burckhardt, Jacob Christoph. *Civilization of the Renaissance in Italy*. trans. S.G.C. Middlemore, London, 1904, and New York, 1958.

Bury, J.P.T. *Napoleon III and the Second Empire*. London : The English Universities Press Ltd., 1964.

Butler, J.R.M., *Grand Strategy : September 1939–June 1941*. Vol. 2, *History of the Second World War*. J.R.M. Butler (ed.), London : Her Majesty's Stationary Office, 1957.

Cambridge Medieval History, Vols. 7 and 8.

Campbell, Thomas. (ed.), *Frederick the Great, His Court and Times*. Vol. 4, London : Henry Colburn Publisher, 1843.

Carlyle, Thomas. *History of Friedrich II of Prussia called Frederick the Great*. 7 Vols. Part III, The Seven Years War and Old Age of Friedrich. Vol. 7, London : Chapman and Hall, 1869.

Carr, Edward Hallett. *German-Soviet Relations Between the Two World Wars*, Baltimore : The John Hopkins Press, 1951.

Case, Lynn M. *Franco-Italian Relations, 1860–1865*. A thesis, Philadelphia, 1932.

Case, Lynn M. *French Opinion on War and Diplomacy during the Second Empire*. Philadelphia : University of Pennsylvania, 1954.

Cheyney, Edward P. *A Short History of England*. rev., enl. edn., New York : Ginn and Co., 1945.

Chilston, Viscount. 'The Occupied Countries in Western Europe : Denmark. *Survey of International Affairs 1939–1946 : Hitler's Europe*. Arnold Toynbee and Veronica M. Toynbee (eds.), London: Oxford University Press, 1954.

Clough, Shepard Bancroft. and Cole, Charles Woolsey. *Economic History of Europe*. Boston : D.C. Heath and Co., 1941.

Cobbet's Reasons for War against Russia in Defence of Turkey. 2nd. edn. London : A. Cobbett, Publisher 137 Strand, May, 1954.

Cochran, M.H. *Germany Not Guilty in 1914* (Examining a Much Prized Book). Boston: Stratford Co., 1931.

Collingwood, R.G. *The Idea of History*, Oxford, 1946.

Corley, T.A.B. *Democratic Despot : A Life of Napoleon III*. London : Barrie and Rockliff, 1961.

Costain, Thomas B. *The Conquerors*. New York : Doubleday and Co. Inc., 1949.

Costain, Thomas B. *The Magnificent Century*. New York: Doubleday and Co. Inc., 1951.

Costain, Thomas B. *The Three Edwards.* New York : Doubleday and Co. Inc., 1962.

Crane, Edward A. (ed.). *The Second French Empire.* Memoirs of Dr. Thomas W. Evans. New York : D. Appleton and Co., 1906.

Crowe, Captain J.W. *Yesterday and Tomorrow or Shadows of the War.* London : T. Hatchard, 167 Piccadily, 1956.

Curzon, Harold Nicholson. *The last Phase 1919–1925 : A Study In PostWar Diplomacy*, New York : Harcourt, Brace and Co., 1929.

D'Abernon, Viscount. *An Ambassador of Peace*, Vol. I, *From Spain (1920) to Rapallo (1922).* With historical notes by Gerothwohl, Maurice Alfred. 3 Vols., London : Hodder and Stoughton, 1929.

D'Abernon, Viscount. *Versailles to Rapallo* 1920–1922. With historical notes by Gerothwohl, Maurice Alfred. New York : Doubleday, Doran and Co., 1929.

Daniels, Emil. 'Frederick the Great and His Successor (1) Home and Foreign Policy (1763–97).' *The Cambridge Modern History.* Planned by Lord Acton, A.W. Ward and others (ed.), Vol. 6 : *The Eighteenth Century.* New York : The Macmillan Co., 1909.

Daniels, H.G. *The Rise of the German Republic.* New York : Charles Scribner's Sons, 1928.

D'Auvergne, Edmund B. *Napoleon the Third.* A Biography. New York : Dodd, Mead and Co., 1929.

Deakin, F.W. 'Great Britain and European Resistance.' *European Resistance Movements 1939–1945.* Proceedings of the Second International Conference on the history of the Resistance Movements held at Milan, March 26–29, 1961. New York : The Macmillan Co., 1964.

Dedijer, Vladimir. *The Road to Sarajevo.* New York : Simon and Schuster, 1966.

Degras, Jane. (ed). *Soviet Documents on Foreign Policy.* Vol. 1, *1917–1924.* London : Oxford University Press, 1951.

Delmer, Sefton. *Black Boomerang.* New York : The Viking Press, 1962.

Deutsh, Harold C. *The Conspiracy against Hitler in the Twilight War.* Minneapolis : The University Press, 1968.

Dickinson, G. Lowes. *The International Anarchy, 1904–1914.* New York, 1926.

Diplomatic Study on the Crimean War (Alexandre Jomini). 2 Vols., Vol. I, London, 1882.

Dorn, Walter L. 'The Prussian Bureaucracy in the Eighteenth Century', Parts I, II and III. *Political Science Quarterly*. Vol. 46 1931, and Vol. 47. 1932.

Dorn, Walter L. *Competition for Empire 1740–1763*. Vol. 9, *The Rise of Modern Europe*. William L. Langer, (ed.) New York : Harper and Brothers Publishers, 1940.

Douglas, David C. *The Norman Achievement 1050–1100*. Berkeley : University of California Press, 1969.

Douglas, David C. *William the Conqueror*, Berkeley : University of California Press, 1964.

Durham, Edith M. *The Sarajevo Crime*. London, 1925.

Edleston, R.H. *Napoleon III*; Speeches from the Throne. Cambridge, 1931.

Ehrman, John. *Grand Strategy August 1943–September 1944*. Vol. 5, *'Hist. Sec. World War.'* J.R.M. Butler (ed.), London : Her Majesty's Stationary Office, 1956.

Eubank, Keith. *Paul Cambon : Master Diplomatist*. Norman : University of Okhlahoma Press, 1960.

Europe Under the Nazi Scourge : A Picture and an Indictment. 'A reprint of some recent articles in the *Times* on conditions in the countries of Europe which have fallen under Nazi oppression. London : The Times Publishing Co., Ltd., 1940.

Fay, Sidney B. *The Rise of Brandenburg Prussia to 1786*. rev. edn. by Klaus Epstein. New York : Holt, Rinehart and Winston, 1964.

Fay, Sidney B. *The Origins of the World War*. 2nd. rev. edn. 2 Vols New York : The Macmillan Co., 1949.

Ferguson, Wallace K. *The Interpretation of the Renaissance*–The Renaissance Essays from the *Journal of the History of Ideas*, P.O. Kristeller, and P.P. Wiener, (eds.), New York, 1968.

Ferguson, Wallace K. *The Reinterpretation of the Renaissance*–Facets of the Renaissance, Werkemister, William H. (ed.), New York, 1959.

Ferguson, Wallace K. *The Renaissance in Historical Thought*, Cambridge, Massachusetts, 1948.

Fischer, Louis. *The Soviets In World Affairs*. Vol. I, New York, 1951.

FitzGibbon, Constantine. *20 July*. New York : W.W. Norton and Co., Inc., 1956.

Flender, Harold. *Rescue in Denmark*. London : Simon and Schustar, 1963.

Florinsky, Michael T. *Russia : A History and an Interpretation* in 2 Vol., Vol. 2. New York : The Macmillan Co., 1953.

Forbes, Archibald. *The Life of Napoleon the Third*. New York : Dodd, Mead and Co., 1897.

Fraser, Lindley Macnaghtan. *Propaganda.* London : Oxford University Press, 1957.

Freeman, Edward A. *A Short History of the Norman Conquest.* 2nd edn., Oxford : Clarendon Press, 1880.

Freeman, Edward A. *Norman Conquest of England.* 2nd edn., Vol. 1, Oxford: Clarendon Press, 1870.

Gaevernitz, Gero V.S. (ed.), *Revolt against Hitler : The Personal Account of Fabian von Schlabrendorff.* London, 1948.

Gagliardo, John G. *From Pariah to Patriot : The Changing Image of the German Peasant 1770–1840.* Kentucky : Kentucky Univ. Press, *1969.*

Gallin, Mother Mary Alice. *Ethical and Religious Factors in the German Resistance to Hitler.* Washington D.C. : Catholic University of California Press, 1970.

Garin, Eugenio. *Science and Civic Life in the Italian Renaissance*, trans. Peter Munz, New York, 1969.

Gaxotte, Pierre. *Frederick the Great.* trans. R.A. Bell, London : G. Bell and Sons Ltd., 1941.

Geiss, Imanuel. (ed). *July 1914 : The Outbreak of the First World War : Selected Documents.* New York : Charles Scribner's Sons, 1967.

Gershoy, Leo. *From Despotism to Revolution 1763–1789.* Vol. 10, *The Rise of Modern Europe.* William L. Langer (ed.). New York : Harper and Brothers Publishers, 1944.

Gibbons, Herbert Adams. *Europe Since 1918.* New York : The Century Co., 1923.

Gillies, John. *A View of the Reign of Frederick II of Prussia with a Parallel between the Prince and Philip II of Macedon.* Dublin : Printed by William Porter, 1789.

Gleason, J. *The Genesis of Russophobia in Great Britain : A Study of the Interpretation of Policy and Opinion.* Cambridge, Mass. London, 1950.

Gombrich, E.H. *Norm and Form* –Studies in the Art of the Renaissance, London, 1966.

Gooch, Brison D. *The Origins of the Crimean War.* Problems in European Civilization. Massachussetts: D.C. Heath and Co.,

1969.

Gooch, Brison D. 'A Century of Historiography on the Origins of the Crimean War.' *The American Historical Review.* Vol. 62 (1), Oct. 1956.

Gooch, G.P. *Before the War : Studies in Diplomacy.* Vol. 2 : The coming of the Storm. London : Longman Green and Co., 1938.

Gooch, G.P. *History of Modern Europe 1878–1919*. London : Cassell and Co., Ltd., 1923.

Gooch, G.P. *Recent Revelations of European Diplomacy. 4th* rev. enl. edn. London: Longman Green and Co., 1940.

Gooch, G.P. *The Second Empire*. London : Longman Green and Co., 1960.

Gooch, G.P. *Frederick the Great : The Ruler, the Writer, the Man.* New York : Alfred A. Knopf, 1947.

Goriainov, Sergei Mikhailovich. *Le Bosphore at les Dardanelles.* Paris : Plon-Nourrit, 1910.

Graml, Hermann and others. *The German Resistance to Hitler.* Berkeley : University of California Press, 1970.

Gudme, Sten. *Denmark : Hitler's 'Model Protectorate.'* trans. from the Danish by Jan Noble. London : Victor Gollancz Ltd., 1942.

Guedella, Phillip. *The Second Empire,* 2nd. rev. edn., New York : G.P. Putnam's Sons, 1922.

Guerard, Albert. *Napoleon III : A Great Life in Brief.* New York : Alfred A. Knopf, 1966.

Guerard, Albert. *Napoleon III : An Interpretation*. Cambridge Assoc Harvard University Press, 1943.

Haestrup, Joerge. 'Denmark's Connection with the Allied Powers during the Occupation.' *European Resistence Movements.* New York : The Macmillan Co., 1964.

Hassell, Ulrich Von *The Von Hassel Diaries 1938–1944 : The Story of the Forces against Hitler inside Germany.* New York : Doubleday and Co. Inc., 1947.

Hay, Denys. *Hans Baron in the Renaissance Historiography*–Renaissance Studies in Honour of Hans Baron, A. Molho, and J.A. Tedeschi, and, G.C. Sansoni, (eds.) 1971.

Hearder, H. *European the Nineteenth Century 1830–1880.* London : Longman, Green and Co., 1966.

Henderson, W.O. *Studies in the Economic Policy of Frederick the Great.* New York : Augustus M. Kelley Publisher, 1965.

Henderson, W.O. *The State and the Industrial Revolution in Prussia 1740–1870.* Liverpool: Liverpool University Press, 1958.

Hilger, Gustav, and Meyer, Alfred G. *The Incompatible Allies – A Memoir-History of German-Soviet Relations 1918–1941.* New York : The Macmillan Co., 1953.

Holborn, Hajo. *The Political Collapse of Europe.* New York : Alfred A. Knopf, 1966.

Horvath, Eugene. *Origins of the Crimean War : Documents Relative to the Russian Intervention in Hungary and Transylvania, 1848–1849.* Budapest, 1937.

Jacobson, Hans-Adolf, (ed.) *July 20, 1944 : The German Opposition to Hitler as viewed by Foreign Historians.* An Anthology. Bonn, 1969.

Jerrold, Blanchard. *The Life of Napoleon III.* Vol. 4, London : Longman Green and Co. 1882.

Journal of The History of Ideas. Vol. 1(4), October 1940.

Journal of The History of Ideas. Vol. 1(1), January 1940.

Karpovich, Michael. *Imperial Russia 1801–1917.* New York : Henry Holt and Co., 1932.

Kennan, George F. *Russia and the West Under Lenin and Stalin.* Boston : Little, Brown and Co., 1961.

Kennan, George F. *Soviet Foreign Policy 1917–1941.* Snyder, Louis L. (gen. ed.), New York : D. Van Nostrand Co. Inc., 1960.

Kesslar, Harry Count. *Walter Rathenau : His LIfe and Work.* Eng. trans. New York : Harcourt, Brace and Co., 1930.

Keynes, J.M. *The Economic Consequences of the Peace.* New York, 1920.

Kinglake, Alexander W. *The Invasion of the Crimea,* 6 Vols. London : Harrison, 1863–1880. Vol. 1.

Kohn, Hans. *Nationalism : Its Meaning and History.* rev. edn., New York : D. Van Nostrand Co., Inc., 1965.

Krabbe, Henning, (ed.) *Voices from Britain : Broadcast History.* London : Goerge Allen and Unwin Ltd., 1947.

Kristeller, Paul Oscar. *The Renaissance Thought II*–Papers on Humanism and the Arts., New York, 1965.

Kuhns, William, *In Pursuit of DietrichBonhoeffer.* Ohio : Pflaum Press, 1967.

La Gorce, Pierre Francois Gustave de. *Histoire du Second Empire.* 7 Vols., Reprint of the edition published in Paris 1899–1905. New York : AMS Press, 1969.

Lafore, Laurence. *The Long Fuse : An Interpretation of the Origins of World War I.* New York : J.B. Lippincott Co., 1965.

Langer, William L. *European Alliances and Alignments 1871–1890.* 2nd. edn. New York : Alfred A. Knopf, 1950.

Langer, William L. *The Diplomacy of Imperialism.* 2nd. edn., New York : Alfred A. Knopf, 1951.

Langford, John Alfred. *The War with Russia : Its Origin and Cause : A Reply to the Letter of J. Bright.* London : R. Theobald, Paternoster Row, 1855.

Lano, Pierre De. *The Emperor Napoleon III –The Secret of an Empire.* trans. from the French by Helen Hunt Johnson. New York : Dodd Mead and Co., 1895.

Layard, Austen Henry. *Diplomatic Mystifications and Popular Credulity; of the Anglo-French Alliance.* London : Harrison, 59 Pall Mall, 1855.

Layard, Austen Henry. *The Turkish Question.* Speeches delivered in the House of Commons, on Aug. 16, 1853 and Feb. 17, 1854. London : John Murray, Albemarle St., 1854.

League of Nations Treaty Series, 1923, Vol. 19, (Nos. 1, 2 and 3). Treaty No. 498. *Germany and Russian Soviet Republic Agreement Signed At Rapallo.* April 16, 1922.

Lengyel, Alfonz. *The Quattrocento:* A Study of the Principles of Art and a Chronological Biography of the Italian 1400's, Lowa, 1971.

Lerner, Daniel. *Sykewar : Psychological Warfare against Germany, D-Day to VE-Day,* New York : George W. Stewart, Publisher, Inc., 1949.

Lockhart, Sir Robert Hamilton Bruce. *Comes the Reckoning.* London : G.P. Putnams' sons, 1947.

Lousse, Emile. 'The True Place of Napoleon III in the History of Europe.' *Napoleon III and Europe.* Oxford : Pergamon Press, 1965.

Lowenstein, Prince Hubertus zu. *What was the German Resistance Movement?* Grafes Bad Godesberg, 1960.

Lyndhurst, Right Hon. Lord. *The Eastern Question.* The substance of a speech delivered in the House of Lords, June 19, 1854. London: John Patheram, 94, High Holborn, 1854.

MacMunn, Sir George. *The Crimea in Perspective.* London : G.Bell and Sons Ltd., 1935.

Malmesbury, Lord, (ed.) *Diaries and Correspondence of James Harris,*

First Earl of Malmesbury. Vol. 1, London, 1945.

Mange, Alyce Edythe. *The Near Eastern Policy of the Emperor Napoleon III*. Studies in the Social Sciences no. 25. Urbana : The Univ. of Illinois Press, 1940.

Manvell, Roger and Fraenkel, Heinrich. *The July Plot*. London : Pan Books Ltd., 1964.

Manvell, Roger. *The Conspirators : July 20th, 1944*. London : Pan Books Ltd., 1972.

Margutti, Albert Alexander. *Emperor Francis Joseph and His Times*. New York, 1922.

Marriott, J.A.R. *The Eastern Question : An Historical Study in European Diplomacy*. 4th edn., Oxford : Clarendon Press, 1940.

Marx Karl. *The Eastern Question :* A Reprint of Letters written between 1853–1856 dealing with the events of the Crimean War. Eleanor Marx Aveling and Edward Aveling (eds.). London : S. Sonnenschein and Co. Ltd, 1897.

Mathew, D.J.A. *The Norman Conquest*. London : B.T. Batsford Ltd., 1966.

McNally, T. 'The Origin of Russophobia in France, 1812–1830.' *American Slavic and East European Review*. Vol. 17(2), 1958.

Miller, William. *The Ottoman Empire and its Successors 1801–1927*. rev. enl. edn., of *The Ottoman Empire 1801–1913*. London : Frank Cass and Co. Ltd, 1966.

Mosely, Philip E. *Russian Diplomacy and the Opening of the Eastern Question in 1838 and 1839*. New York : Russell and Russell, 1969.

Muller, Edwin. 'Waging War with Words.' *Current History*. August, 1939.

Munro, Dana Carletin. *The Middle Age 395–1272*. New York : The Century Co., 1923.

N.E.M.D. *A Word to the British Public before Entering into Hostilities with Russia*. London : W.J. Golbourn, 1854.

Nechkina, M.V. (ed.) *Russia in the Nineteenth Century*, Vol. 2 of the *History of Russia*, trans. from the Russian by Oliver J, Frederiksen and Bernard Pares. Ann Arbor : Published by J.W. Edwards, 1953.

Nolan, E.H. *The History of the War against Russia*. 2 Vols. London : J.S. Virtue, 1857.

Olschki, Leonardo. *The Genius of Italy*. New York, 1949.

Palm, Franklin Charles. *England and Napoleon III : A Study in the Rise of Utopian Dictator.* Durham, N.C. : Duke University Press, 1948.

Palmer, Paul. *Denmark in Nazi Chains.* W.C.Z. : Lindsay Drummond, 1942.

Patterson, R.H. *New Revolution or the Napoleonic Policy in Europe.* Edinburgh : William Blackwood and Sons, 1860.

Pechel, Rudolf. *Freedom in Struggle.* Toronto : The Ryerson Press, 1957.

Pemberton, W. Baring. *Battles of the Crimean War.* New York : The Macmillan Co., 1962.

Powicke, F.M. *King Henry III and the Lord Edward.* 2 Vols. Oxford : Clarendon Press, 1947.

Price, M. Philips, (ed.). *The Diplomatic History of the War : The Texts of the Official Documents of the Various Governments,* New York : Charles Scribner's Sons, 1914.

Prittie, Terence. *Germans against Hitler.* London : Hutchinson, 1964.

Puryear, Vernon John. *International Economics and Diplomacy in the Near East : A Study of British Commercial Policy in the Levant 1834–1853.* Connecticut : Archon Books, 1969.

Puryear, Vernon John. 'New Light on the Origin of the Crimean War.' Vol. 3(2), June, 1931.

Puryear, Vernon John. *England, Russia, and the Straits Question, 1844–1856.* Connecticut : Archon Books, 1965.

Rambaud, Alfred. *A Popular History of Russia from the Earliest Times to 1882,* trans. L.B. Lang, Nathan Haskell Dole (ed.), Vol. 3, Boston: Estes and Lauriat, 1882.

Rasmussen, Larry L. *Dietrich Bonhoeffer : Carl Goerdeler's Struggle against Tyranny.,* trans. R.T. Clark. New York : Frederick A. Praeger, 1958.

Reddaway, W.F. *Frederick The Great : A Biography.,* trans. P.R. Lawrence Wilson. New York : G.P. Putnam's Sons, 1960.

Remak, Joachim. *Sarajevo : The Story of a Political Murder.* New York : Criterion Books, Inc., 1959.

Remak, Joachim. *The Origin of World War 1871–1914.* New York : Holt, Rinehart and Winston, 1967.

Renaissance News. Spring 1956, Vol. 9(1), *Review The Crisis.* Bouwsmn.

Renaissance News. Spring 1954, Vol. 7(1), *Renaissance Historiography in America,* Bradeur, Leicester.

Renouvin, Pierre. *The Immediate Origin of the War (June 28th–August*

4th, 1914), trans. Theodore Carswell Hume. New Haven : Yale University Press, 1928.

Rheinhardt, E.A. *Napoleon and Eugenie.* The Tragicomedy of an Empire. trans. from German by Hannah Waller. New York : Alfred A. Knopf, 1931.

Riasanovsky, Nicholas V. *Nicholas I and Official Nationality in Russia, 1825–1855.* Berkeley : Univ. of California Press, 1961.

Rice, Eugine F. *The Foundations of Early Modern Europe–1460–1559*, New York, 1970.

Richardson, Oliver H. *The National Movement in the Reign of Henry III and its Culmination in the Barons' War.* New York : The Macmillan Co. 1897.

Ritter, Gerhard, *Frederick the Great : A Historical Profile.*, trans. Peter Paret. Berkeley : University of California Press, 1968.

Rolo, Charles J. *Radio goes to War : The 'Fourth Front'.* New Yrok : G.P. Putnam's Sons, 1942.

Romoser, George K. 'The Politics of Uncertainty : The German Resistance Movement.' *Social Research.* Vol. 31, 1964.

Roon, Ger van. *German Resistance to Hitler : Count von Moltke and the Kreisau Circle.*, trans. Peter Ludlow. London : Van Nostrand Reinhold Co., 1971.

Rosenberg, Hans. *Bureaucracy, Aristocracy and Autocrat : The Prussian Experience 1660–1815.* Cambridge : Harvard University Press, 1966.

Rothfels, Hans. *The German Opposition to Hitler : An Appraisal.* Illinois : Henry Regnery Co., 1948.

Russian Turkey; or a Greek Empire : The Inevitable Solution of the 'Eastern Question.' A letter to Lord John Russell by G.D.P. London : Saunders and Stanford, 6, Charing Cross, 1853.

Saint-Amand, Imbert De. *France and Italy.*, trans. Elizabeth Gilbert Martin. New York : Charles Scribner's Sons, 1899.

Sayles, G.O. *The Medieval Foundations of England.* rev. edn. London : Methuen and Co., 1952.

Schevill, Ferdinand. *History of Florence from the Founding of the City through the Renaissance*, New York, 1936.

Schevill, Ferdinand. *History of the Balkan Peninsula*, New York, 1933.

Schlabrendorff, Fabian von. *The Secret War to Tragedy.*, trans. Hilda Simon. New York : Pitman Publishing Corp., 1965.

Schmitt, Bernadotte E. *The Origin of the First World War*, The Historical

Association, London, 1966.

Schmitt, Bernadotte E. 'The Diplomatic Preliminaries of the Crimean War.' *American Historical Review.* Vol. 25(1), Oct., 1919.

Schmitt, Bernadotte E. "The Origin of the First World War." *The Outbreak.* Lee (ed.) Boston : D.C. Heath and Co., 1963.

Schmitt, Bernadotte E. 'Triple Alliance and Triple Entente, 1902–14.' *American Historical Review*, April, 1924.

Schmitt, Bernadotte E. and Barnes, Harry E. *Recent Disclosures Concerning The Origin of the World War I,* Chicago, 1926.

Schmitt, Bernadotte E. *The Coming of the War 1914.* 2 Vol. New York : Howard Fertig, 1966. New edn. (originally published in 1930).

Schnerb, R. 'Napoleon III and the Second French Empire.' *Journal of Modern History.* Sept., 1936.

Schroeder, Paul W. *Austria, Great Britain and the Crimean War : The Destruction of the European Concert.* Ithaca : Cornell Univ. Press, 1972.

Scott, James Brown, (ed.). *Diplomatic Documents Relating to the Outbreak of the European War.* Austrian Red Book, Part I. The Serbian Blue Book, Part II; New York : Oxford University Press, 1916.

Seaman, L.C.B. *From Vienna to Versailles.* New York : Harper and Row Publishers, 1963.

Sellery, George Clarke. *The Renaissance: Its Nature and Origin.* Wisconsin, 1949.

Sencourt, Robert. *Napoleon III : The Modern Emperor.* New York : D. Appleton-Century Co., 1933.

Seton-Watson, R.W. *German Slav and Magyar–A study in the Origin of the Great War,* London, 1916.

Seton-Watson R.W. *The Murder at Sarajevo,* In Foreign Affairs, New York, Vol. 3(3), April, 1925.

Seton-Watson, R.W. *The Rise of Nationality in the Balkans,* London, 1917.

Seton-Watson, R.W. *The Southern Slav Question And The Habsburg Monarchy,* New York, 1969.

Seton-Watson, Hugh. *the Russian Empire.* Oxford : Clarendon Press, 1967.

Seton-Watson, R.W. *Britain in Europe 1789–1914.* A Survey of Foreign Policy. New York : The Macmillan Co., 1937.

Seton-Watson, R.W. *Sarajevo : A Study in the Origin of the Great War.*

London, 1925.

Seymour, Charles. *The Diplomatic Background of the War 1870–1914.* New Haven : Yale University Press, 1927.

Shapirao, Leonard, (ed.). *Soviet Treaty Series.* Vol. I, *1917–1928.* Washington D.C. : The Georgetown Univ. Press.

Simpson, F.A. *Louis Napoleon and the Recovery of France.* London : Longman Green and Co., 1923.

Simpson, F.A. *Louis Napoleon and the Recovery of France.* 3rd edn., London : Longman Green and Co., 1951.

Simpson, F.A. *The Rise of Louis Napoleon,* New edn. London : Longman Green and Co., 1925.

Smucker, Samuel M. *The Life and Reign of Nicholas the First, Emperor of Russia.* Philadelphia : J.W. Bradely, 48 N. Fourth St., 1856.

Sontag, Raymond James. *European Diplomatic History 1871–1932.* New York : The Century Co., 1933.

Southgate, Right Rev. Horatio. *The War : Its Origin and Consequences.* London : James Madden, 8, Leadenhall St., 1855.

Speech of Earl Grey in the House of Lords, on Friday, the 25th of May, on the Negotiations at Vienna. London : Ward and Co., 27, Paternoster Row, 1855.

Speier, Hans. 'Morale and propaganda.' *War in Our Time.* Hans Speier and Alfred Kahler (eds). New York : W.W. Norton and Co., Inc., 1939.

Steed, Wickham. *Through Thirty Years, 1892–1922.* Vol. I, New York : The Century Co., 1924.

Stubbs, William, *Historical Introductions to the Rolls Series.* Coll., ed., Arthur Hassall, New York : Longman Green and Co. Ltd., 1902.

Sumner, B.H. *The Secret Franco-Russian Treaty of March 3, 1859.* HER, 1933.

Symonds, John Addington. *The Renaissance in Italy–The Revival of Learning,* London, 1915.

Taylor, A.J.P. *The Struggle for Mastery in Europe 1848–1918.* Oxford : Clarendon Press, 1954.

Taylor, A.J.P. *The Course of German History : A Survey of the Development of Germany since 1815.* New edn. Coward-McCann, Inc., 1951.

Taylor A.J.P. *The Murder at Sarajevo, The Observer,* Nov. 16, 1958.

Taylor, Edmond. *The Fall of the Dynasties : The Collapse of the Old Order 1905–1922,* New York : Doubleday and Co., Inc., 1963.

Temperley, Harold W.W. *England and the Near East : The Crimea.* London : Longman Green Co., Ltd., 1936.

Temperley, Harold W.W. *History of Serbia,* New York, 1969.

Terkelsen, T.M. *Front Line in Denmark.* London : The Free Danish Publishing Co., 1944.

Thayer, William Roscoe. *The Life and Times of Cavour.* Vol. II. New York: Houghton Mifflin Co., 1911.

The American Historical Review, Vol. 52, Oct. 1946 to July 1947.

The Cambridge Historical Journal. Vol. 5 (1, 2, 3), 1935, 36 and 37.

The Crisis and Way of Escape : An Appeal for the Oldest of the Oppressed Touching the Origin of the Present War, and Conditions of Durable Peace. London : Houlston and Stoneman, 1856.

The Letter of John Bright on the War verified and illustrated by extracts from the Parliamentary Documents. London : W.F.G. Cash, 5 Bishopsgate Str.

The Treaty of Peace Between The Allied And Associated Powers and Germany Signed At Versailles, June 28, 1919. London : H.M. Stationary Office, Imperial House, Kingsway, 1919.

Thompson, James Westfall and Johnson, Edgar Nathaniel. *Medieval Europe 300–1500.* New York : W.W. Norton and Co. Inc., 1937.

Thomson, J.M. *Louis Napoleon and the Second Empire.* Oxford, 1954.

Tipton, C. Leon, (ed). *Nationalism in the Middle Ages.* 'European Problem Studies' New York : Holt, Rinehart and Winston, 1972.

Valentin, Veit. 'Some Interpretations of Frederick the Great.' *History,* Vol. 19, 1934.

Veale, F.J.P. *Frederick the Great : His Life and Place in History.* Rochester : The Stanhope Press Ltd., 1935.

Vernadsky, George. *Political and Diplomatic History of Russia.* Students' edn., Boston : Little, Brown and Co., 1936.

Vucinich, Wayne S. *Serbia Between East and West*–The events of 1903–1908, Stanford : California, 1954.

Vulliamy, C.E. *Crimea : The Campaign of 1854–56 : With an outline of Politics and a Study of the Royal Charter.* London : Jonathan Cape, 1939.

War in the Crimea: Some Observations. Extract from the Duke of Wellington's instructions to Lt. Col. R.E. Fletcher, London: Simpkin, Marshall and Co., 1855.

War Report : A Record of Dispatches Broadcast by the B.B.C.'s War Correspondents with the Allied Expeditionary Force, June 6, 1944–

May 5, 1945. London : Oxford University Press, 1946.

Ward, A.W. and Gooch, G.P., (eds). *The Cambridge History of British Foreign Policy, 1783–1919.* Vol. 2. New York, 1922–23.

Warner, Philip. *The Crimean War : A Reappraisal.* London : Arthur Barker, 1972.

Weill, Herman N. (ed). *European Diplomatic History, 1815–1914 : Documents and Interpretations.* New York : Exposition Press, 1972.

Werstein, Irving. *That Denmark Might Live : the Saga of the Danish Resistance in World War II.* Philadelphia : Macrae Smith Co., 1967.

Wheeler-Bennett, J.W. *Munich : Prologue to Tragedy.* London, 1948.

Wheeler-Bennett, J.W. *The Nemesis of Power : The German Army in Politics. 1918–1945.* New York : St. Martin's Press, Inc., 1954.

Whyte, A.J.B. *The Political Life and Letters of Cavour 1848–1861.* London: Oxford University Press, H.Milford, 1930.

William, Nassau Senior, *Conversations with M. Thiers, M. Guizot, and Other Distinguished Persons during the Second Empire.* 2 Vols. London, 1878.

Woelfel, James W. *Bonhoeffer's Theology, Classical and Revolutionary.* New York : Abingdon Press, 1970.

Woodward, E.L. *The Age of Reform, 1815–1870.* Oxford : Clarendon Press, 1938.

Young, Norwood. *The Life of Frederick the Great.* New York : Henry Holt and Co., 1919.

Zeller, Eberhard. *The Flame of Freedom : The German Struggle against Hitler.* University of Miami Press. 1969.

Zilliacus. K. 'Economic and Social Causes of the War.' *The Outbreak,* Lee (ed.). Boston : D.C. Heath and Co., 1963.

Index

Aberdeen 151, 155-9, 172, 182, 185
Absolutism, Political System of, 94
Adams, George Burton, 62
Administrative Reform, 222
Adrianople, Treaty of, 154, 161
Aehrenthal, Baron, 363
Africa, 152, 263, 428, 430
    Expansion in, 155
Agadir Crisis, 287
Agrarian Economy, 86
Albert, 38
Alfred, 9, 11
America, 152, 312, 432
Anjevin Bureaucracy, 18
    Empire, 20, 24
Anglicus, Robertus, 39
Anglo-Indian Government, 218
Anti-Sabotage Bill, 405
Aquinas, Thomas, 38
Archduke, 251, 271, 274
Aristotle, 38-9
Arms, Assize of, 17
Aron, Raymond, 260
Arthur, 25, 27
Aryan Philology, 225
    Village, 222
Asia, 152, 161, 263, 427-8, 430, 434
    Vacillation of, 189
Augustine, 4
Augustus, Phillip, 20
Austria, 85, 110, 118-9, 122-3, 153-4, 164, 178, 183, 186, 249-50, 263, 267, 269, 271-3, 277, 279, 363, 365
    Defeat of, 128
    Love of, 121
    Policy of, 278
Authoritarianism, 212
Axis Powers, 344

Bacon, Roger, 38-9
Balfour, Michael L G, 252
Balkan Struggle, 287
    Wars, 379
Barnes, Harry Elmer, 259
Baron, Hans, 67, 69, 72-4
Bastaic, Paul, 370
Beck, Ludwig, 305
Becker, Marvin, 73-4
Becket, Thomas A, 23
    Controversy, 18
Bengal, 208
Bennett, Jeremy, 397-400, 402-4, 408, 413-5
Bentham, 214, 223
Berchtold, Count, 269, 272, 277, 279, 283, 292, 383
Berlin, 79-80, 95, 252, 277, 281, 330, 337
    Bunker, 425
Berry, W. Grinton, 109, 133
Best, Werner, 402
Bethlehem, 175
Bethmann-Hollweg, 277-9, 281, 292
Bilinski, 384-5
Bismarck, 244-5, 262, 281

Black Hand, 274-6, 358, 364-7, 370, 373
  Sea, 158, 169
  Stone, 34
Bloch, Marc, 2, 4
Blum, M Leon, 395
Blytgen-Petersen, Emil, 398, 405
Bogicevic, M, 371
Bonaparte, Louis Napolean,108, 117, 126
Bonhoeffer, Dietrich, 320
Bosnia, 263, 274, 362, 365, 367-8, 370-2, 379, 383, 388
  Revolutionary Movement in, 364-5
Bosnian Crisis, 287, 363
Bourgeois, Emile, 165
Bouvines, 7;
  Disaster of, 23
Boveri, Margret, 305
Brakespeare, Nicholas, 23
Brill, Hermann, 314
Brinton, Grane, 223, 241
British Attitude, 205, 212
  Authority, 221
  Broadcasting Corporation, 393-6
  Empire, 221
  Foreign Policy, 189
  Indian Policy, 212
  Policy, 158, 206
  Rule, 208, 220, 234
Brucker, Gene, 73
Bruni, Leonardo, 65
Brunner, Otto, 426
Brunnow ,157
Brutus, Trojan, 25
Buol, 184, 186
Burgundians, 6
Burke, Edmund, 93
Burkhardt, Jacob, 50, 58, 61-2, 64, 66, 68-70
Burry, J P T , 110, 115, 121, 166

Cabrinovic, Nedjelko, 368-9, 378
Cacinovic, Vladimir, 368
Calcutta European Community, 209
Calzabigi, 80
Canning, 172, 207-9
Capital Starvation, 89
Capitalism, Development of, 67
Carlyle, Thomas, 93, 97, 217
Carolingian Empire, 3
Carr, E.H., 334
Castelbajac, 168
Cavour, Camillo di, 112-3, 115, 118-9, 124, 131
Cawnpore Massacre, 206-7
Chabod, Federico, 426, 429
Charlemagne, Empire of, 5
Charter, 33
Cheyney, Edward P, 21, 32-3
Chicherin, Georgi, 330, 337
Chilston, Viscount, 400
China, 92, 432
Christian, 402
Christianity, 3, 17
Churchill, Winston, 344-5, 348, 350-1, 394, 398
Ciganovic, Milan, 370, 388
Civilization, 232
Clarendon, Constitution of, 19
Class Division, 49
Colbert, 91
Collingwood, R G, 52
Colonialism, 313
Conflict, 49
Congress, Formation of, 234
Constantinople, 188, 190
Corley, T A B, 115, 118, 124-6, 131, 166, 168
Corporate Will, 3
Costain, Thomas, 23, 26-7, 35
Cowley, 168, 185
Craig, Gordon Alexander, 245
Crimean War, 111-2, 120-1, 129, 146-7, 153-4, 157, 159, 163-4, 168, 183-4, 188
Crisis, Appearance of, 72
Croce, Benedetto, 429
Crocker, George, 348
Crowe, Eyre, 290

Crown, 16
Danger to, 13
Policy of, 17
Power of, 16
Prime Objective of, 20
Crozier, Michel, 431-2
Curzon, Harol Nicholson, 331
Czar, 157-8, 165, 173, 182, 188-9
Czechoslovakia, 307, 323

D'Abernon, Viscount, 336, 342
Dalhousie, Policies of, 236
Dalrymple, 95
Damocles, Sword of, 330, 334
Daniels, Emil, 79-81, 83-4
Daniels, H G, 331
Danish, 393, 396, 398
Army, 400
Broadcast, 410
Population, 407
Problem, 411
Resistance, 399, 415
Movement, 399
Sabotage, 405, 407
Unity, 407
Wounds, 415
D'Auvergne, Edmund B, 113, 170
DaVinci, Leonardo, 50
De Burgh, Hubert, 27
De Coulanges, Fustel, 2
De Deo, Johannes, 5
Dedijer, Vladimir, 251
De Gaulle, Charles, 424, 432
Dejure, Theory of, 5
De la Gorce, Pierre, 147
De Launay, 83-4
De Lhuys, Drouyn, 111, 182
Delmer, Sefton, 413
Democracy, 214, 222, 225, 232, 235
De Montfort, Simon, 6, 16, 30-2
Denmark, 392-8, 401-5, 411-2
De Reynold, Gonzague, 426
Despotism, 10, 70
De Tocqueville, 424-5
Detrimental Doctrine, 7
D'Hilliers, Baraguay, 182
Dickinson, G Lowes, 273
Dimitrijevic, Dragutin, 366, 374
Diplomacy, 188, 262
Diplomatic History, 244-5, 255
Dismemberment, Principle of, 347
Dogger Bank, 265
Dorn, Walter L, 83, 93
Dossing, Thomas, 411
Douglas, Davis C, 22-3
Duns, 38
Durham, Edith M, 274-5, 375, 381

Earl, Simon, 31
Ecclesiastical Freedom, Struggle for, 19
Economic Crisis, 79
Eden, Anthony, 349-50, 411
Edgar, 9, 11
Edward I, 6, 31, 33-4
Effendi, Fuad, 179
Egypt, 155, 178
Elbe River, 96
Emiliani, Giudici, Paolo, 72
Emmanuel, Victor, 131
England, 2, 5-6, 8-10, 15-18, 22, 25-7, 32, 41, 103, 111-2, 151, 153, 156-60, 162, 182, 186, 207, 213, 218, 221, 227, 229, 231, 263, 279, 287-9, 293
Constitution, Age of, 34
King of, 7, 24
Liberty, 6
English Common Law, 19
Democracy, 225
Liberal Party, 236
Liberty, Critic of, 18
Nationality, 2
Entente Powers, 329, 332-3
Eugene, 117
Europe, 3-5, 67, 79, 83, 108-9, 111, 146, 149-50, 152, 174, 183, 250, 262-3, 266-7, 304-5, 314, 316, 319-21, 328-9, 332, 357, 385, 394, 397-8, 402-3, 424-5, 427, 430-1, 433-4
Destiny of, 250

Idea of, 426
Solidarity of, 186
Unity, Hague Congress of, 429
European Advisory Commission, 346, 349
Civilization, 235
Economy, Rebuilding of, 329
Nationalism, 4, 8
Problems, 218
Resistance Movements, 397
War, 189, 261
Evolution, Doctrine of, 222
Exploitation, Age of, 11

Fanaticism, 187-8
Fatherland, 5
Concept of, 4
Fatwa, 188
Fay, Sidney B, 89, 248, 259, 269, 274, 280, 371, 375, 383, 385
Feis, 354
Ferdinand, Archduke Franz, 251, 271-2, 357, 359, 369, 371, 377, 383
Assassination of, 292
Ferguson, Adam, 52, 54-8, 68, 72
Feudal Anarchy, 15, 31
Society, 4, 49
System, 55
Feudalism, 6, 15, 20, 52
Darkness of, 24
Introduction of, 10
Mercy of, 16
First World War, 248, 253, 257, 259, 261, 265-6, 268, 303, 306, 391
Outbreak of, 286
Fischer, Fritz, 253, 264
Fischer, Louis, 334
Florinsky, 182
Foreign Policy, 110, 153, 244, 304, 314-5
Power, 18
Trade, 158
France, 5-7, 50, 64, 85, 91, 96, 108, 110-1, 121, 128, 155, 158, 160, 168, 175, 183, 186, 263, 267, 286, 288, 293, 303, 314, 329, 349-50, 362, 413
Fate of, 14
Guidance of, 64
Hegemony of, 117
Solidarity of, 154
Franco-Russian Alliance, 246, 262
Frechulf, 3
Frederick, 78-9, 81-5, 87-8, 90-3, 96-7
Freeman, Edward, 11-2
French Revolution, 111

Gagliardo, John G, 89, 105
Galbraith, 39-40
Gallop, Rodney, 406-7
Garin, Eugenio, 59-60, 67, 73-4
Gaxotte, Pierre, 106
Geiss, Imanuel, 260, 271
Genoa Conference, 329-31, 333
Geneva, 320
Geoffrey, Welshman, 8, 25
George, Llyod, 329, 331, 335
German Empire, 244
Foreign Policy, 303, 328
Germanic Invasions, Period of, 2
Germany, 85, 92, 122, 131, 246, 254, 258, 263, 266, 277-9, 290, 292-3, 303, 306-7, 314, 316, 319-21, 327-8, 332-3, 335, 344, 347, 410, 413, 425
Future of, 345
Treaty of, 255
Weakness of, 252
Gershoy, Leo, 78, 91-2, 95, 104
Geyl, Pieter, 262
Gibbon, Fitz, 313
Gibbons, H A, 329
Gillies, John, 89, 103
Gilmore, Myron, 51
Giotto, 50
Global Policy, 264
Gladstone, 212, 214, 249
Liberalism of, 236
Goerdeler, Carl Friedrich, 304-7,

312, 317, 319
Goetz, Walter, 69
Golubic, Mustapha, 370
Gooch, G P, 63, 96, 249, 260, 278
Goriainov, Sergei M, 147, 193
Goschen, William, 290
Government, System of, 15
Grabezh, Trifko, 368-9
Graham, James, 185
Graml, Hermann, 305-6, 310, 314, 319
Grand Council, 188
Granville, Earl, 208
Great Britain, 25, 114, 121-2, 155, 157-9, 162, 172, 183, 186, 189, 217, 230, 232, 234, 255, 263-4, 267, 290, 310, 344, 350, 352, 362, 394-7, 401-3, 407, 411
 Charter, 21
  Russia Party, 160
Greece, 423
 Independence of, 150
Greek Tragedy, 175, 416
Greville, C F G, 184
Grey, Edward, 289-90
Grosseteste, Robert, 28, 37
Guarino, 65
Gudme, Sten, 406, 416
Guedalla, Philip, 97, 119, 121, 126, 131
Guerard, Albert, 108, 117, 125, 131, 168
Guinn, Paul, 254
Gyulay, 126

Haas, Ernst, 427
Habsburg, 359-61
 Monarchy, 266, 270, 272-3
Haestrup, Joerge, 395
Hagiographer, 2
Hale, Mathew, 32
Hallstein, Walter, 434
Harold, 9, 26
Harris, James, 95
Hassell, Ulrich Von, 304, 306, 311-3, 317, 323
Haubach, Theo, 315
Hay, Denis, 66
Hearnshaw, F J C, 180
Heath, Edward, 433
Henderson, Cavin, 156
Henderson, N O, 82, 85, 87, 104
Henry, I, 2, 11, 13, 16, 21, 27
Hindu Joint Family, 224
Hitler, Adolf, 258, 304, 308-9, 425
Hobbes, 220
Holborn, Hajo, 253
Holland, 183
Hollweg, 252
Holstein, Friederich Von, 245-6
Holy Alliance, 165, 186
Home Rule Crisis, 216
Horne, Alistair, 254
House of Lords, 234
Hubertsburg, 86
 Peace of, 78
Huguccio, 4
Huizinga, Johan, 1-2
Humanism, Appraisal of, 70
Hume, David, 72

Ideology, 111
Ilbert Bill, 227-8, 236
Imperial Legislative Council, 235
Imperialism, 305
 Diplomacy of, 246
 Principles of, 236
India, 92, 205-9, 213, 216, 218, 220-1, 224-7, 229, 231, 236
 Threat to, 159
Indian Civil Service, 218, 222-3, 225, 234
 Contract Bill, 223
 Council, 235
 Empire, 212, 227
 Nation, 234
 Social System, 226
 Society, 232
 Conservatism of, 237
 Regeneration of, 206
Industrial Revolution, 85
Insurrection, War to, 188

Irish Home Rule, 236
Iron Chancellor, 245
Italy, 49-50, 58, 64, 70-1, 112, 117, 128, 270, 279
  Future of, 119
  Liberation of, 133
  Unity of, 133

Jamaica Committee, 217
Japan, 293, 344
Jarausch, K H, 252
Jerome, 120
Jerrold, 132
Jerusalem, 175, 180
Jevtic, Borivoje, 374
John, 6, 18, 20
  Reign of, 25
Joll, James, 253
Jorgensen, Robert, 394, 420
Joseph, Francis, 186
Joseph, Franz, 129-30
Jovanovic, M Ljuba, 374-7
Justice, 20

Kaye, J W, 236
Keeney, Barnaby C, 13, 40-1
Kennan, G F, 328-9
Keynes, John Maynard, 254-5
Kinglake, A W, 164
Kohn, Hans, 247
Koht, Halvdan, 3, 8
Kossovo, Battle of, 372
Kreisau Circle, 313-5, 317
  Ideology of, 319
Kremlin, 351-2
Kristeller, Paul Oskar, 54, 75
Kuchuk Kainarji, Treaty of, 176, 181
Kurth, Godefroid, 8

Lafore, Laurence, 250, 266, 290
Laicization, 5
Land Policy, 205
Langer, William L, 246, 286
Langton, Stephen, 23
Larsen, Gunnar, 400
Lawrence, John, 207
League of Nations, 304
Leber, Julius, 315, 320
Lerner, Daniel, 391
Liberal Party, 216, 236
Liberalism, 174, 190, 205, 212-3, 215
Lichnowsky, 290
London, 13, 26, 94, 114, 157, 180, 190, 265, 337, 394-5, 397
Louis, 27
Lousse, Emile, 133
Lowe, Robert, 214-6
Luther, 57

Macaulay, 207, 226, 231
  Vision of, 214
MacMunn, George, 172, 291
Magna Carta, 15, 18-9, 21, 26
Mahmoud, Reign of, 150
Maine, Henry, 213, 222-3, 225, 233, 237
Malone, Kemp, 9
Marriott, J A R, 147
Marshall Plan, 329
Martin, A P, 23, 239
Marx, Karl, 149, 158
Medieval Europe, 4
Menshikov, 177-80, 182, 189
Mercantalism, 94
Michelet, 426
Middle Ages, 1, 6, 8, 17, 50-2, 55, 62, 87, 391
  East, 159
Midlothian Campaign, 215
Milanese Threat, 73
Military Despotism, 17
  Monarchy, 15
  Power, 16
Mill, J S, 213-4, 217-9, 231
Miller, William, 175
Mange, Alyce Edythe, 147
Mitchell, Andrew, 101
Modern Nationalism, 3
Moeller, Christmas, 410, 412, 415
Moltke, Count Von, 315, 320
Mommsen, Hans, 309
Montague-Chelmsford Reforms,

236
Morality, System of, 219
Morandi, Carlo, 426
Morgenthau Plan, 320
Morocco, 263, 267
Moscow, 309-10, 327, 330, 332, 347, 411
Munchengratz, Alliance of, 156
Convention of, 154
Munro, Dana Carletin, 14, 44
Muscovite Rule, 152
Muslim Sultan, 176
Mutiny, 209-11, 236
Influence of, 205

Nana Saheb, 207
Napoleon, Louis, 97, 109, 111-4, 117-8, 120, 125-6
National Cohesion, Principle of, 15
Consciousness, 1, 4, 9, 39
Conservative, 306, 311-2, 317, 319, 321
opposition, 319
Parliament, 8
Separatism, 3
Socialism, 323
Nationalism, 1-3, 5-6, 8-9, 40-1, 314
Nationality, Definition, 3
Nazi Germany, 398
Nazi-Soviet Pact, 309
Negro Revolt, 217
Nesselrode, 177-8, 185, 192
Neumann, Carl, 62
New World, 74
New York, 112
Nicholas, 156-7, 177-8, 180, 182
Nord, Hans, 433
Nordstrom, John, 64
Norman England, 2
Invasion, 26

Obrenovic, Milan, 360
Occam, 38
Ockham, William, 5
Oder River, 87
Olomouc, 186
Oltenitza, 187
Orange, William of, 27
Oriental States, 229
Orsini, 114, 116-7
Affair of, 112
Orthodox Church, 189
Ottoman, Defence of, 146
Empire, 150, 158-9, 181, 190, 262, 267
Integrity of, 147
Oudh, 212
Overseas Trading Corporation, 83, 86
Oxford, 23, 66
University of, 37

Palestine, Peace of, 221
Palmer, Paul, 392
Palmerston, 156-9, 171-2, 185, 189
Paris, 23, 185, 187, 252
Congress, 112
Peace Conference, 254
Treaty of, 120
Pasha, Reschid, 151
Pashitch, Nicholas, 275
Patriotism, 1, 9, 38, 108
Fire of, 24
Patterson, R H, 134
Pax Romana, 221
Peace Conference, 120, 257
Preservation of, 182
Settlement, 254
Philippe, Louis, 165
Phillip, Age of, 6
Pig War, 361
Pilate, Pontius, 221
Pirenne, Henry, 3
Plantagenet, Henry, 20
Poincare, 288-9, 330
Poitevin King, 20
Poland, 88, 309, 318, 350
Fate of, 91
Political Testaments, 81
Theory, 17
Potiorek, 370
Power, Balance of, 260, 307

Price, M P, 278
Primitive Nationalism, 3
    Tribe, 2
Princip, Gavrilo, 268, 272, 368, 370
Propaganda, 391, 393-4, 407, 414
Protestant Reformation, 57
Prussia, 78-80, 83, 85-6, 91, 97, 110, 122, 186, 319, 321
    Constitution of, 90
        Trade of, 81
    Transformation of, 95
Public opinion, 255
Puryear, Vernon J, 149, 153, 156, 160

Racism, 209
Radical Party, 364-5, 376
Rambaud, Alfred, 172, 178, 183
Rapallo, 335-7
    Treaty of, 327
Rathenau, Walther, 329, 332
Ravaillo, Tortures of, 207
Realm, Defence of, 5
Rebellion, 17
Redcliffe, Stratford de, 147-8, 173, 181-2
Reddaway, W F, 89, 182
Redking, 13
Reform Bill, 215
Reformation, 57
    Drama of, 66
Religious Liberty, Principle of, 221
Remak, Joachim, 247, 250-1, 264, 274, 276, 285, 358
Renaissance, 49-51, 57, 64
    Humanism, Study of, 71
    Medieval Society, 1
    Problem of, 54
Renouvin, Pierre, 260
Revolution, 114
    Collapse of, 174
    Failure of, 190
Rheinhardt, E A, 113, 126, 130
Richardson, Oliver, 18-9, 30, 32
Ripon, 235
    Liberalism of, 227
Ritter, Gerhard, 82, 86, 308
Rocca, Della, 116
Rolo, Charles J, 391, 394
Roman Empire, 4
    Dissolution of, 3
    Law, 225
Rome, 19, 27-8, 38, 50, 117, 176
Romoser, George K, 304
Roosevelt, 344-8
Rose, Colonel, 182
Rosenberg, 101
Rothfels, Hans, 322
Royal Disposition Fund, 82
Rufus, William, 21
Russell, John, 171-2
Russell, W H, 209
Russia, 110, 121-3, 147-8, 150-1, 153-5, 157-60, 162, 173-5, 178, 183-4, 186, 189-90, 263, 267-9, 271, 278-9, 281-2, 284-5, 299, 319, 329, 332, 335, 354, 360, 411, 432
    Isolation of, 121
Russian Encroachment, 146-7
    Invasion, 280
Russo-Japanese War, 265

San Francisco Conference, 412
Sarajevo, 357, 370-1, 379, 382, 386
    Affair, 367
        Assassination, 251
    Conference of, 365
        Conspiracy, 365
    Crime of, 276
    Plot, 357-8, 385
Sazonoff, 283-4, 286-7
Schevill, Ferdinand, 362
Schleinitz, 129
Schlieffen Plan, 294
Schmitt, Bernadott, 146, 170, 369, 376, 380, 386
Schramm, Wilhelm Von, 304
Schubart, J C, 89
Schultz, Walter, 101
Science, 35
Scotland, 11, 16
Seaman, L C B, 171-2, 260, 270

Second World War, 65, 315, 431
Outbreak of, 392
Secret Agreement, 157
Committee, 211
Secularism, 49
Sellery, 51, 58, 60
Sencourt, Robert, 111, 133
Serbia, 249-50, 268, 273, 278, 287-8, 359-61, 364, 379
Seton-Watson, 157, 171, 275-6, 359, 363, 368, 371, 376-7, 381, 386
Seven Years War, 82-3, 248
Economic Effect of, 78
Seymour, Hamilton, 177-8
Sheikh-ul-Islam, 188
Siciliano, 64
Silesia, 86
Simpson, F A, 165, 173
Sinope, Massacre of, 187
Smith, Adam, 94
Social Policy, Direction of, 320
Reform, 205
Tensions, 266
Socialism, 223
Sontag, Raymond, 264
Soviet Union, 309, 319, 344-5, 352
Spain, 5, 50
Speier, Hans, 391
Spengler, Oswald, 434
Stalin, Marshall, 320, 344-51, 354
Stauffenberg, Klaus, 320
Steed, Wickham, 380
Stettinius, 345, 351, 353
Stenton, Frank, 23
Stephen, James Fitzjames, 13, 205, 213, 216, 217-9, 221-4, 227, 230-1, 236
Strachey, John, 218, 234
Stratford, Role of, 172-3, 185
Strayer, Joseph R, 5
Stubbs, William, 9, 13-4, 18, 21, 33
Sudeten Crisis, 310
Sultan Salahuddin, 20
Symond, John Addington, 62, 66

Tankovic, Voja, 366-7, 370-1
Taylor, A J P, 118, 176-7, 186, 245, 247, 260, 281
Tehran Proposal, 347
Temperley, Harold, 146, 157-8, 173-4, 178, 187, 363
Terkelsen, TM, 392, 403, 405, 408
Thomas, 39
Thouvenel, Edouard, 189
Tilly, 66
Tipton, 1
Toryism, 225
Tout, Thomas F, 6
Trafalgar, 27
Trevelyan, George Otta, 206, 210, 214
Trevor-Roper, 306
Triple Alliance, 262-3, 279, 290, 360
Turberville, A S, 65
Turkey, 150, 153-8, 160, 162, 172-3, 175, 177, 183-4, 186, 189
Liberalism of, 151
Partition of, 177

Unionism, 236
United Nations, 411-2
Security Council, 349
United States, 344, 352, 411, 434
Constitution, 224
Unkiar, 154
Universalism, 5

Valery, Paul, 426-7
Valient Struggle, 7
Vaughan, Robert, 21
Van Roon, Ger, 315
Veale, F J B, 78, 97
Verdun Sector, 253-4
Versailles Peace Settlement, 254
Treaty of, 258, 291, 327
Vienna, 110, 121, 149, 178, 252
Note, 184-6, 188, 269, 278, 286-9, 291, 375, 383-5
Vitalis, Ordericus, 24
Vittorino, 65
Voigt, George, 61, 66

Von Trott, Adam, 315-6, 320, 325-6
Voyage Home, 218
Vucinich, 361

Walewska, Countess, 112
War, Declaration of, 268
Outbreak of, 310
Threat of, 126
Warner, Philip, 200
Weber, Alfred, 423
Weber, Max, 245
Weisinger, 54
Welshman, 8
Werstein, Irving, 408
Wessex, Ancient Dynasty of, 2
Western Civilization, 233
Power, 323
Wilhelmine, Germany, 252
Williamson, Samuel R, 252
William, 9, 11-2, 122
Wilson, Woodrow, 108-9
Wingfield-Stratford, Esme, 10, 16, 18, 27-8, 32, 38
Wint, Guy, 238
Wisely, 12
World War, 250, 266, 271, 279, 364, 385
Wycliffe, John, 37

Yalta Conference 345, 352-3
Young, G M, 244
Yugoslav Agitation, 269
Nationalism, 367, 378, 386
Unity, 276, 386

Zeller, 314
Zewrajic, 377-8
Ziekursch, 85